Latin American Realities – Who Holds Power?

'You are asking for specific guarantees [against paramilitary forces and death squads] and I cannot give you an adequate response. It is not in my power to promise you a clear-cut solution in your fine European terms. I have been a leading journalist during the years of the military and the repression. I have been threatened and had to go abroad to be safe. Now I am the vice-president, even the acting president of this country. I have written the essential parts of the constitution. Apparently I am invested with all political power. But in fact, my friends, I have to share power with a lot of players, some of them invisible. In this country, the military are still in command. This is Guatemala, my friends, you cannot implement a government programme without their implicit permission. Then, of course, there are the paramilitary forces, the death squads. They are present and absent at the same time. They are nowhere and everywhere; and they ask for their share. Then there are the drug dealers, the mafias. Of course, I should negate their very existence, as I should with the military, the police, the criminals and the drug lords. But we are here in Guatemala and their presence is a reality. And then there is the problem of the CACIF. They consider a small increase of taxation by 2 or 3 per cent as communism, and the military believe them! CACIF controls the entire national economy. So, considering these facts, what kind of guarantees are you asking for?'

A former vice-president of Guatemala

Latin American Studies from Zed Books

Zed Books publishes on international and Third World issues. In addition to our general lists on economics, development, the environment, gender and politics, we also publish area studies in the fields of African Studies, Asian and Pacific Studies, Latin American and Caribbean Studies, and Middle East Studies. Our Latin American titles include:

Frederique Apffel-Marglin with PRATEC (eds), *The Spirit of Regeneration: Andean Culture Confronting Western Notions of Development*

Susan Bassnett (ed.), *Knives and Angels: Women Writers in Latin America*

Cristovam Buarque, *The End of Economics? Ethics and the Disorder of Progress*

Raff Carmen and Miguel Sobrado (eds), *Capacity Building and the Poor: An Introduction to Latin American Approaches to Urban and Rural Development*

Jacques M. Chevalier and Daniel Buckles, *A Land Without Gods: Process Theory, Maldevelopment and the Mexican Nahuas*

Catherine Davies (ed.), *A Place in the Sun? Women Writers in Twentieth Century Cuba*

Gustavo Esteva and Madhu Suri Prakash, *Grassroots Post-Modernism: Remaking the Soil of Cultures*

Stefano Harney, *Nationalism and Identity: Culture and the Imagination in a Caribbean Diaspora*

Clare Hargreaves, *Snowfields: The War on Cocaine in the Andes*

Elizabeth Jelin (ed.), *Women and Social Change in Latin America*

Michael Kaufman and Alfonso Dilla (eds), *Community Power and Grassroots Democracy: The Transformation of Social Life*

Kees Koonings and Dirk Kruijt (eds), *Societies of Fear: The Legacy of Civil War, Violence and Terror in Latin America*

Peter Mayo, *Gramsci, Freire and Adult Education: Possibilities for Transformative Action*

Ronaldo Munck, *Latin America: The Transition to Democracy*

Rhoda E. Reddock, *Women, Labour and Politics in Trinidad and Tobago*

Oscar Ugarteche, *The False Dilemma: Is Globalization the Only Choice?*

Bill Weinberg, *War on the Land: Ecology and Politics in Central America*

For full details of this list and Zed's other subject and general catalogues, please write to: The Marketing Department, Zed Books, 7 Cynthia Street, London N1 9JF, UK or email: sales@zedbooks.demon.co.uk

Visit our website at: http://www.zedbooks.demon.co.uk

SOCIETIES OF FEAR

The Legacy of Civil War, Violence and Terror in Latin America

EDITED BY
KEES KOONINGS AND
DIRK KRUIJT

Zed Books
LONDON · NEW YORK

Societies of Fear: The Legacy of Civil War, Violence and Terror in Latin America was first published by Zed Books Ltd, 7 Cynthia Street, London N1 9JF, UK and Room 400, 175 Fifth Avenue, New York, NY 10010, USA in 1999.

Distributed in the USA exclusively by St Martin's Press, Inc., 175 Fifth Avenue, New York, NY 10010, USA.

Cover designed by Andrew Corbett
Set in Monotype Garamond by Ewan Smith
Printed and bound in Malaysia

A catalogue record for this book is available from the British Library

Library of Congess Cataloging-in-Publication-Data

Societies of fear: the legacy of civil war, violence and terror in Latin America / Kees Koonings, Dirk Kruijt [eds].
        p.   cm.
includes bibliographical references (p.) and index.
ISBN 1 85649 766 6 (hardcover). – ISBN 1 85649 767 4 (pbk)
   1. Violence–Latin America.   2. Political violence–Latin America.   3. Terror–Latin America.   4. State-sponsored terrorism–Latin America.   I. Koonings, Kees.   II. Kruijt, Dirk.
HN110.5.Z9V575   1999
303.6'098–dc21
                                                  99-2572
                                                  CIP

ISBN 1 85649 766 6 cased
ISBN 1 85649 767 4 limp

Contents

Acknowledgements

This volume is the result of an international conference at Utrecht University in September 1995, organized by the editors, together with Professor Raymond Buve from Leiden University. We originally organized this conference in order to address the ways in which different kinds of social and political violence – especially civil war and state terror – have affected social and political developments in Latin America. It is, as we felt, a legitimate concern, because debates on the current Latin American situation have been focusing to a large extent on the prospects for democratic consolidation and on the so-called 'adjustment and governance' agenda.

With the demise of almost all of the authoritarian military regimes in the region, and with the formalization of peace agreements in Central America drawing to a conclusion after the December 1996 comprehensive peace treaty in Guatemala, it is tempting to think of violence, repression and civil war as something of the Latin American past. However, decades of violence, state terror and civil war cannot be expected to vanish with one pencil stroke. The Utrecht conference, under the title 'Societies of Fear', was designed to review the possible impact of recent and current forms of violence on the broader social and political dynamics in the region, especially with respect to the core issue of democratic governance. In total, twenty-eight papers, by scholars from France, Germany, Guatemala, Mexico, the Netherlands, Peru, Spain, Surinam, the United Kingdom and the United States were presented at the conference, in sessions on issues such as ethnic civil wars, political transitions, violence and civil society, and country sessions on Argentina, Central America, Mexico and Surinam. This volume offers a selection of ten of the papers, all of them substantially revised or rewritten. Three papers had been submitted in a language other than English, and were translated especially for this volume. The chapter on Brazil was not originally presented as a paper at the conference but was written afterwards for inclusion in the book. We added a general introduction to serve as the opening chapter of the volume.

In the course of a large project such as this, conference organizers and volume editors incur a variety of debts, scholarly and otherwise. First of all, we would like to express our gratitude to a number of entities that made the original conference financially possible: the Netherlands Foundation for the Advancement of Tropical Research (WOTRO), the Royal Netherlands Academy of Science (KNAW), the Netherlands Association for Latin American and Caribbean Studies (NALACS), the Board of Governors of Utrecht University, the Faculty of Social Science of Utrecht University, its Department of Anthropology, CERES Research School, the Centre for Latin American and Caribbean Studies at Utrecht University, the Department for Latin American Studies at Leiden University, and the Centre for Non-Western Studies Research School at Leiden University.

Secondly, a great many people assisted us with time and effort before and during the conference and in the course of the preparation of this book. We are indebted to Raymond Buve for the pleasant joint effort of organizing the conference. Lieteke van Vucht-Tijssen, member of the Board of Governors of Utrecht University, offered permanent support. Suzette de Boer, Camie van de Brug and Machteld Ooijens provided invaluable organizational support, dealing with the turmoil of conference details.

In preparing the manuscript, we are grateful to the authors for accepting our suggestions for revision of the papers, and for allowing us ample manoeuvring space in harnessing their final texts. We could count on the valuable effort and fine work of Chris Follett, Mario Fumerton, Helen Hintjens, Jo Kingsfield, Patrick Loftman and John Schaechter for translations and proof-reading of English. Flora de Groot provided bibliographic assistance at a crucial moment. Petra Nesselaar skilfully and patiently took care of text processing. Finally we would like to acknowledge the warm and efficient way in which Robert Molteno and his colleagues at Zed Books took care of the final preparation and production of the book.

Utrecht, December 1998
Kees Koonings, Dirk Kruijt

About the Contributors

CARLOS IVÁN DEGREGORI is professor of anthropology at San Marcos University and senior researcher at the Instituto de Estudios Peruanos (IEP), Lima. He has published on a variety of subjects: Andean society, ethnicity, the origins of Shining Path, the peasant militia and post-war Peru.

ALAN KNIGHT is professor of Latin American history at Oxford University. His many books and articles examine the Mexican revolution and post-revolutionary Mexican social and political life.

KEES KOONINGS is associate professor of Latin American development at Utrecht University. An anthropologist and sociologist, he has written on development issues, Brazilian industrialization, and militarism in Latin America.

DIRK KRUIJT is professor of development studies at Utrecht University. A political sociologist and social anthropologist, his published work is mostly about poverty and informality, war and peace, and military governments.

GERT OOSTINDIE is professor of Caribbean studies at Utrecht University and head of the Caribbean Department of the Royal Institute of Linguistics and Anthropology, Leiden. Historian and social anthropologist, he has published extensively on plantation societies, and on ethnicity and nation-building in the Caribbean.

ARIJ OUWENEEL is senior researcher at the Centre for Study and Documentation of Latin America (CEDLA), Amsterdam, and professor of the history of indigenous peoples in Latin America at Utrecht University. He has written on various issues relating to the indigenous population in colonial and post-colonial Mexico, Guatemala and the Andean countries.

WIL PANSTERS is associate professor of Latin American studies at Utrecht University. A human geographist, he has published works on regional history, regional development and political culture in Mexico.

DANIEL PÉCAUT is professor of Latin American studies at the Ecole des Hautes Etudes en Sciences Sociales, Paris. A sociologist, he has published extensively on issues related to political violence in Latin America, especially in Colombia.

ANTONIUS ROBBEN is professor of Latin American studies at Utrecht

University. A cultural anthropologist, he has written about local communities in Brazil and on the psycho-anthropological effects of violence in Latin America.

PATRICIO SILVA is associate professor of Latin American politics at Leiden University. A political scientist, he has published extensively on the (post-) authoritarian regimes in the southern cone, especially on issues related to democratization and the role of technocrats.

EDELBERTO TORRES-RIVAS is currently a senior researcher at UNRISD. A sociologist and former secretary general of FLACSO, he has published widely on general Latin American political issues, the social and political history of Central America, and on Guatemala's civil war and peace process.

ONE

Introduction: Violence and Fear in Latin America

DIRK KRUIJT AND KEES KOONINGS

In September 1989, one of the authors, acting as a member of a negotiating mission to the Christian Democratic government of Guatemala, participated in a lengthy dialogue with the then vice-president of the country, Lic. Roberto Carpio Nicolle. The national government, the first civilian one after a long period of military rule, was trying to attract technical and financial support from European donor countries. Guatemala had become eligible for European aid, not only because the country needed to be rebuilt after the gruesome civil war and the crisis of the 1980s, but also because it had become a politically fashionable recipient, after all those years of pariah status within the international community. Mr Carpio had been the president of the constitutional reform committee during the transition period from military rule to a civilian government. As the constitutional vice-president, he was the head of the national public sector, and, at the very moment of the interview, the acting president as well. At the end of the last negotiating session – the topic was a support project for his ambitious national anti-poverty and micro-enterprise programme – the delicate theme of human rights was touched upon. When the delegation leader insisted upon guarantees against paramilitary forces and death squads while executing the agreed project, the Guatemalan vice-president turned red and, with his face flushed, began to argue in the following way:

> You are asking for specific guarantees and I cannot give you an adequate response. It is not in my power to promise you a clear-cut solution in your fine European terms. I have been a leading journalist during the years of the military and the repression. I have been threatened and had to go abroad to be safe. Now I am the vice-president, even the acting president of this country. I have written the essential parts of the constitution. Apparently I am invested with all political power. But in fact, my friends, I have to share power with a

lot of players, some of them invisible. In this country, the military are still in command. This is Guatemala, my friends, you cannot implement a government programme without their implicit permission. Then, of course, there are the paramilitary forces, the death squads, as you said. OK, can you suggest something I can do with them? They are present and absent at the same time. They are nowhere and everywhere; and they ask for their share. Then there are the drug dealers, the mafias. Of course, I should negate their very existence, as I should with the military, the police, the criminals and the drug lords. But we are here in Guatemala and their presence is a reality. And then there is the problem of CACIF.[1] They consider a small increase of taxation by 2 or 3 per cent as communism, and the military believe them! CACIF controls the entire national economy. So, reconsidering these facts, what kind of guarantees are you asking for?

Thus he expressed in a nutshell the problem under study. Latin America has a legacy of terror, of violence, of fear. Of all the countries on the continent, Guatemala is one of the most significant examples of a 'society of fear'. The constitution of this kind of society and the persistence of its characteristics – in other words, the long-term consequences of violence, repression and arbitrariness – are recurrent features of the Latin American political landscape. Unfortunately, these problems have not vanished from the continent's social and political scene despite almost two decades of efforts to end authoritarianism and civil war and to rebuild democracy and legitimate civil governance.

Since the late 1970s, Latin America has been experiencing profound and often painful processes of economic, social and political change. The region had to face the double challenge of coping with the worst economic crisis since the 1930s, while also having to move forwards along the road of democratic transition and consolidation. At the same time, these changes were complicated by numerous internal social and political contradictions and conflicts. It is therefore not surprising that the advances made along the way have in many cases been ambiguous, partial and unstable. In most cases the transition towards 'normality' has taken a zig-zag movement. Economic recovery came late; it proved to be fragile and did not produce the expected result of rapidly reducing poverty and inequality. Formal democratization has proceeded in often quite impressive ways, but the process has been permanently bedeviled by institutional confusion, political turmoil, conflicts and violence.

Toward the end of the present century, the region finds itself at a crossroads, marked by a fundamental dilemma. On the one hand, most countries in the region have been working to establish civic democratic governments during the past ten to fifteen years with which to replace authoritarian regimes that governed partially or wholly on the basis of arbitrariness and institutionalized violence. This so-called 'democratic consolidation' has been

followed, in a number of countries, by an apparent economic recovery which
marked the end of the cycle of stagnation, debt and impoverishment of the
1980s. On the other hand, many social and political problems continue to
haunt Latin America. These problems do not go unnoticed, as they cast a
shadow on the status of Latin America as a promising region of 'new
democracies' and 'emerging markets',[2] but they are still relatively ignored in
the recent boom of literature on Latin American re-democratization.

The scholarly discussion of contemporary Latin American development
has focused mainly, up till now, on the political economy of adjustment,
upon the mechanisms of democratic transition and consolidation, or on the
relationships between the two (especially through the notions of governance
and governability).[3] Much less attention has been given to the recent and
current manifestations of conflict, violence, repression and terror, their
consequences, and their social, political and cultural preconditions. These
phenomena seem to be at odds with the image of gradual economic and
political development towards a supposed status of liberal and democratic
'modernity'. It is by no means certain that stable, civic forms of rule and
social integration will prevail or endure in Latin America. This caution is
inspired by the legacies of repressive dictatorships and civil wars, as well as
by the persistence of poverty, inequality, and social and political exclusion.
The latter form the backdrop to new and perturbing forms of violence that
seem to be on the rise in post-authoritarian Latin American societies.

This volume aims to address one particularly distressing aspect of this
problem: past and present forms of violence, conflict and terror. In the
chapters that follow, a number of authors deal with violent social and political
conflicts in Latin America by analysing the variety of its backgrounds,
manifestations and consequences. In this introductory chapter, we will try to
provide a first demarcation of the issues of conflict, violence and fear that
have plagued Latin American societies in the past and continue to do so in
the present. In fact, it is our assertion that social and political violence has
been an endemic and permanent feature of the pattern of nation-building in
Latin America and the conflicts generated by this process. We will suggest
a typological distinction between three kinds of violence in the history of
Latin America: violence related to maintaining the traditional rural and
oligarchic social order; violence related to the problem of the modernization
of the state and the incorporation of the masses in politics; and, finally,
violence related to the present-day difficulties of consolidating democratic
stability, economic progress and social inclusion. We then proceed to discuss
two enduring background features that underly, in our understanding, the
tenacity of social and political violence in Latin America. In the first place,
it is nurtured by long-lasting patterns of social exclusion of large parts of
the population. It has been observed that Latin America has experienced
relatively few fundamental social revolutions despite the almost permanent
'pre-revolutionary' nature of the profound social cleavages within the region's

social fabric.[4] It may be true that current social inequalities seldom lead to massive violent reactions by the poor and excluded; violent protests seem to be localized, focused and of short duration.[5] Still, as we will argue, these cleavages lead to what we call the 'informalization' of society and the subsequent erosion of the notion of citizenship. We feel that this tendency runs counter to the prospect of institutionalizing and pacifying political life. Second, we point at the legacy of violence engrained in the dynamics of the state and politics. We especially refer to the institutionalization of arbitrary violence within the state and the effects this has, in terms of generalized fear, on politics and on social life in general. Finally, we present the outline of the book, using our discussion of violence and fear as a conceptual framework to situate the issues discussed in each of the remaining chapters of the book.

Violence and Nation-building in Latin America

Of course, the problem of violence and the tenacity of violent conflicts in thwarting democracy, stable institutions and hence, in the end, undermining social consensus, is not new in the history of modern state formation and nation-building. Nor is it unique for Latin America. Indeed, the past decade has witnessed a new wave of violence that was part and parcel of varied manifestations of social, regional, ethnic or religious contentions that have been challenging established forms of 'national' legitimate authority. Such tendencies run counter to conventional images of 'nation-building' that stress the cumulative pacification and institutionalization of conflicts within modern societies. The state is supposed to embody this kind of progress, not only by taking charge of the monopoly of the legitimate means of collective violence, but also by forming the frame of reference for the notion of citizenship and the peaceful settlement of social differences within civil society.[6]

From this point of view it is tempting but erroneous to see the recent forms of violence either as 'deviant', that is to say, as being related to underdevelopment or incomplete modernity, or as transitory, meaning a return to a 'normal' legitimate civic order in some near future, once its basic conditions have been restored. In fact, a number of scholars have been paying attention to the violence intrinsically involved in the construction of the modern world. Moore, echoing the classics, has shown that so-called 'modernization', the transition from agricultural societies to urbanizing nation-states, typically involved violent forms of elimination and re-accommodation of social classes. The complex processes of modern state formation were to a large extent based on the deployment of military violence by contending polities, as has been demonstrated by Tilly. Still, he sees this as the prelude to modernity in which the 'relative non-violence of civil life' prevails. Keane, in contrast, offers us a transcending image of the delicate balance between 'civility' and violence that runs through modern history from the Enlightenment up till the post-Cold War present.[7] In this light, the persistence of violence in Latin America is not particularly unique, but it has had quite specific characteristics, as we shall demonstrate below.

Social and political violence have been recurrent elements of social change in Latin America. This is especially noteworthy because the often violent nature of Latin American society has to be placed against the backdrop of the 'modern' norm of civil consensus and institutional stability to which the Latin American nations themselves formally adhere. Violence has of course been present anywhere. But in (Western) Europe, for instance, violence, during the first half of the twentieth century, has mainly taken the form of military conflicts between states. More recently, violence in parts of Eastern Europe, Africa and Asia has emerged in the absence or because of the collapse of accepted societal and political institutions and rules. In contrast, violence in Latin America, has been endemic in spite of stable state systems and the existence of formal institutional frameworks that, on paper, ought to guarantee order, stability and a basis for consensus.

In fact, violence has historically been a central feature in the evolution of Latin American societies. The European conquest of the region was mainly based on the destruction of existing social patterns and the systematic use of violence (in both physical and psychological terms) against the native population, in order to subject them to the new colonial order. Repression was essential for the domination of slaves, peasants and forced labourers. Repression was also a tool to express social discontent and desire for change among parts of the population, by means of Indian rebellions, peasant and artisan uprisings, and slave resistance. Colonial society, while formally organized along lines of hierarchy and monopolistic control, in practice presented an often fragile texture. Latin American independence often passed through episodes of violence. In Spanish America (but also in Haiti) the formation of independent states was won on the battlefield. After independence, violence was a key mechanism for the struggle between various pretenders to power: regional *caudillos*, political factions, insurgent groups, or contending elites and classes. The consolidation of a national state was a slow process in the face of continuous challenges to its institutional integrity and its monopoly of the legitimate means of violence. During the present century, the use of political and military violence to achieve or conserve power has been characteristic of a great variety of political systems, regimes and movements: from the *caudillo* regimes from the turn of the century until the depression years, to the bureaucratic–authoritarian military regimes and the revolutionary movements of the 1960s and 1970s.

Violence, however, has not been confined solely to the domain of political power and governmental institutions, although this kind of violence tended to attract the greatest attention. Nor are the physical or open forms of violence the only ones that affect social relations in Latin America. Socio-economic inequality and deprivation, ethnic discrimination, criminal violence, death squads, kidnapping and so on, can be mentioned alongside the stereotyped *pronunciamientos, cuartelazos* and *golpes* perpetrated by the military, with their accompanying political assassinations, repression, torture and disappearances, revolutionary armed struggle, and outside interventions frequently associated with politics in Latin America. Together, these forms present a broad array of threats to what can be called 'livelihood security'. A consistent lack of the basic parameters of such security leads to the creation of fear as an endemic condition. Fear related to livelihood insecurity is an often latent but at times manifest phenomenon affecting a large part of the population up till the present day. Here we deal, however, not so much with these kinds of what some would call 'structural violence', but with violence and fear that are more directly related to the way political power has been used. In fact, we would suggest that three broad types, or cycles, of violence can be discerned in the social and political history of Latin America since the mid-nineteenth century. These cycles are characterized not only by the nature of the violence involved, but especially by the way it is related to patterns of social and political domination and interaction. These patterns are historical as well, but it is not easy to set them in a chronological order, as we will see below.

Violence in the Traditional Order

The first cycle refers to the kind of violence that underlies, almost as if it were taken for granted, the social and political domination of rather closed and restricted elites predicated upon the systematic exclusion of the 'masses, castes, and classes'. This type of violence, with certain roots in colonial history, came to the fore in the course of the nineteenth century. As such, it was imbued with a basic ambivalence that remained a distinctive feature of Latin American societies up till the present. On the one hand, we see elite adherence to European civility, progress, liberalism, bourgeois society; on the other hand, this civility was founded upon extreme social hierarchies led by the logic of exclusion. After a half century following the 1810–20 in-dependence decade of formative violence (civil wars, *caudillo* contestation and scattered popular uprisings), state formation was stabilized under an oligarchic order. Consensus between politically relevant groups was established in many Latin American countries. Some even speak of a situation of oligarchic hegemony.[8] Roughly between 1870 and 1930, most Latin American countries demonstrated an apparent supremacy of civil rule and domestic order (Mexico after 1910 being the great exception). Even Colombia ex-perienced a rare interlude of political tranquillity under the rule of the Conservative party, interrupted only by the *Guerra de los Mil Dias* (1899–1902).

Nevertheless, this order was a violent one. Force and coercion were manifest on different levels and in various forms. The interaction between patrons and clients across hierarchical class divisions usually combined loyalty, based on the extension of resources, with allegiance produced by coercion. Clientelism has been analysed as being one important mechanism in reproducing class hierarchies in Latin America.[9] Labour systems, especially in the countryside, often involved coercive recruitment methods, such as forced or indentured field labour. Strikes carried out by the nascent urban working classes and their organizations were generally met with repressive action.[10] The popular adage among politicians in Brazil's Old Republic was: 'the social problem is a police problem'.

The violent repression of social, regional and ethnic uprisings was commonplace throughout the nineteenth and early twentieth centuries. We could point to the regional rebellions in Brazil prior to 1850, peasant uprisings in Mexico and the Andean countries, localized uprisings either inspired by ethnic politics (the Oriente uprising in Cuba) or popular religious fervour (the Canudos campaign in Bahia, Brazil).[11] One general feature of this kind of sociopolitical violence may be that the fragile process of state consolidation was easily seen as being threatened by the mobilization of the 'dangerous' classes. In so far as the mass of the population was socially and culturally excluded from the national projects of the *criollo* elites, the latter were unable to perceive the collective expressions of the popular masses in any other way than as putting the oligarchic states in great peril. In addition, despite the hegemony sometimes attributed to oligarchic rule, the resource of military coercion to back it up was never forfeited: the Mexican Porfiriato, Brazil's Old Republic, Colombia's Pax Conservadora, Peru's Aristocratic Republic, and the personalized dictatorships in countries like Venezuela, Nicaragua, Cuba or the Dominican Republic, were founded upon alliances between the oligarchies and the military. As a result, there was an iron-clad civility for the privileged few, and violence against the underprivileged masses was a routine affair. The notion of citizenship was inoperative.

It is tempting to consider this kind of violence as 'traditional', as something of the nineteenth and early twentieth centuries. But one need not adopt the full thrust of the cultural determinist argument, as presented, by among others, Wiarda,[12] to see that this kind of violence persists up till the present in many shapes and forms. As a matter of fact, in recognizing the specific trajectory of Latin America's Iberic path to modernity, Wiarda considers this kind of violence as culturally predetermined. He argues that it is rooted in the Catholic and Iberic legacy of warfare, patrimonialism, corporate autonomy of the armed forces, and so on. Without entering here into this debate, it seems to us that it is more relevant to consider this issue in terms of the persistence of the problem of the 'private appropriation of public power'. This may have some roots in Iberic and colonial patrimonialism, but has been reproduced under changing conditions employing old as well as new social and political artefacts and justifications. Hagopian argues that many of the practices of so-called 'traditional rule' have been constantly modernized

to adapt to changing social and political conditions, including the recent
wave of democratic transitions.[13]

Mass Politics, Political Violence and 'Internal Warfare'

The second cycle of violence we would like to distinguish was brought about
by what Weffort calls the 'problem of the incorporation of the masses' into
the Latin American political process.[14] The rise of anti-oligarchic counter-
elites and the growing pressure from organized popular sectors to take part
in power arrangements challenged the prevailing oligarchic order.[15] The
transition – sometimes abrupt, sometimes gradual – to wider (popular) political
participation generally led to the emergence of populist regimes marked by
corporatism and limited formal democracy.[16] But whatever the manner in
which populist regimes came to power or their subsequent characteristics,
some degree of violence was almost always involved. Violence was generated
not only to overthrow the so-called old order, but also, as in Argentina or
Peru in the 1930s, to fend off populist or reformist intrusions into the
political arena. What is important for our discussion, however, is that social
violence became more politicized, and even ideologically charged, concomitant
with the opening up of the political domain.

The typical cycle of violence between, roughly, the 1930s and the 1970s
ran from the advent of what Touraine calls 'national-popular' regimes and
alliances, through a period of their instability and breakdown, and on to the
rise of 'counter-revolutionary' authoritarian regimes dominated by the armed
forces.[17] This cycle is typical but not emblematic of every Latin American
country: Colombia, Costa Rica, Mexico, Peru and Venezuela deviate in a
number of important ways. On the other hand, the typical trajectory can be
seen to shimmer behind the historical experiences of Argentina, Bolivia,
Brazil, Chile, Guatemala, Honduras and Uruguay. Classical populism was not
equally manifest in all these countries, but in some way the problem of
popular participation and social and political reform was addressed, its limits
were reached, and a reaction followed in which the logic of political violence
was brought to its most extreme consequences. Let us look closer at the
violence within this infamous cycle of populism and authoritarianism.

Except for the case of Mexico, the violence involved in the rise of populist
regimes was rather limited in scope and duration. In countries like Chile,
Costa Rica and Uruguay the process was gradual and institutional. In
Argentina, the rise of Perón was accompanied by a number of short outbursts
of urban protest against his opponents. In Brazil, the revolutionary movement
led by Vargas in 1930 achieved state power after a limited military campaign.
In Colombia, the end of the Pax Conservadora rekindled the previously
existing endemic political and social violence, in which parts of the Liberal
party adopted a populist–reformist platform. In Costa Rica, a short and
small-scale civil war in 1948 had the happy consequence of abolishing the

army, with notable political consequences to this day. In Bolivia and Guatemala, reformist overtures during the 1950s marked the start of a long period of protracted low-intensity violence and repression, which in Guatemala erupted in the 1970s into one of the most brutal civil conflicts of this century.

The novelty, perhaps, was that violence was now employed to gain access to, or to secure, political power. The ideological substratum was increasingly formed by 'nationalism', but of this Latin American nationalism, a number of (conflicting) varieties came to the fore. Under populism, nationalistic sentiments were directed towards forming a broad and fairly inclusive alliance which tried to foster national import substitution and gave some political space to new (mainly urban) social categories such as the industrialists, the middle-class professionals and organized labour. The military were actively incorporated into these alliances and, as such, they began to assume their typical political role as arbiters of national order, stability and progress. In many cases, some level of formal democracy was built into the political process. But at a deeper level, and most relevant to the present discussion, the shadow of ongoing political conflict and violence loomed. This has to do with one of the most notable characteristics of these kinds of inclusive political models (generally dubbed *estado de compromiso* or 'compromise state'): the lack of long-term consensus and the potential or actual instability this brought on. This fragility and instability can be related to the lack of trust between the principal societal and political actors under populism. Due to conflicting agendas – continuity against reform, different economic sectors against each other, elitism against broadening popular participation – the principal protagonists seemed to get locked into some sort of zero-sum stalemate. This was exacerbated by the predominance of the state in defining and mediating the relationships between social groups. Put differently, the access to state power was seen as crucial by all politically activated social sectors. This might have led to the widespread perception that gains by some would mean losses for others, in absolute and eventually catastrophic terms. The loss of control of the state was seen as an imminent threat to a group's or class's position within the national order.[18]

It is perhaps significant that the country that best solved the problem of populist political instability, Mexico, was the country that experienced the most violent initial eruption of the masses into the national political arena. The Mexican revolution was a massive and protracted display of social and political violence, whose complexities often obscured its long-term implications.[19] What is important to note here is that two decades of internal warfare and widespread political violence were wilfully ended by a momentous and long-lasting effort to bring about political institutionalization and social reform. The terms of the Mexican compromise – both in its formal and informal dimensions – wrought under the aegis of the PRI, are (or were) unique and were largely responsible for the relative absence of politically inspired violence

at the national level until 1994. As a result, Mexico was also the major
exception to the paradigm pioneered by O'Donnell that relatively advanced
processes of modernization and industrial development in Latin America led
to the establishment of repressive (hence violent) bureaucratic-authoritarian
regimes.[20] We need not repeat the arguments against the original formulation
of this thesis[21] to agree that the tensions incorporated in the populist alliances
led, in a number of cases, to the rise to power of institutional military-civil
dictatorships that resorted to systematic violence to stay in power, to neutralize
opponents, and to push forward specific projects of economic and social
development. Once again, the logic of exclusion surfaced, this time based on
the structural propensities of the developmental models adopted by the
authoritarian regimes, compounded by the closure of the political system to
groups and interests that opposed these regimes and their projects.

Regardless of the differences between the various bureaucratic-authoritarian 'projects' (there are, for instance, basic differences between the Brazilian
and the Chilean variety), they had in common a certain conservative notion
of the 'national interest' or 'permanent national objectives', that were seen
as threatened by radical (communist) internal enemies. These enemies (the
former populists and the newly arriving radical leftists inspired by the Cuban
revolution) were confronted with the logic of internal warfare, regardless of
the actual strength of left-wing armed struggle.[22] From Guatemala to
Argentina, the dictatorships declared war on their populations in the name
of freedom and the preservation of western-Christian civilization.[23] This
violence was based on clear doctrinal guidelines and strategic notions, as in
a genuine war, but its perverse effects were inevitable in the sense that
internal warfare led to state terrorism. One of the key characteristics of
systematic state terrorism is the proliferation of arbitrariness. No national
security doctrine or 'strong democracy' concept will ever manage to restrain
the perpetrators of state violence on the level of the day-to-day practices of
the *guerra sucia*. The leading military political strategist of the Brazilian regime,
General Golbery do Couto e Silva, referred to this problem in terms of the
'black hole' created by Brazil's security apparatus: beyond all control, without
any sensible direction, eventually turning into a threat to the sustainability of
military rule itself.[24]

As we will argue below, this problem of the continuity of the logic of
arbitrary repression by security forces is one of the tricky problems still
present in the legacy of the authoritarian regimes of the recent past. This
does not mean that the process of (re)building institutional democracy, and
in some cases of ending open civil war through reconciliation and formal
peace treaties, may not be successful. On the contrary, what seems to be
fairly indisputable is that the past experiences of repression and violence
have injected all relevant actors and groups with the strong conviction that
institutional democracy is relevant and desirable to solve Latin America's
long-term problems. Equally, a lot of progress has been made towards

consolidating the institutional framework for democratic politics, and the basic consensus among political forces that is necessary to sustain it. Still, this does not mean that all conditions for effective governance are now progressively met.[25] Governance is jeopardized by a number of problems. The persistence of violence and social conflicts is one of them.

Violence in Post-authoritarian Latin America

The advent of democracy, now formally prevailing everywhere except Cuba, did not mean the end of violence as a social and political problem. On the contrary, one might cynically state that violence is being democratized in Latin America. It ceased to be the resource of only the traditionally powerful or of the grim uniformed guardians of the nation. Violence increasingly appears as an option for a multitude of actors in pursuit of all kind of goals.

The textbook example of this trend is, of course, Colombia. The deployment of violence has become so customary that to a certain extent the Colombian state has ceased to exist in its Weberian quality of the monopolizer of the legitimate use of violence. Not only the military, the paramilitaries, the guerrillas, and the drug cartels use violence as a matter of course; also at lower levels of society, violence can mean a career or an instrument for social mobility, or even an instrument for reversing traditional social hierarchies. For instance, in the city of Medellín, the spread of violence not only enabled the ascent of 'marginal' youngsters from the *tugurios* (the shantytowns), but also created new spaces for neighbourhood associations to confront a traditionally conservative municipal administration.[26] Further illustrations can be derived from the case of Brazil. Brazil presents the ambivalent situation of a country in which, on the one hand, formal redemocratization has proceeded considerably and enjoys widespread support and legitimacy. During the past decades, Brazilian society has been thoroughly politicized and a lively civil society has been mushrooming. At the same time, however, violence and arbitrariness remain prominent features of national life.

These forms of violence in Brazil and elsewhere are not new, but apprehension has clearly been rising over the past ten years or so. In addition, it nurtures an overall climate in which (especially on the level of daily law enforcement) random and arbitrary violence persists in spite of the demise of authoritarian rule. This kind of violence is not only directed at common criminals, but also at social activists such as landless peasants occupying an estate, metal-workers on strike, or gold miners (*garimpeiros*) being expelled from their site. Especially on Brazil's Amazon frontier, daily violence is endemic and testifies to the incapacity of the state to uphold a legitimate and peaceful internal order. This may well contribute to a general climate (as a matter of fact to a large extent created by the introduction of everyday arbitrariness during the dictatorship) in which violence is seen as a normal option with which to pursue interests, attain power or resolve conflicts.

The 'new violence' in Latin America pits the repressive instincts of the traditional elites and the security forces against an increasingly wide variety of actors who also have recourse to violence, despite the establishment of formal democratic rule. This new kind of social and political insecurity is, in the first place, exacerbated by the continuation and even deepening of social cleavages in virtually every Latin American country during the past two decades. In the second place, the end of military rule did not abolish the prerogatives and the self-appointed role of the armed forces to deal with 'threats', as has been systematically demonstrated by Lovemann.[27] This means that violent backlashes in response to social mobilization or 'upheavals' remain a common feature of post-authoritarian Latin America. In addition, years or decades of arbitrary rule contributed to an overall climate of impunity among incumbents of the security forces (most notably the police and the special anti-subversive units) which very often gave law enforcement under the new democracies a grim and, in fact, criminal overtone. We witness state representatives who resort to arbitrary violence despite the installation of democracy and the adoption of pro-active human rights policies by central governments. We see the mushrooming of (organized) criminal violence at the same time as grassroots civic organizations with peaceful agendas proliferate. The perilous trend seems to be that the basic ambiguity of Latin America we mentioned earlier is being reproduced: progress towards democratization and citizens' empowerment goes hand in hand with the erosion of state legitimacy due to the state's failure to promote social participation and the rule of law. This leaves what could be called 'governance voids', which are inevitably occupied by actors who obey the law of the jungle. In turn, new authoritarian backlashes, or the perversion of civil governance, may eventually result. In the next two sections, we will discuss both components of present-day 'societies of fear' in more detail.

Threatening a Peaceful Social Order: Poverty, Informality and Exclusion

Pauperization, mass poverty, informality and social exclusion became increasingly intense phenomena during the aftermath of the military dictatorships in the early 1980s. They sprang up as the result of the economic crisis, aggravated in the short term by the structural adjustment packages in most Latin American countries. Already historically characterized by endemic poverty and extreme patterns of inequality, Latin America saw the numbers of those living in misery swelled by the 'new poor', the lower middle and formal working classes that recently fell victim to the economic crisis and the adjustment policies carried out in the mid- and late 1980s. The new poor are the members of what used to be the working class and the urban middle classes, together with former rural smallholders and peasants.

Since the 1970s, poverty in Latin America has become an increasingly urban phenomenon, which increases its potential to provoke social conflict, disturbances of order and political radicalization. However, if one thing stands out with regard to the strategies employed by the urban poor, it is the peaceful and inventive nature of their strategies for daily survival. Poverty is identified largely with the 'informal sector', a social and economic complex within the national economy and society. From Monterrey in Mexico to Puerto Mont in Chile, the informal sector has been growing, reflected in the multitude of small-scale activities of all kinds which have taken the capital cities and other urban localities by storm. Half of the inhabitants of the capital cities of Mexico, Central America and most Andean countries describe themselves as 'informal'. Seen from the inside, 'informality' operates separately from the formal economic and social institutions, and from the elementary civil rights associated with them: employment, a regular income, labour unions, social legislation, and access to the social institutions that provide such basic needs as health services, education and housing. Seen from the outside, the Latin American 'private sector of the poor' (the domain of social exclusion and poverty) is growing at an astonishing rate; and it is now challenging national governments, whatever the ideology of the president or the composition of the cabinet.

Although not directly conducive to violence, the social and political consequence of this long-term process of informalization and social exclusion is the erosion of the legitimacy of the formal civil, political and public order. It contributes to the emergence of parallel institutions and the 'privatization' of public administration. For instance, in Central America and most Andean countries, the 'Chambers' of the entrepreneurs, the *gremios* of the lawyers and other middle-class professions, and the all-powerful labour confederations began to decline during the 1980s in terms of both membership and political presence.[28] In Argentina, Brazil and Mexico the same process was observed, albeit on a less dramatic scale. In the early 1980s the Peruvian anthropologist Matos Mar[29] wrote a prophetic essay on 'the other face of society'. In it he describes the decline of the organizations that make up civil society and sketches the timid emergence of a variety of micro-entrepreneurial organizations: local and regional chambers of artisans, the institutionalized soup kitchen and other organizations which provide cheap food in the metropolitan slums, all of them bound by dependency to private development organizations, churches and welfare institutions funded by external donor agencies rather than by the local or national authorities.

Informalization is penetrating the political arena. During the 1980s, in Peru and other Latin American countries, the political parties lost the confidence of the voters. In view of the social and economic crisis, and in response to the erosion of the traditional political parties, the public turned its attention to 'politicians without a party', who entered the scene offering to form hard-working governments. The first electoral manifestation of this change in direction was the election of the mayor of Lima, a television company entrepreneur. During the presidential election of 1990, Mario Vargas Llosa, a celebrated writer but completely apolitical, unexpectedly put together a movement and stood as a non-political candidate. However, he came on to the scene quite early and, in the course of his campaign, he came to be seen as part of the formal political system due to his alliance with the traditional parties. At the last minute another candidate entered the race. He was an unknown professor named Alberto Fujimori, with no political programme and no candidates for ministerial posts. The election of Fujimori was the expression, in its simplest form, of the feelings of an entire nation, and their message was the rejection of the political parties. But there were other factors at work here, not only in Peru, but also in Guatemala where the phenomenon of the outsider elected to the presidency was repeated with the victory of Serrano. It is a curious fact that in both countries the outsider won with the open support of the informal sector and the new evangelical churches which have been creating a substantial following among the poor urban masses.

The risk posed by the growing political weight of the 'informals' for democratic consolidation comes to the fore in the so-called neo-populist tendency in contemporary Latin American politics. The anti-politicians who came to power upon the waves of a direct appeal to the masses, while rejecting the political establishment, may well side-step the institutions of democracy and reinstate a kind of exceptionary rule. The plebiscitary nature of their legitimacy can be reinforced by an alliance with the security forces in an effort to address pressing national problems. Clearly, the *autogolpe* carried out in 1992 by Fujimori, in connivance with the army – especially the intelligence service controlled by the ex-army captain Vladimiro Montesinos – exemplifies this possibility. With this move, Fujimori neutralized parliament, the judiciary, and the political parties, in order to 'end corruption and ineffectiveness' and to get a free hand in implementing austerity and fighting Shining Path. Subsequently, Fujimori obtained widespread support among the Limeño urban masses.

The informalization of society also results in the restructuring of the forces of public order. In Peru, one example has been the semi-institutionalization of the *rondas campesinas* as a forward arm of the police and armed forces. In their transformation into private armies in the early 1990s, they followed the same road as the armed bands of workers attached to the poorer districts or to the unions of the legal Left, armed first with sticks, then with home-made weapons, and finally with conventional weapons. Alongside these popular self-defence and peace-keeping groups, private organizations of a similar type began to be formed. These are private sector security institutions, companies with personnel recruited from within the formal and informal sectors, from among servicemen who are retired, discharged or on leave from the army or from the police. These private *vigilantes* find employment and income guarding banks, houses, districts, supermarkets, even ministries and public buildings. Mention must be made, too, of the paramilitary bands, sometimes closely related to the existing political parties, sometimes belonging to the complicated networks of the *narco*-economy. Finally, one must consider the consequences of the introduction in Lima of the *serenazgo*, the district police made up of self-armed metropolitan inhabitants. These are the armed middle class, protecting their belongings, functioning as a complement to the capital's police forces.

In Colombia, *milicianos* or armed vigilantes, whose members come from the ranks of ex-guerrillas have found a new niche in recent years in the poorer neighbourhoods of the big cities, where neither the army nor the police dare enter.[30] One of the most disturbing problems is that of the existence of the so-called *escuadrones de la muerte*. Who knows all the details of the links that exist between the forces of law and order and the sinister paramilitary and quasi-police organizations that have operated, or are operating, in Brazil, in Colombia, in El Salvador, in Guatemala? They are growing in strength, established in the interstices of counter-insurgency warfare and the struggle to control crime, eliminating not only the enemies of the state but also petty criminals, whether these be minors or even young children. In order to complement this sketch of the informalization process affecting the forces of law and order, it is necessary to emphasize the part played by the *narcos*, whose aforementioned armed bands virtually administer whole departments of Latin American countries.

It is perhaps cynical to argue that a certain 'democratization of violence' has been under way in Latin America. Formerly the use of violence was restricted to certain sectors: the aristocracy, the elite, the army, the police. Nowadays most of Latin America's urban society (and part of rural society) has access to small arms equipment. The proliferation of violence, even in its more anomic forms, has reached the stage of mass production and mass consumption.

Societies of Fear: Their Causes and Consequences

Fear is the institutional, cultural and psychological repercussion of violence. Fear is a response to institutional destabilization, social exclusion, individual ambiguity and uncertainty. In Latin America, a latent though sometimes open 'culture of fear' has obtained institutional characteristics, induced by systematic yet at the same time arbitrary violence, often organized from above by the state apparatus or by central authorities and reproduced within the *fuerzas del orden*. Then, as is argued by Edelberto Torres-Rivas in the final chapter of this volume, the culture of fear is embedded in a generalized climate marked by the 'trivialization of horror'. The second cycle of political violence and internal warfare mentioned above was marked by the perfecting of state terrorism and the proliferation of arbitrary repression with systemic logic. Without the supporting doctrines of low-intensity warfare against the internal enemies of the state, Latin America could not have developed its 'harvest of violence'[31] and its 'psychoanalysis of violence'.[32] The near-anomic environment of anxiety, characteristic of the third cycle of violence we distinguished above, would be much less pronounced without Latin America's heyday of armoured repression, terror and torture. Several chapters of this book will be dedicated to the machinery and legacy of the 'dirty war' in Argentina, Chile, Brazil, the ethnic civil wars in Guatemala and the draconic guerrilla and counter-insurgency campaigns in Peru.

The creation of an apparatus of systematic repression and a concomitant climate of fear, sanctioned by the armed forces, but permitted to exist by civil governments and the justice apparatus, was the result of a combination of explicit policies and implicit routines. Although rooted in the process of state formation during the second half of the nineteenth century, the principles of a police state, where the forces of law and order are transformed into the battalions of brutality and repression, were fully elaborated during the cycle of authoritarianism from the 1960s to the 1980s. This formed the backbone of 'societies of fear' in which a climate of insecurity, anxiety and suspense overshadowed all other feelings. Ultimately, the power centre of the terror machinery was localized in the legitimized (and sometimes legalized) independent working of the armed forces and their more sinister extended arms and legs: the intelligence community, the security forces, the paramilitary organizations, the different, subordinated local police bodies and sometimes even the death squads.[33] After transitions to formal democratic government, substantial parts of this apparatus remained untouched. Lovemann rightly stresses the threat to strengthening democracy posed by the continuing supervision of social and political life by the military, based upon their guardianship of 'permanent national objectives' and anchored in exceptional legislation: 'Maintaining the essential features of national security legislation ... has significantly altered the meaning of democracy in Latin America by imposing severe constraints, both psychological and legal, on the extent to which public life can be carried out, whether in areas of public contestation, electoral competition, and/or opposition to the incumbent government.'[34]

Not only do the constitutional and juridical mechanisms upon which military tutelage is founded cast shadows over democracy and civic life; the de facto autonomy of the security forces and the subordination of civil law enforcement to military security doctrines also contribute to the perpetuity of violence and fear. During the delicate efforts of dismantling the terror machines (a task that has only recently been taken up) one should always remember the ubiquitous presence of the military powers who oppose the mechanisms of civilian control.[35]

The superiority of the security forces over Latin American civil society during the decades of the military and civil-military dictatorships was based upon the internal logic of military organization and its post-World War II notion of 'new professionalism'. This entailed a moral appropriation by the armed forces of the core values and destiny of the nation, and led the military to spearhead a technocratic approach towards national ('strategic') planning and public ('hierarchical') administration.[36] These strategies were founded upon comprehensive doctrines of national security or national stability devised by military intellectuals and disseminated through civil-military training institutions. It is remarkable that three of the Latin American countries deeply affected by their military governments in the past decades, Brazil, Guatemala and Peru, created influential postgraduate study centres where military intellectuals lectured, wrote, thought and prospered. After the end of military rule, the influence of the war colleges waned somewhat in Brazil and Peru, but their role was taken over by their heirs, the military intelligence agencies. In Brazil, the National Intelligence Service (SNI) played a key role in policy formulation both during the last military government of João Figueiredo (1979–85) and during the civilian government of José Sarney (1985–90). The Peruvian intelligence chief Montesinos remains a powerful factor behind the Fujimori government. In Guatemala, the Centro ESTNA (Centro de Estudios de La Estabilidad Nacional) was founded in the late 1980s. Contrary to its counterparts in other Latin American countries, this centre aims to develop a doctrine for post-authoritarian civil–military relations, rather than for underpinning exceptional rule by the armed forces. Still, the supervisory role of the Guatemalan military over democratic consolidation is institutionalized.

As a consequence, the military retained substantial control over the formulation of policy in 'sensitive' areas using the intelligence system as their principal vehicle. Except in the clear case of Mexico,[37] the ties between military and civilian intelligence in most other Latin American countries are very close, generally in the context of military predominance. As a consequence of the 'internal enemy' concept, military and civilian intelligence is mainly directed against potential 'subversive forces' *within* the national territory. In countries such as Brazil, Chile, Guatemala and Peru (at least until 1989), the elected or appointed presidents are the ideological hostages of their intelligence advisers. Chile's linkage committee with the commander-in-chief maintains an easy advisory relation with the president and the senior civilian cabinet members. Brazil's military *ministros da casa*, of which the *ministro-chefe* of the national intelligence system was part, exerted decisive influence both during the 1964–85 years of dictatorship and the civilian regime of Sarney (1985–90). In Guatemala, the defence ministers have an army general as presidential chief-of-staff/chief of the advisory group. Civilian presidents Cereso, Serrano, De Leon Carpio, and Arzú received, from their obligatory intelligence advisers, 'consultative briefings' on the long-term national development and security priorities, as perceived by the army. Fujimori, Peruvian president-elect in 1990 without a list of cabinet members and a coherent government plan, received warm hospitality in the *Círculo Militar* during the transition period and the first weeks of his presidency. There he was extensively briefed by military intelligence about anti-guerrilla tactics, human rights, development strategies and long-term economic and political priorities. His intelligence mentor Montesinos, president of the newly created Strategic Council of State, acts as virtual president of the national intelligence system. Military intelligence provides the results of the bi-weekly opinion polls about the presidential popularity: *vox populi, vox Dei.*

A further element bequeathed by the militarization of politics in most Latin American countries – this time Chile being the exception – is military predominance over the national and local police. It is common for army officers to hold sensitive posts in the police hierarchy, and the political responsibility for the national police is often a matter of civil–military power distribution. Sometimes an army general is the minister of interior affairs or public safety. In other cases only the vice-minister or the national police director is a former army officer. In some cases – Guatemala, for instance – the police are subordinated to the military not only at the national, but also at the regional and local levels; the local police have to coordinate, in detail, with the local army commander and depend completely on army intelligence and army information. This is closely linked to the problem of immunity and impunity enjoyed by the security forces. In the case of the military there is a legal base. The formal juxtaposition of the armed forces and civilians, the existence of military courts, the thin but always valid excuse of the 'emergency situation' prevent adequate persecution of human rights violations by secluded offenders. The inviolability of the officers corps during the anti-guerrilla and anti-narcotics campaigns of the last decades in Colombia, El Salvador, Guatemala and Peru has to be remembered as a chronic obstacle to effective reforms. In post-authoritarian Latin America, the involvement of the various police forces in brutal acts of violence and the failure of the civil authorities to punish such acts properly are important factors in the reproduction of fear among the citizenry of the authorities.[38]

The problem of fear at the societal and individual level has only recently begun to be addressed. The present state of scholarly research is that of comparative case studies. In some cases, the build-up of the specialized instruments and routines of state terrorism are described in detail, as well as the responses of individual victims.[39] The traumatic consequences of violent experiences, such as torture and intimidation, disappearances, executions, and arbitrary arrests, and the minute description of ethnographical experiences of violent situations, contribute mainly to the phenomenology of individual responses to collective violence.[40] However, the subjective and initially in-dividual responses are, during the next stages of state terrorism, collective answers that take on, in the long run, the shape of societal characteristics.[41] House searches and arrests, followed by lack of information about the prisoner's whereabouts and by apparently random accusations, torture and the widespread knowledge of indiscriminate torturing of captured victims, contribute to a generalized climate of individual weakness, of permanent alertness without the possibility of escape, of collective powerlessness, of lack of control over daily life and the near future, and of a distorted perception of reality. Facts and certainties become blurred, all news is threatening, and the boundaries between good and evil are veiled. Felicity and hope are substituted by fantasies of suffering, feelings of vulnerability, worries and phobias, and self-blame. Self-blame is followed by self-censorship and the culture of silence, an avoidance of discussion, and secrecy about trivialities. Horror becomes a routine social phenomenon.

A recently published anthropological description of daily life in war-torn Guatemala describes explicitly how the routinization of terror and the socialization of violence determine daily life in Indian *municipios* in the department of Chimaltenango.[42] Routinization, as the author remarks, allows people to live in a chronic state of fear with a façade of normality. Fear surfaces in dreams and chronic illness. Whisperings, innuendos and rumours of death lists circulate. Ambiguity becomes institutionalized. The people live under constant surveillance. The military encampment, camouflaged, is situated on a nearby hillside. Spies, military commissioners and civil patrollers provide the backbone of military scrutiny. Traditional village authorities are subordinated to the local military commander. Terror becomes defused through subtle messages. Language and symbols are utilized to mitigate military vigilance and presence. The militarization of the mind affects the children; the use of camouflage cloth for civilian clothing, military wallets, key chains, belts, caps and toy helicopters reproduces the intertwining of military and civilian life. Former enforced recruits, having left as Maya Indians, return home to become the military commissioners, paid informers or heads of the civil patrols. Families' loyalties are divided; a fragile integrity of village life is apparently maintained. Silence and secrecy serve as a protective shield, and the villages have been transformed into a kind of micro-cosmos of fear.

It is not easy to overcome the legacy of violence and fear in post-authoritarian Latin America. Not only is this due to the continuing situation of political instability and institutional uncertainty, which continues to make the threat of the resurrection of violent and arbitrary regimes a real one; the current civil and democratic governments also find it difficult to remove the legacy of institutionalized and arbitrary violence embedded in the state. Furthermore, the deepening of social inequalities, and the appearance of new governance voids with respect to maintaining a peaceful social order and the rule of law, provide new fuel to the long-lasting fire of violence and fear in Latin America.

Outline of the Book

The chapters that are brought together in this book all treat distinctive aspects of the problems presented so far. As we have already argued, concrete cases of violence and fear in Latin America are not confined by the analytical typology of violence suggested above. Although there are compelling reasons to regard them as temporal cycles, in practice different forms of violence, as well as their causes and consequences, are rather superimposed one on the other: new forms appear while altering the existing ones. This means that the spectre of violence in Latin America has grown increasingly complex, especially during the past decades. For this reason, the contributions in this book look at a diverse range of cases and salient features of the problem under study, adopting in most cases a historical perspective to elucidate recent and current dimensions of violence and fear.

Rather than trying to use our typology of violence as a framework for the organization of the book, we opted for a slightly different approach based on an empirical distinction between different contemporary political settings. In Part I, the book addresses various examples drawn from open civil wars. These situations are distinctive in that they involve the confrontation of two clearly identified parties in an armed struggle for control of the state. Part II analyses cases in which systematic violence is a much more covert phenomenon, either because it is officially ignored or denied, or because the confrontations at hand are between the secretive counter-insurgency forces of the state and ill-defined, sometimes elusive and perhaps even imagined opponents. In Part III, the book focuses on a number of cases in which recent or future regime transitions appear to run along orderly, institutional lines. The contributions will query the possibilities and problems of exorcizing the phantoms of violence and fear through the installation of civil democratic governance and the rule of law.

Throughout the book, the different chapters also show different ways of addressing the issues at hand. Some are based on systematic primary (field) research or on a thorough reinterpretation of existing (secondary) sources. Others take a more essayistic approach based on long-term acquaintance with the respective cases or topics. In the rest of this introductory chapter, we will briefly elucidate the choice of chapters in each of these three parts.

The first part of the book deals with the various dimensions of recent civil wars in Latin America. One of the most outstanding features of these conflicts is that a gradual change can be observed, from the 1970s to the 1990s, in which the classical confrontation between conservative right-wing authoritarian governments and revolutionary socialist guerrilla forces gave way to more diverse and complex fields of contention. The three chapters focus upon the increasingly variegated social, political and cultural dimensions of the conflicts in southern Mexico, Central America and Peru. On the side of the state forces in these conflicts, we observe that a gradual shift from authoritarian intransigency to a more compromise-like approach has occurred in the Central American civil wars, especially in El Salvador and Guatemala. This has been the result of the regional peace process and the democratization process that has been slowly making headway in this region. At the same time, the armed opposition largely shed its socialist revolutionary stance and adopted a new platform based on notions such as civil democracy, human rights, social justice and multiculturalism. The net result was a gradual convergence between the warring parties and the signing of formal peace treaties under the auspices of the international community.

A quite different scenario is offered in the case of Peru. There, precisely after the restoration of civil rule in 1980, a fierce guerrilla war broke out. In Peru, the guerrilla forces were especially intransigent and not at all interested in a negotiated settlement with the state. In response, the democratically elected governments of Belaúnde, García, and Fujimori resorted to grim counter-insurgency tactics that gave free rein to the counter-insurgency forces. Chapter 2, by Dirk Kruijt, traces the comparison between the Peruvian and Guatemalan examples. He especially focuses on the strategies employed by the security forces, bringing to light that despite the differences in the overall political dynamics of both civil wars the virtual autonomy of the security forces leads to strong and disturbing parallels with regard to brutality and human rights violations.

Another similarity between the Peruvian and Guatemalan cases is the significance of ethnicity. Recently, it has become common usage to highlight the role of ethnicity in conflicts and violent situations all around the world. In Latin America, socio-economic inequalities have, in many countries, co-incided with the subordination of ethnic categories, usually defined in terms of 'colour'. Curiously enough, the deeply rooted divisions along ethnic lines within Latin American societies have not given rise to very frequent or large scale outbursts of ethnic rebellion. During the 1960s and 1970s, the main lines of conflict identified by guerrilla rebels were drawn along socio-economic or class lines, and the emancipatory platform adopted was that of socialism and anti-imperialism. Only during the past ten or fifteen years has ethnicity been more frequently called upon by the contending sides in armed con-frontations. In Peru and Guatemala, the ethnic element has been partly introduced from the outside: indigenous communities were mainly victims but also became protagonists, either forced to become so by the state or in self-defence. Chapter 3, by Carlos Iván Degregori, deals with the role of peasant armies, the *rondas campesinas*, in the Peruvian civil war. It is noteworthy that Shining Path itself never abandoned its rigid Maoist revolutionary doctrine, which included a certain amount of disdain for the indigenous population. This runs counter to frequent assertions as to the Indian nature of Shining Path's rebellion, which is probably inspired by its efforts to build up its own structures of political and military control and support in the highland communities. Instead, the armed groups of the indigenous peasantry entered the conflict as an opponent of Shining Path, in large part due to the intensification of violence propagated by the guerrillas as an end in itself and its eventual failure to come to grips with crucial aspects of Andean community culture.

The deliberate ethnic component of armed opposition has been much clearer in the case of the Chiapas rebellion of the EZLN, that erupted in January 1994. Although the uprising started with invocations of imperialism and capitalist oppression, the rebels quickly shifted to a stance that stressed the social and cultural dimensions of the exclusion of the indigenous population of Chiapas. In addition, the *zapatistas* called for the 'democratization' of the Mexican political system as a precondition for emancipating the indigenous peasantry. Till now, most of the literature on the Chiapas uprising has focused on the socio-economic context of the rebellion and on its wider political implications. In these discussions, the ethnic dimension of the rebellion is often questioned, for it is seen as a strategic artefact employed by professional revolutionaries with an urban, middle-class, intellectual background, cleverly communicated by fax, e-mail and internet to a largely sympathetic international audience. In Chapter 4, Arij Ouweneel takes a quite different point of departure in exploring the connections between the platform and discourse of the EZLN and the legacy of Maya cosmology and symbolism. He argues that the latter has been decisive in shaping the eventual position of the EZLN, thereby adapting or absorbing other more conventional revolutionary doctrines such as Marxism or liberation theology. Present-day violence in Chiapas is thus seen as part of the cycles of right and wrong, order and chaos, destruction and reconstruction that are prominent in the classical Maya world-view. Ouweneel argues that this fusion of doctrines is part of the construction of a new Mayan emancipatory identity in both Chiapas and Guatemala.

The second part of this book contains three chapters that discuss cases of conflict and violence in specific national settings. The common denominator of these settings is that there is no open civil war in which the armed opposition is in a serious position to overthrow the regime in power. Instead, the use of violence to underscore social and political conflicts or to preserve the prevailing political order has been, or still is, more covert and veiled in a number of countries, including Argentina, Colombia and Mexico. In these countries the power position of established regimes has not been decisively challenged despite the considerable degree of violence that prevailed. How-ever, these three countries serve to illustrate a possible continuum of violence, terror and non-declared war. The role of violence was either downplayed or hidden, such as in Mexico, or portrayed as a temporary problem of 'internal security' as during Argentina's dirty war. The confrontations between the state and the revolutionary movements in Colombia probably come closest to a situation of open civil war, although the Colombian state and its political elites have never relinquished their formal adherence to democratic and institutional 'normality'. So the violent conflicts seemed somehow relegated to an unreal shadow side of national life.

In Mexico, the PRI has always boasted the orderly, civil and peaceful nature of its rule, legitimized by the legacy of the revolution and the structures of popular incorporation. Still, as demonstrated by Alan Knight in Chapter 5, this one-party model of corporatist domination was based on covert (everyday) and overt (rebellious) forms of violence, especially *after* the formal consolidation of the revolutionary movement under Calles and Cárdenas in the 1930s. Knight highlights the complex interweaving of the various types of violence discussed above. Local power-holders (the *caciques*) continued to rely on coercion to bolster their positions while, at the same time, conforming to the pacification arranged at the federal level. The central state, in turn, by and large managed to uphold its peaceful appearance (at least until the 1980s), while at the same time disposing of a discrete apparatus of repression. Lastly, a variety of local and regional actors took recourse to armed actions in the interstices of the *'pax priísta'*.

Unlike Mexico, Argentina has been marked by constant political instability since the 1930s. This can, to a large extent, be traced back to the deepening of fundamental cleavages between the main politically activated social sectors. In fact, Argentina offers a rather puzzling scenario for it combines, since the end of the nineteenth century, a legacy of European-styled economic, social and cultural development – including a supposedly ordered civil society – with a peculiar legacy of social and political polarization which became especially sharpened after World War II. This process resulted in a period of state repression, called the 'dirty war' (1976–82), that was probably unmatched (with the exception of the civil wars in El Salvador and Guatemala) in its scale, brutality and number of casualties. Chapter 6, by Antonius Robben, explores the implications of the Argentine dirty war for the constitution of a generalized climate of fear and anxiety in the country. His analysis shows that the apparent limits of the conflict were, in fact, transcended as the brutality of the violence and the singlemindedness of the opponents eliminated social and cultural spaces of neutrality. The anxiety of the combatants threatened to engulf the neutral citizenry in a vortex of fear which made the struggle for the restoration of democracy and the rule of law in Argentina a delicate endeavour.

The Colombian case represents a situation in which an almost complete routinization of violence has permeated virtually all spheres of social and political life. Since its independence, in fact, Colombian society and politics have been conflict- and violence-ridden. The country has been permanently on (or over) the brink of violent anarchy and civil war. After an interlude of relative internal stability after the end of the War of a Thousand Days (1899–1902), violence re-emerged due to the tensions between the followers of the Liberal and the Conservative parties during the 1940s. The liberals were set to embrace a reformist and populist platform, while the conservatives defended the interests of the established elite. The ensuing civil war, known as La Violencia, pitted political opponents against each other, but the conflict was also marked by family feuding, community antagonism and banditry.[43] With the formal end of the civil war in 1958, the banner of violent resistance against the consecutive National Front governments was taken over by a number of Marxist-Maoist-Castrist guerrilla movements.[44] But from the 1970s onwards, and especially after 1980, violence in Colombia took on an increasingly complex morphology. In Chapter 7, Daniel Pécaut shows in detail how the violence has been generalized and, at the same time, has become so highly diverse that it is increasingly difficult to make any sense of the patterns of conflict and violence in Colombia. Pécaut calls this the 'banality of violence', involving not only the existing guerrilla forces but also the drug cartels, urban criminal gangs, death squads, paramilitary forces defending the *hacendados*, and the security forces of the state. Violence was directed at political opponents, rivalling drug lords, prosecutors and judges, labour, peasant and indigenous leaders, journalists, and even the public at large when the *narcotraficantes* started to use car bombs in their campaign to dissuade the government from extraditing arrested drug barons. In the process, the Colombian state has lost a significant degree of control over its territory and of its monopoly of the legitimate use of violence. As a result, Colombia now witnesses the erosion of public institutions, the dumbfounding of public opinion, and the routinization of terror in everyday life.

Part III of the volume addresses the prospects and problems of what supposedly are peaceful democratic transitions. The success of a number of countries in consolidating the political and institutional dimensions of democracy after having recently emerged from situations of (military) authoritarianism suggests that the spectre of instability and violence does not exhaustively describe the current Latin American experience. Countries that went through civil-military dictatorships that employed the kind of violence and terror linked to the second type, presented above, not only reinstalled civilian rule, they also reformed their political institutions while managing to preserve the rhythm of pluralism, elections and peaceful changes in government during the past one or two decades. As a result, a modicum of internal political stability was restored. Brazil, the southern cone countries – Argentina, Chile and Uruguay – Bolivia and Ecuador belong to the group of countries that seem to have made a relatively successful and peaceful transition to democracy. The third part of the book examines the prospects of (non-violent) transitions out of a situation of dictatorship and repression, not only in the case of two countries drawn from this group (Chile and Brazil), but also for two other countries (Mexico and Cuba) in which a transition seems to be under way or to be unavoidable.

The steadily growing body of literature on democratic transitions and consolidation generally focuses on the mechanisms that erode authoritarian regimes while promoting viable democratic alternatives on the basis of the construction of a broad social and political consensus.[45] Different trajectories and stages in the transition process have been identified, whereby progress in the fields of liberalization and democratization has been combined in various forms.[46] After the full restoration of democratic rule, analysis shifted to the long-term conditions that determine the consolidation of democracy (such as the problem of poverty and exclusion, the incorporation of conservative elites into the democratic project, and the role of the military) as well as to the issue of broadening citizenship through the incorporation of popular movements.[47] Remaining obstacles in the field of party structures, political institutions and political culture have also been highlighted.[48] There is no need to proceed, at this point, with a review of all the highly relevant work done in these fields. We contend that little attention has been paid to the questions of past and present violence, fear and uncertainty, within the conceptual work and country case studies that deal with the democratization process.

The chapters included in Part III are intended to address this relative lacuna. The four chapters review Chile and Brazil, two cases commonly included among the examples of successful democratization, and offer interpretations of Mexico and Cuba, two cases that could be considered 'future transitions'. Chile and Brazil passed through fairly clear-cut transitions from military authoritarianism to civil democratic rule. Mexico and Cuba have in common that, until recently, these countries were marked by a relatively stable political order based on a project and discourse of national revolution, dominated by a single political party. In these cases, although the old order was far from being free of coercion and repression, the imminent transition expected to follow current processes of political erosion and disintegration of the underlying relative societal consensus is likely to exacerbate not only the problem of instability and violence, but also the anxieties and fears this brings along – at least in the short and medium term.

The Chilean case, analysed in Chapter 8 by Patricio Silva, suggests that this country seems to have recovered its democratic civil stability which had made it an outstanding example in South America until 1973. The country's political forces have emerged out of the autocracy of the military under Pinochet (1973–90) to reconstruct a seemingly exemplary form of civil–democratic consensus. However, Silva shows that the construction of this consensus has itself passed through various moments of fear and anxiety that were important in shaping the eventual political outcome. This consensus, moreover, has to contend with the legacy of fear and human rights violations left behind by the military regime. In Chile (at least until the late 1990s) matters have been complicated by the preservation of some important military prerogatives under the command of General Pinochet. The democratic governments since 1990 have had to take this factor into account, especially with regard to the sensitive issue of human rights violations perpetrated during the dictatorship.

In Brazil, the legacy of repression and human rights violations did not play a very prominent role in the process of democratic consolidation up till now. As shown by Kees Koonings in Chapter 9, the Brazilian military governments

(1964–85) were basically founded upon a complex re-engineering of the existing political and institutional structure that had been brought under firm military control. Although this militarization of state and politics after 1964 was, to a significant degree, based on the logic of internal warfare, the scale of actual armed conflicts and the number of victims were low if compared with those in Argentina or Chile. As a result, the Brazilian military embarked on the road to a limited and controlled democratic opening at quite an early stage. This led to a protracted period of transition during which the realignment of political forces and the gradual reintroduction of civil political pluralism as a substitute for repression and arbitrariness were the core features. From 1985 till the present, the civilian governments oversaw the steady deepening of the re-democratization of political life, despite some weaknesses and uncertainties that characterized this process. The Brazilian paradox resides in the fact that despite this relatively successful democratic transition, the problems of violence and fear have not disappeared. On the contrary, to many observers they seem to have grown more ominous and have become increasingly complex after the return to civil rule. In addition to the continuation of violence perpetrated by state-linked agencies and actors that defy the manifest intentions of the government, violence also has spread to include organized crime, petty political confrontations, violence due to general lawlessness, and violence employed against social movements. Brazil seems to be the clearest example where the third type, that of post-authoritarian violence, is on the rise. The efforts to broaden democratic consensus and, in particular, to expand the effective rule of law and true social and political participation through the notion of citizenship are plagued by the backlashes of current violence and fear that seem almost out of control.

In Mexico, the issue of citizenship has also recently been discovered, amidst growing uncertainty as to the future of the political system dominated by the Institutional Revolutionary Party (PRI). Wil Pansters argues, in Chapter 10, that Mexico is faced with the complex multiple dilemmas of reforming its civil (albeit authoritarian) political structure, and of doing away with the engrained patterns of social exclusion and routine violence. The notion of citizenship is advanced by political and intellectual opponents to the PRI to replace the old concepts of the *patria* and the revolution that have, up till now, dominated state–society relationships. Few doubt that some transition affecting the Mexican political system is under way, but few would also accept as a certainty that the interests organized around and within the PRI will quickly give way to effective party pluralism and electoral changes to the control of government. The Mexican scenario, as Pansters shows, is one of oppositional advances met by PRI re-entrenchment. One particularly noteworthy consequence is that these dynamics seem to erode the relative political peace that had existed, at least at the (federal) institutional level. Pansters takes the arguments made by Knight in Chapter 5 one step further in showing that political violence has become more common, especially after 1988.

Mexico might yet face the prospect of ongoing destabilization if the current situation of the 'swamped transition' prolongs itself.

The case of Cuba is a special one, for the communist regime has been resisting the forces that have been pressing it to change since the early 1990s. As argued by Gert Oostindie in Chapter 11, the Cuban case combines the continuation of one-party rule and revolutionary loyalties within certain segments of the population with economic disintegration and rising dissatisfaction, especially among the younger generations. The regime seems to meet these developments with intransigency, yet under growing external pressure. Oostindie discusses the recent background to the erosion of the Cuban revolutionary model: the collapse of the Soviet system and the economic crisis that grips Cuba. Amid growing public dissatisfaction, the regime is faced with a complicated dilemma. Stepping up repression will not help to counteract the decline in legitimacy, but allowing real spaces for political opening will quite likely bring the regime to its knees. In this protracted political limbo, Cubans have to cope with the intensification of economic hardships and the very real threat of social, cultural and moral disintegration. Fear of an uncertain future, but also fear of losing the legacy of the revolution, now seem to dominate Cuba's daily reality.

In the Epilogue, formed by the twelfth and last chapter of the volume, Edelberto Torres-Rivas offers a long-term view of the significance of violence and fear in Latin American society and politics. He calls for caution with respect to the idea that recent democratization in Latin America has been firmly established and that the rule of violence will be a thing of the past. The long-term effect of violence, as produced by the wielding of state power, is the insertion of fear as a permanent social and cultural ingredient. The 'trivialization of horror', as Torres-Rivas calls it, extends well beyond the formal ending of political authoritarianism. As shown in most of the chapters of the book and restated in this final chapter, the 'trivialistation of horror' has been spreading to other areas of social life in which the legacy of past terror mingles with the fears caused by present insecurity. This poses a major obstacle to the real consolidation of democracy and to the establishment of politics without violence. In order to come closer to this ideal, Latin Americans (and indeed all concerned) will have to give precedence to the protection of human rights, and to punishing and controlling those who violated them in the past as well as in the present, so that effective political citizenship may prevail.

Notes and References

1. CACIF is the national Chamber of Commerce and Industry, unifying the landowning, financial and commercial bourgeoisie.

2. See *The Economist* 30 November 1996, pp. 23–6. *The Economist* applauds the 'victory

of sound policies over populism' (referring to the structural adjustment policies sustained by almost every government in the region) but calls attention to the endemic problems of poverty, social exclusion and widespread violence.

3. For the intricate problems of combining democratization and economic adjustment, see especially Stallings and Kaufman, *Debt and Democracy*, Haggard and Kaufman, *Political Economy*, Smith, Acuña and Gamarra, *Latin American Political Economy*. One of the basic problems that emerges is the threat that socially unsustainable adjustment policies may pose to the viability of political democracy, given the patterns of poverty and inequality in Latin America.

4. See Touraine, *America Latina*.

5. One could think of the so-called bread riots against structural adjustment policies that took place in countries such as Argentina, Brazil and Venezuela during the 1980s and early 1990s. Other examples may be the indigenous uprisings in Ecuador in the early 1990s, or the landless movement in Brazil. It is debatable to what extent the movement of the Ejercito Zapatista de Liberación Nacional (Zapatista Army of National Liberation, EZLN) in Chiapas, Mexico, can be seen as a limited and focused violent reaction, since they not only advocate the specific demands of the Chiapas (and other) indigenous populations, but have also called for a reform of the Mexican political system. Only the guerrilla wars fought in Central America, Peru and, to a lesser degree, Colombia in the 1980s were closer to constituting 'revolutionary projects'.

6. See Giddens, *Nation-State and Violence*, for a lucid overview of the core elements of modern state formation. He refers, *inter alia*, to the importance of military organization for the constitution of modern states but also to the relevance of modern warfare for the internal strengthening of national societies and citizenship. In consolidated nation-states, citizenship forms the central domain of contention through which contesting class and other interests are played out along orderly and legitimate channels. See Turner, *Citizenship and Capitalism*, for a useful introduction to the debate on citizenship.

7. See Moore, *Social Origins*; Tilly, *Coercion* (p. 68 for the quotation); Keane, *Reflections on Violence*.

8. See Nun, 'Middle class military coup'.

9. See Flynn, 'Class, clientelism and coercion'.

10. See Koonings, Kruijt and Wils, 'Very long march'.

11. See Baud et al., *Etnicidad como estrategia*.

12. See Wiarda, *Corporatism*; also Wiarda, *Politics*.

13. See Hagopian, 'Traditional power structures'.

14. See Weffort, *Populismo*.

15. One of the original formulations of this issue was given by Tella, 'Populism and reform'.

16. For an illuminating distinction between democratic and authoritarian varieties of Latin American populism see Dix, 'Populism'.

17. See Touraine, *America Latina*.

18. See the relevant discussion by Lechner, 'Some people die of fear', particularly pp. 28–9.

19. See Knight, *Mexican Revolution*.

20. See O'Donnell, *Modernization*.

21. See the various contributions to Collier, *New Authoritarianism*.

22. See Wickham-Crowley, *Guerrillas and Revolution*, for a detailed analysis of armed rebellions during the second half of the twentieth century. The armed struggle of the Latin American Left was largely unsuccessful and contributed to the incorporation of the Left in the pro-democracy forces in many countries after 1980. Also see Angell, 'Incorporating the left'.

23. In this book emphasis is placed on the domestic dimensions of the authoritarian and repressive regimes of the 1960s, 1970s and 1980s. This does not mean, however, that external influences were not relevant for the rise and consolidation of these regimes and the shaping of their repressive practices. During the 1960s and 1970s, it was common usage to stress the pervasive influence of the United States in putting into power a long list of military dictatorships and also in staging counter-insurgency campaigns. There is no doubt that the USA gave various forms of support to the Latin American military through military assistance programmes, development cooperation and diplomatic and intelligence liaisons. However, Rouquié argues that this does not mean that the Latin American military regimes were merely 'the sixth side of the Pentagon' (see Rouquié, *Military*). Especially in Brazil and the southern cone countries, the USA basically offered a *nihil obstat* kind of support to the militarization of politics that was well founded in nationally developed geo-political thinking and related doctrines on the role of the military in politics (see Child, 'Geopolitical thinking'). On the other hand, the hand of the USA can be clearly seen in Central America and the Caribbean. From the adventures of William Walker in nineteenth-century Nicaragua to the interventions in Panama and Haiti in the early 1990s, the USA has followed a constant and systematic practice of direct interference with politics and civil wars. Finally, since the 1980s, the Pentagon and the CIA have been gradually superseded by the US Drug Enforcement Agency (DEA) whose high-profile activities include involving the military of a number of countries (especially in the Andean region) in its 'war on drugs'.

24. See Alves, *Estado e oposição*.

25. We refer to governance not only in the strict sense used by, among others, the World Bank (meaning the ability to carry out sensible adjustment programmes and creating the long-term conditions for market-led growth) but also in terms of deepening democratic participation, accountability and legitimacy.

26. Argued by Roldán, 'Citizenship, class and violence'.

27. See Lovemann, 'Protected democracies'.

28. See Koonings, Kruijt and Wils, 'Very long march'; Kruijt et al., *Changing Labour Relations*.

29. See Matos Mar, *Desborde popular*.

30. For the Colombian situation, see Chapter 7 of this book by Daniel Pécaut. Recent publications in Spanish are Bétancourt and García, *Contrabandistas*; Guerrero, *Años del Olvído*; Lara, *Siembra vientos*; Palacio, *Irrupción*; Salazar, *No nacimos pa' semilla*; Salazar, *Mujeres*; Salazar and Jaramillo, *Medellín*; Torres Arias, *Mercaderes*.

31. *Harvest of Violence* is the title of Carmack's splendid reader on the Guatemalan tragedy.

32. See Rodríguez Rabal, *Violencia*.

33. See Garretón, 'Fear in military regimes'; also Alves, *Estado e oposição*, pp. 166ff.

34. See Lovemann, 'Protected democracies', p. 141.

35. See Stepan, *Rethinking Military Politics*; also Kruijt, 'Politicians in uniform'.

36. See Rial, 'Armed forces'; Lovemann, 'Protected democracies'.

37. Although the armed forces are formally incorporated in the corporativist structure supervised by the PRI, the influence of the Mexican military has been growing since the erosion of the power monopoly of the PRI and the Chiapas rebellion. See Piñeyro, 'Fuerzas Armadas'.

38. See NACLA, 'Injustice for all'.

39. See Weiss Fagen, 'Repression'; also Rial, 'Makers and guardians of fear'.

40. See Nordstrom and Robben, *Fieldwork under Fire*.

41. As remarked by Salimovich, Lira and Weinstein, 'Victims of fear', p. 72, in reference to their analysis of experiences in authoritarian and post-authoritarian Chile.

42. See Green, 'Living in a state of fear'.

43. See Guzmán Campos, Fals Borda, and Umaña Luna, *Violencia en Colombia*.

44. The principal ones still existing are the Colombian Revolutionary Armed Forces (FARC), the Revolutionary Peoples Army (ERP), and the National Liberation Army (ELN).

45. See in particular the seminal work brought together in O'Donnell, Schmitter and Whitehead, *Transitions: Latin America*; O'Donnell, Schmitter and Whitehead, *Transitions: Comparative Perspectives*; and O'Donnell and Schmitter *Transitions: Tentative Conclusions*. See also Higley and Guenther, *Elites and Democratic Consolidation*.

46. See Lopez and Stohl, 'Liberalization'; Baloyra, 'Democratic transitions'.

47. See Diamond, Linz and Lipset, *Democracy: Latin America*; Domínguez and Lowenthal, *Constructing Democratic Governance* (3 vols).

48. See Alcántara and Crespo, *Límites*.

PART I

The Social, Political and Ethnic Dimensions of Civil War

Exercises in State Terrorism: the Counter-insurgency Campaigns in Guatemala and Peru[1]

DIRK KRUIJT

The objective of this chapter is to present in a comparative study the political and military ingredients of the civil wars in Guatemala and Peru, two of the most sanguinary and devastating conflicts in Latin America during the last fifty years. The analytical framework for this chapter is formed by a chronological account of politico-military guerrilla and counter-insurgency strategy and tactics in Guatemala and Peru. The theatre of 'Revolutionary Wars' and 'People's Wars', was fought out mainly in the remote rural and indigenous Indian zones of the Quiché and the Petén in Guatemala, and in the departments of Ayacucho and Junín in Peru. The wars could be interpreted as ethnic civil wars; they originated on behalf of the indigenous population and led to their incorporation in the guerrilla columns, in the paramilitary 'defence'-organizations and in the regular army. However, the final outcome of the wars has been the massive slaughtering of the indigenous Indian population. In both nations, the local and regional conflicts originated from an orthodox ideology of class and class conflict. Thereafter, these conflicts developed into nation-wide, low-intensity civil wars with strong ethnic dimensions.

The analysis of Guatemala and Peru follows on from the aftermath of the 'Military Revolutions' of Arbenz and Velasco, the years of nationalistic and leftist military governments.[1] During this period the government attempted to carry out a programme of land reform and other economic and social reforms; to liquidate the economic and political base of the ruling oligarchy; to integrate the indigenous population into the nation-state; and to modernize the economy, society and the political order to build a strong state and an efficient public development sector with a presence in the remotest areas of the national territory. The guerrilla movement in Guatemala was born during the restorative period thereafter, when the government's land and other reforms stagnated or were reduced; when the hope of a generation of indigenous Indian peasants and the urban working classes had been shattered. In Peru, the guerrillas of Shining Path manifested themselves at the very moment of the re-establishment of the civilian regime. In both countries, it took a long time before the military established an outline of an 'efficient' counter-insurgency strategy. Only when the military incorporated the paramilitary 'voluntary' peasant defence organizations – the *patrullas de autodefensa civil* in Guatemala and the *rondas campesinas* in Peru – did they start to take the strategic initiative. However, the anti-guerrilla campaigns, especially in Guatemala, resulted in a savage and ruthless destruction of the guerrilla movement *and* their supposed Indian allies.

During most of the period of the guerrilla and the anti-guerrilla campaigns, both Guatemala and Peru were stigmatized by international political isolation. In both countries, the guerrilla and the counter-insurgency campaigns were carried out in the sordid misery of remoteness: in the inaccessible and secluded indigenous regions of the country, without noticeable external support or intervention, with home-made weapons and without sophisticated technology.

Peru: the Civil War, Shining Path and the Military[2]

The indigenous population of Peru is generally characterized as being extremely serene and unwarlike. There have been, however, various periods of remarkable rebellion and resistance associated with the group.[3] During the sixteenth century, the Spanish conquest and the civil wars thereafter were followed by long-lasting and stubborn Indian guerrilla campaigns. The rebellion movement of Tupac Amaru II at the end of the eighteenth century, had an impact on most countries of Latin America. The last of several significant rural protest movements in the nineteenth and twentieth centuries, before World War II, was the Rumi Maqui revolt in 1914, a movement that was headed by a former army major and which spread into over eight departments in Southern Peru before it was brutally crushed by troops sent from the capital.

In the 1960s, three 'conventional' Che Guevara-like guerrilla movements, headed by intellectuals from Lima and operating without major coordination, tried to launch a Popular and Peasants' Revolution in the indigenous highlands.[4] The Peruvian army – its intelligence having strongly infiltrated these movements[5] – crushed the three incipient guerrilla armies in the northern, the central and the southern part of the Andes in surprisingly short campaigns, and without major bloodshed. Nevertheless, the anti-guerrilla campaign left its mark on the army officers, who had to fight adversaries who were not really enemies. It was felt that what caused the development of guerrilla movements had deep roots in the underdeveloped Peruvian economy and society; that the political system had failed; and that it was just a matter of time before a new wave of guerrillas and rebellion would sweep the country.[6] The reform programme of Velasco's Revolutionary Government of the Armed Forces was drafted by a group of officers who played a leading role in the anti-guerrilla campaigns. In fact, the reform programme, carried out during the Velasco years (1968–75), was conceptualized as a coherent national development and anti-poverty strategy to prevent another guerrilla uprising in the near future. From 1975 to 1980, a second military government was seen to be implementing the 'second phase' of the revolution. In those years, most of the reform programme stagnated or was restructured 'to real proportions'. It has to be said, however, that during the benevolent Velasco years and the more dictatorial, right-wing military period thereafter, the public sector was present everywhere in the country. Indeed, the last military reform was even concerned with the creation of regional development ministries, established in the provincial capitals, with control of the local and regional development projects in the underdeveloped regions.

In the light of what followed, this chapter mainly emphasizes the strong points of the military reform programme: nation-building through development, and guerrilla prevention through good governance. Building up a strong 'Peruvianized' economy through expropriations and nationalizations, the Velasco military governed via a strong public sector, the instrument for their 'Revolution from Above', with an authoritarian and paternalistic rule. The public sector was a command structure for 'development' and for 'people's participation'. Through the public sector the military brought security to the capital, cities elsewhere and in the provinces; it provided water and sewerage in the urban slums; it sent the peace judges to the indigenous communities; it launched the national alphabetization campaigns; it paid the salary of nurses in the highland villages; and it supervized community workers in the jungle. In addition, the military utilized the public sector to enforce the law and establish order for every citizen. It treated the labour unions with sympathy, the poor with compassion, the Indians with reverence; Quechua was recognized as the second official language of the country.

Government officials were anxious to 're-associate the already organized and to organize the marginalized'.[7] They assisted in the creation of mass organizations for the indigenous peasants, deeply influencing the formation of the national peasant federation, CNA, which in 1977 had unified 160 peasant leagues with 4,500 local unions and a total of 675,000 members. Government officials also helped to set up workers' communities in industry, trade, and in the mining and fishing industries, organized 'federations for landless peasants', and unified local squatter movements in the urban and metropolitan slums. The years of the military government probably formed the only decade of this century in which the public sector was present in the most remote regions of Peru, the most forgotten villages of the country.

The infrastructure for local and regional development in Peru was to be considerably reduced over the next few years, as a result of two factors with mutually reinforcing effects. First, the indifference to, and disregard of poverty and development issues outside the capital by the new civilian governments – Belaúnde first and then García;[8] and second, the destructive tactics of the guerrilla movements, emerging in the 1980s. Of the guerrilla movements, Shining Path has been the most important and the most devastating. Since its first public manifestations, Shining Path has directed its destructive energy against the local representatives of the state, the local police, the local universities and, in general, the local public sector and local development authorities.

Shining Path emerged in the department of Ayacucho, a region stigmatized with the wounds of poverty, illiteracy, exploitation and underdevelopment.[9] The land reform of the Velasco government was withheld in these parts of the Andean highlands. The city of Ayacucho, for centuries the capital of a miserable region of medium-sized haciendas and forgotten indigenous communities, obtained a regional university in the 1950s. Soon, the *alumni* would compete with the students of twenty other provincial universities. Most of the latter group of students were better connected to structural sources of income and employment, while most of the indigenous students returned to their villages. In the early 1960s, a parochial philosopher, Abimael Guzmán, went to teach the students at the university in Ayacucho and its affiliated teacher training school. Guzmán became the undisputed leader of a Maoist splinter group of the Peruvian Communist Party, Shining Path.[10] While the pro-Moscow wing of the Peruvian Left, allied with the Velasco government and other neo-Marxist party leaders, participated with success in the elections of the 1980s, Shining Path's leadership chose the anonymity of a diligent cell structure, the cocoons to be matured for a final 'People's War'. Guzmán took his time to strengthen his organization and to acquire strong roots in the peasantry. The timing of his first armed presence was inspired. It took place in the provincial market town of Chuschi in Ayacucho on 17 May 1980, during the national elections for the first civilian president, when the military was weakened and the future civilian government in Lima would be powerless.[11]

Shining Path matured slowly but steadily during the relatively prosperous years of the military governments. Guzmán bided his time, nurturing the semi-clandestine movement over a period of fifteen years before he launched the armed struggle. The emphasis on cell structure, ideological purity, slow proselytism, absolute loyalty and· devotion, and strict morality – an iron discipline imposed upon the university students by their charismatic and quasi-religious leader Guzmán – provided the movement with a protective ambience and contributed mostly to the movement's impenetrability during the following years. Shining Path had sought, and had acquired, a strong popular base. It initiated the 'People's War' in its home region.

Two facts, mentioned previously, contributed to the sustained growth of the guerrilla movement in the short period between 1980 and 1982. First, the new Belaúnde civilian government did not trust the Peruvian army and thought it better to keep them quiet. Velasquista generals commanded the army, and army intelligence was considered to be the heir of the Velasco team. Belaúnde played down the subject of armed attacks and peasant rebellion in the indigenous heartlands, depicting the movement in cabinet sessions as 'petty cattle-lifters'. Thus, instead of the army, the police force from the capital Lima, untrained and unfit for guerrilla fighting, was mobilized. The indolent president transformed the metropolitan police, in fact, into Shining Path's principal arms supplier. Second, the movement's tactics, blindly destroying the public sector's infrastructure, and the continuous expulsion, or execution, of local magistrates, teachers, rural police officers and public health officials, provided the guerrillas with a real monopoly of power, violence and legality in the Ayacucho region and the surrounding departments.

Two other factors help to explain the consolidation of Shining Path during the years between 1982 and 1988/89 when the movement extended its power over the remaining departments of the Peruvian highlands; and the columns of Shining Path established partial control over the Upper Huallaga Valley, the region that produces 60 per cent of the world's coca. First, the economic opportunities arising from coca production and the trafficking of cocaine paste provided financial resources for the movement, estimated to be between US$30 million and US$100 million per year.[12] Second, the government, even after 1982 when the military took the *plaza* of Ayacucho and most of the politico-military responsibilities were delegated to the army's high command, delayed making a coherent action plan for years. The civilian presidents of the 1980s, Belaúnde and García, and their advisers, refused to consider the presence and the activities of Shining Path as a serious threat. When the government explicitly required action, it asked for military manifestations, indiscriminate military operations rather than for the combination of local development, local confidence-building and tactical military counter-insurgency. General Jarama, the youngest of Peru's geo-politicians and the director of the Centro de Altos Estudios Militares in the late 1980s, expressed the problem in the following terms:

> I'm sure Guzmán has licked his fingers, has licked his hands, to have had political leaders such as Belaúnde and García as his adversaries. To fight against a government, that sent in the police instead of the army. As I said the other day: 'Gúzman is playing chess whereas the government is preparing itself for a tennis match, a game with other rules, other instruments, another playoff, another public and even other uniforms.'[13]

Without doubt, the ideology and the activities of Shining Path have attracted differing groups of people. The party's leadership was formed mainly by the sons and daughters of the provincial elites. Most of the original party members came from the urban provincial youth; some had entered the university system for a couple of years, most of them dropped out later.

Recruitment of the lower echelons took place primarily from the young and the marginalized, the Indians, the peasants and the slum dwellers. The guerrilla columns included large numbers of fourteen-to-eighteen-year-olds and women.[14] Shining Path's ideological message was the crude and simple 'abracadabra' of a movement in the desolate milieu of extremely poor indigenous peasants and slum dwellers. The organization symbolized a crude and violent justice, displayed by the selective assassination of 'bad' people and a cruel morality that included the public punishing of adulterers and drinkers. A crude and merciless redistribution that emphasized the necessity for small plots of land and the minimum of food and cattle for survival; and a crude and haranguing pedagogy – teaching humble and acquiescent people, with a tradition of deep respect for teachers and apostles.[15] Shining Path used a vocabulary that varied from region to region, from one population segment to another. It incorporated sympathizers and recruited new members using inducement and coercion, gradually applying more terror and violence. The procedures utilized by Shining Path in the provinces were as follows.

The rural bases are real military training camps *in situ*. Their members receive theory and practice as well, based upon Guzmán's reflections and the characteristics of the local situation. They are trained in the identification of friends and foes. In the use of fire arms, dynamite and home-made bombs. In espionage and surveillance, proselytism and intimidation. Finally, they participate in combat operations and urban terrorism. They form assault groups of six to eight persons, based on cell structure and fragmented command. [...] Rural control is stricter than urban rule. Landowners or medium-size proprietors are forced out. Independent leaders of the Indian communities have been replaced by more obedient officials. Smallholders pay regular tribute. Local market people do business according to Shining Path's regulations, otherwise they risk losing their trade or their lives. Regional Offices of the Ministry of Agriculture, Education and Public Health are threatened or paralysed, their technical assistance reduced to zero. The clergy is under control. Church services and mass celebrations are permitted, but the sermon's global content should be previously authorized. [...] The basic objective is to establish political and military control over agricultural production and distribution, and control over the regional centres to facilitate posterior domination of the regional urban population. They proceed in the following order:

- by discovering conflicts between leaders and members of cooperatives, between landlords and tenants, between proprietors and peasants without land, and between rich and poor community leaders;
- by military presence to influence the conflict in a favourable way towards groups or persons whose sympathies can be counted on;
- by armed support for the loyal individuals and groups, followed by continuous marginalization of the opposition: by local land reform, by privatization and

distribution of land and animals, and legitimized by a 'popular assembly', organized by Shining Path's representatives;

- by imposition of *mitimaes*, i.e. the migration of loyal peasants and military from other zones already under control (bases), who receive the best land and who act as leaders of the assault groups and as political supervisors in the new zones;
- by transformation of the new zones into regular 'bases', where they regulate the production process, the consumption process and the distribution process, the social and political life style, as well as the public and private morality;
- and by consolidation of the bases as self-supporting defensive zones.[16]

These were the procedures in the provinces utilized by Shining Path. With the extension of Shining Path's realm to the metropolitan areas of Arequipa, Trujillo and Lima, the ingredients of the 'persuasion and terror cocktail' changed. The first areas of infiltration to be selected were the urban slums and the industrial cordons. The first category of persons to be intimidated were the independent or leftist union leaders, slum leaders, local mayors and councillors, and the directorate of the local development organizations. Sometimes they were 'persuaded' to retire, sometimes a 'popular tribunal' had to be organized to condemn the obstinate representatives and execute them with dynamite after the trial. With the appointment of a more co-operative leadership, Shining Path then established training schools and selected supervisors thereafter. Public sector officials, NGO-officers, lawyers, doctors and journalists were paid a warning visit at home or in the office. The '1,000 eyes and 1,000 ears' of the movement were rumoured to be omnipresent. And to demonstrate their potential for public control, Shining Path periodically organized 'armed strikes' in metropolitan areas – organizing selective punishing by killing disobedient taxi-drivers and shopkeepers.

Shining Path, at least until Guzmán's arrest, was directed by a strong political Central Committee with a personal cult towards the sacralized leader, with direct links with a network of regional and provincial committees. In principle, military and operational planning were (and remain) realized at the regional level. Although the overall strategy was a matter of national – Guzmán's – concern, most of the movement's flexibility and perseverance can be attributed to regional and local decentralization. Shining Path remains strong where the government (the military, the police, the public sector) is weak, that is mainly in the poor highland villages and the metropolitan poverty belts. During the twelve years of the 'People's War', Shining Path operated, in the strictly military sense, prudently. That is, defensively against military formations, avoiding direct contact, and allowing only *ad hoc* raids against isolated units and provincial police-stations.

Until the late 1980s, the Shining Path movement basically followed an uncomplicated attack–defence strategy, operating through a loose structure of 'military columns'. There were a few ranks without uniforms or a complicated command hierarchy. A *comandante* – women's representation in the higher ranks was surprisingly high – controlled a small, versatile unit of ideologically immaculate and highly motivated loyalists. This nucleus – an estimated hard core of 3,000 to 7,000 persons in 1992 – was supported by local sympathizers and novices, and mostly recruited in the 'liberated' areas in the highland departments or in the pauperized metropolitan slums. A secondary support structure consisted of a network of lawyers, medical personnel and paramedics, students and other sympathetic organizations, including a sort of diplomatic representation in foreign countries. When Shining Path tried to expand its range of operations to Bolivia, Ecuador and Chile in 1992, the first organizations and persons to be 'touched' for sympathy and support were the local NGOs and the local doctors.[17]

During the first years of the 'People's War', the counter-insurgency strategy was based upon some vague ideas about anti-subversive warfare.[18] Moreover, until December 1982, the government was not at all interested in a specific anti-guerrilla strategy. Gustavo Gorriti, a scholar with access both to the written statements of Shining Path's politburo sessions in the early 1980s and to the confidential government reports of the same period, repeatedly describes almost unbelievable incidents: complicated power struggles within the police forces; instructions 'to gather information about Cuban, Chilean, Ecuadorean and Russian advisers' of the guerrilla movement; the blunt refusal of the Ministry of the Air Force to put helicopters at the disposal of the police force in Ayacucho; and the instruction to the intelligence services of the military and the police 'to make use of public telephones' when calling their headquarters.[19]

Even after the armed forces were made responsible for the anti-guerrilla campaign in December 1982, the situation did not change substantially. Belaúnde, afraid of the army and deeply resented by it, deliberately decreased its intelligence capabilities, considering military intelligence a Velasquista stronghold. However, without any anti-subversive strategy being formulated by the government, the military made things worse, entering the anti-guerrilla arena without knowing what subversive war and anti-subversive campaigns were about. Obando relates that the conceptual base of the campaigns against Shining Path in the 1980s consisted of two anti-subversive manuals of the US army, dating back to the 1950s and translated into Spanish.[20] The military chiefs in the emergency zones – first Ayacucho, then most of the Andean departments – acted on their own in the absence of a coherent strategic concept. Consequently, most of the local and regional activities were carried out without the slightest coordination with other military chiefs in other regions.

In fact, the strategy that began to predominate empirically was the indiscriminate use of military force against the guerrillas and their supposed civilian allies, which were mostly indigenous *comuneros*. In the beginning of 1981, the government sent the Sinchis into the city of Ayacucho 'to restore order'. These 'special anti-subversive troops', specially created and trained to deal with urban violence, labour unrest, popular manifestations and civil disorders, organized a ten-day orgy of murder, violence and rape, providing Shining Path with a yardstick for the future of excessive brutality against the civilian population that they could not easily match. General Huamán, appointed as the military chief in the emergency zone of Ayacucho, started with a policy of trying to win the sympathy of the regional population:

> The government had ordered a curfew. That meant, that people should be at home from ten o'clock on. 'For what reason?' I asked myself. One of the first things I did was to get back to normality. People want to have the perspective of music, of dance, of a *fiesta*. Not of control. What they want is confidence restored. Well, if I give them confidence and security, I begin winning the war.[21]

General Huamán, however, asked also for fresh funds for local development projects. The government decided not to allocate new money for development, but asked for sustained actions to challenge the guerrillas and their followers. When the military chief of Ayacucho criticized the decision, Huamán found himself substituted by a new regional commander who quickly returned to the 'normal' policy of mass destruction and 'disappearing' of suspects. A similar treatment was received by General Arciniega, appointed as the military commander of the Upper Huallaga, while attempting to win the confidence of the coca-cultivating peasants, who were controlled by Shining Path. Accused of drug trafficking by the DEA, he was forced to resign. Several months afterwards, Shining Path reinforced its control over the Upper Huallaga region.

In general, the anti-guerrilla strategy implemented during the 1980s was a policy of harsh, indiscriminate violence against 'the subversive population', considered to be the Quechua ethnicities in the Peruvian highlands.[22] The Quechua population, not necessarily attracted to Shining Path's ideology unless under force, also declined to choose in favour of the government or the military. But at the end of the 1980s, Shining Path started to alienate their support base drawn from the local indigenous population. When the movement, in order to cut off Lima and other metropolitan areas from its 'food-producing hinterland', first prohibited selling the local surpluses, then started to terrorize the peasants who did, and consequently organized a killing campaign in order to establish the obedience of the indigenous population, the local population started to revolt. Shining Path's answer was to exterminate whole communities.

This strategy probably signified, in retrospect, the turning point of the civil war. The general animosity towards Shining Path forced the peasants into self-defence organizations, the so-called *rondas campesinas*.[23] These peasant organizations emerged spontaneously in the mid-1970s, basically as defense organizations during the land reform of Velasco in the northern regions of

Peru. From the 1980s on, they acted as local, then regional, low-level law-enforcers and self-protection organizations. The organized Left and García's APRA party disputed with each other over the political control of the *rondas* during the local elections. When the *rondas* proliferated all over the indigenous regions, in the absence of any other institutions of the public sector, their leaders asked for arms. The government, thinking about a rural militia, distributed old firearms under the peasant leaders.

In 1990 a political novice, Alberto Fujimori, won the presidential campaign against all the odds. Fujimori, the president-elect in 1990 without a list of cabinet members and a coherent government plan, looked for long-term allies. Of course he received warm hospitality from the *Círculo Militar* during the transition period and the first week of his presidency. He was extensively briefed by military intelligence about anti-guerrilla tactics and human rights, development strategies and long-term economic and political priorities. Fujimori's political guide and intelligence mentor Vladimiro Montesinos, president of the newly created Strategic Council of State, has acted since then as the virtual president of the national intelligence system. One of the first initiatives that the new government took was to recognize the *rondas campesinas* as the semi-institutionalized fourth branch of the armed forces. Armed peasants now marched alongside the regular army, the navy and the air force on Independence Day. Since then, the *rondas* have mostly become influenced by, and subordinated to, the regional military command structure.

From the early 1990s on, Shining Path lost the strategic initiative within the Indian highlands. Guzmán, apparently understanding that he was losing the war in the Andes, decided to concentrate his efforts in Lima. From then on, Shining Path tried to surround and penetrate Lima, making its presence visible in the metropolitan slums and distributing land and animals within some of Lima's rural coastal valleys. The movement, however, could not easily penetrate the labour unions and the industrial organizations. Thus a selective wave of terror against the legal Left and the fabric of independent slum organizations added to an armed strike that paralysed Lima around Independence Day in 1992, contributing to a generalized sense of demoralization. Then, suddenly, in September 1992, Guzmán himself and most members of the Central Committee were arrested. Following the arrest of Guzmán, the character and the intensity of the civil war has changed substantially. Sixty per cent of the Central Committee of Shining Path was captured: of the twenty-five members, nine are free.[24] At the regional level, most of the fighting machine of Shining Path remained intact: only the Comité Norte was 'neutralized', whereas the other four are virtually undetected. The same can be said about the zonal and sub-zonal committees. It was estimated by DINCOTE in February 1994 that the number of guerrillas totalled 3,000, mostly organized in small columns and cells.

The arrest of Guzmán was the result of meticulous detective work by DINCOTE, a special anti-terrorist police division, created in the early 1980s.

When Fujimori became president, DINCOTE decided to concentrate its activities only upon the high-ranking members of Shining Path. This decision was part of a more general shift in the anti-subversive strategy as a whole. The new strategy, prepared by the combined 'intelligence and strategic' forces, attributed much more importance to the *rondas campesinas*. The results of this strategy were almost immediately apparent. First, the strategy provided much more initiative for DINCOTE and the military system of intelligence; and second, it made a distinction between the military and the more encompassing political aspects of the war.[25] The key principles of the new anti-subversive doctrine were to try to obtain the sympathy and the confidence of the population; to provide local development programmes; to provide local protection; and to re-establish law and order locally. Especially since Fujimori's coup in 1992, the new strategy and its supporting new organizational structures – a unified national intelligence system, a unified national anti-subversive command structure, and the creation of a National Defence Council – have proved to be successful. Inside the armed forces, it is estimated that the strict military aftermath will be a question of one, maybe two years. Shining Path, as a coherent clandestine political organization, has broken into smaller components. As a military organization at the national level, Shining Path has been reduced to an organization of regional significance, although some of its brigades, under new names, display the same violence and surprise tactics as before.

Guatemala: the Permanent Low Intensity Warfare

When US President Eisenhower, Vice-President Nixon and Secretary of State Dulles authorized the CIA in 1954 to carry out a plan called 'Operation Success', to remove the constitutional president of Guatemala, Jacobo Arbenz, it was not the interests of the Indian ethnicities of Guatemala, nor those of the population of that country, that they tried to defend. The decision to substitute Guatemala's constitutional presidency by a regime headed by a virtually unknown military 'strawman', named Castillo Armas, basically served the interests of a US company, the United Fruit Corporation. In the early 1950s, United Fruit's land-holdings in Guatemala were threatened with confiscation under Arbenz's land reform. Twenty years later, in 1972, the same company sold all of its remaining Guatemalan holdings to the Del Monte corporation, during its not so successful merger with another conglomerate, United Brands.

Toriello, Guatemala's ambassador to the United States and, during the last months of Arbenz's government, Guatemala's Minister of Foreign Affairs, reveals in his memoirs the abysmal ignorance of the US leaders of the situation in Guatemala.[27] In the light of the sad series of military dictators, fraudulent 'constitutional' general-presidents and the bitter guerrilla warfare which followed shortly after Arbenz's fall producing a nation-wide civil war,

'Operation Success' should have been renamed 'Operation Disaster'. A government that had given hope to the indigenous people of the country; that had initiated a much-needed land reform; and that had produced a timid presence in the Guatemalan countryside, was replaced by a restorative regime, the very transition 'from *Guatemala* to *Guatepeor*'. Even the 'official' historian of the coup, Schneider, concluded afterwards: 'While the short-run outcome of the intervention in 1954 was viewed at the time as a success for the United States in the Cold War, in a larger perspective it is increasingly difficult to see it as such. Indeed, in light of subsequent events it might reasonably be considered little short of disaster.'[27]

In later years, the State Department had to staff the American Embassy in Guatemala with counter-insurgency specialists from South Vietnam; twenty-five foreign service experts with experience in this singular profession were posted to Guatemala between 1964 and 1974.[28] The Guatemalan guerrilla campaign was initiated during the last government years of Castillo Armas' successor Ydígoras, in the early 1960s. Nevertheless, the most important guerrilla groups of that time reflected the years of the Guatemalan revolution (1944–54).[29] The three guerrilla commanders, Marco Aurelio Yon Sosa, Luis Turcios Lima and Carlos Paz Tejada, were army officers; and Paz Tejada had been the Minister of Defence under Arbenz. As various authors have pointed out, the overthrow of Arbenz not only frustrated the Left, but also the progressive sectors of the Guatemalan army.[30] The influence of the USA, via its embassy and military assistance, but especially via the CIA and its not so covert use of Guatemalan facilities for what later became known as the Bay of Pigs invasion, caused an uneasy feeling among the young officials who had graduated from the Escuela Politécnica, the military academy. The army, slowly professionalizing since the 1950s,[31] maintained a *nolens volens* combat relation with the incipient guerrilla movement. The basic anti-guerrilla strategy declared a state of siege, launching at certain moments a short but massive military campaign against the guerrilla movement and limiting direct warfare to the disputed regions of Zacapa, Izabal and the Sierra de las Minas. Most of the national military interest was directed towards the political scenario.

Having unseated the unpopular Ydígoras in 1963, the higher military echelons appointed Colonel Peralta Azurdia as head of state; he refused to use the title of president. Peralta primarily tried to put the country's political house in order: reorganizing the public sector's bureaucracy; producing new labour and electoral legislation; establishing a new constitution; and preparing for the election of a civilian government in 1966.[32] The military head of state, a fierce anti-communist but an 'apolitical' military politician, was particularly concerned about ridding the armed forces of party politics and political clientalism. Worried about schisms within the military since 1954, and trying to reinforce the unity of the armed forces, the survival of the military government – and of the future civil–military and military-dominated regimes – depended on a precarious equilibrium with the guerrilla movement.

The Peralta government seemed content to depict the guerrillas as 'bandits' and no real major effort was made to combat them.

In these years, the guerrilla campaigns appeared to be guided by the concept of fighting a limited war. In a military sense, the guerrilla attacks were mostly of local significance. The leadership consisted of ex-army officials, ex-university students and former student representatives. Some of the leadership attended university seminars during the week and fought a 'weekend war' on Friday, Saturday and Sunday. With a certain frequency, the *comandantes* were interviewed in the national press and most people in Zacapa knew where to find them in a local bar or a restaurant. Ordinary members were recruited from the urban areas and the smaller regional cities, mixed with peasants from the southern and eastern Ladino regions. Yon Sosa and Turcios Lima maintained contacts with their former brothers-in-arms in the army, sometimes visiting their classmates at the Politécnica, privately at home, in a cinema or in a bar.[33] This gentlemanlike behaviour was extended to posthumous military honours. After Turcios Lima's death in a car accident, when his coffin was carried through the streets of Guatemala City during the funeral ceremony, it was halted before the Politécnica to receive the last salutation by his *compañeros de promoción* and his fellow officers.

However, the relatively comfortable (comfortable in a strict military sense) anti-guerrilla campaigns during the 1960s had an outcome for the national social and political order, that in the long run had much more far-reaching consequences: the creation of a 'society of fear'. Using the threat of a communist overthrow as a pretext or as a virtual reality, the military in-stitutions began to monopolize their institutional strength against all other organized segments of the civil society: against the public sector, against the political parties and social movements, gradually producing a hybrid civil–military political regime of violence and repression. An alliance between the political leaders and the military became the most 'natural' solution for a new government, constitutional or imposed.[34] As it has been expressed by a keen observer of this scene:

> It reached to the extreme situation that all political parties, looking desperately after a General who could be their presidential candidate. Later, when the higher army echelons appointed the military successor of the former military presid-ent, an opaque process of electoral fraud began to take shape. After all, the direct damage was limited to the members of the officers' corps: one military man won the presidential elections and was replaced by another officer with better credentials to the armed forces.[35]

In the political arena, the already strong national tradition of military presidentialism was reinforced into a political paradigm of military super-vision. From 1958 to 1985, Guatemala's head of state was an army officer; between 1970 and 1982, the elected or appointed military president was succeeded by a new general, who had served his predecessor as Minister of

Defence. The only apparent exception was the formally civilian government period of Méndez Montenegro (1966–70), the period within which the military supervision and repression structure was established. Méndez Montenegro, coming from a political family of moderate, even 'socialist', reputation, had to prove his patriotic credentials to the armed forces. At the beginning of his period in government he was approached by the younger, more moderate and modernizing segment of the officers' corps, and by the old guard of fervent anti-communist colonels.[36] Montenegro made a pact with the old colonels, an alliance that in Guatemalan terms signified a pact with the devil. From the mid-1960s to the mid-1980s, Guatemala's social and political formula was to be a combination of violence, repression and fear.[37]

The armed forces – a modest army,[38] a very small navy and a supporting air force, under the unified command of the (army) chief of staff – expanded their domain over some of the essential parts of the public sector.[39] The intelligence sector holds, even today, an undisputed monopoly over the armed forces. Intelligence support was mostly provided by US assistance; however, in the late 1970s, the Israelis entered as advisers on such sensitive areas as counter-intelligence and intelligence-processing.[40] The police, for instance, was militarized, a situation that is maintained to this day (1996). The police were subordinated to the military not only at the national but also at the regional and local levels; and the local police had to coordinate in detail with the local army commander and were completely dependent on army intelligence and army information.[41] In addition, the presidential house was militarized. Since the last decades of the nineteenth century, the Minister of Defence provided an army general as presidential chief of staff/chief of the presidential advisory group. During the decades of the military presidents, this situation appeared to be 'normal' in terms of providing services within the armed forces. However, from 1986 on, the civilian presidents Cereso, Serrano, De Leon Carpio and Arzú also received from their obligatory intelligence advisers 'consultative briefings on the long-term national development and security priorities', as perceived by the armed forces.

A vital mission was established and consolidated in the rural departments of Guatemala. With the prolongation of the armed conflict and its extension towards other departments in the 1970s, the armed forces began to behave, first *de facto* and then *de jure*, as the only legitimate representatives of the central government. Outside the urban centres, the army, and sometimes the navy, acted (and still act) as the representatives of the public sector, with army nurses and medics, army dentists, army veterinarians, army engineers, army lawyers and army administrators. The links between civilian and military functions in the undeveloped and the indigenous regions were reinforced by a 'traditional' military development mission; the 'military civic action' programme, provided and financed by US military and civilian assistance;[42] and the local development programmes for the civilian population, designed and executed by the armed forces.

However, the most violent and dramatic institutional change was the partially hidden, and partially unveiled, shaping of a machinery of control, persecution, oppression and murder. This machinery was apparently directed against the 'communist threat of the guerrilla', but was in fact expanded towards all segments of civil society that, maybe, one day, would or could support the guerrillas. To acquire more direct control over the peasants and the regional population, the military expanded the role of the *comisionados militares* – up until that time an army reserve in each village and in each *latifundio* in charge of delivering the quota of conscripts – into the local *jefe* of a spy and control network, which reported about the political and military activities of the local population to the army representative. In some localities, the army began experimentally forming and training paramilitary peasant militia units. A network of paramilitary officers was formed to control and terrorize the supposed urban guerrilla support structure: the political parties of the Left (defined as such by the extreme conservatives), the labour movement, the movement of the university students and the leadership of the secondary school students, the leadership of the urban slum movements and so on. Torture, disappearances, violent murders and local massacres were thought to be an efficient deterrent strategy.

By the time Méndez Montenegro came to power, the government and the military were considering the elimination of the guerrilla movement, and the strategy for eliminating their support structure became a top national priority. The result of a ferocious counter-insurgency campaign, called 'Operation Guatemala',[43] was that the guerrilla movement seemed to be crushed: several hundred *guerrilleros* were killed, but at the cost of the lives of thousands of innocent peasants and of the destruction of their villages. Colonel Carlos Arana, the commanding officer of the successful anti-guerrilla campaign in Zacapa and the eastern regions, was promoted to general and sent as the ambassador of Guatemala to Managua. There, Anastasio Somosa helped him form a successful coalition for his presidential campaign in 1970.[44] After the Anara government's period of office, the combination of the massive destruction of the guerrilla movement and its supposed support structure became the strategic recipe of the counter-insurgency doctrine. As a secondary 'sweetening' option, some local development projects, mostly in the form of 'strategic hamlets' and other mechanisms for controlling the peasants and the regional population, were implemented by the state.[45] However, the basic ingredients of the anti-insurgency strategy were intimidation, attack, violence, torture, and blind destruction. An independent US-sponsored study group concluded:

> Meanwhile, the insurgency continued to grow. But rather than reassess counter-insurgency tactics that contrived to the growing number of guerrilla recruits, the government simply intensified them. [...] Two major opposition leaders were assassinated: Manuel Colóm [...] and Alberto Fuentes [...] Their deaths

clearly indicated that Opposition leaders —no matter how responsible, patriotic, or nonviolent— were considered a threat to the *esquema politico*. To the list of the assassinated were added labor and peasant leaders, party officials, student activists, lawyers, doctors and teachers. And their number grew alarmingly: in 1972 'political' deaths averaged 30 to 50 a month; by 1980, 80 to 100 a month; by 1981, 250 to 300 a month.[46]

From Méndez Montenegro's government onwards, the guerrilla and counter-insurgency campaigns had transformed Guatemala into a theatre of low-intensity civil war. The civil war was still to acquire its strong ethnic component.[47] During the 1970s, a new guerrilla group, the EGP (1972), emerged, starting with operations in Ixcán, the northern frontier of the Mayan Quiché-region. Many of their *comandantes* had already participated in campaigns in the Ladino regions, were of middle-class Ladino descent and had studied for at least several years at university. A second group, the ORPA (1971), entered the Maya regions as well. In contrast to the older guerrilla movements of the 1960s, the new guerrillas were from the start inclined to recruit the Maya Indians. They received support from the Maya communities and acquired roots in the socio-economic and cultural affairs of the Maya ethnicities. After several years of living in the Maya communities, and after slow and persistent recruiting and collaborating in the local economy and society, the EGP and the ORPA gained and consolidated the sympathy of the Indian communities and the regional population. From the second half of the 1970s onwards, the guerrillas' initiatives and their political and reform manifestos were basically indigenous. During the following years, the guerrillas succeeded in gaining territorial advances in the Maya departments at an impressive pace.

The growth of the guerrillas, their expansion over the Indian departments, and the success of their campaigns would never have been so sensational without the national climate of the harsh and embittering counter-insurgency campaigns and the generalized atmosphere of violence and persecution which existed in the last years of the presidency of Laugerud, culminating in the presidential period of Lucas García (1978–82). It was during this period that President Lucas García referred to the President of the United States as 'Jimmy Castro' in public speeches and received warm applause. In those years, when violence was structural, and torture and murder were seen to be correction mechanisms against existing, future and potential insurgents, the army and the government drove a deep wedge into the social and political order of the country. Whoever was considered not to be a '100 per cent government loyalist' was regarded as an enemy, an insurgent, a criminal, and thus a communist.

The social cleavage produced by the government's induced 'society of fear', delivered to the guerrillas a stream of fresh recruits and embittered sympathizers. At the end of the Lucas García regime, in early 1982, guerrilla units operated in at least half of Guatemala's twenty-two departments, controlling a well-established infrastructure in a region consisting of six connected departments in the Indian highlands.[48] The guerrilla units operated in columns of up to 200 combatants, systematically attacking police stations, military outposts, and sometimes occupying entire regional municipalities and urban centres. In Guatemala City, at the Ministry of Defence, commanding officers were deeply concerned about the possibility of the encirclement of more important urban areas.[49] The ORPA and the EGP together consisted of an estimated 6,000 guerrillas, supported by an estimated 250,000 civilian, mostly Maya, peasants.[50] In army circles, the indigenous support was considered to be the result of a master plan, conceptualized by the guerrilla leadership in order to provide their troops with logistic support:

> In fact we have to thank them for the conception of what later was our system of *Patrullas de Autodefensa Civil*. The guerrillas organized the peasants in *Fuerzas Irregulares Locales*, the so-called FIL. [...] But in the long run, they overextended themselves. Let me give you an example: only in Chimaltenango, some 45 minutes from the capital, they had organized more than 70,000 *Fuerzas Irregulares Locales*. The army had only 27,000 regular troops. What I think is that, with so many people, they lost the capacity of minimum supply, of minimum command, of minimum control.[51]

The government knew only one solution: to intensify the counter-insurgency campaign, to build up the capacity for destruction, and to apply the tactics of 'scorched-earth' to the indigenous communities. In the period between 1980 and 1985 (the years 1982 and 1983 being the most violent), approximately 100,000 civilians were killed; 450 villages and hamlets were completely destroyed; 60,000 indigenous peasants were 'relocated' in 'strategic hamlets';[52] one milllion people had chosen 'internal displacement'; 500,000 migrated abroad; and several thousands were 'disappeared'.[53] General Benedicto Lucas García, brother of President General Romeo Lucas García and the army chief of staff, requested the triplication of the armed forces, in terms of officers and conscripts, to launch a more efficient counter-campaign. It was then, at the end of the Lucas García period of government, that a group of army officers, calling themselves the Young Officers Movement, staged a coup to replace the megalomaniac warrior brothers with a more sophisticated military leadership. General Ríos Montt[54] was appointed as the new head of state, in order to clear the sphere of corruption, to remove the most violent military leaders and politicians from the national arena,[56] and to come to better terms with the guerrillas and civil society.

In terms of the counter-insurgency strategy and tactics, some substantive changes took place. Ríos Montt made the first steps in a negotiating process with the guerrillas.[56] Then he offered amnesty to the guerrillas – official declarations mentioned a number of several hundreds who had turned in their arms to army posts or the Red Cross. After the expiration of the amnesty, Montt declared a state of siege, followed by draconic laws that expanded the already vast powers of the army. In early 1983, after six months of relative tranquillity, the army launched a new counter-insurgency offensive, based upon another concept of anti-guerrilla fighting.[57] The younger army elite, who soon removed Ríos Montt because of his personal ambitions and replaced him with a more 'decent' army general, formulated the strategy which consisted of a mixture of political, military and development ideas. The main idea of the new strategy was to establish a more legitimate presence in the disputed regions, with 'positive actions', local development projects, and protection of allied peasants, etc. Strengthening the politico-military position would require more control of 'extra-governmental' violence, more control over the peasantry as a whole, and a larger presence through other, paramilitary, means. The new strategy also required a more legitimate national and international context, a better understanding with the United States and other relevant countries, and, finally, a civilian government that would agree with the global content of these concepts. It is from these ideas that the slow transition towards the civilian governments of Cereso (1986–91) and his successors can be explained.

In more military terms, the counter-insurgency strategy contained three elements.[58] The first was to increase the number of men, basically conscripts, under arms and to deploy smaller, more mobile, units in the disputed regions. The second element was to expand and consolidate a system of paramilitary, civilian defence forces. This resulted in the creation of the so-called Patrullas de Autodefensa Civil (PACs), a system used to such a degree within the national territory that, at one time, approximately 900,000 men out of the total population of 9 million Guatemalans were enlisted in the PACs. The third was to re-initiate the former civic-action plans of local development: involving food, services and the improvement of the local infrastructure. In practice, the members of the PACs were mostly the beneficiaries of the civic-action plans and the local development activities. The peasants who joined were rewarded with food, housing and jobs. Those who refused to join the patrols were 'disappeared' or simply shot.

The social costs of the civil war remained extremely high in terms of civilian victims, widows and orphans, and in terms of displaced and 'resettled' persons. In a series of shock-and-pacification campaigns, called *Fusiles y Frijoles* (beans and rifles) and *Techo, Tortilla y Trabajo* (roof, tortilla and work) the army acquired the strategic initiative. The number of killed or wounded civilians was, although less than in former years, estimated to be in excess of 10,000. The army and the guerrillas were said to kill those who were suspected to have sympathy for the other side. As a consequence the guerrillas were slowly pushed into the defensive, no longer capable of protecting friendly villages from army reprisals or defending their indigenous supporters in the disputed areas. A human rights researcher reported the following explanation in an interview (1990) with General Gramajo, the principal designer of the new strategy:

A: Rather than killing 100 per cent, we provided food for 70 per cent [of war refugees], while killing 30 per cent. Before, the doctrine was [killing] 100 per cent.

Q: But what's the difference [between 100 and 30/70 per cent], then? There were many people killed between 1982–84, right?

A: Ah, but fewer than in 1980, or in 1979 [...] We aren't going to return to the killing zones [matazonas], we aren't going to return to that.

Q: How long will this stage of transition [in which the 30/70 per cent formula will be used] continue?

A: We don't know. When the opponent is no longer significant enough to impose actions against the State.[59]

In retrospect, he made the following summary of the campaign:

In fact we applied Mao, but then from the other side. It was pure Mao, counter-insurgency and development. We organized *fiestas*. A Saturday night in Pajachel requires rock, you know? Well, we organized the festivities. The *feria* of Mazatenango is famous for its carnival. Well, we organized the carnival. When the tourists came, we had removed the burned trucks, the destroyed houses, we had painted again the *plaza*, the roads had been cleaned, you could see only peace and tranquillity. That's the way you do it, together with the CACIF, the local chamber of industry and commerce, the municipality, the churches, using volunteers. Psychological action! And we paid for it, with food, with development projects. Everybody participated and everybody was a participant of the victory. Then we got, through our intelligence, access to reports, sent to MISEREOR. As you know, MISEREOR is the organization of the German bishops. The report stated: 'The army, and not the guerrillas, is winning.' And that was information obtained from independent sources. Another day I met by pure coincidence a professor of Georgetown University, an anthropologist. He told me that he was paid by the State Department to provide an analysis of the situation. And I asked him: 'The peasant population, is it supporting the guerrillas or the army?' He told me frankly: 'What I believe is, that you are winning the war. It is the system of the self-defence committees that's working, the small local infrastructure projects, the food-for-work programme.'[60]

The counter-insurgency strategy was maintained during most of Cereso's years in government. At the end of his term, in the late 1980s, the military considered the strategic defeat of the guerrilla movement as consolidated; they also considered Cereso's government to be a military transitional one:

In that context the extreme anticommunism in Guatemala and [the extreme conservatism of the ruling classes], we transferred, after the elections the year before, in 1986 the power to Cereso. In name of the armed forces I transferred to him on January 17 the power. It was a long and strained session, it took more than six hours of discussion. We gave him an exposition about the national reality and explained to him the matters of national priority. He received an analysis of everything: the social situation, the economical, the political, the military, he got to hear everything. At last I told him: 'Sir, are you aware of the fact that you are a transition president?' Cereso was pretty nervous, he thought we would begin reducing his political power [as in the case of Méndez Montenegro]. But he didn't know that the thesis of national security and stability exactly prescribed a democratic leadership for the nation, a strong democracy, protected by the armed forces. We didn't conceal anything, we told him everything straightforward: 'President, there are only 3,000 to 3,500 *guerrilleros* left, all parties included. They are supported by Cuba, by Nicaragua, by the Swedish, by Spain, by the Nordic countries. We are going to prevent their regrouping and their expansion [their scale of operations] again. We have developed our plans and we request from you your full support.' 'OK' he told us. 'Let me go my way, let me initiate my international work.'[61]

The past decade, the period of the civilian presidents Cereso, Serrano and De Leon Carpio, were the years of a civil–military government *de facto*. The anti-guerrilla campaigns gradually lost their intensity and wild violence. Serrano initiated a series of negotiating rounds with the guerrillas; most of his participating ministers and vice-ministers who were directly engaged, were later dismissed at the request of the army command.[62] Recently, under the presidency of De Leon Carpio, a slow, semi-public process of 'end of war' negotiations was initiated from both sides. The peace accords were negotiated subject by subject[63] and a formal agreement, followed by a planned re-insertion of the former combatants into civil society, was discussed during the years of the De Leon Carpio government. The final peace agreement was signed by his successor, President Arzú, in December 1996.

Concluding Remarks

In 1821 and 1824, two decisive battles took place in Junín and Ayacucho, the last fighting during the Latin American Wars of Liberation. Two armies, that of the 'Spanish Royalists' and that of the 'Peruvian Liberators', fought against each other. Of course, the soldiers of both armies were Indian conscripts, while the officer corps was composed of *blancones* and *criollos*. What is more peculiar, however, is the distribution of the nationalities within the officer corps. Nearly all officers in the liberation army were foreigners: from Argentina, from Chile, from Venezuela and from Colombia. There were some British and other Europeans, even an American officer was noticed. The loyalists' army was commanded by Peruvian officers.

The intriguing question remains of who liberated whom from whose dominance? The question was formulated by the Peruvian author José de la Riva Agüero in the 1940s; Mario Vargas Llosa re-examines the problem in his political memoirs.[64] Nevertheless, another controversial issue about the armies of the Spanish crown and of those of the Liberators in the battles of Junín and Ayacucho remains unclarified: the position of the Indian troops. These troops were the cannon-fodder of the military campaigns in the early nineteenth century, during the later decades of the nineteenth century, and in the military and paramilitary operations of the twentieth century. Ultimately, the question refers to one of the major ambiguities of Peru's political history: the issue of the Peruvian nationality.

Peru is not the only Latin American country whose 'Indian soul' has been separated from its 'political corpse'. In Guatemala, the long-term tendencies of the history of Peru seem to have been reproduced in a similar picture. Only in two nations of Latin America – Guatemala and Peru – have the indigenous peoples been so completely and so systematically degraded. In most Latin American countries, the colonial heritage produced a second-class citizenship, based upon ethnic characteristics and colour. The ruling classes of Guatemala and Peru have none the less succeeded in the creation of a kind of third-class citizenship for their Mayan and Quechua population.

The colonial history of both countries, and the greater part of the post-colonial history as well, could be summarized in identical phrases: enslavement of the original ethnic population, disintegration of the indigenous civilizations, languages and cultural identities. Where the indigenous peoples have been integrated in the national economies of Guatemala and Peru, it happened in the form of communal *minifundistas* or as landless or dependent peasants, employed on the huge *latifundios* in the highlands of Guatemala and Peru. In both countries, a vigorous segregation system has emerged, based upon a complicated stratification in terms of class, race and ethnicity. During the nineteenth and the greater part of the twentieth century, social relations were determined by the oligarchy and the armed forces. The former was made up mostly of land-owning dynasties. During the late twentieth century, the social structure of both countries, in which wealth, power and prestige were based on the possession of land, amounted to a perpetuation of the colonial order.[65] The political structure, based upon the ex-colonial economy and society and basically unaltered in Peru until the years of the 'Revolutionary Government of the Armed Forces' led by Velasco, has been wryly typified by the Peruvian historian Basadre as the 'Aristocratic Republic'.[66] In Guatemala, an all-permeating structure of social relations had originated in colonial times, called the *ladino–indio* segregation.[67] This quasi-apartheid system continues to determine the everyday life of Guatemala. The revolutionary period of 1944–54, the government years of Arévalo and Arbenz, did not change the basic structure of social relations in Guatemala, despite all intentions. There are arguments for the thesis of Solares that Guatemala is a 'State without being a Nation'.[68] In terms of official pretensions about a national identity in Guatemala and Peru, both countries represent the cultures, sentiments and hopes of fragmented societies.

When it comes to national reconciliation and national reconstruction after the civil war, the ethnic components of both Guatemalan and Peruvian society will play a prominent role. The integration of the ethnic legacy, the indigenous heritage into the national culture and society, and the substitution of the racial second- or third-class citizenship for at least an ideological concept of 'Guatemalidad' and 'Peruanidad' will be one of the basic priorities.[69] In the short run, the attitude of the military, both in Guatemala and in Peru – the triumphant victors of the civil war – does not give any reason for extreme optimism. In the sardonic words of General Gramajo, commander of the decisive Guatemalan counter-insurgency campaigns in the 1980s: 'In Guatemala, the Indian ethnicities still harbour a strong resentment due to the *Conquista*. In fact, if you think about it, during the years of 1982 and 1983, the conquering process that the Spanish initiated in the 1520s, was consolidated.'[70]

There are, however, differences in the development of the peace process in both countries. Guatemala's civil war ended at least in a series of negotiated peace agreements. There has been a minimum dialogue, a consolidated participation of the civil, the guerrilla and the public sectors, and the military. A kind of international forum has been provided by the presence of 'friendly nations' such as Mexico, Norway and Spain. As in the case of its neighbour country El Salvador, the role played by the United Nations (UN) system has been a positive one, and UN vigilance over the peace treaty will ensure a certain kind of respectability during the tenuous process of national reconstruction and regrouping of the main social forces. In such a context, the re-dimensioning of the armed forces, the reform of the police, the re-legitimation of law and order will have a fair chance. Although, by and large, the army has been drafting most of the transition and peace scenarios since the mid-1980s, a gradual re-emergence of civil society is to be expected. In Peru, in comparison, the implemented peace is the Pax Fujimoricana, a *sui generis* civil–military government formula by which an 'enlightened' civilian president 'understands' the urban informal masses and the peasant population with the backing of the higher military echelons and the support of the intelligence community. In terms of a reconstruction of civil society, the regime's dissolution of all formal pre-1990 institutions leaves doubts about the unaffectedness of Peru's future civil society.

One can only formulate open-ended questions about the very nature of the peasant movements and the informal masses in both Guatemala and Peru. What will be the legacy of the peasant armies in the indigenous Indian Maya and Quechua homelands? What will be the long-term effects of the war upon the collective memory of the urban masses, the urbanized Indian slum dwellers, micro-entrepreneurs and the self-employed? The neglected ethnic dimensions of the war, the identity claims during the guerrilla and the counter-insurgency campaigns, will play a latent and not to be forgotten role in the future years of peace and reconstruction.

Appendix I National Executives of Peru, 1930–99

Character of governance	National executive	Years in office	Form of succession
military	Gen. Manuel Ponce	1930–31	overthrown
military	Lt. Col. Luis Sanchez Cerro [I]	1931	resigned
junta of prominent citizens	Ricardo Leoncio Elias	1931	overthrown
military	Lt. Col. Gustavo Jimenez	1931	resigned
junta of prominent citizens	Gen. David Samanez Ocampo	1931	concluded term with elections
constitutional	Gen. Luis Sanchez Cerro [II]	1931–33	assassinated
appointed by congress	Gen. Oscar Benavides	1933–39	concluded term with elections
constitutional	Manuel Prado Ugarteche [I]	1939–45	served electoral term
constitutional	José Luis Bustamante y Rivero	1945–48	overthrown
military, later elected	Gen. Manuel Odria	1948–56	concluded term with elections
constitutional	Manuel Prado Ugarteche [II]	1956–62	overthrown
provisional	Gen. Ricardo Pérez Godoy	1962–63	overthrown
provisional	Gen. Nicolás Lindley	1963	concluded term with elections
constitutional	Fernande Belaúnde Terry [I]	1963–68	overthrown
military	Gen. Juan Velasco Alvarado	1968–75	overthrown
military	Gen. Francisco Morales Bermúdez	1975–80	concluded term with elections
constitutional	Fernando Belaúnde Terry [II]	1980–85	served electoral term
constitutional	Alán García	1985–90	served electoral term
constitutional	Alberto Fujimori [I]	1990–92	self-coup
legitimized by *constituyente*	Alberto Fujimori [II]	1992–95	served electoral term
constitutional	Alberto Fujimori [III]	1995–	served electoral term

Appendix II National Executives of Guatemala, 1930–99

Character of governance	National executive	Years in office	Form of succession
provisional	Gen. Manuel Orellana	1930	resigned
provisional	José María Reina Andrade	1930–31	resigned
dictatorship	Gen. Jorge Ubico y Castañeda	1931–44	resigned
provisional	Gen. Federico Ponce Vaides	1944	overthrown
provisional triumvirate	Major Francisco Arana / Captain Jacobo Arbenz / Jorge Toriello Garrido	1944–45	concluded term with elections
constitutional	Juan José Arévalo Bermejo	1945–50	served electoral term
constitutional	Col. Jacobo Arbenz	1950–54	overthrown
military junta	Col. Elfego Mozon / Col. Carlos Castillo Armas	1954	phased out
self-appointed	Col. Carlos Castillo Armas	1954–57	assassinated
provisional	Luis Arturo González Lopez	1957	resigned
provisional	Guillermo Flores Avendaño	1957–58	concluded term with elections
constitutional	Gen. Miguel Ydígoras Fuentes	1958–63	overthrown
provisional	Col. Enrique Peralta Azurdia	1963–65	concluded term with elections
constitutional	Julio César Méndez Montenegro	1966–70	served electoral term
elected	Gen. Carlos Arana Osorio	1970–74	served electoral term
elected	Gen. Eugenio Kjell Laugerud García	1974–78	served electoral term
elected	Gen. Romeo Lucas García	1978–82	overthrown
provisional military triumvirate	Gen. Efrain Rios Montt / Gen. Horacio Maldonado Schaad / Col. Francisco Luis Gordillo	1982	phased out

Gen. Efrain Rios Montt	1982–83	appointed	overthrown
Gen. Oscar Humberto Mejia Victores	1983–86	appointed	concluded term with elections
Marco Vinicio Cerezo Arevalo	1986–91	constitutional	served electoral term
Jorge Serrano	1991–93	constitutional	resigned after failed self-coup
Ramiro de Leon Carpio	1993–96	appointed by congress	served electoral term
Alvaro Arzú	1996–	constitutional	served electoral term

Notes and References

With thanks to Mario Fumerton, Henri Gooren and Simone Remeynse, who revised the details of the Peruvian and Guatemalan war scenario's.

1. See Gleijeses, *Shattered Hope*, for the Guatemalan, and Kruijt, *Revolution by Decree*, for the Peruvian, revolutions.

2. For analytical reasons, this chapter refers only to the case of Shining Path. While another guerrilla movement, the Movimiento Revolucionario Tupac Amaru (MRTA) emerged in 1984, its importance cannot be compared with that of Shining Path. If there is officialdom in guerrilla warfare, Tupac Amaru belonged to the 'formal sector' with their uniforms, military-style command and 'normal' behaviour, which included their public appearances and the romanesque bravado of its leadership. Being the smaller, the weaker, the more predictable and the more 'civilized' of the two guerrilla movements, the performance of Tupac Amaru was considered by most analysts to be less significant than the more mysterious Shining Path. For details, see Kruijt, 'Perú'. And then, when the movement was officially declared disappeared and dissolved, and its leaders imprisoned, the MRTA re-emerged in a spectacular assault on the Japanese Embassy in Lima, capturing a significant number of hostages among high-profile political, entrepreneurial and diplomatic figures. After the equally spectacular commando raid on the embassy building by Peruvian elite troops, the MRTA was again declared to be 'virtually non-existent'. A reborn phoenix flying high again?

3. See Fisher, *Last Inca Revolt*; O'Phelan Godoy, *Rebellions and Revolts*; Golte, *Repartos y rebeliones*; Klaiber and Jeffrey, *Religion and Revolution*; Lockhart, *Spanish Peru*; Martinez Peláez, *Patria*; and Stern, *Resistance*.

4. See Wickham-Crowley, 'Terror and guerrilla warfare'; Wickham-Crowley, *Guerillas and Revolution*; and Masterson, *Militarism and Politics*, for an analysis of the guerrilla movements in Latin America.

5. General Jorge Fernández Maldonado, co-founder of the military intelligence system; co-author of Velasco's reform programme, Plan Inca, and during the 1960s in charge of most of the anti-guerrilla campaigns recalled: 'The guerrilla effort was short-lived; we had infiltrated them thoroughly. Also, the three fronts operated without any coordination. One of Hugo Blanco's lieutenants worked for Intelligence. In the camp of De la Puente we had people as well. Technically it was not difficult to wipe out the guerrilla. They were idealists to the point that they practically committed suicide. It was a bunch of idealists who took to the Andes without knowing what the place was like, without having worked there, remaining alien. They came from Lima and wanted to be brethren to the peasants without really knowing them. The guerrilla did not inspire. Today things are different with *Sendero*; it is based there, knows the area and emerged at least in part from the peasants. In those days it was easy, every group was infiltrated by people of our side.' Quoted in Kruijt, *Revolution by Decree*, p. 55 (the interview took place in June 1986).

6. In an interesting study Payne indicates some of the roots of military reformist thinking in Peru. See Payne, *Peruvian Coup d'Etat*.

7. As Stepan rightly describes the process taking place in those years. See Stepan, *The State and Society*, pp. 158, 190.

8. See for more details Kruijt, 'Perú'. It is interesting to note that the army commanders between 1981 and 1990 – and I conducted long interviews with nearly all of them – blame Belaúnde explicitly and García in somewhat less harsh terms for their lack of interest in indigenous and ethnic emancipation, in local and regional development, the military, and even in the political aspects of the guerrilla campaigns and the civil war.

9. For a general analysis, see Degregori, *Ayacucho*, Goritti, *Sendero Luminoso*, Herthoghe and Labrousse, *Sentier Lumineux*, Palmer, *Shining Path*, Strong, *Shining Path*, Tarazona-Sevillano and Reuter, *Sendero Luminoso*, Tello, *Sobre el Volcán*, Tello, *Perú*. Two excellent essays about Shining Path have been published by Degregori, *Qué difícil es ser Dios*, and Flores Galindo, *Buscando un Inca*, pp. 287–320. See also Degregori's Chapter 3 of this book.

10. Officially called the Communist Party of Peru, by the *Shining Path of José Carlos Mariátegui*, in honour of Peru's most original and influential Marxist theorist. The splintering of the Peruvian Left has been described by Letts, *Izquierda peruana*.

11. The military high command in Lima, confronted with the burning of the ballot boxes in Chuschi, consulted with the presidential palace and obtained a 'Don't worry'. The army commander nevertheless sent troops in by helicopter to restore law and order and let the population vote again. (Interview with an, at his request, anonymous commander-general in Kruijt, 'Perú', p. 105.)

12. Palmer, 'Shining Path'; Palmer, 'Peru'.

13. Author's interview with General Sinesio Jarama on 4 February 1991, quoted in Kruijt, 'Perú', p. 107.

14. For an essay about the attraction of Shining Path for young women, see Kirk, *Grabado en Piedra*.

15. Degregori, *Qué difícil es ser Dios*, p. 19, emphasizes the fact that in Shining Path's hagiographic manuscripts Guzmán is always depected as an unarmed teacher.

16. Quoted from *Sendero Luminoso en el norte del país*, an extensive unpublished document written by a United Nations official, in May 1991, who was a sociologist with family ties in the departments dominated by Shining Path.

17. I used some specific articles in *Sí* and I interviewed diplomatic and development representatives in September and October 1992.

18. The best description of the counter-insurgency strategy is given by Obando Arbulú, 'Diéz años de guerra'; and Obando Arbulú, 'Subversion and antisubversion'. Another good piece of information is provided by Basombrío Iglesias, 'Estrategia del chino'.

19. Gorriti, *Sendero Luminoso*, pp. 71–6, 117–21, 223, 225, 308ff.

20. Obando Arbulú, 'Subversion and antisubversion', p. 321.

21. Author's interview with General Adrián Huamán on 4 February 1991, quoted in Kruijt, 'Perú', p. 109.

22. See Kruijt, 'Ethnic civil war', for more details.

23. See Starn, *Rondas Campesinas*, Starn, 'Noches de ronda'; Starn, *Con los llanques*, Starn, *Hablan los Ronderos*, for the origin and evolution of these organizations.

24. The following data are quoted from a confidential briefing, offered by General Carlos Dominguez Solis, national director of DINCOTE, to representatives of the Diplomatic Corps on 8 February 1994.

25. See Obando Arbulú, 'Subversion and antisubversion', p. 326.

26. Toriello, *Batalla*. A similar statement was made by Edgar Ponce, then academic director of the Centro ESTNA in a series of interviews with the author in July 1994.

27. Schneider, *Communism in Guatemala*, quoted *verbatim* in Schlesinger and Kinzer, *Bitter Fruit*, p. 227.

28. Schlesinger and Kinzer, *Bitter Fruit*, p. 228.

29. The 'October 20 Front' was given to commemorate the revolution of 1944; the name of the other front, 'Alejandro de Leon November 13 Guerrilla Movement', reflects the day of the revolt against Yvígoras in 1960.

30. Aguilera et al., *Dialectica del terror*, pp. 37ff.; Millett, 'Central American militaries', pp. 211–16; Sesereses, 'Guatemalan legacy', pp. 21–2; Sexton, *Campesino*, pp. 397–428; and Yurrita, 'Transition', pp. 77ff.

31. The best analysis on this subject is provided by Aguilera, *El fusil y el olivo*; Aguilera, *Propuestas*; and Aguilera et al., *Reconversión militar en América Latina*. See also Kruijt, 'Futuro' for additional details.

32. The following is based upon Sesereses, 'Guatemalan legacy', pp. 22ff.

33. Author's interview with Edgar Ponce, then academic director of the Centro ESTNA on 7 July 1994.

34. The most detailed analysis of the political pacts is given by Villagran Kramer, *Bibliografía política*. Villagran, himself a politician who – in an unhappy alliance – as 'running mate' for Lucas García became the civilian vice-president of the country during the most repressive military government in Guatemala of this century, was invited to appear before a military tribunal in his third year of government. However, he thought it better to stay in the United States, where he was attending a meeting. As vice-president, he was succeeded by a colonel.

35. Author's interview with General Ricardo Peralta Mendez, on 13 July 1994.

36. Author's interview with Edgar Ponce, then academic director of the Centro ESTNA, on 7 July 1994, and with General Ricardo Peralta Mendez on 13 July 1994. Peralta Mendez, a nephew of the former head of state, Colonel Peralta Azurdia, and the founder and first director of the Centro de Estudios Militares, was later the presidential candidate of the Christian Democrats in the election campaign against Lucas García. He is a member of the board of the Centro ESTNA. In the 1970s, he studied at the Peruvian Centro de Altos Estudios Militares (CAEM), where he met with the generals Mercado Jarrin, Jorge Fernández Maldonado, Ramón Miranda and with other Velasquistas. Ponce was at that time the personal assistant of Manuel Colóm, the social-democratic mayor of Guatemala City, who was later assassinated.

37. The following stems from Barry, *Guatemala*; Calvert, *Guatemala*; Delli Sante, *Nightmare or Reality?*, Fauriol and Loser, *Guatemala's Political Puzzle*; Gleijeses, 'Guatemala'; Jonas, *Battle for Guatemala*; Painter, *Guatemala*; Plant, *Guatemala*; Simon, *Guatemala*; Torres-Rivas, *Centroamérica*; Torres-Rivas, *Repression and Resistance*.

38. The total number of division generals is two (the Minister of Defence and the Chief of Staff), whereas the total number of brigadier generals is twelve. The armed forces were, at the time, anticipating a gradual reduction process to take place after 1996 (author's interview with General Mario René Enriquez Morales, Minister of Defence, on 2 September 1993, and with General Sergio Camargo, commander of the elite brigade *Mariscal Zavala*, on 11 July 1994. Note the contrast with the eighty-eight three- and one-star generals of the Peruvian army (in 1994).

39. Author's interview with Captain Rafael Rottman Chang, former intelligence adviser to President Cereso and on the day of the interview (23 March 1994) president of the Guatemalan Congress Committee on Defence and the Police.

40. Mossad still maintains a special relationship with the Guatemalan administration. When, in 1994, for instance, General Quilo, then Vice-Minister of Defence, prepared plans for a coup, the presidency was alerted by the Israelis.

41. In the early 1980s the army was studying a project to incorporate the Policía Nacional and the Policía de Hacienda formally within the structure of the Ministerio de la Defensa. Besides these civilian police forces, there existed during the 1980s other semi-militarized police forces: the Policía Militar Ambulante, the Comisionados Militares, the Guardia Nacional, and the Batallón de Reacción de Operaciones Especiales; see Vargas Foronda, *Guatemala*, pp. 86–7.

42. Described in detail by Barber and Ronning, *Internal Security*.

43. Designed with reference to 'Operation Phoenix' in Vietnam, with strong support from the CIA; see Schlesinger and Kinzer, *Bitter Fruit*, p. 246.

44. Poor Guatemala! In 1970, Anastasio Somosa formed, in Managua, Guatemala's national cabinet. In 1982, Fidel Castro concluded in La Habana the unification of the four hitherto independently operating guerrilla movements into the Unidad Revolucionaria Nacional Guatemalteca (URNG). The URNG is composed of the EGP (Ejercito Guerrillero de los Pobres), the ORPA (Organización del Pueblo en Armas), the FAR (Fuerzas Armadas Rebeldes) and the PGT (Partido Guatemalteco del Trabajo).

45. A good and detailed analysis is given by Manz, *Refugees*.

46. *Report on Guatemala*, pp. 26–7.

47. See the excellent analysis of Le Bot, *La guerre*, pp. 109ff.

48. Sesereses, 'Guatemalan legacy', p. 37.

49. Author's interview with General Alejandro Gramajo on 13 July 1994. Gramajo was chief of staff during most of the time of the 1982/85 campaigns, and Minister of Defence during the Cereso government. He is the author of Guatemala's security ('stability') thesis and the founder of the Centro ESTNA. See Gramajo Morales, *Tesis*; Gramajo Morales, *Liderazgo militar*.

50. Le Bot, *La guerre*, p. 195.

51. Author's interview with General Jaime Rabanales on 12 July 1994. Rabanales was the commander of the Guatemalan army in the Quiché and the other Maya regions in the period between 1986 and 1988. Since then, he was the director of the Centro de Estudios Militares; he is now a member of the board of the Centro ESTNA.

52. See Montejo, *Testimony*; and Stoll, *Between Two Armies*, for detailed descriptions of the effects on the Maya communities.

53. See Sexton, *Campesino*; and Delli Sante, *Nightmare or Reality?* for sources in their annotated biography.

54. Ríos Montt had formerly been a presidential candidate for the Christian Democrats. He probably won the elections, but the army decided in favour of another general. Ríos Montt shifted colours and participated in various other party formulae. He then turned out to be a 'born-again Christian'. His political biography (by Anfuso and Sczepanski, *Efrain Ríos Montt*) was distributed by his new church. Ríos Montt, whatever the final judgement about his government years, possessed, and still possesses, charismatic traits. During the parliamentary elections of March 1995, he and his party obtained more than 30 per cent of the vote.

55. Benedicto Lucas García, for instance, was placed under house arrest, but was later appointed chief of the counter-insurgency operations in the Petén; see Sexton, *Campesino*, p. 420.

56. An offer of initial negotiations was prudently channelled through the Colegios Profesionales of the Lawyers, the Doctors and the Engineers, who were represented in Ríos Montt's new Consejo del Estado. However, the representatives of the guerrillas in New York refused to accept the offer. (Author's interview with Edgar Ponce on 7 July 1994. Ponce was then the vice-president of the political committee of the *Consejo*.)

57. Author's interview with General Alejandro Gramajo on 13 July 1994.

58. See Sesereses, 'Guatemalan legacy', pp. 41ff., for a more detailed description.

59. See Schirmer, 'The looting', p. 9. See also Schirmer, 'Guatemalan military project'; and Schirmer, 'Guatemala'.

60. Author's interview with General Alejandro Gramajo on 13 July 1994.

61. Ibid.

62. Personal communication during a series of author's interviews with Abel Girón, in 1991 and 1992 Vice-Minister of Development and, together with his Minister, in charge of the logistics of the expected surrender procedures. The interviews took place in March and July 1994.

63. Author's interview with Dr Hector Rosada-Granados, government negotiator on behalf of the president, on 14 March and 8 July 1994. See also Aguilera and Ponciano, *El espejo*; and Poitevin, *Guatemala*.

64. Vargas Llosa, *El pez en el agua*. Some years before, Flores Galindo, *Buscando un Inca*, pp. 281ff., raised the same question.

65. Spalding, 'Class structures', has documented this process for Peru.

66. The term, coined by Basadre, has been used by succeeding generations of historians to typify the social and political formula of the years before the 1960s; see Burga and Flores, *República aristocrática*.

67. For an interpretation, see Adams, *Crucifixion by Power*; Carmack, *Harvest of Violence*; Martínez Peláez, *Patria*; Perera, *Unfinished Conquest*; Rosada Granados, *Indios y Ladinos*; and Smith, *Guatemalan Indians*.

68. Solares, 'Guatemala', pp. 50ff.

69. Comparable to the ideological concept of *Méxicanidad*, as discussed in Bartra, *Jaula de la melancolía*; Bartra, *Oficio méxicano*; and Bonfil Batalla, *México profundo*.

70. Author's interview with General Gramajo on 13 July 1994.

THREE

Reaping the Whirlwind: the *Rondas Campesinas* and the Defeat of *Sendero Luminoso* in Ayacucho

CARLOS IVÁN DEGREGORI

When *Sendero Luminoso* (Shining Path) began its war in 1980, it was a party formed mainly of schoolmasters and university teachers and students. Its presence among the local peasantry was weak. However, when, after Christmas 1982, the Peruvian armed forces assumed political and military control of Ayacucho, Shining Path had easily managed to dislodge the police from broad areas of the countryside in the northern provinces of the department, and was preparing to take control of the departmental capital.[1]

The Rural Young and the Peasantry

The key factor facilitating the rapid expansion of Shining Path was a significant number of rural young people with education to secondary level or, in some cases, only up to the last year of primary school, that swelled the party ranks. This group of people constituted the most active sector of the 'bodies generated' by Shining Path in the countryside and, later, of the organs of power of the *senderista* 'new state' under construction. It may be stated unequivocally that Shining Path *needed* this stratum. In regions where it did not exist, it was very difficult to establish solid links with the peasantry.

These young people were politically and socially 'available', exposed at school to instruction in *senderista* ideas, or at least to what has been called the *idea crítica del Perú* – questioning the social and political order in a confrontational but authoritarian manner.[2] The presence of other left-wing parties, although tenuous, in some parts of the region, fertilized youthful radicalism. The rural young people were, at the same time, a group of people in search of an identity, to the degree that the traditional Andean identity of their parents had begun to seem distant to them, after their exposure to the 'myth of progress' disseminated by the schools and the media, and also

63

subscribed to by their parents. Finally, they were young people with few expectations of progress via the marketplace, whether assisted by migration or a higher level of education. To these young people was suddenly offered the concrete possibility of ascending socially through the ranks of the (new) *senderista* state. Militancy in the party, then, can be seen also as a channel of social mobility. Arturo, a young man from the community of Rumi, relates: 'They said that Ayacucho was going to be a liberated zone by 1985. A splendid dream they created in the kids was that – well you know we're in 1981 now – by 1985 this is going to be an independent republic. Wouldn't you like to be a minister, or a military chief: to be something?'

Power seduced these young school students, recruited in turn by other young people, the university students turned guerrillas, who were the main support of the *senderista* columns. Nicario, also from Rumi, relates his encounter with one of them:

> When I was in the second year of secondary school I was invited by a person from the University of San Cristóbal. So I, well, I readily accepted [...] because at that time – it was 1982 – Sendero had already staged a lot of operations. At the Assembly he was a military commander, a leader. He came with his machine gun. I went up to him full of fear still. He introduced himself with his thick voice: 'Yes, comrade,' just like that, with his boots and all, he greeted me.

Power appeared in all its terrifying splendour, and seduced most of the young people of Rumi, promising to invest them with the same attributes. The young people played around with this power. Their first actions were to paint walls and explode dynamite in the village, disturbing the peace of the rural nights. According to Arturo, 'they caused explosions just for the hell of it'.

For the university students that formed the nucleus of *Sendero*, the party was a 'total identity'. A sector of rural young people also came to be active in Shining Path in this way.[3] But for many, the fact that the possibility of social mobility was associated with the concrete exercise of power in their own localities – and, besides, with elements of youthful adventure, especially in the first years, when the violence was still under control – played an important role. Arturo relates: 'They were young people who studied at Cangallo. Teenage boys who were suddenly desperate to handle arms, a submachine gun for example; handling dynamite too was a great thing for them. Only the brave ones did it [...] for them to get their hands on weapons was something on another level, a rung above the rest.'

Finally, an important role was played by something that might be called the demonstration effect. The rural young people joined an organization on the way up, with prestige, that was proving itself effective, that was giving them power and transforming them. Becoming a member of Shining Path had a lot in common with a rite of passage or initiation into a religious sect: the armed sect.

From this juvenile beachhead, the movement made incursions among the peasantry and met with most success in places where there was a significant educational generation gap. This gap placed the young people not so close to their parents as to be fully subjected to the dictates of tradition, and not so far from them as to lack interest in the fate of their villages: they wanted to transform them. Once the rural young people had become the armed generation, in many regions and communities they seduced, convinced or subjugated the adults, who had sent their children to school so that they could find a way to get ahead in a complex and discriminating society. If these educated youngsters said so, there must be something in it. They were *nawiyoq* (they had eyes), they *saw* things their parents, 'ignorant people', had perhaps not noticed.[4] Even when, in their heart of hearts, they rejected the discourse of the young, the reaction of the parents was ambivalent because of the family and cultural ties binding the generations.

Beyond the ties of family relationships, the party (PCP-SL) was always ready to display its capacity for coercion, which included, from the beginning, doses of terror. Shining Path thus occupied the place of the traditional Andean *patrón*, hard and inflexible, but 'just', pushing aside the existing ones, generally unjust or abusive. From this position, the movement tried to secure concrete benefits for the peasants. On the one hand, the party straddled the existing contradictions in the region;[5] on the other hand, it imposed a very strict moral code.

In Ayacucho – where among the ruins of *gamonalismo*, abusive local *misti* (white 'Lord') strongmen persisted – Shining Path found a particularly favour-able scenario, with a peasantry relatively disposed to accept it as the new *patrón*, one, besides, that seemed to be more powerful than the old local powers and the existing state boss, whose repressive representatives, the armed forces, had been swept away. This was a region with a low number of peasant organizations and a high density of students, where education enjoyed a particular prestige, and where the principal social movement in the previous decades had not been a movement in demand of land, but one demanding free education.[6] The local peasants' acceptance of Shining Path was a basically pragmatic one, given in exchange for highly concrete personal, family and communal advantages.[7] But on the basis of this tactical acceptance, the pos-sibility of a long-term strategic identification opened up for the *Sendero* project.

This widespread acceptance of Shining Path seemed almost inevitable in the second half of 1982, which was a very special period for the region. For the party it was a moment of euphoria. It had held its second national conference and had begun to develop the second stage of its plan 'Unfold the Guerrilla War', that consisted in 'Advance towards Support Bases'.[8] The influence of the party was rapidly spreading in the rural zones and also grew in the departmental capital where, in March 1982, guerrillas had successfully attacked the prison and liberated dozens of imprisoned cadres; and when the young *Sendero* leader Edith Lagos was buried in September of that year, more than 10,000 people congregated.

But as often happens, unnoticed in the midst of success, failure was being incubated. To begin with, neither the young people nor the cadres seemed to have a concrete idea of long-term consequences. They lived in a triumphant present and dreamed of a future tinged with the concept of a peasant Utopia: the armed forces would suffer massive desertions; the helicopters could be brought down with slingshot; Lima would be put in a stranglehold and the urban poor would flock back to the new rural republic.[9]

The concept of a 'peasant's Utopia' engraved itself in fire on the imagination of the cadres, but scarcely and/or only for moments ignited the enthusiasm of the masses. Shining Path was successful in 'beating and combing the countryside';[10] nevertheless, its problems started when it began to build its new power on this cleared terrain. It was then that, on various levels, several of the structural faults in the *senderista* project began to be noticed: fissures opening between the party strategy and the dynamics of regional and peasant society and economy.

The Organization of Production

Shining Path gave pride of place to collective forms of organization and, on this level – at least in late 1982, at the moment of the sowing – it seemed to meet with little resistance. Nicario took part in the first party sowing in Chuschi (Cangallo), a community where the movement began its armed struggle on 17 May 1980. His account brings to mind the pre-Columbian states or the colonial *mitas* (forced labour): sowing the land of the sun, of the Inca or the big land-owner. On the 8 hectares of communal land, sixty yokes were gathered from Chuschi and neighbouring communities. At each of the four corners of the farm (*chacra*) they set a red flag: 'On beginning work they set off twelve sticks of dynamite; at twelve o'clock, six sticks, and in the evening twelve sticks. The work was successful, but the Party was never able to harvest, because the army moved in' (Nicario). In other geographical areas the party did harvest, and there were cases where that was the moment of breakdown – as the peasants noticed that what had been produced collectively was appropriated by the party.

Finally, in other places, the problems began when the party ordained that sowing was to be carried out only for the party and for family subsistence, and proceeded to close down fairs. Here the strategy of conquering territories and closing them off in order to block the flow of products and asphyxiate the cities, came into collision with the majority strategies that transcend questions of payments and extend beyond the limits of the community. These are strategies involving extensive networks of family and *paisanaje* relationships and including a series of nexus in different parts of the country and the cities.[11] The cities, on the other hand, are not supplied exclusively nor even, in all cases, primarily from their own rural hinterland.[12] The difficulties experienced by Shining Path when it closed the fair at Lirio in the

Huanta highlands, where Iquichano peasants, supposedly isolated, supplied themselves with an array of manufactured products, have been mentioned elsewhere;[13] but the fissures on this level began to deepen irremediably towards the end of the decade.

The New Power

It was in the construction of the new power that Shining Path first experienced major difficulties. In the second half of 1982, and as part of its plan to 'beat and comb the countryside', the movement decided to replace the communal authorities by commissars representing the new power.

According to Mao's Little Red Book (*el libreto maoista*), in order to carry the people's war to a successful conclusion, the party must have as its base the poor peasants, 'those most disposed to accept the direction of the Communist Party'. Surprisingly for Shining Path, their greatest problems occurred in the poorest regions that were at the same time the most 'traditional'. This was the case in the Iquichana communities, where the system of *varas* (yardsticks) still functioned. This is a system of hierarchical and ritualized authority, at whose pinnacle is the *varayoq* or *alcalde vara*, who personifies the community and reaches this position at an advanced age, after ascending a scale of civic and religious responsibilities.[14] The substitution of young *senderista* cadres for these authorities was not only an attack on a communal order, but also an affront against a whole-world view. For the party, however, the peasant world seemed flat, two-dimensional, without historical density or social complexity, divided simply into rich, middle or poor peasants. It seems fair to say that, as a result of adopting this approach, applying its mistaken economistic categories, the movement often ended up with a base of young people from the middle and rich strata, winning over or neutralizing some sectors of the adults of these same strata, and imposing its line on, or repressing and finally massacring, the poor peasants.

It was especially after Shining Path's disavowal of the communal authorities that the first open rebellions against the organization occurred. But, even in communities where the election of the *varayoq* had already been abandoned and local government was carried out in line with national legislation, the take-over by the new authorities tended to give rise to problems. In some communities, family ties between the 'old and new powers' (to use Shining Path's terminology) at first neutralized any resistance, as at Rumi, where 'Already at that time we were appointing new authorities. We convoked [an assembly] to name our true community authorities. The old authorities didn't complain because the Chairman's own son had already made up his mind and was in the Party. His son had won *him* over as well.' But in many other areas, the youth of the *senderista* commanders came as a shock. Not only because it contradicted the hierarchy of age, but because 'Gonzalo's thought' was not in itself sufficient to disentangle the rural young, who were taking

charge of their villages, from the thick web of family and *paisanaje* relationships – with their own dynamics of reciprocation, vendettas, hatreds and
preferences – in which they were submerged. The representatives of the new
power were often drawn into intra-communal disputes. An account from the
community of Tambo/La Mar, describes one of the ways in which these
dynamics worked themselves out:

> Perhaps the worse thing *Sendero* could have done was to put its trust in very
> young people from each locality – people with very little experience [...]
> These youngsters at times totally distorted *Sendero's* plans of government, at
> others took on revengeful attitudes, got involved in vendettas: for example,
> one father had a quarrel with another father over a question of boundaries
> between their plots, or over animals, theft or loss; or it might be a matter
> between husband and wife. So, as *Sendero* had given the local people responsi-
> bility in their affairs, they began to take reprisals, vengeance; this is what led to
> the killings, this is what caused all the dissatisfaction of the people. (José, a
> teacher)

And so the column set off without being aware that, in the rear, there was
a wasps' nest of contradictions that it would be unable to resolve.

In other cases, dissatisfaction was felt against outsiders posted as cadres
in a locality, while the local militiamen appeared more accessible. Alejandro,
a young university student from a peasant family, gave his opinion on one
of these cases, in which one also notes the irresponsible way in which the
cadres approached the armed struggle: 'It seems that the people directing
the Allpachaca group weren't good cadres; they imagined themselves winning
the war, capturing the enemy's helicopters, without thinking what kind of
arms there were going to be for everyone. [...] I think it depended on the
zone: in other areas, there were good people.' This remark is important
because it highlights the wide variation in the concrete situations that existed.
While it is true that, in these cases, no instances of open rebellion are
recorded, it was after the imposition of new authorities that the first resent-
ments appeared, along with the first peasant allies of the armed forces:
informers or *soplones*, according to *senderista* terminology.

Andean vs *Senderista* Rationality

By 1980, the great 'semi-feudal' scenario in which Shining Path imagined
itself carrying out its epic battles had already in fact fallen apart, due to the
action of the market, the state, pressures from the peasants, the great
migrations and Velasco's land reform. Taking its inspiration from Mao, the
movement programmed for 1980–81 'collective harvests' and land invasions.
The results were unimpressive, since only a few remaining haciendas were
taken over.[15] In 1982, in the only action that, on account of its large scale
though under a radically different flag, recalled the land mobilizations of the

1960s, the *Senderistas* destroyed Allpachaca, the university's experimental farm. Then they attacked certain cooperatives originating in the agrarian reform. But apart from police driven away by dynamite from their rural posts, the most important targets were abusive traders, animal thieves, corrupt magistrates and drunken husbands.

All these were no doubt real enough problems for the peasants. However, in order to deal with them it was hardly necessary to build a 'war machine' and, still less, to mount a scenario of horror beyond reason that was to leave the region swimming in blood. This is shown by the *rondas* of Piura and Cajamarca that dealt with similar problems with success, and practically without violence.[16]

Shining Path, however, had three characteristics that differentiated it from the *rondas* of the north: an ideology that accorded violence an absolute value; a 'molecular' strategy of construction of a counter-power; and a totalitarian political project. *Senderista* ideology took violence beyond the classical Maoist limits of the people's war. *Senderista* violence was a purifying violence, through which the old and bad was to be extirpated by blood and fire. The ideological zeal of the activists was constantly encouraged by the leaders and the supreme chief, himself given to real flights of ecstasy on the purifying virtues of violence.[17] In view of the absence of important targets in the region, big land-owners, for example, the movement ended up concentrating all this purifying zeal on the dynamics of power at the lowest level: on day-to-day life and 'social cleansing'. On the other hand, Shining Path's strategy was to go 'sweeping the country' and liberating zones for the construction not only of a new state but also a new society controlled by the party down to the smallest details.

Ideological zeal, military strategy and totalitarian project were brought together at the Fourth Plenum of the Central Committee, held in May 1981, where Guzmán took up the subject of the portion of blood, or *cuota*, necessary for the triumph of the revolution, and warned of the need to prepare for the 'blood bath' that would inevitably take place. Members would have to be prepared to cross the 'river of blood' of the revolution. 'Living on the knife edge', the fourth plenary session then agreed to a 'radical intensification of the violence', justifying this escalation in the following terms: 'they (the reaction) form lakes (of blood), we soak our handkerchiefs.'

It is in this context that one must set the decision to 'beat the countryside', taken in 1982: '"In beating, the key is to destroy. And to leave nothing behind." The task in hand was "to de-articulate the power of the *gamonales*, put out of order the power of the authorities and hit the living forces of the enemy [...] clean the zone, leave a wasteland (*pampa*) behind."'[18]

The two following accounts, from the provinces of Huancasancos and Cangallo respectively, refer to the *Senderista* 'people's trials', in which the strategy of 'beating the countryside' was put into practice with appalling results:

Then they punished the woman with fifty lashes because she had complained about the bad distribution of the harvests. She was from a poor family and was also given to drinking. Then they cut her hair all *cachi* and gave the other fellow fifty lashes too and cut off one of his ears with scissors. He's still going around today all *qoro rinri* [truncated].

And the people, what did they say?

Well nothing: 'Punish, but don't kill'; that's all they said. (Juvenal, a peasant of mature years)

Now the people are unhappy because the Party people have committed a lot of mindless atrocities. They've killed innocent people saying they were informers. I think that if they had made a mistake, they could have just punished them, couldn't they?, they could have lashed them with whips, cut their hair [...] but not like they did, like the filthy way they killed the mayor.

And the people, what did they say?

Well nothing; as they were armed, what were we going to do? Nothing obviously. That's why I'd say they've committed a lot of barbarities. (Mariano, a small trader)

The phrase 'Punish but don't kill' marks the limit of the peasants' acceptance, at least in the context of the so-called people's trials. It was a limit that drove some of the *senderista* cadres to desperation, as is seen in the following account from a community in Cangallo, given by a young teacher who, at the time, was also a member of a 'body' created by Shining Path:

Then there were some people who had been collecting money in *Sendero's* name and they'd captured them. They held a trial of these people in the village square. It was a short time ago, and they asked the people: 'These men have done this, this and this. What do you say; should we kill them, or should we punish them?' And immediately the people answered: 'Why kill them? Let them be subjected to a punishment' – that's what the community said. 'Ah you people are always with those archaic ideas of defending yourselves still. From now on, we won't ask your opinion again; we already knew you were going to defend. We have to take their heads off, because weeds must be completely exterminated, because if we are going to be pardoning the weeds we shall never triumph, never get ahead' — that's what the *Senderistas* said. (Cesáreo, a teacher)

One thing that comes to light from this account is the tragic out-of-phasedness between the young cadres' anxiousness to 'get ahead', and what they regarded as the 'archaic ideas' of the community, between the *senderista* project and Andean rationality. The *Senderistas* – ideologized to the extremes of fundamentalism, ready to kill and to die for their project – neither understood nor respected the peasant codes. Theirs was a cadres' Utopia that could never become one for the masses; they were priests of a god who spoke, at times literally, Chinese.

An explanation would be useful at this point. In a context in which *gamonalismo*, although in decay, still continued (to some extent, to sustain the codes of domination and subordination − in a region with a scarcity of new peasant organizations, little development of the market, and lacking opportunities to explore the democratic spaces opened in other parts of the country after 1980 with the municipal elections), the peasants seemed disposed to accept a new boss, and even his punishments. Neither the built-in violence nor the harsh policies were alien to them. The corporal punishments, the whipping, the haircutting, are simply a continuation of the old aristocratic Andean society and the old *misti* power. The peasants were accustomed to bearing it and knew how to resist it. Shining Path's hyper-ideologized political violence, which developed in contradiction with traditional codes, was, on the other hand, alien to them. In the account just cited above, the dialogue with Cesáreo continues as follows: '"But, if they were criminals, why did the people not want them to be killed?" "What about their children? Who was going to look after their families?"' In other words, death is considered to be the limit of punishment, but not only because the peasants have a 'culture of life'. The primary reasons are, rather, the very pragmatic ones proper to a society whose economic basis is precarious; one that lays down intricate relationship networks and highly complex strategies of reproduction, a society that must look after its work force with great care. To kill, to eliminate a node in these networks, has repercussions that go beyond the nuclear family of the condemned person. As noted previously in this chapter, when Shining Path began its war, the big land-owners had already practically disappeared from Ayacucho. In many cases, therefore, the 'targets of the revolution' were small local exploiters, overbearing and often abusive, but linked, nevertheless, by ties of relationship, *paisanaje* and daily life to their communities, or at least to certain groups within the community. A comment on Allpachaca, collected after its destruction, corroborates this: 'In Allpachaca, there were many rustlers and they killed them. After this, their families became anti-*Senderista* and began to denounce innocent people as *Senderistas*. I think they should not have killed them but rather punished them so that they should learn to correct their behavior' (Alejandro, university student from a peasant family). 'To punish *in order to correct*' is one of the basic powers of legitimate authority, whether of the community or of the *mistis*. By killing, Shining Path was tearing apart an extremely delicate social fabric and opening a Pandora's box that it was then unable to control.

In today's fashionable jargon, one could argue, in reference to the economy of violence, that the party's macro-economic assumptions were 'out of synch' with the micro-economic behaviour of the agents. The starting point of *Sendero's* macro-economic analysis of violence is that 'structural' violence, that built into the *status quo*, is deadlier still. Criticizing the speech by Monsignor Dammert at the opening of the Consejo por la Paz, Guzmán remarks:

He is preaching the peace of those dead of hunger [...] In Peru, as a result of the iniquitous system prevailing, 60,000 children of less than one year old die each year; of course these figures are partly a result of the effect of recent cholera epidemics. But compare this figure with the official statistics for deaths as a result of the people's war: in ten years, the number of deaths is only a third of that for children less than a year old in just one year. Who, then, is murdering infants in the cradle? Who else but Fujimori and the old reactionary state?[19]

Shining Path claimed that its model was more efficient and, in the medium term, less costly in human lives to the degree that the revolution would eliminate poverty, hunger and 'structural' violence in general. From the point of view of the peasants, however, political violence was something added to structural violence (already by itself more than sufficient) that rendered the short term intolerable, while – in Keynes's words – in the long term (that of the *senderista* Utopia), we are all dead anyway.

In legal terms, on the other hand, the sentences imposed by the *Senderistas* were increasingly out of proportion with the alleged crimes. Moreover, these alleged crimes were classified according to a legal code of the movement's own making, totally alien both to what is known as customary or common law and to national legislation. According to Gálvez,[20] in what he calls, for merely descriptive purposes, 'peasant law', punishments often entail physical force but very rarely death. The latter is contemplated only when the security of the whole group is felt to be in danger, especially in relation to rustling, and then only as a last resort. The basis of the so-called Andean customary law is persuasion, convincing the offender to make restitution and so restore the unity of the group.[21] Thus, when appointing the communal authorities and justices of the peace (who are proposed by the community and recognized by the state), the communal assembly takes into account above all the question of whether a candidate is considered 'just', 'upright', and is recognized as such by the whole group. The authorities are people who know the people and their customs.

This is of course a somewhat idealized situation: one that has, besides, been eroded by the conflicts caused —among other developments— by the expansion of the market, the increasing differentiation between peasants, the growing weight of family interests over and above those of the community, and the consolidation of new power groups within it. However, in this terrain, on the one hand, Shining Path showed itself so alien to the reality surrounding it that, instead of taking advantage of these contradictions, it stumbled over them and became trapped in conflicts within and between communities. On the other hand, the cracks opening in rural society were not so deep as to annul the general principles of peasant comunal life and Andean highland culture.

There were other reasons, as it happens, of equal or greater weight for the rejection of the *senderista* project by the peasants, going beyond the economic ones. Nicario recounts an episode during the destruction of Allpachaca, that reveals the complexity of the subject.

> Of the livestock, we killed all we could. But when we were slaughtering, the peasant women began to cry: 'The poor animals! Why are you killing them like that? What have they done?'. As the women began to cry – 'Poor creatures [...] one thing and the other' – we stopped [...] Our intention was to kill all the livestock, but we couldn't finish doing it because the women began to cry.

The image of milkmaids and herders embracing cows and bulls to save them from death is not only romantic and strangely bucolic – these women are, after all, herders, and the death of the livestock is, for them, the equivalent of the closure of a factory for the workers employed in it; but if the herders were not just bucolic figures, lovers of life in the abstract, they were *also* human beings, who appreciated the life of *their* animals.

Both in Umaro and in Purus (Huanta), I have seen elderly women, former authorities, cry inconsolably when remembering the appalling, unbearable way in which the *Senderistas* killed people, as if they were pigs, making the victim kneel down and cutting his throat, letting his blood drain away and even, at times, smashing his skull with a stone. In the party's language this was to 'crush like a toad under a rock'. This was done on the insane pretext of the need to 'save munitions'. Then, they would often refuse to allow the burial of the victims, the universal rituals of mourning. If account is taken of the violence perpetrated by the armed forces that, in the period 1983–85 and in many areas until 1988, greatly exceeded the *senderista* violence, it is possible to begin to gain an idea of the hell in which the region was submerged.[22] It should always be borne in mind that, if the whole of Peru had undergone the same level of violence as Ayacucho, the death toll would have amounted to 450,000 Peruvians and not 'only' 25,000.

It is Ponciano del Pino, however, which presents the most extraordinary case of rejection of Shining Path by the peasants, for reasons that go beyond that of mere 'rational choice'. It was the Pentecostal Evangelical Church of the Apurímac Valley which took on Shining Path from the viewpoint of another 'total identity'. The result: a not-so-holy war that ended in the victory of the Evangelicals and which, although this was not their intention, turned out to be a victory for the coca business as well.

The frequency of the executions, the closeness of the victims to the rest of the community because of family ties, and the traumatic manner of their deaths also affected the young rural people, stretched between the ideologization of the party and their own family ties, their links to the community, their common sense:

> Of course, their families were sad [...] but they didn't know [...] When this kind of execution was carried out – and it might happen at any moment – the people would look and say to themselves, 'If we find out about something, or

see someone who's doing things for the Party, we'd do better to shut up. If the police come we have to say: we don't know, we don't know.' We too had to give that recommendation. Some disagreed but they put up with it, they said nothing, they shut their mouths, and some peasants, some peasant women, cried. It always caused fear and grief when we killed in front of the people.

Pain and grief were two of the loose threads by means of which, in the following years, the extended family, and later the *rondas*, began to unravel the clothing of the *senderista* project, gradually revealing its nakedness. Nicanor, for example, torn between his younger brother who persuaded him to join the organization and his other brothers and sisters who called him from *el otro sendero* in Lima, decided in 1983 to respond to the latter call and began a career as a micro-entrepreneur.[23] In the following years there were sporadic cases of *arrepentidos*, that became a flood as the *rondas* went to work *en masse*.

The Security of the Population

The entry of the armed forces revealed a fourth fissure in the strategy of Shining Path towards the peasant communities, a product of the discrepancy between the traditional strategies of domination and that of the people's war. According to the rules of the Maoist war, 'when the enemy advances, we withdraw'. Therefore, when the armed forces entered Ayacucho, Shining Path withdrew in order to protect its cadres. Nevertheless, on doing so, it came into contradiction with the role of the traditional *patrón*, who protects his clients. For this reason, when the movement withdrew, the disappointment in many places was very great. The following account of what happened in one district of the Valley of Huanta is echoed with slight variations in several other testimonies: 'They told us, "you must be prepared for war, to defeat the enemy". We believed them, but once they attacked Huanta and, after attacking and killing two guards, they escaped, coming back through here, and left us in the lurch, they handed us over to the enemy, they sold us practically; that's not how men should behave' (Walter, a peasant).

For those sections of the population that Shining Path was unable to protect, the army gradually came to be the 'lesser evil', or, in any case, a more powerful *patrón* than the party; one with whom one had to be on good terms. To drive home this lesson was one of the aims of the genocidal offensive of 1983–84: 'to drain the pond' serving as environment for the *senderista* fish, by terrorizing the peasants and inhibiting their support for Shining Path. What is surprising is that, in spite of its harshness, in many places this strategy also failed to achieve its objectives.

The main consequence of the armed forces' strategy in those years, while it did serve to make some already existing fissures fully visible, was to block the development of the contradictions between Shining Path and the peasantry. The *Senderistas* were able to gloss over this first breaking point, since by letting loose what can truly be described as genocide the armed forces converted the countryside around Ayacucho into an Armageddon in which it was often the party that seemed the 'lesser evil'. Such was the case in the Valley of Huanta, as José Coronel argues. To describe what happened in the language used by the Party: while the latter set the prairie on fire, 'the reaction' provided the bellows.

Adaptation-in-resistance

However, the 'lesser evil' was seen as external; it did not generate a sense of identity other than what Stern calls 'adaptation-in-resistance'.[24] The step from the pragmatic acceptance of the first years to a long-term identification with Shining Path was never made. Except for some pockets, the relation froze into that adaptation-in-resistance, situated between acceptance and open rebellion. The following testimony, from a community in the province of Sucre, neatly exemplifies what is generally considered to be 'adaptation-in-resistance':

> The *Teniente Gobernador* is still at his post, but clandestinely; in other words, when the comrades come, we say we have no *Teniente*, that we've had no *Teniente* for a long time; that they've taken away our seals, so [...] when the 'reaction' comes, the authorities come out of their hiding places so that there are no problems for the people — they were there all along, but in hiding. (Pedro, a young man)

The concept is akin, in some degree, to what Scott calls 'the arms of the weak', that, in the liminal situation of those years, were the only weapons available to the peasantry.[25] In the following account by a sixty-one-year-old peasant woman from Acos-Vinchos, collected by Celina Salcedo,[26] the shrewdness of the adaptation-in-resistance takes on a hint of the picaresque:

> When the *tuta puriq* came, they told us: 'Tomorrow in the afternoon you're going to line up and then we'll see.' That's what they told us, and all of us were afraid, thinking 'what are they going to do to us? surely they're going to kill us all.' So when they went away we all got together, men and women, young and old, and we said, 'Let's go and line up like they said, and we'll tell them that we're going to keep a watch out, and then when they're all there, the ones who are keeping the watch will yell out, "The *Cabitos*[27] are coming!" and they'll run away,' we said. So then the next day just like we decided, the ones keeping watch began to shout, 'The *Cabitos* are coming! The *Cabitos* are coming!' When they heard that, the *tuta puriq* set about escaping, running like madmen. Since then they haven't come back.

Externalization

A terrifying episode symbolizes Shining Path's withdrawal, once again, to the position of an external actor. This was the massacre of eighty peasants in the community of Lucanamarca (Víctor Fajardo) in April 1983, responsibility for which was acknowledged by Abimael Guzmán himself:

> In view of the use of armed retinues and reactionary military action, we responded with an overwhelming action: Lucanamarca. Neither they nor we will forget it, of course, because there they saw a response that they never imagined, more than 80 were annihilated there; that was what really happened, and we say it, there was excess [...] our problem was how to give a decisive blow to restrain them, to make them understand that things were not so easy. On certain occasions, such as this one, it was the Central Directorate that planned the action and ordered things, that is how it was [...] I repeat, the main thing was to make them understand that we were a hard nut to crack, and that we were prepared to do anything, anything.[28]

Shining Path decided to compete with the army on an equal footing as regards the meting out of violence against the rural population, to defeat it on that ground too. Following this logic, years later, Guzmán himself began to proclaim that 'the triumph of the revolution will cost a million lives'.

Thus, exceptions apart, the region was devastated, from 1983 onwards, by two objectively external armies. Each set off for the battlefield, however, with opposite points of view. One of the main *senderista* slogans was, 'the party has a thousand eyes and a thousand ears'. To put it more brutally, in those days, Shining Path generally knew who to kill, even at Lucanamarca, and if the peasantry submitted to its dictates, it could survive. But while the party had a thousand eyes and a thousand ears, the armed forces were blind or, rather, blind to everything but colour. Having recently arrived in the region, and trying to reproduce in the Andes strategies that had been effective in the countries of the southern cone, they had no means of distinguishing the enemy from anyone else in the area and wherever they saw dark skin, they fired.

The path taken by the rural young people in the years following the military intervention may serve as a thread to guide us in an attempt to understand the course taken by Shining Path. These young people, a key link for the *senderista* expansion in the countryside, were always torn between two logics and two worlds. They were torn in Allpachaca between the party's order to slaughter the livestock and the crying of the female cow-hands; torn in La Mar between the party's logic of government, local loyalties and family vendettas; and torn between the party and the market as possible ways towards 'progress' and social mobility. The entry of the army on the scene increased these tensions and, when the party decided to respond to the state using the same weapons on the military terrain, producing a mirror-image of the army's violence, a decisive disillusionment took place among them.

What happened with the young people of Rumi is a microcosm of this decanting process. Nicario 'broke', but others, including his younger brother, opted to join the party, becoming the seed that, along with other factors, allowed Shining Path to propagate itself throughout different parts of the country. In this process Shining Path lost its peasant masses but won young cadres. Once again it converted what was a social defeat into a political victory.[29] But nowhere else in Peru was the Ayacucho scenario of the early 1980s – Shining Path's most 'social' and consensual period – to be repeated. In later years, as the organization expanded into other zones, its tendency to resort to terror and its 'anti-social' nature tended to increase.

In Ayacucho, Shining Path continued to exist in a kind of limbo, on the frontiers of a peasant society that either adapted to it or resisted it, or did both at the same time. In these circumstances the party then became one actor among others, armed and therefore powerful, but without the hegemony of the initial stage; or it became a faction firmly ensconced in certain communities at war with others within the broader area, immersed in contradictions that at times went back to the pre-Hispanic era; or it became a faction capturing and subjugating villages, forcing them to become its 'support bases' that only, in the medium term, served to reveal its coercive and artificial nature.

Peasant Resistance and the *Rondas Campesinas*

This situation of uncertainty and change lasted for about five years in the region. What was, for large sections of the local population, a destructive and exhausting war of attrition was, for the movement, simply the normal development of the strategy of the prolonged war:

> '83 and '84 were years of struggle around [the process of] re-establishment/counter-re-establishment, in other words, between the counter-revolutionary war to crush the new Power and re-establish the Old, and the people's war to defend, develop and construct the recently emerged Popular Power [...] From '85 to today, [we have been engaged in] the continuation of the defense, development and construction for the maintenance of the support bases and the expansion of the people's war to the entire context of our Northern and Southern *sierras*.[30]

This is how the pamphlet *Desarrollar la guerra popular sirviendo a la revolución mundial* talks about those years, in an account of six years of violence from which the contradictions, mentioned above, are made to disappear. It is true, nevertheless, that Shining Path continued to keep parts of the region barred to the army and even managed to expand into other parts of the country, particularly the Huallaga Valley, the world's most important coca-producing zone, and to Lima itself. In 1988 the party held its first congress. Not long afterwards, it felt the time had come to conquer 'the strategic equilibrium'. According to Mao (as interpreted by Guzmán), the 'prolonged war' was to be developed through three major strategic phases: defensive, equilibrium and offensive. From 1989 onwards, Shining Path believed the moment had arrived to pass from the defensive to the equilibrium phase.[31] To do so, it would be necessary to recruit more combatants; these could be obtained from the juvenile fringe that had always been its main seedbed for new recruits, or by the use of force in the rural areas where its presence was established. Furthermore, the movement needed more and better arms, which it could also obtain via its posts in the Huallaga Valley and its connections with the narcotics traffickers.

However, if (as Mao used to say) the guerrilla army must move among the masses 'like a fish in water', then Shining Path needed not simply the neutrality or the passive acceptance of the peasantry, but its active consensus. However, this was where its problems began with the population because, as the movement's demands grew, they put in jeopardy the fragile equilibrium of the adaptation-in-resistance prevailing in many communities. Recruitment of a greater number of young people, greater supplies of food and so on, a greater participation of the population as a 'mass' in military actions, a tightening of senderista discipline with its propensity for rapid and summary trials with frequent application of the death penalty: all these new require-ments made peasant adaptation difficult and favoured resistance. The rejection became all the more emphatic when, during 1989–90, a prolonged drought compounded the effect of the national economic crisis.[32]

Shining Path then stepped up the violence against the peasantry. However, the only thing it achieved by this was a multiplication of the rondas until, as the new decade began, Shining Path found itself trapped in a kind of trench war against the civil defence committees (Comités de Defensa Civil). This was the first strategic victory of the armed forces and the first real defeat for Shining Path in a whole decade of war, although this fact was partly eclipsed by its advances in Amazonia – especially in the coca-producing zones – and in the cities, particularly Lima.

Why, then, this defeat for the Senderistas? If this period is examined from the peasants' point of view, Shining Path and the armed forces were set on opposite courses. As the former became more distant, the latter became closer; as Shining Path became more external, the armed forces became more internal to the population.

In 1983 the armed forces entered an unknown territory in which they dealt out indiscriminate repression: anything that moved was a potential enemy. The navy, the branch of the armed forces which recruited mostly from the coastal areas and personnel with the most racist outlook (its recruits were mainly whites or mestízos), played in those years an outstanding role in the provinces of Huanta and La Mar. From 1985 onwards the navy was replaced by the army, with contingents mainly drawn from the sierra. Towards the end of the decade, when the change of approach from indiscriminate repression to selective repression came about, the armed forces can be described as installing themselves on the frontier of peasant society in order to make incursions into it. First, the army used those peasants who had spent some time in the armed forces on compulsory military service as intermediaries. Then, second, in the present decade, they increasingly engaged in policies of assistance to the community, carrying out infrastructure works, as representatives of a state that, in spite of its crises, had at the time more 'aces up its sleeve' than Shining Path, which could offer nothing but the most radical austerity. Finally, the recruitment of young men to do their military service in their home districts and the distribution of arms to the *rondas*, even when these were only shotguns,[33] showed that the armed forces – and via them the state – had won the upper hand in the zone.

An important element in this re-conquest is worth mentioning: the armed forces did not attempt to control 'everything without exception', as did Shining Path. While the weekly visits by the peasant 'commandos' to the barracks, participating in parades and attending to the needs of the patrols in the villages, might be a burden, the armed forces did not interfere in local life in the oppressive way that Shining Path had done.

Shining Path, in contrast, grew ever more distant from the peasantry, while the latter's attitude tended to change from one of pragmatic acceptance to one of adaptation-in-resistance and finally to open rebellion against the party. So it was that, while in the first years of the war names such as Pucayuca, Accomarca, Umaro, Bellavista, Ccayara – villages razed to the ground by the armed forces – won an invidious fame, from 1988 onwards it was the massacres perpetrated by Shining Path that sowed the land with corpses. In little over four years, between December 1987 and February 1992, a far-from-exhaustive check of the available data yields a total of sixteen massacres committed by Shining Path in which more than twelve victims were involved.[34] If it were attempted to plot this horror on a graph, Shining Path's ascending curve and the armed forces' descending curve would be seen to cross definitively at Ccayara. On 14 May 1988, twenty-eight peasants died in this community in the last large-scale massacre perpetrated by the armed forces in the region. A few days before, Shining Path had murdered eighteen *ronderos* at Azángaro, Huanta. While engaged in this macabre accountancy, it is worthy of note that, as the repression unleashed by the armed forces became more selective,[35] repression directed by Shining Path evolved from the 'selective annihilations' justified (according to the *Senderistas*) as the carrying out 'without any degree of cruelty, of a simple and efficient justice'[36] to large-scale massacres. In many areas, decisive sections of the peasantry opted then for a pragmatic alliance with the armed forces.

Two facts illustrate this evolution graphically. In the first years of the military intervention a whole mythology was formed round the navy. It was said that they had foreign mercenaries, Argentines perhaps, because not even the most prejudiced peasants imagined that their own countrymen could treat them in the way they did. In April 1994, in a van heading for the fair at Chaca, in the highlands of Huanta, I conversed with a leader of that community who had been in the River Apurímac region during the worst years of the violence and remembered the panic created by those supposed mercenaries:

> They came out of the helicopter firing bursts from their sub-machine guns. They fired at anything, even if it was just a leaf falling from the tree, they were already firing. They didn't know how to walk properly, [you could see] they weren't familiar with the mountain terrain; they were a leftover from the Falklands that they'd brought in to advise them. When they stopped, they threw themselves on the ground listening to some other kind of music. They also had the Killers. In a cage they were, just standing there, they didn't come out of it. They gave them their food through a little window. They were men, but they had long hair down to here [indicating his waist]. Once they put a *tucu* in the cage and they opened his heart and the blood that flowed out they lapped it up, lapped it up, saying 'how nice!'[37]

Once we arrived in Chaca, we found a solitary army officer taking a stroll among hundreds of fairgoers, peasants and traders, 'like a fish in water', with only a pistol and two *piñitas* (hand grenades) at his belt, 'just in case'. A lot of water had passed under the bridge. In San José de Secce, the district administrative centre, the conscripts doing their military service in the garrison were local Quechua-speaking peasants.

Shining Path, on the other hand, ended up in many places identified with the antichrist or the terrible *ñakaq* or *pishtaco*.[38] At least as much as the massacres of villagers, what best exemplifies Shining Path's 'externalization' in the region is the sort of Russian roulette to which they submitted the truckers on the Ayacucho–San Francisco route around 1991. At one of the frequent road blocks Shining Path was in the habit of setting up on this highway to exact tolls and settle accounts in blood, one of the drivers escaped and reported the guerrillas' presence to a military detachment. The army then descended on the *Senderistas*, causing them a number of casualties. In reprisal, Shining Path began an indiscriminate campaign of killing truckers on different roads, selecting its victims practically at random.[39] This kind of reflex action was only displayed by the armed forces in the 1983–84 period.

Blind Spots and the Defeat of Shining Path

It seems strange how the significance of the spread of the *rondas* and the emergence of a new relationship binding the peasantry to the armed forces was lost on the *Senderistas* themselves. The guerrillas failed to see it for the important defeat it was, proclaiming that same year that they were still on the way to achieving 'strategic equilibrium'.

Until 1991, documents issued by Shining Path showed no in-depth analysis of the spread of the *rondas*. That year, in a document entitled ¡*Que el equilibrio estratégico remezca más el país*!, the *rondas* are defined as one of the mechanisms of the counter-revolutionary 'low-intensity war', developed by Fujimori, the military and the 'Yankee imperialists'.[40] This is followed by a tedious legal analysis (of all things!) of the decree legalizing the Comités de Defensa Civil, at that time under discussion.[41] The year-end edition of the party's official organ, *El Diario*, goes beyond the mere definition to give a balance, far removed from the real situation, in which it is stated that the *rondas* had 'touched bottom': 'Only 5 percent have kept going intact since they were created by the Navy or the Army; the rest have been revamped many times and lately scores of them have been undecided whether to dissolve or to turn against their mentors.' Only in 1992 did Shining Path seem to begin to realize the danger the *rondas* represented for it, when, at the Third Plenum of the Central Committee, it was stated:

> The problem is that things have taken a change of direction, that is the problem [...] they have occupied some points and pushed us out. Then they have subjected the masses [...] threatening them with death, and now these are masses under pressure from the enemy. Our problem here, then, is what? That we are restricted in our aim of infiltrating the *mesnadas*[42] and this is something we must correct so we can penetrate them, unmask them, stifle them, even blow them apart.[43]

The directive, that also included a greater emphasis on persuasion, arrived too late.

This complete disorientation has to do with a number of blind spots in the party line (which was pointed out when analysing the period 1982–83), and which now seem to have become more acute. These 'blind spots' included: the exaggerated cult of violence; the 'optimistic fatalism' of its teleological view of history; its conception of social and political actors as 'essences in action', bearers of structures that determine, willy-nilly, their trajectory; its conception of the peasantry as an actor incapable of initiative; its strategy of prolonged war through the construction of support bases and liberated zones; and its contempt for Andean culture.[44]

This chapter has already referred to the subject of violence and the discordance between the party's logic and the dynamics of society. It is now clear that, in 1982, the decision of the party apparatus to step up a violence that did not serve any real purpose, and the consequent beginning of a campaign of rough 'justice', contributed to the widening of fissures between Shining Path and the general population. Towards the end of the 1980s, the escalation of violence against the *rondas* was an important factor in reaffirming the belief of those already convinced, convincing the undecided, and pushing entire communities into an alliance with the armed forces.

Essences in Action

According to the literature issued by Shining Path, history does not advance along a straight line, but via a series of zigzags and temporary retrogressions.

These occur, however, strictly within a general, predetermined and inevitable trajectory: more than just a libretto – a destiny.

The armed forces, for example – labelled again and again in the *senderista* literature as 'specialists in defeat' – could not change. Rather the armed forces could only make ever more manifest their genocidal essence and their dependence on imperialism. In concrete reality, however, the armed forces left Shining Path off-side when they halted the increase of indiscriminate repression many would have expected to continue into the present decade. I do not wish to overestimate the changes in the armed forces, nor to forget the degree of demoralization to which they were subjected towards the turn of the decade. Nor is it possible to say what might have happened if Guzmán had not been captured. Towards the end of the 1980s it appeared as if the type of counter-insurgency adopted by the armed forces was heading for a 'Guatemalan solution'. Happily, history took another direction and the armed forces developed, instead, a strategy that could be described as 'non-genocidal authoritarian'.[45]

The peasants, on the other hand, were 'an arena of struggle between revolution and counter-revolution',[46] passive actors, zeros that acquired value only when added to one or other of the warring bands. Shining Path was the depository of the Truth, with a leader who was the 'guarantee of triumph', in as much as he was favoured with the ability to interpret the laws of history: it was 'condemned to triumph'. Sooner or later, however, through the development of the prolonged people's war, the peasants would at last find their way along the path mapped out for them by destiny and would gravitate towards Shining Path like moths towards a light, because 'Objectively, they [the counter-revolution] do not represent the interests of the people; we, on the other hand, do. They cannot win over the masses; they have to force them, oppress them in order to make them follow, and this engenders resistance. In our case we can make them follow us by showing them what is objective: that we represent their interests.' There was no problem then. At least no very serious problem. According to Shining Path, the establishment of the 'new power' in a particular zone could be followed by the *re*-establishment of the old power for a period, then by the counter-*re*-establishment of the new power and so on, until the definitive establishment of the liberated zones and the New Order. The growth of the *rondas* as mass organizations was seen as just one more episode in the (temporary) 're-establishment'.

Conceptions of Time and Space

Shining Path did not notice that the prolonged nature of the war and its strategy of constructing support bases was in direct contradiction with the peasants' conceptions of time and space, since, after all, such conceptions were of little or no importance to the guerrillas. The outcome of the story of Nicario is in some measure a paradigm of the peasantry, whose reproduction – despite its poverty – depends to an important extent on the market. The young, in particular, have aspirations of social mobility instilled in them through school and the media. The lapses of time for which families make their plans have to do with their own life cycle and the growth of their children, not with a 'people's war' that, in the late 1980s, appeared to be extending into infinity through interminable cycles of establishment, re-establishment and counter-re-establishment. When Shining Path tried to impress an even harder rhythm on the war – precisely in years of drought and economic crisis – the thread of adaptation finally snapped.

On the other hand, the spaces in which peasant society reproduces itself are extensive, taking in the city as well as the countryside, via networks of family relationships and *paisanaje*, and may also include mines in the bleak uplands and coca plantations in the jungle. This could only entail a collision with the *senderista* strategy of imposing its dominion over confined areas, forcing them to become support bases that would of necessity tend towards isolation. After the first years and especially when the armed forces came into action, the peasants were trapped in the crossfire and all who could do so fled. In many areas, Shining Path ended up the master of almost empty spaces, in which only the weakest remained: poverty-stricken, monolingual peasants without links in the cities, members of the Asháninka minority, all subject to the 'all-embracing domination' of Shining Path.

Andean Culture

The collision between Shining Path and the peasantry's notions of time and space forms part of a more general conflict with Andean culture. I am referring here to a constellation of institutions of great importance for the Quechua peasantry of Ayacucho, in particular: the extended family, the community, the rules of reciprocation, the hierarchy of age, rituals, festivals and the religious dimension in general. The *Senderistas* abhorred the beliefs of the native Andean religion and of popular Catholicism (which they regarded as archaic), and the rituals and festivals (which they tried to suppress). The cadres justified this by referring to the costs such events entailed.

However, the party was also uncomfortable with the aspect of the 'world turned upside down' that these *fiestas* represented. 'Absolute power' could not consent to such potential opportunities for escaping its control; and not without reason. In several places – Huancasancos, Huaychao – it was during local festivals that the population rebelled against Shining Path. In one community in Vilcashuamán, the *Senderistas* suppressed the festivals because, '"suddenly, in the middle of a festival, we may be betrayed; problems can occur". That's what they told us' (Pedro).

The contempt felt by the *Senderistas* for the cultural manifestations of the Quechua peasantry has a theoretical basis: 'Maoism teaches us that a given culture is the reflection – on the ideological plane – of the politics and economy of a given society', says *El Diario* on 13 September 1989. This being the case, the artistic and cultural manifestations of the Andean people are a mere hangover from the past: '[...] a reflection of the existence of mankind under the oppression of the landowners, that reflects the customs, beliefs, superstitions, feudal and anti-scientific ideas of the peasantry: the product of centuries of oppression and exploitation that have submerged it in ignorance.'[47]

On the basis of this theory and this practice, it still seems valid to describe the *Senderistas* as new *mistis*, influenced by school and Marxism.[48] In an earlier work[49] the *Senderistas* were likened to the third of the Aragón de Peralta brothers, the protagonists of Arguedas' *Todas las sangres*. Taking the example of another novel by Arguedas, *Yawar fiesta*, it is easy to identify Don Bruno with the traditional *mistis* (Julián Aranguëna, for example) who are in favour of the 'Indian *corrida*'; and Don Fermín with the national authorities and the 'progressive' *mistis*, who are against the Indian *corrida* and try to 'civilize' it by bringing a Spanish bullfighter to Puquio. This group would include the *cholo* university students who seek the 'progress of the people' and help to contract the bullfighter. But the Indians of the Qayau *ayllu* manage to capture the ferocious bull Misitu; the students change their opinion, convinced by the strength of the villagers, filled with joy and pride and forgetting their 'concern for progress'; the Spaniard fails in the bullfight and the Indians are the ones who stream into the ring to the joy of even the 'progressive' *mistis*. In the last line of the novel, the mayor whispers in the ear of the deputy prefect: 'Do you see that sir? These are our *corridas*. The genuine *yawar fiesta*!'

If the third brother had been there the outcome would surely have been different. This character is easily recognizable in certain *senderista* students or teachers, who would not have succumbed to the strength of the *runas* of Qayau. If the party had been present, Misitu would probably have been killed and the *fiesta* would have been prohibited. If it had been permitted, this would have been a strictly tactical decision, and the event would probably not have been accompanied by the pride that took hold of the Puquian students.

It is somewhat shocking to note how, in the 1980s, in the Peruvian sierra, the conflict between the *mistis* and Indians of *Yawar fiesta* is in some way reproduced, and how, once again, the *mistis*-turned-revolutionaries are defeated by the 'Indians' transformed into *ronderos*.

Notes and References

1. The organization's weakness was, in part, the consequence of an option that Shining Path developed throughout the 1970s and which made it into a fundamentalist project on the ideological level; socially, an 'anti-movement' (see Wieviorka, *Société et terrorisme*) on the political level; and a 'war machine' on the level of organization. The movement did not give priority to political work in social organizations, communities or federations, but rather

to what it referred to as 'bodies generated' by the party: entities constituting the 'drive belt' between the latter and the 'masses'. Regarding the composition of Shining Path up to 1980 and the evolution of the *Sendero* project, see Degregori, *Última tentación*.

2. Portocarrero and Oliart, *Perú desde la escuela*.

3. Nicario's younger brother, for example. He joined the guerrillas and lived as a *tuta puriq* (one who walks at night) from 1983 to 1986 until, having fallen ill, he heeded the call of his family and went to Lima. However, although a long time had passed and he no longer had any organic links with Shining Path, he would not tell me anything about his experience, preferring just to repeat the official party line.

4. In the way that, for a peasant, going to school and obtaining an education – understood above all as becoming literate in Spanish – meant passing from blindness to sightedness, or from night to day, see Montoya, *Capitalismo*; Degregori, *Qué difícil es ser Dios*.

5. Berg has stressed the manner in which Shining Path exploited the contradictions between communities and cooperatives in some areas of Andahuaylas, see Berg, 'Peasant response'; Isbell has made note of how Shining Path concentrated its attacks on certain rustlers in Chuschi, see Isbell, 'Shining Path'; Manrique has paid attention to Shining Path's work based on the contradictions between the peasantry and the SAIS (enlarged rural cooperative) *Cahuide* in the highlands of Junín; see Manrique, 'Década'.

6. Degregori, *Ayacucho*.

7. As Berg has shown for Andahuaylas, see Berg, 'Peasant response'.

8. Gorriti, *Sendero Luminoso*.

9. Absolutely the opposite took place: a massive migration to the cities in the zones affected by violence and where the dirty war was beginning.

10. Described in Gorriti, *Sendero Luminoso*.

11. Golte and Adams, *Caballos de Troya*; Steinhauf, 'Diferenciación étnica'.

12. Lima is an extreme case, but not even the medium-sized towns of the *sierra* depend basically on their rural surroundings (see Gonzales, *Economía regional*).

13. Degregori, *Sendero Luminoso*.

14. See Vergara et al., 'Culluchaca'.

15. Gorriti, *Sendero Luminoso*; Tapia, *Autodefensa armada*.

16. Starn, *Hablan los Ronderos*; Huber, *Después de Dios*.

17. Speaking of those within the party who held positions opposed to beginning the armed struggle, Guzmán stated: 'Let us pull out the poisonous weeds, this is pure poison, a cancer of the bones, it would eat us up from within; we cannot permit this [...] let us begin to burn, to pull out that pus, that poison, it is urgent to burn it'; see Guzmán, 'Nueva bandera'. On the *senderista* discourse and purifying violence in the context previous to the outbreak of the armed struggle, see Degregori, *Última tentación*; on the need to step up the violence in order to advance the revolution before 1982, see Gorriti, *Sendero Luminoso*, ch. 8.

18. In Gorriti, *Sendero Luminoso*, p. 283; the author quotes the PCP-SL document *Pensamiento militar del partido*, December 1982.

19. Guzmán, 'Nueva bandera', p. 17.

20. Galvéz, 'El derecho'.

21. Often conflicts are resolved by competitions or even ritualized battles, for example in carnivals. Behind this predilection for the restoration of group unity through conflict is the concept of *tinkuy*, see Ansión, 'Violencia y cultura'.

22. An analysis of the violence of the armed forces goes beyond the limits of this chapter. An account of the demented and racially motivated violence committed by the armed forces in the same period can be found in an unpublished manuscript by Degregori and López Ricci.

23. *El otro sendero* (the other path) refers to the title of Hernando de Soto's book *The Other Path*, highlighting the merits of Lima's informal sector (editors' note).

24. Stern, 'Nuevas aproximaciones'.

25. Scott, *Weapons of the Weak*.

26. In *Ideología* 10, September 1987, Ayacucho.

27. *Cabitos* is the name given to the soldiers in the region and comes from the name of the garrison, *Los Cabitos*, located outside the departmental capital.

28. Guzmán, 'Presidente Gonzalo'.

29. On this process during the 1970s, see Kruijt, *Sendero Luminoso*.

30. PCP, 'Documentos fundamentales'.

31. A discussion of the extreme 'voluntarism' that led Guzmán to consider that Shining Path was already in a position to reach strategic equilibrium exceeds the scope of this chapter. Tapia analyses in detail the differences between equilibrium in Mao's China and the situation in Peru around 1990, see Tapia, *Equilibrio estratégico*, and also Manrique, 'Caída'.

32. In Junín and other departments of the central sierra with a greater commercial development, events took on a faster rhythm. Up to 1987–88, the peasants had observed with stupor, and not without sympathy, how Shining Path destroyed the great Super-cooperatives ('SAIS') of the region. But soon the population passed over, for the most part, to the opposition, especially in the valleys of Mantaro, Cunas and Tullumayo, grain suppliers to Lima, when Shining Path tried to restrict their access to the market, directly or indirectly, by means of blowing up bridges and destroying roads; see Manrique, 'Década'.

33. The distribution of arms began in 1990, in the closing period of Alán García's government. The situation was legalized in 1992 with the Legislative Decree 741, recognizing the civil defence committees and permitting the 'holding and use of guns and munitions for civil use'.

34. See *Ideéle*, IDL, for the detailed accounts.

35. The repression continued to claim its victims. Thus during those same five years of massacres by the *Senderistas*, Peru occupied the first place in world statistics for disappearances in detention, see *Ideéle*, IDL.

36. PCP, 'Documentos fundamentales'.

37. If anybody thinks these characters, a combination of the traditional *pishtaco* and video Rambos, were a mere product of the hallucinated imagination of our informant, I suggest they read the 'hair-raising' account by 'Pancho' – a marine who served during those years in Ayacucho – in a forthcoming manuscript by Degregori and López Ricci.

38. In Purus, in 1994, remembering Shining Path's way of killing, a former community leader insisted that the *Senderistas* were not human beings but demons.

39. *TV Cultura* filmed on video a column of vehicles that had been attacked, several of them in flames, on the *Los Libertadores* highway (Ayacucho–Pisco) in 1991.

40. PCP, 'Equilibrio estratégico', p. 52.

41. It is obvious that at least this part of the document is a literal transcription of an oral address by Guzmán. The decree is analysed almost article by article, with numerous very detailed and precise notes.

42. Shining Path's expression for *rondas*, literally meaning 'armed retinues'.

43. PCP, 'III Pleno del Comité Central'.

44. In other words, Shining Path's reading of the Peruvian and international situations did not fit at all the real dynamics at work in Peru and the outside world.

45. Degregori and Rivera, *Perú 1980–1990*.

46. PCP, 'Equilibro estratégico', p. 4.

47. Márquez, '¿Cuál arte alienante?'

48. It might also be interesting to examine the use of the Quechua language, the music

of Ayacucho and the *música chicha* by the *Senderistas*. The use of Quechua seems to be instrumental. The *huaynos*, with a simple change of text, were converted into 'new type art'. But it is difficult to know to what extent the *cholo* who enjoyed the music 'enjoying without wanting to' (*sin querer queriendo*) is lurking here. In any case, the Montoya brothers, the master interpreters of the regional 'Quechua songs', have noted shrewdly: 'What a strange and terrible place is ours! The dominant class that despises and abuses the Indians uses their language to express its finest emotions.' (See Montoya, *Sangre de los cerros*, p. 40.)

49. Degregori, *Qué difícil es ser Dios*.

FOUR

'Welcome to the Nightmare': Thoughts on the Faceless Warriors of the Lacandona Revolt of 1994 (Chiapas, Mexico)

ARIJ OUWENEEL

Why do peasants take up arms? This question has occupied social scientists and historians for decades. If a Mexicanist, any Mexicanist, is invited for a talk, he or she will be confronted with this classic problem and be asked about the Chiapas uprising of New Year's Day 1994.[1] Chiapas, which has already received more anthropologists than it has communities, is now the topic of a publication craze comparable to those for the Cuban and Nicaraguan revolutions, the Central American guerrillas or the Bolivar and Colombus commemorations a few years ago.[2] Apparently, the revolt is relatively easy to explain, and its origins easy to trace.[3]

Inside and Outside

In spite of this, some differences have emerged in the literature on the topic of the revolt. It is possible to identify two groups of analysts: one 'from-the-inside perspective' and one 'from-the-outside perspective'. The first group of analysts build their account of the revolt on the problems in the Selva Lacandona, the cloud forest on the border with Guatemala. They concentrate on the problems of the peasantry in a real frontier area. Most important was the area of Las Cañadas in the western part of the Lacandón. Another revolutionary area was to the north of San Cristóbal de Las Casas, near the town of Simojovel.[4] The 'from-the-inside' analysts sketch the impact of poverty and overpopulation and end with a detailed narrative of the origins of the EZLN, the Zapatista Army of National Liberation. The 'from-the-outside' group of writers, on the other hand, build their account of history on the economic disasters of past decades in the state of Chiapas in general. They paint a sorry picture of the development of poverty and exploitation in all rural townships of the state, and see the Zapatista revolt as one of its main consequences. From a review of the literature, I detect a preference by the first group to speak of 'The Lacandona Revolt', and by the second group to stick to the designation of 'The Chiapas Revolt'.

In this chapter I have adopted the perspective of the 'from-the-inside' analysts. After all, the rebels *did* come from the north-eastern cloud forest and not from the highlands (or Altos, as they are labelled in Chiapas). True, the rebels seem to have had their roots in the highlands once, because the peasants in the Selva Lacandona are migrants or children of migrants, who have left the overpopulated highland communities during the 1950s, 1960s and 1970s. It was a diaspora of Tzeltales and Tzotziles from the Altos, who had based themselves in the forest, and saw the area as their last resort. It was their promised land. Nevertheless, it seems somewhat inept to call a book on the revolt *Los Altos de Chiapas*, as Romero Jacobo has done, because this is missing the crux of the issue.

The radical solution to go to war was particular to the Lacandón area. True, misery all over Chiapas had intensified. The cruelties and inequalities of the state are shocking: Chiapas leads in infant mortality, illiteracy, and lack of running water and electricity. Life in the state is violent because of poverty and repression. Guillermoprieto writes: 'The river-rich state provides one-fifth of the country's electricity and a third of its coffee production, but none of this wealth trickles down to the various Maya peoples.'[5] But despite being the 'most shamefully neglected of all Mexico's poor', the inhabitants of the Altos de Chiapas did *not* take the radical solution of going to war. Rather they tried to opt for legal mechanisms to address their problems: court cases, elections, political protests and marches. Some communities had arms, but left them unused. Even the occupation of town councils was endured without open warfare. In fact, during the second armed attack of January and February 1995, the EZLN received no armed support from highland communities. On the contrary, in most villages that could be visited by journalists, white flags were waving from the tiny peasant shacks. And we all know, poverty itself does not cause armed rebellion.

Reading most of the works of the second group of analysts – correct though their narratives about Chiapas are – I increasingly tend to disagree with their presentation. It seems as if something is missing, as if their analyses are overly economistic. It is my opinion that the 'from-the-inside' social scientists are scholars most likely to know Chiapas best. They have long lists of publications, know entire families personally, and have lived there for years in a row. But above all their focus has been upon the communities that lie on the central highlands, the mountain area of the Altos. For example, George Collier, Neil Harvey and Jan Rus (among others) point to the problems of development in general: population growth, the unequal distribution of national resources, the collapse of coffee prices, and the administration's abrogation of agrarian reform.[6] They also ensure that the policy of President Carlos Salinas de Gortari (1988–94) to develop Mexico in a neo-liberal direction and officially join the North American economy via the North American Free Trade Agreement (NAFTA) gets all the attention it deserves to explain rural problems all over Mexico, and in Chiapas in particular. Fortunately, in these works there is hardly any analysis based on the Black Legend discourse that was popular in the days of authors such as Gerrit Huizer or Ernest Feder, who more than thirty years ago traced all the problems of Mexico's rural areas back to the period of the Conquistadores and *hacendados*, or to some latifundium/minifundium conflict, which was stated to be the essence of Mexico's heritage.[7]

But despite its modern focus, viewing Latin American development as *one* particular society, without underestimating the inequality and repression that are part of Mexico today, the main question here remains: did the peasants from the Selva Lacandona take up arms to fight NAFTA or the globalization of the Mexican economy? What were their motives? Why did their possible brothers-in-arms outside the forest area not participate? To answer these questions, the Chiapas publication craze mentioned above comes to my aid. Most of the books in Spanish are round-ups of newspaper articles, consisting of reports of life in the jungle and of interviews with individual rebels. Also hundreds of pages of the Mexico City newspaper *La Jornada*, published in the first months of 1994, can be used thoroughly as historical documentation. Its journalists, still bewildered by what had happened during this period, penetrated deep into the jungle to interview any Indian they met and wrote page after page full of impressions. They reproduced peasants' statements and published all EZLN and government messages. Historians rarely find such a wealth of information about such a small group of persons. It gives the researcher the best opportunity possible to read the material critically and make cross-documentary comparisons.

Voices from the Jungle

The EZLN was not just an army. Several of its young soldiers made declarations similar to one given by Captain Elisa: 'When I lived in my house, with my family, I did not know anything. I did not know how to read, I did not go to school. But when I joined the EZLN, I learned how to read, I learned all of the Spanish I know, how to write, and I was trained for war.'[8]

The *guerrilleros* offered education, especially on language, history and politics. Another woman stated to have been recruited while working on the land in the forest: 'And then study advisers came and we understood and advanced.' The type of education offered to them is not known, but deducing from the EZLN declarations and 'laws', it must have had a radical, utopian, though very Mexican and nationalistic, character. In the end, all soldiers said they had learned that they had to struggle for the so-called 'Ten Points': land, work, housing, health-care, bread, dignified education, freedom, democracy, peace and justice.

The declarations made in the jungle on the content of these Ten Points make clear the utopian character of the indigenous voices. Of course, survival in difficult surroundings requires a utopian vision. But in the Lacandón three groups had been strengthening or, indeed, constituting this character. First, liberation theology lay-deacons and fieldworkers had entered the lowland jungle on the initiative of Bishop Samuel Ruiz García of San Cristóbal. From the late 1960s onwards, the bishop was one of the principal liberation theologians of Mexico, indeed of Latin America. In October 1974, he had organized an Indigenous Congress in San Cristóbal to commemorate the 500th anniversary of the birth of Fray Bartolomé de Las Casas. Since then, a network of lay-preachers has worked among the pioneers in the jungle to work out Catholic liberation theology and support the poor. The message was that only radical egalitarianism could lead to 'salvation'. The lay-deacons hoped to create a society free of what they call the social sin of Mexico's society.

Second came the Maoists, on the initiative of Mexico City University professor, Adolfo Orive Berlinguer.[9] These political fieldworkers spent a decade (from 1974 to 1984) organizing the colonists' communities to win bureaucratic battles, press for credits, subsidies, education and land. It was an unarmed struggle. The Maoist fieldworkers also set up a system for decision-making that included every voice in the community, including those of children. This is what is meant by 'democracy' in the Ten Points. However, small assemblies (*asambleas chicas*) consisting of some five to ten leaders from the Maoist vanguard worked out proposals. Obviously, some leaders were 'more equal' than others: the Maoists had started to direct the peasants,[10] otherwise, decisions could take weeks or months of debate. In short, the Maoists had created a distinctive political mentality among the people of the Selva Lacandona.

The Catholic lay-preachers and Maoist groups formed a union, called the Unión de Uniones (UU) to coordinate their socio-political struggle. But over the years the union split several times. One faction, dominated by the lay-preachers and supported by the church, saw its primary demand as land. They were utterly distrustful of the government and pleaded for the most radical road to 'salvation'. The other main faction saw that, given the rate of increase of the population, land alone would not solve the problems, but marketing and credit mechanisms as well as skilful negotiations with the government might do so. The Maoists, leading this faction, presumed that precisely such reformist actions could bring 'salvation', and reorganized their members into the Asociación Rural de Interés Colectivo (Rural Association of Collective Interest, ARIC).[11] The UU later split once again, this time over the issue of violent resistance. Guillermoprieto thinks the most radical group, opting for armed struggle in 1989, incorporated about 60 per cent of the population in the area.[12]

By then a third group, which had been strengthening or constituting the utopian character of the communities, had done its work. This group consisted of guerrilla fighters and, at present, forms the leadership of the EZLN. They were and remain independent of UU and ARIC and include a small group of twelve – or five, as Subcomandante Marcos, its leader, repeatedly stated – political activists from the central Mexican highlands. From 1983 on, they offered to train the local population in guerrilla warfare and pleaded for a new armed revolution in Mexico. They awaited in the mountainous area of the cloud forest until the indigenous leaders would express their willingness to go to war. They had to wait almost a full decade, because during most of the 1970s and 1980s the peasants fought for a better future with the help of the church's and Maoists' outsiders. Only after 1992, after the 500 Years of Struggle Movement, in the wake of the Columbus Memorials and the reforms of the Salinas administration – especially the revision of Article 27 of the constitution early in 1992, intended to 'modern-ize' Mexican agriculture and abolish the *ejido*-system of collective agriculture because, in the eyes of Salinas' technocrats, by the end of the twentieth century the *ejido* was considered an anachronism, impeding economic progress in the countryside[13] – made a future in the cloud forest more difficult and expansion impossible, youngsters joined the *guerrilleros*. They joined the men and women of the most radical UU split. Only about 40 per cent of the ARIC left-over and the tiny Protestant groups refused to vote for war.

By the end of the 1980s, two other measures had radicalized peasants' attitudes. As early as 1972, President Luis Echeverría had issued a decree granting seventy Lacandón Maya families control over a large tract of the cloud forest. It was meant to be an ecological measure in favour of preserving the jungle, but the measure deprived the first settlers of further room for expansion. Then, some fifteen years later, the Salinas administration refrained from stepping in with subsidized prices for coffee after the collapse of world prices in 1989. This was a blow to the small coffee-farmers in Chiapas, who produce one-third of the country's coffee exports. Of course, global developments, NAFTA, and neo-liberal policies were behind this, but for the peasants it was just more evidence of *mal gobierno*. After decades of support, they felt betrayed. Indeed, the revolution was betrayed. The Article 27 reform, to free *ejidos* for sale, brought above all confirmation of this: 'chaos' was approximate. Surely, the utopian answer to this situation makes the Lacandón communities unique to the Mexican context. Revolutionary education appealed to the people's desperation with the glorious past of Aztecs and Maya, a terrible present in a forgotten corner of Mexico and a non-existent future. At the same time, it brought them to anger at recent defeats and humiliation in Mexico City.

Voices from the Mountain

The Zapatista movement is not only politically utopian, it is also straight-forwardly indigenous. At first, this was not made too explicit in the EZLN's proclamations, but the combatants themselves were quite conscious of it. On the first day of the revolt one of the combatants declared to a journalist: 'Don't forget this: this is an ethnic movement.'[14] In fact, the new indigenous members had changed the character of Marcos' original EZLN. The EZLN's white leaders had to adjust their vision. The Tzeltales, Tzotziles, Tojolabales and Mames did not explain their struggle in terms of 'bourgeois and proletarians', rather in terms of 'wrong and right'.

This point is illustrated by a quote (cited below) from a communiqué released by the Clandestine Indigenous Revolutionary Committee (CIRC), on 27 February 1994. The CIRC consist of indigenous leaders from the Lacandona communities. In this declaration, they refer to the non-indigenous leaders, Maoists, lay-preachers and EZLN *guerrilleros* who came to their rescue in the time of chaos, described by them as the time of the night:

When the EZLN was only a shadow, creeping through the mist and darkness of the jungle, when the words 'justice,' 'liberty' and 'democracy' were only that: words; barely a dream that the elders of our communities, true guardians of the words of our dead ancestors, had given us in the moment when day gives way to night, when hatred and fear began to grow in our hearts, when there was nothing but desperation; when the times repeated themselves, with no way out, with no door, no tomorrow, when all was injustice, as it was, the true men spoke, the faceless ones, the ones who go by night, the ones who are jungle. [...]

The world is another world, reason no longer governs and we true men and women are few and forgotten and death walks upon us, we are despised, we are small, our word is muffled, silence has inhabited our houses for a long time, the time has come to speak for our hearts, for the hearts of others, from the night and from the earth our dead should come, the faceless ones, those who are jungle, who dress with war so their voice will be heard, that their word later falls silent and they return once again to the night and to the earth, that other men and women may speak, who walk other lands, whose words carry the truth, who do not become lost in lies.[15]

All major Maya rebellions – the Tzeltal revolt of 1712, Cuzcat's revolt of 1868–69, the Caste War of Yucatán of 1848–1901 – have been characterized by important supernatural and sacred aspects.[16] It was always a restoration of the sacred order that these warriors strived for; the 'right' ordering of society, avoiding and, indeed, fighting 'chaos' itself.[17] And 'chaos' was obviously coming in the form of: hunger (and I mean real hunger), disease (pneumonia, the flu, anaemia), lack of education and good clothing, despair and anger, and a government policy that excluded the Lacandona poor. 'Welcome to the nightmare,' the EZLN's Subcomandante Marcos wrote to Mexico's new president, Ernesto Zedillo Ponce de León, just before his inauguration in December 1994. The Indians of the Lacandón knew precisely what he meant.

But why 'the faceless ones'? Anthropologist Munro Edmonson, known for his editing of two of the most important indigenous documents on the Mayan faith, the *Popol Vuh* and the *Book of Chilam Balam of Chumayel*, writes that the Maya see the face as one's visible self.[18] It is not only one's physiognomy and costume but the behaviour one presents to the world. It is the most important projection of one's ego, and must be carefully protected from insult, criticism and ridicule. To destroy the enemy is to destroy his face. Mayan art is known for its destroyed faces, the literal defacement of the portraits of deified rulers at the end of a dynasty. Because appearance and speech are perceived in Mayan faith as the external manifestations of the soul, the face is strongly linked to the mouth. The prominence of masks and disguises in Mayan ritual, Edmonson continues, and the rigid formalization of speech militate against the easy assumption that things are what they seem. Faceless and masked men are not only shielded against insult and ridicule or, indeed, against violent assaults, by their masks, they can also act as men ritually transformed into deified warriors. Then, these warriors are men sacrificed to God and the Saints; the spiritual powers who command life and death, the very existence of human families and the rebirth of society. The sacrifice of the warriors is at the very centre of Maya belief. In ancient Maya language, sacrifice is not summed up in a unitary word, Edmonson concludes, because it is the point of nothingness, the point at which the zero of death equals the one of life.

Man, the Maya believe, cannot deal with the opaque nature of human access to reality.[19] It is the human condition that, in the great scheme of things, people are never to have easy admission to the 'true scheme of things'. Man can merely respond to an approximation of reality. The Maya believe that there is always something beyond and outside this. Therefore, it is vital for us to realize that the notion of chance happenings or accidents is foreign to them. Despite utopian education on combating 'social sin', Maoist education and guerrilla tactics, the Lacandona immigrants likewise know that anything that occurs is potentially subject to interpretation in spiritual terms. It is as if they are looking for the world through a steamed-up window.

This brings me to the realization that I may be interpreting some EZLN expressions incorrectly because of my Western mode of understanding. For example, the EZLN is not just based in the cloud forest, it is above all based on a mountain. Soldiers repeatedly stated: 'The mountain protects us, the mountain has been our *compañera* for many years.'[20] A mountain in the indigenous vision is not just a strategic place to hide away from the helicopters of Mexico's federal army. On the contrary, most soldiers interviewed by the press continuously confirmed that on the mountain they could not be spotted. According to military information coming from their opponents, this is not true; the Mexican army showed photographs of their camps on the mountain. But the Indians insist that the mountain, a female creature, is like their mother in childhood. She is the source of all life, she is even the gate to 'heaven'. In her womb, they will never be defeated. In the mountain itself, men live on.

Then there is the figure of Emiliano Zapata, introduced by the EZLN white leadership. Has this symbol of the Mexican Revolution of 1910 any appeal to the indigenous members of the Lacandona movement? Anthropologist Evon Zogt was surprised to learn that no small chapel in the cloud forest, containing an image of a new *santo* in the form of Zapata called San Emiliano, has been found yet.[21] In the sources, I only found one personal reference: soldier Ángel, a Tzeltal Maya, was proud to have read the Spanish translation of John Womack's book on Zapata. It took him three years of struggle to finish it.[22] Certainly, for the non-indigenous commanders, Zapata might be viewed as a kind of apotheosized embodiment of twentieth-century revolutionary ideology, but not for the Indians. The *mestízo* leadership might have carried Womack's book around and might have used the symbol of Zapata to discredit the presidential administration in Mexico City. Every new president presents himself as a new phase of the revolution and the Zapatistas denied this by turning to the same symbols. In general, I imagine that for the Lacandona migrants this symbol does not work at all. Where Marcos pointed to Mexico's historical heritage, rarely did I come across references to Zapata as the revolutionary hero of ordinary rebel fighters.

However, in an official, *collective* statement of the CCRI-CG of 10 April 1994, Zapata did appear as the major deified warrior of the EZLN. In fact, he has materialized as the source of life itself:

> Votán Zapata, light from afar, came and was born here in our land. Votán Zapata, always among our people, timid fire who lived 501 years in our death. Faceless man, tender light that gives us shelter. Name without name, Votán Zapata watched in Miguel, walked in José María, was Vincente, was named Benito, flew in bird, mounted in Emiliano, shouted in Francisco, visited Pedro. He is and is not all in us. He is one and many. None and all. Living, he comes. Without name he is named, face without face, all and none, one and many, living dead. Tapacamino bird, always in front of us. Votán, guardian and heart of the people. He is the sky in the mountains.[23]

We also learn that this Votán Zapata came to 'our mountain' to be reborn. It was Votán Zapata who took the face of those without faces. Because of his presence, the CCRI-CG explained, an unjust peace was transformed into a just war: death that is born. This is order reborn out of chaos, a classic theme of Mesoamerican culture.[24]

The references to the 'just moment' of the actions to 'beat the night' refer to what anthropologist Gary Gossen calls the 'tyranny of time'.[25] The divine mandate of solar and lunar cylces, and Venus, in combination with the 260-day calendar cycles, intimately affected the unfolding of each day for each individual and the community in the ancient Mayan world. This chrono-visionary perspective does not imply a deification of time, but an acknowledgement that all things, human and natural, are programmed with shifting valences of cause and effect as divine cycles, located outside the body, dictate. Humans have no choice but to adjust their behaviour accordingly. Gossen concludes that here emerges 'an almost unlimited opening for the interpretive skills and political control of shamans and secular leaders who claim to have a less opaque vision than ordinary people'.

That these leaders can be white should not amaze us, Gossen writes in another essay.[26] For according to the Tzotzil cosmology of Chamula – mother-town of many Lacandona colonists – the creators of life, the Moon/Virgin Mary and the Sun/Christ, are white, the overseers and guardians of life, the Saints, are white, and so are the earth lords who control land and water. Gossen shows that none of the earlier leaders of indigenous movements is remembered seriously by the Indians themselves, to the contrast of *mestízo* commanders. This is not, he warns us, because Chamula should be viewed as a colonial creation: 'The plot is not that simple.' One answer may lie in the cyclical time-reckoning, for this allows for selective accommodation and comprehension of new actors and new ideas by placing them morally in the past. In fact, in some past cycle. Each destruction in a period of chaos and each restoration of order yield a new and better truly indigenous reality. The white men of a previous epoch have become Sun and Moon, Saints and earth lords. These 'former men and women' are historicized in order to foreground and frame an always emergent Indian present. It is renewal in time that equals the rebirth of the indigenous present. In sum, during the period of chaos, destruction has already set in and thus has already produced 'historicized men', like the men who had become Saints after a prior cycle.

This brings me to Marcos himself. Marcos communicated the written statements to the outside world and debated furiously with the Mexican media. Apparently, he read everything that was published in Mexico on the movement and reacted to it. Marcos saw himself as a servant of the CCRI-CG and perhaps he was nothing more than this. In interviews, other *comandantes* of the EZLN confirmed this role. However, some common soldiers described him as a cat who could escape from soldier's attacks through the jungle, or as an eagle, flying high in the air to judge the development of the struggle. Obviously, as in typical Maya thinking on the metaphysics of personhood, he was seen as Marcos the military leader, and as his 'co-essence' at the same time. The co-essence of the person consists of his spiritual companion that resides outside the body, usually identified with animals. These spirits are given at birth and share with each individual the trajectory of his life, from birth to death.[27] Man's destiny is shared with this co-essence, it is perhaps even known to his spiritual companion. Hence, a 'faceless' Marcos is seen as a spiritual being who comprehends the world 'behind' the tangible and immediately accessible senses. White 'non-humans' like Marcos were indispensable to lead the faceless ones into this divine combat. Because reality is opaque, trusted interpreters and leaders are indispensable to influence or even alter that reality. Accordingly, the whites of the previous cycle, who operate in times of chaos, are the ones to follow.

Now, these trusted-ones need to 'know' the hidden reality to do so, including the 'sacred tyranny of time'. They do so because, as white historicized humans, they already belong to the previous cycle. In short, Marcos' actions could not have been so successful without being cast as something that was somehow destined to happen in the first place, and destined to be initiated by some supra-human leadership from the spiritual world. The overthrow of 'chaos' and the re-creation of 'order' were perceived as part of a magical, transcendental struggle in which human fighters transformed themselves into divine warriors. These warriors themselves are part of the cycle that is being destroyed during the transition from chaos to order. They vanish into the other world when the new order no longer needs them. Remember what the CCRI-CG had to say on this, as quoted above:

> from the night and from the earth our dead should come, the faceless ones, those who are jungle, who dress with war so their voice will be heard, that their word later falls silent and they return once again to the night and to the earth, that other men and women may speak, who walk other lands, whose words carry the truth, who do not become lost in lies.

Here then is a curious congruency of indigenous sacred and predestined fate and the Maoist theory of the transition from socialism to communism. According to both ideological constructions, Marcos and his faceless warriors will eventually make themselves superfluous.

Restoring Order

Seen from this perspective, we may agree with Gossen that the Zapatista Operation is but one dramatic move in a general pan-Maya cultural and political affirmation movement that is well under way in Mexico and Guatemala.[28] 'Only on rare occasions', Gossen writes, 'have Indian political and religious movements [...] crossed ethnic and linguistic lines in terms of their constituencies and military mobilization.'[29] This is happening nowadays in Chiapas and Guatemala. Gossen notes: 'Pan-Indian groups range from intellectual, educational, and religious organizations to craft guilds [...] catering to the tourist and export trade. There are also numerous writers' and artists' cooperatives whose members are working to create a corpus of literature in Maya languages, as well as graphic and performing arts that express traditional and contemporary Maya themes.'[30] The pan-Indian movement is in search of a new indigenous social order, discipline and hierarchy. Guatemala is moving towards the creation of a parallel indigenous education system.

As was made clear from the outset, the programme of the Zapatistas – i.e. the movement in general, not just its military arm, the EZLN – is substantially political. Think of what occurred in mid-March 1994, when shamans representing the five major Maya groups in Chiapas arrived at Palenque, the ancient town of Lord Pacal (Shield). Pacal was entombed in the well-known Temple of Inscriptions there in the year 683. More than 1,300 years later, these shamans set up a sacred shrine with multicoloured candles, copan incense – seen as 'the heart of heaven and the heart of earth' and the 'food for the ancestors inside the mountain'— and wild plants. The Fifth Sun had ended, they stated later, hunger and disease were over soon. The Sixth Sun had begun, an era of hope and unity for the *pueblos de indios*.[31]

Independent of this, but not really to be seen apart from it, was the issue of a Declaration of Autonomy on 12 October 1994, Dia de la Raza or Columbus Day. The declaration included the projection of so-called 'regional parliamentary groups'. Indeed, most important and constantly repeated, the EZLN demands a separate status for indigenous communities. By December 1994, more than forty Maya communities, most of them outside the EZLN zone, had responded with the formation of four autonomous regions. These regions were to be governed by a directorate of local indigenous groups from various townships.

But why such a political issue, legitimized with sacred rituals, if the main problems are overpopulation, poverty and neglect? Above all, the return of traditional *pueblos de indios* means a return of *order* and the defeat of chaos. Order means self-governing institutions, a 'just' distribution of land, modern health-care and good education. However, order also means the establishment of commercial centres for the benefit of the peasants to buy and sell at a 'just price', as well as amusement centres for a 'dignified' rest, without *cantinas* or brothels. One of the CCRI-CG members declared to *La Jornada* in February 1994, that there is 'no need to hold our hand. We believe that our people are capable of governing themselves because our people are aware. That is why we do not need a government that only wants to manipulate us, to have us under its feet. As Indians, we need our own autonomy, we need that identity, that dignity.'[32] The *pueblo* is autonomy, identity and dignity; it means social order. Those words were heard previously in the eighteenth century.

The CCRI-CG is responsible for establishing order in the communities.[33] There is a loud echo of the traditional *cabildo de indios*, known from the colonial period, in the tasks this governing committee sees ahead of itself. Committee members have to resolve problems that may arise in their communities. They see to it that people attend the town meetings. The committees prohibited alcohol throughout the zone and do not permit their *compañeros* to get drunk. They punish men who beat their wives, by fining them or requiring them to undertake activities such as cutting wood. Homosexual acts lead to public self-criticism.

In January 1994, the EZLN issued a series of laws and regulations, valid for 'all the national territory'. These 'laws' also echo former *pueblo* regulations:

communal ownership of all land to distribute small plots among all members of the organization. The Agrarian Reform Law stated that all land-holdings greater than 100 hectares of poor quality land or 50 of good quality land were subject to such redistribution. The owners were allowed to remain as smallholders and were advised to join the cooperatives the EZLN wanted to set up. In short, this meant self-determination in the area of land management and distribution.

One book on the Lacandona Revolt began with the phrase: 'The time of the revolution has not passed.'[34] As true as this might be, I nevertheless have my doubts about the Mexican case. True, general discontent with the Mexican government, anger about repression and despair after many years of economic crisis stood at the root of rural movements, organized or not, in the state of Chiapas; but only in the Selva Lacandona did these factors lead to armed resistance. The isolated situation in the cloud forest made it a playground for radical groups to transform the mentality of the people. Maoist ideology, liberation theology and traditional Maya faith in predestined time, came together in a unique stance towards the fear of chaos and the end of the world. This brought the faceless warriors of the EZLN to the fore. Poor youth, men and women, were prepared to 'transform' themselves, as they expressed it, to defeat the night and vanish with the 'past cycle'. This unique ideological combination is not present in the other areas of Chiapas. The decision to opt for a radical solution was made on the micro-level of the Selva Lacandona.

Notes and References

1. See Ouweneel, *Alweer die Indianen*, and Gosner and Ouweneel, *Indigenous Revolts*, for more details.

2. See, among others, Aubry, 'Lenta acumulación'; (Autonomedia), *¡Zapatistas!*, Camú Urzúa and Tótoro Taulis, *EZLN*, Collier, *Basta!*, Guillermoprieto, 'Letter from Mexico'; Harvey, *Rebellion*; Romero Jacobo, *Altos de Chiapas*, Ross, *Rebellion*, Rovira, *¡Zapata vive!*, Rus, 'Local adaptation'.

3. One of the best recent histories, powerful in its brevity, is by Alma Guillermoprieto, 'The shadow war'.

4. Personal communication by Jan de Vos to the author.

5. Guillermoprieto, 'The shadow war', p. 34.

6. For example, Collier, *Basta!*, Collier, 'Background'; Rus, 'Local adaptation'; Harvey, *Rebellion*.

7. Feder, *Rape of the Peasantry*, Huizer, 'Emiliano Zapata'. On this, see Ouweneel, *Onderbroken groei in Anáhuac*.

8. *La Jornada*, 18 January 1994.

9. Curiously, Orive later served the Salinas administration as the coordinator of advisers on Social and Rural Policies, and, later still, the Zedillo administration.

10. Officially, the Zapatistas' highest authority is called the Comité Clandestino Revolucionario Indígena–Coordinadora General (Indigenous Clandestine Revolutionary Committee), or CCRI-CG. Reading the newspapers, I have the impression that every community has several representatives in this body.

11. In another stage of its development ARIC was referred to as Asociación Rural de Iniciativa Colectiva (Rural Association for Collective Initiative), or even as Asociación Regional Indígena Campesina (Regional Indigenous Peasant Association). On the discourse of 'salvation', see a paper delivered by Jan de Vos, 'Encuentro de los Mayas de Chiapas'.

12. Guillermoprieto, 'The shadow war', p. 38.

13. See Ouweneel, 'Away from prying eyes'.

14. (Autonomedia), ¡Zapatistas!, p. 71.

15. 'Communiqué from the Clandestine Indigenous Revolutionary Committee High Command of the Zapatista National Liberation Army (CCRI-CG del EZLN)', made public by telefax, e-mail and on paper on 27 February 1994. Also published in Cultural Survival Quarterly 18 (1), 1994, p. 12.

16. See the essays in Gosner and Ouweneel, Indigenous Revolts; also Bricker, Indian Christ; Vogt, 'Possible sacred aspects'; also, Ouweneel, 'Verleden leefde voort'.

17. On this mentality, see Gossen's work.

18. Edmonson, 'Mayan faith', p. 71.

19. This is from Tedlock, Breath on the Mirror; also, Gossen, 'Who is the Comandante'; and Gossen, 'Maya Zapatistas'.

20. From the second communiqué packet that the EZLN released to the press. This is a packet that circulates among many journalists and even scientists. It contains letters and documents dated between 17 and 26 January 1994.

21. Vogt, 'Possible sacred aspects', p. 34.

22. Womack, Zapata. Despite its age (1969), the book is still considered to be the major study on Emiliano Zapata.

23. La Jornada, 11 April 1994. Included are the names of Miguel Hidalgo, José María Morelos and Vicente Guerrero, heroes of the Independence Movement of 1810–21. Also mentioned are Benito Juárez of the Reform Movement in the 1870s, the great hero of the Mexican nation, and Emiliano Zapata and Francisco Villa. The name of Votán is known from the work of Fray Ramón de Ordoñez y Aguilar. In 1773, this canon of the cathedral town of Ciudad-real in Chiapas (now: San Cristóbal Las Casas) went to visit Palenque. The ruins had such impact on him that he decided to write a book on the place and its history. He claimed to have received the material from a book written by Votán himself in Quiché. Votán was said to have travelled from the land of Chivim, somewhere in the Near East, to the Americas and to have settled in Palenque. He is said to have subjugated the Indians and founded the cities of which the present ruins are all that remain. According to Ordoñez, Chivim must have been the city of Tripoli in Phoenicia. This story intrigued speculative writers such as Constance Irwin, Fair Gods and Stone Faces (1963), and Peter Tompkins, Mysteries of the Mexican Pyramids (1976). Curiously, Votán's name was preserved among the Indians of the area; or must indeed have been known there before and inspired Ordoñez to write his awkward narrative.

24. Tedlock, Breath on the Mirror; also the essays in Danien and Sharer, New Theories.

25. Gossen, 'Who is the Comandante'.

26. Gossen, 'Other in Chamula Tzotzil cosmology', pp. 462–8.

27. On this, see the summary in Gossen, 'Who is the Comandante'.

28. Gossen, 'Who is the Comandante'.

29. Gossen, 'Maya Zapatistas', p. 536.

30. Ibid.

31. Vogt, 'Possible sacred aspects'.

32. La Jornada, 4 Februray 1994.

33. (Autonomedia), ¡Zapatistas!, pp. 283–9. For reasons of methodology and historical criticism I have left Marcos' statements on the CCRI-CG and on life in the cloud forest in

general aside, and concentrated entirely on interviews with other people, preferably on occasions when Marcos was not around. The role of Marcos, nicely treated by Guillermoprieto in her 'The shadow war', requires a separate analysis. On the *Cabildo de Indios*, see Ouweneel, *Shadows over Anáhuac*.

34. (Autonomedia), *¡Zapatistas!*, p. 11.

PART II

The Long-term Consequences of Violence, Terror and Fear

FIVE

Political Violence in Post-revolutionary Mexico

ALAN KNIGHT

Historically, Latin American countries have experienced sharp swings in the scale and incidence of political violence. Perhaps violence in society at large has displayed greater continuity; the relationship between political and societal violence is clearly an important, though difficult, question to consider.[1] If the question is confined to *political* violence – that is, violence perpetrated in the pursuit of political goals[2] – however, the discontinuities over time are striking, and may, for a start, call into question theories which posit a deep, deterministic predisposition to violence (or its opposite: political pacifism – or civility?) coursing through the veins of the body politic like blood laden with character-forming DNA.

During the nineteenth century, Mexico and Venezuela were notoriously unstable and violent places, victims of recurrent civil war and foreign intervention. During the twentieth century, they became more stable and violence-free (which is not to say impeccably democratic). In Mexico, the process began with the institutionalization of the revolutionary government after 1917; in Venezuela, with the National Front accord of 1958. Both countries avoided the turn to praetorian government which affected much of the continent in the 1960s and 1970s, bringing a sharp increase in top-down, official violence. Conversely, the chief proponents of that praetorian, or 'bureaucratic authoritarian', approach included Chile and Uruguay, which for much of their histories have been over-enthusiastically celebrated as stable, peaceful, civilian polities. Yet Uruguay, the erstwhile 'Switzerland of South America', had the highest relative number of political prisoners of any nation in the world in the early 1970s.[3] Now, Chile and Uruguay are generally seen as among the more stable, 'consolidated', civilian democracies, while Venezuela has had several close encounters with military insurgency and Mexico has witnessed a spate of high-level political assassinations. Is the wheel turning again?

In the Mexican case, the decline of political violence after 1920 cannot be denied, but it should be qualified. It is true, the last successful armed insurrection was seventy-five years ago (the Agua Prieta rebellion of 1920, which installed the Sonoran dynasty). The De la Huerta revolt of 1923–24 was overcome, narrowly; the would-be military rebels of 1927 and the actual rebels of 1929 were crushed; the Cristeros, who mounted a sustained rebellion for three years, were fought to a standstill (and, however popular and powerful in their west/central strongholds, they never threatened to topple the national government). Thereafter, insurgent challenges to the regime were relatively few and feeble. Cedillo was easily put down in 1938; a handful of Almazanista rebels, spurned by their exiled chief, were eliminated in 1940. Celestino Gasca's quixotic conspiracy of 1961 represented the virtual last gasp of the long cycle of revolutionary *pronunciamientos*.[4] Although popular revolts continued after 1961, particularly in the fractious state of Guerrero, the conventional picture of a regime which, unlike its predecessors, has achieved stability and solved the problem of succession, is generally convincing.

Indeed, under this new political dispensation, disgruntled members of the political elite came to see the wisdom of pacific self-abnegation. Whereas disappointed presidential hopefuls and their allies rebelled in 1920, 1923, 1927 and 1929, the tendency thereafter was for political losers to accept defeat gracefully, thereby ensuring their physical survival and, perhaps, making possible their subsequent political rehabilitation. Thus, from 1934 to 1952, a key phase in the evolution of the political system, electoral challenges to the dominant party came from 'out' politicians who had split from the PNR/PRM/PRI to lead improvised opposition *partidos electoreros*: Villareal in 1934, Almazán in 1940, Padilla in 1946, Henriquez Guzmán in 1952.[5] They were all defeated, though Almazán and Henriquez Guzmán gave the official party a scare, and their partisans all suffered official harassment; 1940 and 1952 were particularly rough elections. Unlike their 1920s predecessors (De la Huerta, Gomez, Serrano, Escobar), they did not risk an armed challenge to the regime which had now – in Weberian terms – established a rough 'monopoly of coercive violence', particularly at the national level. And the regime itself recognized and acknowledged this change: Calles' brutal suppression of the 1927 conspirators – fourteen senior officers shot at sunset in the woods near Huitzilac – contrasted with Cárdenas' firm but benign treatment of Calles himself nine years later, when the old *jefe máximo*, instead of greeting the sunrise with a blindfold and his back to the wall, was bundled on a plane to the USA and a comfortable exile. He eventually returned to stand shoulder-to-shoulder with Cárdenas and Avila Camacho on the balcony of the National Palace for the 1943 military *desfile*.

We can therefore discern three stages in the evolution of the official party, which led to its consolidation during the heyday of the PRI in the 1950s and 1960s: first, a Darwinian period (1917–29) of internal conflict, punctuated by revolts from within the ranks of the revolutionary army, during which, with the recurrent victories of the central government, the ranks of the dissidents were thinned and the penalties of insurgency rammed home. Second, a long transitional period (1929–52) when revolts were few or feeble and PNR/ PRM/PRI dissidents mounted significant but unsuccessful electoral challenges to the official candidate. Third, the heyday of the PRI (1952–87), when the party machine, possessed of enormous powers of patronage, maintained party cohesion, avoided schisms and defeated the genuine opposition parties with relative ease.[6] The PRI split of 1987, followed by the highly contentious 1988 election, represented, in some ways, a return to the second phase, although in very different socio-economic circumstances. Meanwhile, this evolution embodied obvious structural changes. There was a professional-ization and domestication of the military, incipient in the 1920s, consummated in the 1940s; and, as a counterweight, the rise of new civilian political and technocratic elites who supplanted the older generation of revolutionary military cadres. This included Pani, Gómez Morin and the other Callista technocrats of the 1920s, Cárdenas' secondary tier of trained civilian experts in the 1930s (Ramón Beteta being a classic case), and the cadre of younger, educated civilians who swept to power with Miguel Alemán (a younger, educated civilian himself) in the later 1940s. The skills required of government also changed. Lawyers, and later economists, replaced soldiers. Mexico became, at the national level, a kinder and a gentler place.

But this was a national or *cupular* phenomenon. As argued elsewhere, this progressive stabilization and civilianization did not uniformly penetrate to the grassroots or to the provinces.[7] Of course, the latter were profoundly affected by the new rules of the political game. But these rules, while they vetoed violence at national level, allowed it, sometimes even encouraged it, at the local level. The sixth commandment lost its force beyond the bound-aries of the federal district. Indeed, it might even be argued that the successful elimination of violence at the national level involved its displacement to the provinces; local people fought and feuded so that the national elites might bask in stable civility.

Of course, the high incidence of local violence was in large measure a consequence of the armed revolution of 1910–17. But in this, as in all things, we must be careful not to exaggerate the causal role of the revolution. Perhaps the Porfiriato was not so peaceful; and certainly there were regions where the violence of the 1910s ('revolutionary' violence) was exceeded by that of the 1920s and 1930s ('post-revolutionary' violence). The Porfiriato deliberately cultivated an image of peace and stability (the PRI of the 1980s and 1990s displayed 'neo-Porfirian' traits in terms not only of its neo-liberal, 'neo-Científico' economic policy, but also of its – quite successful – rhetorical appeals to social peace and stability).

In foreign eyes, for example, the *rurales* were exemplars of effective and reassuring Porfirian peace-keeping, Mexican counterparts, as an unwittingly ironic observer put it, of 'the Irish Constabulary or [...] that splendid corps, the Guardias Civiles in Spain'.[8] The Pax Porfiriana was such that travellers could cross most of Mexico without entertaining the fear of bandits and bushwhackers which had been endemic earlier in the nineteenth century. But if criminal and popular violence had declined, this was at least in part because state violence had increased.

The Pax Porfiriana was, in part, a Roman peace: the Porfirian regime – possessed of railways, telegraphs, machine guns, artillery and even gunboats (in fact, most of the weaponry of contemporary colonialist states) – could repress more effectively than any previous regime. The Yaqui and Maya were bludgeoned into submission. Sporadic peasant and working-class protests were put down; even middle-class oppositionists felt the flat of cavalry sabres when they went too far – for example, at Monterrey in 1903.[9] It is impossible to compute the incidence of Porfirian violence, to weigh the enhanced security of the better-off against the coercion, actual or threatened, suffered by the popular classes. Doubtless, the paeans to the Pax Porfiriana sung by sympathetic observers, especially foreigners, involved turning a blind eye to a great deal of actual or threatened coercion, especially in the countryside; the image of a benign, bucolic, paternalist Porfiriato – the kind of image promoted by ranchero comedies and some recent revisionist historiography – is, if not entirely false, at least greatly exaggerated. As against supposedly happy folksy estates like La Gavia one must set harsh and coercive haciendas like La Guaracha, not to mention the plantations of the Valle Nacional or the *monterias* of Chiapas.[10] And the latter did not need to constitute the majority for severe social tensions to be generated, both within haciendas and, more important, between haciendas and neighbouring communities. Hence, I would argue, the sudden and surprising collapse of the regime in 1910–11; by then, it was a regime dependent, in many regions, on coercion combined with a kind of faltering prescription – not a deep and enduring legitimacy.

The revolution – *huelva decir* – involved extensive violence, which eventually extended throughout the country, that took multiple forms: guerrilla campaigns, conventional warfare, social and unsocial banditry, riots and urban crime.[11] The obvious transformation of the Pax Porfiriana into the hurricane of revolution was striking: it involved not only a quantum leap in the rate of violence, but also a shift in the terms of trade, in that elites now suffered as well as perpetrated violence; or, to put it the other way round, popular groups, for a while, gave as good as they got. Peasants seized lands, often in local, 'spontaneous' fashion;[12] bandits readily metamorphosed into political rebels; the artisans of the declining Bajío towns rioted, looting pawnshops, attacking local officials and *gachupin* shopkeepers. Landlords found that they could not resist and, in many cases, fled: to the cities, to the United States. The federal army, resurgent and reinforced by Huerta, was finally defeated and disbanded in 1914; in its place, a host of *caudillos* and their motley forces now ruled; there was no state, let alone a state monopoly of violence. Even the liberal leaders of the revolution, from Madero down, recoiled from the consequences of their actions; they began to echo Sarmiento, lamenting the barbarism which lay beneath Mexico's veneer of civilization;[13] and they increasingly countenanced tough measures – infringements of liberal principle – in order to crush their conservative opponents and control their popular followers: forced recruitment, summary executions, press censorship, fixed elections. The early, 'doveish' liberalism of 1911–13 gave way to a more hawkish *realpolitik*, which infected Mexican politics from top to bottom.[14] Madero yielded to Machiavelli as a political model.[15]

The casualties of the revolutionary period were, of course, enormous, although, as in most wars, the great majority derived from illness, allied to malnutrition, in the later phase of the conflict, rather than from outright combat.[16] If the common people suffered severely, they did not (in my somewhat 'traditional' opinion) suffer wholly in vain, since the revolution involved autonomous popular mobilization, linked to genuine popular goals; revolutionary recruitment was, at least until the later years (c. 1915–20), voluntary; and if the revolutionary army (a notional concept) attracted its fair share of time-servers, opportunists and even psychopaths (such as Margarito of *Los de Abajo*, or José Inés Chavez Garcia, the scourge of the Bajío),[17] the majority of combatants fought for political reasons, often related to local social and political grievances. Revolutionary violence was, therefore, rational rather than gratuitous;[18] it also had a loosely democratic quality, as had the violence of the mid-nineteenth-century civil wars.[19] This was a product, chiefly, of political circumstances – the collapse of the state, the widespread mobilization of local, popular forces – and, secondarily, of the military requirements of the day: a horse and a .303 were the chief *desiderata* (not that they were always easy to get); air power was incipient, naval power fairly irrelevant, artillery was the most crucial, costly, high-tech weaponry which revolutionary forces needed but often lacked.

This 'democratization' of violence carried over into the post-1917 period of reconstruction and institutionalization. As Cobb put it, of the French Revolution: 'it is likely always to take some time to push or ease the people out of a revolutionary situation once they are no longer needed'.[20] So, too, with Mexico after 1917. Quite simply, there were too many people with too many weapons for the state swiftly to reassert a monopoly of violence. When the Huasteca town of Pisaflores came under rebel attack in October 1922, the local garrison was joined, an eye-witness recalled, 'by many of our own boys here who still had guns from the Revolution'.[21] Weaponry aside, the revolution left a psychological and political legacy. Some of the younger generation, the 'generation of the volcano' at San José de Gracia, grown up amid violence and upheaval, were disrespectful, swaggering and rough.[22] The tough times of the revolution, now recaptured in dozens of graphic oral accounts, conspired with miserable childhoods to produce a breed of hard men who, like Paul Friedrich's 'Princes of Naranja', subscribed to a harsh ethic of struggle and self-interest.[23] Grassroots revolutionary politics were, one might say, the politics of the limited good, premised on the notion that *la vida es una lucha.*[24] The new revolutionary elite, schooled in warfare, was also very distinct from the preceding generation of Porfirian technocrats and *licenciados*. Amaro, risen from provincial obscurity, a self-made general who went on to tame the revolutionary army in the 1920s, thought nothing of having his amatory rivals castrated and left lying in the gutters of Mexico City.[25] Zuno, the revolutionary boss of Jalisco, personally attended violent police interrogations.[26] Local *caciques*, some of them erstwhile plebeians risen from the ranks, some of them local bigwigs convincingly affecting popular manners and appearance, regularly used violence, intimidation and even torture to get their way.[27] If their Porfirian precedecessors had done the same, they had probably done so on a smaller scale and they had certainly covered their tracks better; the Porfirian recourse to covert intimidation was less necessary and less publicized.

Not that Porfirian *caciques* were any more saintly than their revolutionary successors; rather, times had changed, and politics had become more violent, rowdy and rumbustious. Intimidation had a part to play in these new politics; sometimes it had to be known and exemplary; and, anyway, press coverage and political gossip – both more open and extensive than they had been pre-1910 – guaranteed publicity.[28] Throughout the country, local 'defence' forces (*defensas sociales*) proliferated. Formed in order to protect communities from 'bandit' attack, which they sometimes did, the *defensas sociales* became key institutions of political socialization, promotion and struggle. Impressive political careers – for example, that of Jesus Antonio Almeida, governor of Chihuahua, 1924–27 – began in the ranks of the *defensas*; Almeida's chief rival, Ignacio Enriquez, though not a product of the *defensas* himself, 'based his political strength on the control of the *defensas sociales* [...] in the western sierras'.[29] Durable *cacicazgos*, such as that of the Prado family in the Chilchota region of Michoacan, similarly depended on control of the local *defensa social*, whose members were sometimes indistinguishable from the broader population of *pistoleros* (political hired guns) who surrounded local *caciques*.[30] Not surprisingly, protagonists of this form of political domination were – irrespective of their formal ideological labels, Left or Right[31] – rough, tough, political pachyderms. Allegations of illiteracy, brutality and immorality were legion.[32] At the grassroots, they practised a kind of hardball politics, *política cochina*,[33] which offended respectable opinion, but which proved hard to eradicate. Local hardball involved recurrent use of force and intimidation; murders, ambushes and 'punitive expeditions'; a special vocabulary, far removed from the high-minded, progressive rhetoric of the revolution, which teemed with *azotes, atropellos balaceados, chanchullos, esbirros, mangoneadores, mozos de confianza, puñaladas* and *zafarranchos*; a cast of villains, each with his (and they are invariably men) evocative *apodo* (Bones, Scarface, Death, The Toad, Black Hand, etc.); even a warped sense of humour, elements of which are to be found in the graphic pages of the memoirs of Gonzalo N. Santos.[34]

During the 1920s and 1930s, this *política cochina* was not confined to the rural backwoods; it characterized state and national political life too. Chihuahua, a relatively 'modern' mestizo, northern state, experienced recurrent violence: rebellions, coups, assassinations.[35] Throughout Mexico, state elections regularly produced conflict, confrontation, dual legislatures and, frequently, federal intervention.[36] Even the federal government was not immune. It weathered the major revolt of 1923 (thanks partly to its widespread recruitment of local armed forces, *defensas, agraristas,* red batallions, which, of course, maintained the cycle of local violence); and, thereafter, it was never really at risk of losing power at gunpoint. But national politics was far from dignified, decorous and civilian. Obregon was assassinated in 1928, Pascual Ortiz Rubio was shot in the jaw as he emerged from the Palacio Nacional on his first day in office (hence Dulles' delightfully deadpan chapter heading: 'A Sad Inauguration Day for President Ortiz Rubio').[37] Provincial violence often welled up in the federal capital itself, in part because local *caciques* and bosses, advancing to coveted federal posts in Congress, brought their provincial feuds with them into the heart of the D.F. In 1936 two Huasteca *agraristas* – one a federal deputy – were gunned down in a restaurant in Mexico City where they had gone to seek an interview with Cárdenas; in the same year, the Veracruz radical, Manlio Fabio Altamirano, was shot to death in the chic Café Tacuba by *pistoleros* in the pay of the Armenta family.[38]

Over time, as I have said, the federal government gradually curtailed its own exposure to the threat of violence. Sporadic incidents occurred: the *priísta* Jorge Meixueiro blew out his brains while on the podium at the party congress in 1943; *priístas* were still toting guns in Congress in the 1970s.[39] But, at least until recently, the level of national, 'cupular' violence remained low. After the 1940s a new generation of civilian, technocratic *políticos* came to the fore. Even those provincial *caciques* who achieved national careers – Gonzalo Santos being the classic case – developed a kind of schizoid political persona: urbane and enlightened when they hobnobbed with presidents and national *políticos* in the capital, rustic and ruthless when they returned to their political *patrias chicas* to make money, build clienteles, swap crude jokes and eliminate opponents.[40] A key aspect of this process of national civilianization was, therefore, the relationship between the central government and its provincial backers. There is no doubt that the balance shifted dramatically after the 1930s, in favour of the former. This did not mean that peace prevailed, or that a *Rechtsstaat* ruled in place of the old, fractious polity of the 1920s and early 1930s. Provincial *caciques* had to come to terms with the burgeoning central government or – as Cedillo found in 1938–39 – they risked elimination. But by judicious bargaining they could survive, updating their *cacicazgos*, even exploiting the expanded federal power to their own advantage. Smart *caciques* thus realized early on that it made sense to work with, not against, the federal government: an early pioneer was Gabriel Barrios in Puebla; a collective, generational example was provided by the Figueroas of Guerrero who, having failed to re-create a nineteenth-century style *cacicazgo* along the line of Juan Alvarez's, more realistically settled for a division of power with the burgeoning federal government.[41] Santos drew similar conclusions from the fall of his *potosino* predecessor Cedillo.[42]

Thus, the growth of central power, evidenced in peaceful presidential successions and an expanding federal payroll, did not eliminate local *caciques*, but rather 'modernized' them. *Caciques*, and the bundle of interests and practices they represented, thus came to terms with the new order, colonizing and cannibalizing it. One key aspect of this dialectical process was the continued incidence of violence, particularly, though not solely, in the countryside.[43] The 1930s, years of significant federal government initiative, were also years of endemic violence, as *agraristas* clashed with landlords and 'white guards', villagers with villagers, anti-clericals with Catholics, Sinarquistas with Jacobins, syndical and *ejido* factions with their local rivals. Far from constituting a new Leviathan as some analysts would have us think, the central government exercised only limited control over a seething civil society; its front-line agents, such as the federal schoolteachers, were less instruments of totalitarian control than victims of an excessive federal ambition which ran up against dogged, often violent, local resistance. Hence the endless record of bloodshed during the 1930s: schools torched; teachers killed, raped and *desorejados*; communities fighting pitched battles with rivals; endemic factional conflicts within communities; ubiquitous repression by hacienda 'white guards' mounting a rearguard action against *agrarismo*; inter- and intra-union fights (notably in the textile regions of Orizaba and Atlixco).[44]

The expansion of the state thus created new arenas and forms of conflict: Cardenista *agrarismo* introduced conflict to regions which had hitherto been, at least on the face of it, relatively quiet; if, in doing so, it did not introduce the apple of discord into a pre-existing rural paradise (as some revisionist romantics seem to think), it certainly served to generalize violence, perhaps in part by 'democratizing' it and, literally, putting guns into the hands of the previously unarmed poor. But *agrarismo* also afforded the basis for durable *cacicazgos* – some genuinely popular, some thoroughly cynical, but all dependent in part on the successful prosecution of local violence. Federal schooling – a long-term engine of national integration – was, in the short term, often divisive and conflictual. The enhanced power of the trade unions, especially the CTM, also generated widespread violence: as the CTM sought to eliminate rivals (notably the CROM); and as local *políticos* and interests – the Monterrey group, governors like Yocupicio in Sonora, Avila Camacho in Puebla – fought to keep Lombardo and the CTM at bay, often quite successfully.[45] Even the Juntas de Conciliación y Arbitraje, harbingers of greater central control of labour, tended to produce, as well as to inhibit, conflict, as local interests – unions, bosses, politicians – struggled to impose their authority on these nascent nodules of power.

Federal assertions of power, though broadly successful in the long term, were regularly stymied by local resistance or, more insidiously, local cooption.

Sometimes, therefore, we should think, not of the state coopting social groups (the familiar Mexican formula), but rather of social groups coopting the state. It was one thing to get rid of an egregious and unsubtle *caudillo* like Cedillo, who invited his own downfall; but more canny *caciques* survived for decades, developing that schizoid political persona which, I have suggested, could deflect federal presidential displeasure;[46] displaying, from time to time, their utility to the central government. Cárdenas, for example, needed cacical support, even from unsavoury characters like Ernesto Prado (as did Felipe Carrillo Puerto during his brief radical governorship of Yucatán).[47] During the 1940s and 1950s, too, the federal government tolerated entrenched local *caciques*: positively, because they were useful agents of control and electoral mobilization; negatively, because their removal was messy and contentious. Of course, *caciques* were removed, in an almost regular, rhythmic cycle: they outstayed their usefulness, excited local opposition (often middle-class, student opposition), and they were eventually thrown to the wolves by a central government whose pragmatic Realpolitik was legendary. As a result, the postwar history of Mexico is punctuated with episodes, partially violent, in which ageing *caciques* have been toppled; the system thus embodies a necessary quantum of violence, the inevitable product of a tenaciously lingering *caciquismo*.[48]

Caciquismo therefore ensured that violence would remain a staple feature of Mexican politics long after national praetorianism was eliminated. *Caciques* practised violence – it was a traditional part of their political armoury, they ensured a regular recruitment of young *pistoleros*[49] – and their overthrow often involved a degree of violence which, even if it did not achieve the immediate objective of toppling the *cacique*, at least secured the attention of the federal government. (This applies to provincial, political *caciquismo*; the same might also be true of syndical *caciquismo*: e.g. the electricians, teachers, even the celebrated *telefonistas*.) Violence, far from being a psychopathic deviation from political normality, was therefore an integral part of Mexican political culture, particularly at the grassroots, where the politics of hardball prevailed, fostering cynical attitudes towards those in authority and, perhaps, drawing upon a deep reservoir of (apolitical) *machismo*.[50] Indeed, the legitimacy of the federal government was probably enhanced by occasional strategic strikes against faltering *caciques*, which displayed both the superior force and the superior morality of the national executive and sometimes came sweetened with reformist handouts (compare Cardenas' *reparto* in San Luis in 1938–39 and Echeverria's in Sonora in 1976). If, in Mexico in 1968, the federal government appeared as a repressive, reactionary force, in the provinces – Chiapas in the 1930s, Sonora in the 1970s, the Huasteca in the 1980s – it could appear in a more progressive, peace-making guise. However, the removal of one egregious *cacique* did not change the entire system: in unions as well as *municipios*, incoming 'reformers' sometimes started to replicate the sins of their *caciquista* predecessors.

But post-1945 violence went beyond this specifically political rationale. It had a disinct – and, in some respects, novel – socio-economic rationale. During the 1920s and 1930s commercial agriculture went through a lean period (especially from *c.* 1926 onwards). *Agrarismo* threatened property rights, the Cristiada devastated the centre-west; world depression lowered prices, and also lowered the opportunity cost of land reform. As a result, the Cardenista expropriations of the later 1930s were less bitterly contested than they would have been fifteen years earlier, and the government itself was more prepared to confiscate properties – e.g. the Laguna cotton plantations – which were teetering on the brink of bankruptcy. During and after the 1940s the picture changed: with the eclipse of Cardenismo the agrarian reform lost its impetus; the war boosted external markets; the Cold War further blackened the reputation of *agrarismo*. Commercial landlords made a political, economic, even ideological comeback. As the collective *ejidos* – Cárdenas' attempt to socialize cash crop farming – faced external hostility and internal schism (e.g. Zacatepec, Atencingo, the Laguna), commercial capitalist farming revived: in the north-west, where irrigation served its interests and the USA afforded a vast market; in the Huasteca, where the production of coffee and tropical fruit expanded; in the south and south-east, where (again) coffee and cattle flourished; finally, along the western spine of the Sierra Madre, where marijuana and poppies bloomed in response to US consumer demand. Commercial farming soon began to clash with peasant communities, which had themselves been given a new lease of life by the Cardenista reforms. The result was a protracted phase of agrarian 'compression' (to borrow Tutino's term): a collision between capitalist and peasant farming which repeated some of the features of the earlier, Porfirian, phase of 'compression'.[51] But there were also differences. First, crops and localities had changed: pastoral farming was now more important, as were coffee, fruit, vegetables, later drugs; while industrial crops, such as rubber and henequen, were things of the past. Non-agrarian activities, such as tourism, also counted. Second, hitherto marginal zones were now rapidly incorporated into capitalist markets, some of them Indian 'regions of refuge':[52] parts of Oaxaca, Nayarit, the Huasteca, the Lacandón forest of Chiapas. The resulting conflict thus tended to assume an ethnic and racist caste. Third, given the marked shift in the land/labour ratio since the Porfiriato, capitalist farmers did not usually lack for labour, but they coveted peasant resources in the shape of land and water. Hence the progressive assault on the *ejido*, and on peasant communities more generally, which took the form of illegal alienations, sales, sub-renting and outright expropriation. Or – a pattern to be seen throughout Latin America – monopsonistic buyers and middlemen battened on to peasant producers who survived, but at the cost of becoming quasi-proletarians working for piece rates (*a destajo*).[53] Fourth – the most obvious difference – the political system had been transformed; and, while the 'revolutionary' regime seemed decreasingly 'revolutionary' and even increasingly 'neo-

Porfirian', it did not, until the late 1980s, dare terminate the agrarian reform or wind up the *ejido*. Reform therefore remained: a constant incentive to peasants, a threat to land-owners, and a temptation to politicians. Some *políticos* espoused it with genuine, if confused, idealism; some capitulated to popular pressure; some saw it as a useful instrument to control peasant votes and, perhaps, to clobber landlord opponents. Landlords did not enjoy a political blank cheque as they had during the Porfiriato.[54] Now, they had to work to secure political favours: competing for office themselves, promoting their friends, cronies and clients, lobbying for support from state and national bigwigs, colonizing the federal agencies which proliferated throughout the countryside, especially during the 1970s.[55] They also resorted to forms of freelance local repression: they had *rurales* to whistle up, no Guatemalan army to do their bidding; so they relied, where necessary, on *pistoleros* and *guardias blancas.*

Given the variety of motives and local experiences, outcomes also varied widely. Sheridan, studying a frontier peasant community in northern Sonora, notes an atmosphere of tension but an absence of significant violence; ethnic conflict was largely absent, social mobility occurred, and the political system afforded some openings for protest and redress.[56] In contrast, the Juquila district of southern Oaxaca researched by Greenberg, as well as Schryer's Huasteca Hidalguense, both became hotbeds of violence in recent decades. The Huasteca was the site of major land seizures, political conflict and repression in the 1980s (it roughly paralleled what had happened in southern Sonora, as well as other northwestern regions a decade before); the Juquila villages were caught up in a Hobbesian war of all against all – community against community, faction against faction, family against family – in which, while no single causal factor prevailed, the growth of coffee cultivation played a major part.[57] Thus, while the Zapatista revolt of 1994 was exceptional in terms of its scale, success and sophistication, it formed part of a familiar syndrome: a growing class and ethnic tension, characterized by agrarian commercialization, peasant dispossession, land seizures, *pistolerismo*, and a rising incidence of violence and protest. In Chiapas, the PRI's legendary capacity for mediation collapsed, chiefly because the party was hijacked by local vested interests – the Chiapas *ganaderos* and their political allies – who set their face against reform, and whom the distant federal government, its eyes on the prize of NAFTA, complacently tolerated. This stands in contrast to the situation in the Huasteca or Sonora, where, in the 1970s and 1980s, reform and repression coexisted and the PRI proved capable of generating progressive, interventionist measures, rather than simply shoring up the power of hard-nosed provincial elites.

These recurrent cycles of rural protest and repression ensured that the countryside would never be at peace. The endemic conflict of the 1930s subsided somewhat, and the consolidation of the central government meant that major national schisms, like the 1940 and 1952 presidential elections, were avoided, at least until 1987–88. Mexico came to be seen as a textbook case of stable, civilian rule, contrasting with the authoritarian regimes of the southern cone. But Mexican stability, while it was not mythical, was built upon flawed foundations. National stability coexisted with – sometimes depended on – grassroots violence and repression. The latter, I would argue, helped maintain the internal discipline of the PRI, while reminding both elites and people of the perils of social conflict. Fear of civil disorder depended not just on fading memories of revolution, or the cautionary tale of Central America, but also on events taking place – peripherally, and anonymously – in Mexico itself. The PRI's appeal for *paz social* capitalized on this fear, which recent events have clearly augmented. In addition, the central government derived advantage from local conflict which, perhaps, it could not entirely stop anyway. Selective interventions by the executive, even by the federal army, reminded local actors who was boss. The president became the supreme arbiter in local quarrels which were allowed to go so far, but no further (in particular, I suspect, quarrels in northern states were not allowed to go so far as southern conflicts: good relations with the USA required that political abuses and armed collisions be mitigated in, say, Sonora, but neglected in Chiapas). A moderate infringement of the central government's theoretical monopoly of violence could therefore be tolerated, since it redounded to the discretionary power of the executive.

In light of these observations, we could finally hazard some brief comparisons with other Latin American regimes and, perhaps, ponder the significance of recent events in Mexico. As I said at the outset, Mexico, in contrast to Argentina, Brazil, Chile and Uruguay in the 1960s and 1970s, avoided military coups and 'bureaucratic–authoritarian' rule. The Mexican government prided itself on its civilian and institutional status and Mexico became a haven for political refugees from the southern cone. Mexico also avoided the prolonged popular rebellion and military repression which characterized El Salvador and Guatemala and, again, played a moderately progressive role in its relations with Central America. How, in light of my previous argument, can this (relative) commitment to civilian, institutional (and some would say democratic) government be interpreted, particularly when one considers that the Mexico of Santa Anna, Diaz, even of Obregon and Calles, did not look particularly civilian, institutional or democratic compared, say, to the Argentina of Sarmiento and Irigoyen, or Batlle's Uruguay?

Among the many arguments which can be advanced there are, I think, contrasting positive and negative approaches to be distinguished. The positive approach, which would also be the official line (and which should not be discarded simply because it is the official line), would stress Mexico's distinctive political culture, nurtured by the revolution, and committed to social reform, popular participation and institutional government. Compared to the red-baiting and racism which informed the politics of the Guatemalan ruling elite, or the doctrine of national security which, drawing on old cultural traditions,[58] justified the Argentine dirty war, Mexico's official ideology was relatively progressive, enlightened, inclusionary and reformist. This ideology, of course, is conveyed in the country's official 'public transcript', tirelessly enunciated in speeches, the press and the electronic media. Practice is another matter (as I shall mention shortly). But, like most 'public transcripts', it is not wholly hypocritical; it is sometimes translated into action (e.g. with bursts of agrarian reform); and it can to a degree constrain political actors, deterring them from actions which, like the Tlatelolco massacre of 1968, blatantly contravene the public transcript and thus carry the risk of delegitimization. (To put it differently, the gap between public transcript and public policy cannot be allowed to yawn too wide for too long, or the former will lose all legitimacy, as it did, for example, in Eastern Europe).[59] Thus, during its heyday, c. 1950–70 (a briefer heyday than often realized), the PRI did manage to live up to some of its professed ideals, while grossly reneging on others. Even under Salinas the Solidarity programme, for all its hype, bias and discretionality, represented an attempt, not wholly unsuccessful, to soften the blows of neo-liberal macro-economics and refurbish the tarnished scutcheon of presidential authority.[60] Thus, while I would not place huge explanatory weight on this factor, I think the ideology of the revolution, shaping decision-making at least to a degree, helped steer Mexico away from the outright military authoritarianism of, say, Argentina or Guatemala.

But there is also a negative argument, of probably greater force. Roughly, Mexico did not experience a shift to bureaucratic authoritarianism, with its attendant violence and repression, because it did not need to; it already possessed a more discreetly authoritarian system - 'inclusionary', civilian and institutional, but still authoritarian. A *dictablanda* à la Mexicana was the best guarantee against a *dictadura* à la Argentina (recall Vargas Llosa's notorious comment).[61] I do not want to get into the thorny question of the historical origins of southern cone 'bureaucratic authoritarian' regimes. O'Donnell's thesis – that bureaucratic authoritarianism offered the way out of a capitalist cul-de-sac, as the easy phase of import-substitution industrialization came to an end – seems overly schematic and functional, and possibly empirically wrong.[62] However, it hardly seems coincidental that the turn to authoritarianism was experienced in the more 'developed' southern cone countries, which had enjoyed competitive electoral politics since the early twentieth century (which Mexico had not). The problem of incorporating the labour movement into the political system became acute as early as the First World War; in Argentina, the subsequent advent of Peronism made the problem apparently insoluble. In Brazil and Chile, the belated incorporation of the peasantry in the 1950s and 1960s added to political competition, polarization, tension and instability. And these, in turn, aggravated the old investment/consumption dilemma: politicians bidding for electoral support in an expanding political arena were prone to print money and boost public sector employment beyond what economic logic dictated. In Mexico, by contrast, the revolution and its institutionalization produced an unusual outcome: a regime which incorporated a large chunk of civil society, particularly the trade unions and the peasantry, within its massy bulk. Labour incorporation – the Colliers' explanatory key[63] – promoted stability and controlled wage demands. Early peasant incorporation, in the 1920s and 1930s, ensured that there would not be a belated crisis of *campesino* incorporation, as in Brazil or Chile in the 1960s and 1970s. The inclusionary ideology of the Mexican revolution thus had its organizational counterpart; and the regime of the revolution – while it certainly marginalized important sectors of the population[64] – had sufficient monopolistic political power and patronage resources to maintain a broad, majoritarian coalition. It combined, as it were, Colombia's Liberal and Conservative parties in one broad church; it buried a potential Peronism deep in the entrails of the party, in the shape of the CTM.

However, maintaining this coalition involved a good deal of violence actual or threatened. Like Diaz, the PRI brandished the stick as well as the carrot. Thus, as I have briefly suggested, the regime has perpetrated, or tolerated, a constant quantum of political violence: against dissident political groups (Almazanistas, Henriquistas); against independent unions (railwaymen in the late 1950s, electricians in the mid-1970s); against journalists (Manuel Buendia being the most celebrated); against students (1968 being the most notorious); and, pervasively and endemically, against peasants, both individually and collectively. How this quantum of violence might be totalled, and how it might compare to, say, southern cone levels of repression, it is impossible to say in this short chapter. Mexican political violence appears less extreme and significant, but that is partly because it is more discreet, anonymous, prolonged and quotidian. It involves numerous small, often local, acts of violence, rather than massive, centralized campaigns of repression. It is perpetrated by freelance specialists (*pistoleros, guardias blancas, halcones*) more often than by the federal army – which may, in some cases, act as a peace-keeping force. And, since it is at odds with the public transcript, it is not shouted from the political rooftops, but officially denied, decried, evaded or overlooked. Argentinian generals may publicly justify their dirty war; Mexican generals keep their mouths shut, leaving their civilian masters – possibly genuinely concerned civilian masters like Jorge Carpizo – to do the public talking and hand-wringing. In Mexico, the public debate over Tlatelolco involves a good deal of official buckpassing; in some countries and cultures – e.g. China – it would be a question of taking the credit, rather than copping the blame. In short, the Mexican system has evolved subtle mechanisms for intimidating dissidents without recourse to full-scale repression, which would severely damage the dwindling legitimacy of the regime: Echeverría desperately sought to build bridges to the opposition after 1968; and, after its initial, inept response to the Zapatista revolt, the Salinas administration opted for dialogue rather than repression. But 1968 and 1994 were deviations from the norm, failures of an otherwise successful 'stick and carrot' system. For most of its long institutional life, the PRI – by sanctioning violence *a gotitas*, little by little, covertly, anonymously, provincially – has deterred opposition, shored up its national political monopoly, and avoided the need for dramatic and draconian repression. A regular, discreet aspirin-a-day of violence has helped prevent the major cardiac arrest of bureaucratic authoritarianism.

It is impossible, in conclusion, to overlook the recent episodes of violence which have affected Mexico: Chiapas (and lesser outbreaks elsewhere, such as Guerrero); and the assassinations of Colosio and Ruiz Massieu, *inter alia*. Chiapas – and, *a fortiori* Guerrero – are extreme cases of a recurrent problem: agrarian 'compression', popular protest and repression. Subcomandante Marcos' use of fax and modem may maximize publicity and charm the American new Left; but the roots of the Chiapas revolt run deep and even the chosen nomenclature – *Ejercito Zapatista* – suggests historical precedents and traditions. To some extent, therefore, the regime is dealing with a known quantity. The novelty of the situation resides partly in the scale and duration of the revolt (no rebel force has achieved such success since the Cristeros of the 1920s) and partly in the character of the regime which confronts it. (One might say, polemically, that it is not the Zapatistas but the Salinistas who are the revolutionaries of the 1990s.) Whereas previous governments could respond to popular protest with the traditional combination of repression, cooption and social reform (witness how the Cristero rebellion ended, in 1929, with a renewed *reparto de tierras*, a tactic which Echeverría emulated in Sonora in 1976), the present government is less well placed, is perhaps even unable, to pursue such methods. It has wound up the agrarian reform, privatized the *ejido*, placed its faith in NAFTA and neo-liberalism, and struck an alliance with big business and transnational capital. The political logic of neo-liberal macro-economics urges that the traditional peasant vote – Mexico's *voto cabreste* – be forfeited, in favour of the urban middle classes (a strategy which succeeded in August 1994). But, having embraced neo-liberalism and ditched 'populism', it will be harder for the regime to combine stick *and* carrot in its treatment of rural discontent; and, as Chiapas, Guerrero, El Barzon, and the entire logic of NAFTA suggest, that discontent is likely to wax, not wane. Chiapas is therefore a litmus test of official policy: will the PRI resuscitate traditional ('populist') policies, even at a time of renewed austerity, assuaging discontent without recourse to widespread repression? Or, as Riordan Roett seemed to say, does the new economic model require a tough response, more stick than carrot? Solidarity showed, I think, that neo-populist politics were, to a degree, and for a time, compatible with neo-liberal economics.[65] But by 1995, with renewed economic crisis and continued social tension, it has become harder to square the circle. It seems likely, therefore, that the stick will be more in evidence than the carrot.

This sombre conclusion is reinforced by the recent political assassinations. Between 1920 and 1950, inter-elite political violence declined dramatically:

presidents began to serve their terms and pick their successors without fear of rebellion; even state governors and federal legislators, victims and perpetrators of regular violence in earlier years, could now regard their jobs as relatively safe, civilian and secure.[66] *Políticos* could take coffee in the Café Tacuba without looking over their shoulders. Violence had been displaced from the *cúpulas* to the rank-and-file, from the cities to the provinces. Now, however, the *cúpulas* themselves have been reacquainted with violence; *políticos* emerging from Mexico City hotels have to look over the shoulders. The causes of this trend – if trend it is – are obviously murky, and may never be fully known. It is not even clear whether the causes are to be found within the political elite itself – as 'dinosaurs' strive to fend off reform – or whether the elite's Faustian bargain with drug traffickers is now claiming a price in excess of political connivance and tolerance. Either way (and the two are not, of course, mutually exclusive explanations), there is a certain macabre irony: if members of the elite are now shooting each other for political reasons, they are merely catching up with their rank-and-file, who have been doing this for decades. 'The soldiers die, the generals live', as the old *cacique* 'Scarface' told Paul Friedrich:[67] now the generals are dying too. And if their narco-paymasters are engaging in selective violence, removing actual threats, or discouraging potential ones, they are, in a sense, taking a leaf out of the dog-eared Mexican political manual.

Even if these trends involve a kind of perverse equity, they are worrying for the PRI: they threaten individual security; they alarm public opinion; and they suggest a breakdown in elite party discipline which has been one of the regime's longstanding strengths. External delegitimization thus combines with internal factionalism. For years, violence has trickled down, like molten lava, chiefly affecting the lower slopes of the political volcano, while the crater at the summit has remained dormant; now, we see eruptions at the top, though the pall of smoke prevents us discerning their scale or significance. It is therefore not clear whether the volcano will relapse into dormancy again, or completely blow its top.

Notes and References

1. In this chapter I shall not try to address the complex question of 'societal' violence: what Romanucci-Ross terms 'unbound' violence, i.e. violence (such as barroom brawls) where 'individuals act in their own personal behalf and not as members of a larger unit'; see Romanucci-Ross, *Conflict*, pp. 28–9. This is, for Mexico, a big subject with an extensive bibliography. It is worth noting, however, that 'societal' or 'unbound' violence cannot be neatly separated from 'political', 'bound' violence. Political and personal animosities may feed on one another; and, as archival evidence makes abundantly clear, plenty of political violence occurs when individuals get tanked up

2. Again, the boundaries of what is 'political' may be debated. My own working definition is sufficiently broad to include conflicts which involve political parties, factions, and *sindicatos*, as well as class, ethnic, religious and residential groups; it does not – for want of

space and expertise – include, say, 'patriarchal' violence (e.g. wife-beating), which some might also consider 'political'.

3. Lowenthal, *Partners in Conflict*, p. 4.

4. Martínez Assad, 'Nava', p. 61.

5. Molinar Horcasitas, *Tiempo de la legitimidad*.

6. Dating the 'heyday' of the PRI as 1952–87 arguably stretches the period: 1952 – the defeat of Henriquismo and the onset of the period of *desarrollo estabilizador* – is an appropriate starting point, but the end of the *priísta* heyday is open to debate: 1968 (Tlatelolco)? 1976 (the end-of-sexenio crisis)? 1982 (end-of-sexenio *and* economic crisis)? 1987 (the schism within the PRI leading to the 1988 election)? even 1994–95 (Chiapas, Colosio, economic crisis again)? Clearly, we are dealing with an incremental, though far from smooth, political decline; the choice of terminal date will probably require more time, hindsight and research.

7. See also Knight, 'Habitus and homicide'.

8. Hans Gadow, quoted in Knight, *Mexican Revolution* (vol. 1), p. 35.

9. Knight, *Mexican Revolution* (vol. 1), p. 49.

10. See Avila Palafox, *Revolución*, pp. 244–5; Gledhill, *Casi nada*, pp. 72–80.

11. Knight, *Mexican Revolution* (vol. 1), pp. 208–27, 333–81.

12. Actually, armed peasant protest was rarely 'spontaneous' in the sense of being sudden and unexpected; usually it had been brewing for years or decades, during which pacific forms of protest had been exhausted; but it was 'spontaneous' in the sense of being autonomous, relying on local resources, and having little to do with 'vanguard parties' or 'outside agitators' – those exogenous variables beloved of commentators from Left and Right respectively.

13. Apart from Madero himself, José Vasconcelos and Martín Luis Guzmán raised such plaints: Knight, *Mexican Revolution* (vol. 2), pp. 291, 297.

14. Knight, *Mexican Revolution* (vol. 2), pp. 13, 102.

15. Hence Machiavelli figures as both an emic reference and an etic model for Friedrich, *Princes of Naranja*, p. 195.

16. Mexico's population in 1910 was 15.2 million; in 1921 it was 14.3 million when, had the growth rate of the 1900s been maintained, it should have been around 17 million. However, the 1921 census probably seriously under-counted the population. The revolution may have resulted in a population fall of some 2 million, in terms of deaths suffered and births foregone, disease, economic hardship and outright malnutrition, especially in the later years, were the main contributors. See Knight, *Mexican Revolution* (vol. 2), pp. 419–22.

17. Knight, *Mexican Revolution* (vol. 2), pp. 397–402, on Chávez García, who, like Margarito in Azuela's *Los de abajo*, appears to have been a particularly unsocial bandit, fond of bloodshed.

18. In general, the armed phase of the revolution, while replete with casualties, does not seem to have produced much gratuitous, sadistic violence; in this, it seems to resemble the contemporary World War I. In contrast, the endemic – largely rural – violence of the 1920s and 1930s clearly did, perhaps because it attracted full-time 'career' *pistoleros*, Mexican counterparts of Colombia's sanguinary *pájaros*: e.g. Friedrich, *Princes of Naranja*, pp. 7, 156; Knight, 'Habitus and homicide'.

19. Buve, 'Peasant movements', p. 118.

20. Cobb, *Police*, p. 85.

21. Schryer, *Rancheros*, p. 79.

22. González y González, *San José de Gracia*, pp. 129–38.

23. Friedrich, *Princes of Naranja*; Romanucci-Ross, *Conflict*, pp. 14–20; González and Patiño, *Memoria campesina*, pp. 23, 69ff.

24. Foster, *Tztintzuntzán*, p. 94.

25. The central character of Guzmán's *La sombra del caudillo* is reputedly based on Amaro.

26. *Acta levantada* of Genovevo Alatorre, 22 March 1927, Dirección General de Información Política y Social (Gobernación), caja 34, 095.0–62, Archivo General de la Nación, Mexico City.

27. Schryer, *Rancheros*, pp. 89–92, 99–100.

28. Press coverage was certainly fuller post-1910; political gossip, of course, is hard to measure; but there are good – albeit somewhat intuitive – grounds for believing that the socio-political transformation wrought by the revolution involved greater political activity, participation and – one would assume – gossip.

29. Wasserman, *Persistent Oligarchs*, pp. 37, 45, 96, 127.

30. On the Prados: Jiménez Castillo, *Huáncito*, pp. 137–65; and correspondence in AGN, Fondo Presidentes–Lázaro Cárdenas, 541/1783.

31. *Caciquismo* was essentially a form of local domination, involving violence, personalism and clientelism: it could devote the means at its disposal to quite different political ends. *Caciques* therefore came in various political hues: some popular, *agrarista* and leftist (e.g. under Cárdenas), many conservative and pro-landlord. Smart *caciques* bent with the political wind; fierce ideological consistency was not a typical virtue.

32. AGN, Fondo Presidentes–Lázaro Cárdenas, 541/1783 (Ernesto Prado of Chilchota and Heliodoro Charis of Juchitan).

33. Schryer, *Rancheros*, p. 95.

34. Knight, 'Habitus and homicide'; Santos, *Memorias*.

35. Wasserman, *Persistent Oligarchs*. I mention this case in part because it is well documented, in part to dispel the notion that political violence and mayhem were essentially features of 'old', 'traditional', 'backward', 'Indian', central and southern Mexico; an assumption, sometimes grounded in the shaky soil of modernization theory, which is still frequently made today, not least by PRIistas seeking to justify electoral shenanigans in, say, Michoacan.

36. Gruening, *Mexico*, pp. 399ff.

37. Dulles, *Yesterday in Mexico*, p. 481.

38. Schryer, *Rancheros*, p. 91.

39. Meixueiro's suicide was a protest against the PRI's support for a rival (independent) candidate in a Oaxacan election. For the recent case: Sanderson, *Agrarian Populism*, p. 173. Fernando Amilpa, secretary-general of the CTM, 'managed to pick up additional adverse publicity' during the 1946 presidential election by 'knocking senseless the president of a polling booth who asked him to surrender his pistol before entering': Dickinson, Mexico City, 25 May 1948, State Department records, Internal Affairs of Mexico, 812.5043/5–2548. Much more recently, a celebrated Mexican *político* was reputedly involved in a similar incident in the car park of the United Nations building in New York.

40. In Congress, Santos 'moved like a fish in water'; and he enjoyed the esteem and respect of President Ruiz Cortines (who was no fool): Loret de Mola, *Caciques*, pp. 43, 55.

41. Brewster, 'Caciquismo'; Jacobs, 'Rancheros', pp. 76–91.

42. Márquez, 'Gonzalo N. Santos', pp. 385–94.

43. *Caciquismo* – or, if you prefer, 'boss' politics – forms part of a national political structure and is to be found in cities (e.g. in municipal government and trade unions) as well as in the countryside. It is not, therefore, an atavistic throwback or a vestigial remnant of a moribund primitive 'culture', doomed by urbanization and modernization. If its more brazen – and violent – features tend to be rural, this derives from the balance of contending political forces, the attention of the media, and, as this chapter argues, the federal government's tendency to be more concerned about its urban, metropolitan image than its rural, provincial one.

44. Raby, *Educación*, ch. 5; Burt, Veracruz, 3 February 1938, SD 812.504/1703 offers a good resumé of one particularly rough textile factory – Cocolapán, Veracruz.

45. Saragoza, *Monterrey Elite*, pp. 186–91; Bantjes, *Politics*, chs 6 and 7; Pansters, *Politics and Power*, ch 3.

46. Loret de Mola, *Caciques*, ch. 1. A collective example of survival is afforded by the celebrated Atlacomulca group of Mexico State, who have succesfully straddled national and local politics, producing a clutch of *caciques* and cabinet ministers.

47. See Gilbert, 'Caciquismo'.

48. Juchitan is a classic case of cycles of *caciquismo*, protest and renovation.

49. Schryer, *Ethnicity*, pp. 124, 140, 143; Greenberg, *Blood Ties*, pp. 195–6, on the recruitment of *pistoleros*.

50. I shall not try to plumb the murky depths of *machismo*, nor to evaluate its contribution to political violence *per se*, suffice to say, *macho* attitudes – irrespective of whether these are cause or effect of antecedent conditions – fit snugly within the *política cochina* which I am discussing. On *machismo* and violence, see Romanucci-Ross, *Conflict*, pp. 76–8; Friedrich, *Princes of Naranja*, pp. 182–3; Greenberg, *Blood Ties*, pp. 63–4.

51. Tutino, *Insurrection*.

52. Aguirre Beltrán, *Regiones de refugio*.

53. Paré, *Proletariado*.

54. I may exaggerate somewhat, but not a lot. The Porfirian regime was very much a government of landlords, by landlords, for landlords; or, to put it differently, the Porfirian state enjoyed only a very limited 'relative autonomy' *vis-à-vis* the dominant class. The revolution by no means instituted a 'worker-and-peasant' state; but it did severely weaken the landlord class's political leverage and, to a degree, enhance the state's relative autonomy of all social classes.

55. The relationship of local landlords to the political apparatus would repay further research: in some cases, landlords continued to exert control through proxies; in some, they held power themselves; in some, they were politically marginalized. Schryer, *Rancheros*, p. 138, shows how, by the 1970s, rich *rancheros* in the Huasteca Hidalguense no longer had to soil their hands in local politics; the system respected their interests anyway. On local reactions to federal organizations and agencies, see Jiménez Castillo, *Huáncito*, pp. 267–88.

56. Sheridan, *Where the Dove Calls*, pp. 143–5.

57. Schryer, *Ethnicity*, Greenberg, *Blood Ties*. The presence of coffee in Juquila – as well as in Schryer's Huasteca Hidalguense – raises some interesting comparative questions, given the correlation between coffee cultivation and the regions most affected by the Colombian Violencia, and the importance of coffee in Peru's La Convención Valley. Coffee is a crop well suited to peasant cultivation; it grows well on temperate hillsides, often previously marginal to arable farming; it is therefore something of a frontier crop; and it enjoyed buoyant markets through the 1940s and 1950s. It seems reasonable to infer that these factors could lead to acute tension between peasant cultivators, rival rich landlords, and commercial middlemen, within the context of recent, sometimes ill-defined, areas of settlement.

58. Shumway, *Invention of Argentina*.

59. Przeworski, *Democracy*, pp. 2–6.

60. Dresser, 'Bringing the poor back in', pp. 143–66.

61. To the effect that the PRI was the 'perfect dictatorship'. This glib phrase overlooks the fact that, even if the Mexican regime *were* a *dictablanda*, a *dictablanda*, is still significantly different from a *dictadura*.

62. Collier, *New Authoritarianism*.

63. Collier and Collier, *Shaping the Political Arena*.

64. For example, political Catholics and middle-class liberals.

65. Dresser, 'Bringing the poor back in'; Knight, 'Obrigo', pp. 69–72.

66. There have, of course, been some unfortunate plane and car crashes, Carlos Madrazo and Manuel Clouthier being notable victims. The evidence does not allow us to assume that these were political assassinations, although the allegation has been made.

67. Friedrich, *Princes of Naranja*, p. 11.

SIX

The Fear of Indifference: Combatants' Anxieties about the Political Identity of Civilians during Argentina's Dirty War

ANTONIUS ROBBEN

Armed combatants, locked in violent dispute, expect civilians to take a stand on their conflict. They want people to be forthright about their political sympathies, and declare who has truth, justice and morality on their side. As is the case in all major outbreaks of violence, so too in Argentina during the 1970s, each party believed that its use of violence was justified. The commanders of the armed forces and the guerrilla organizations considered it immoral *not* to choose sides. Each party tried to draw the Argentine people into its camp and persuade them that the use of violence was of historical necessity. This public discourse was so predominant that it concealed the deep anxiety which hesitant civilians provoked among the disputants of power.

Much has been written about state terror and cultures of fear in Latin America, but next to nothing has appeared about the fears and anxieties of the protagonists of violence themselves. These fears and anxieties, however, are dwarfed in comparison to the immeasurably greater suffering of the civilian victims of state terror. Nevertheless, such sentiments among the victimizers deserve to be studied, because an analysis of the complex and ambiguous relation between combating forces and a civilian population will add another dimension to our understanding of Latin American societies of fear.

Seemingly indifferent civilians provoked contempt and anxiety, as well as fear and uneasy feelings, among the government forces and revolutionary guerrilla forces in Argentina during their conflict in the 1970s. This fear was not a fear of terror – of which, in different degrees, they were its masters – but a fear of defeat, fed by an anxiety over the large number of un-committed civilians. The Argentine protagonists were troubled by people who refused to rally actively behind either party. These uncommitted civilians fell outside the social categories that had been established with so much bloodshed. They undermined the structure of enmity that characterized a violent conflict presented as an historical inevitability. Their aloofness, it was felt by the protagonists, could result in a defeat by default. Such civilians were the inversion of the men of action, the military and the revolutionary; those who took their own fate and that of others in their hands. I shall use Derrida's neology *undecidable* to describe those civilians.[1] I prefer the term undecidable to the term indecisive, because undecidability does not necessarily imply indecisiveness, passiveness or even paralysis. Undecidability can also be motivated by an active moral stance against violence. The majority of the Argentine people may be characterized as uncommitted undecidables. The Argentine human rights activists who actively opposed the violence of the military and guerrilla forces represent the involved undecidables.

The Emergence of Political Violence in Argentina

'War', so writes Elaine Scarry, 'is [...] a huge structure for the derealization of cultural constructs and, simultaneously, for their eventual reconstitution. The purpose of the war is to designate as an outcome which of the two competing cultural constructs will by both sides be allowed to become real.'[2] The revolution which the Argentine *guerrilleros* tried to achieve in the 1970s, and the cultural and political institutions which the military were defending, were conflicting cultural constructs.[3] Theirs was not a contest about power but a contest about the space of culture, about the cultural confines and conditions within which the Argentine people could lead their lives. These lives were manifested in social institutions, conventions and mores, beliefs, symbols and meanings. In the words of General Díaz Bessone: 'I insist that war becomes inevitable when values are diametrically opposed. There is no other way. They cannot coexist. That's why war intervenes, because the values are contrary [...] Subversion means the changing of values, the changing of a national culture. Culture is not just sculpture and painting. No, no. Culture is everything.'[4] The Argentine military officers and revolutionaries risked their lives to impose a particular cultural construct on society. Victory could be achieved only at the cost of great sacrifice, because both parties were convinced that the political ills of Argentina were deep-seated.

Political opposition as enmity can be traced back in Argentina to the first half of the nineteenth century, when civil wars plagued a country that at the same time was fighting a war of independence from Spain. Regional *caudillos* disputed the hegemony of the post-colonial elite in Buenos Aires, and violent conflicts about the terms of government and political representation were waged for decades between federalists and centralists. Argentina was to suffer several more outbreaks of violence during the twentieth century in the form of *coups d'état* and bloodily repressed labour strikes and student demonstrations. The political violence reached an unprecedented level during the

1970s, a period which is comparable only to the civil wars of the nineteenth century. Political tensions that had been mounting since the overthrow of the populist president Juan Domingo Perón in a military coup in 1955, gestated into stark enmity during the 1960s as military dictators tightened their grip on the working class and the student body. This political conflict erupted into open violence during the 1970s.

Following the overthrow of Perón, there was a ground swell of political dissatisfaction in Argentina.[5] The continued frustration among the working class at the proscription of the Peronist movement, and the emergence of a class-conscious younger generation that desired political participation, coalesced between 1969 and 1973 into an unstoppable force of opposition to the then ruling military government. Labour unions organized massive strikes. Peronist youth organizations held street demonstrations, and a handful of small paramilitary groups, under the encouragement of Perón, bombed large foreign-owned corporations and would for several hours take control of small towns to create a general sense of insecurity in the country. This popular mobilization was effective. By late 1972 the military government negotiated with Perón about the cession of power through free elections in March 1973.

Several Marxist groups rode the wave of the Peronist protest with success, and managed to attract a small but highly motivated following. They believed that the revolutionary consciousness of the popular masses had reached a decisive level. The People's Revolutionary Army (ERP) – the military branch of the Workers Revolutionary Party (PRT) – emerged from the early-1970s as the most important guerrilla organization.[6] This organization continued with its armed attacks, even after the dictatorship in 1973 made place for a democratic Peronist government. The commanders were convinced that a popular insurrection was within reach, although they knew that it might still take years before a final victory could be achieved. The Marxist organizations based this optimism on what they believed to be an objective and scientific assessment of the political forces in Argentina.[7] The former ERP member Pedro Cazes Camarero explained this political scenario two decades later as follows:

> What happens is that in addition to this [assessment] we believed in a dialectic of power accumulation. This dialectic of power accumulation occurred partly because the fight against the enemy would tend to strengthen instead of weaken us. Even though we would receive some blows, we would produce a visible political effect that would tend to polarize the political forces around our own force.[8]

This belief in the inevitability of a dialectical political process and the certainty of a revolutionary outcome was communicated to the armed forces and the Argentine people: 'We must attack the enemy army at once, now, always, until it is destroyed, in order to have a real, popular, workers' government.'[9]

The armed forces took such threats seriously. Ever since the 1959 Cuban revolution, and especially after the Argentine Ernesto 'Che' Guevara had begun a guerrilla war in Bolivia in the mid-1960s, the Argentine military had foreseen the likelihood of similar actions on native soil. The ERP guerrilla attack in September 1973 on an army base near Buenos Aires convinced the armed forces that the turn to democracy had not appeased Argentine society.

The political atmosphere was grim at the end of 1973. Perón could not provide the political stability desired by the military and the ruling class. There was a factional confrontation inside the Peronist movement that manifested itself in: political machinations and in-fighting among the government, street protests, strikes, the intimidation of union members and sectarian assassinations.[10] Meanwhile, the Marxist organization PRT-ERP announced that it was setting up a liberated zone in the northern province of Tucumán, and that it would continue attacking military bases in the rest of the country. The armed forces were feeling increasingly vulnerable, and began to prepare for a counter-attack.

The spiral of violence moved into higher gear after the death of Perón on 1 July 1974. There were more than 2,000 armed actions and over 1,000 people were killed in political violence between July 1974 and March 1976.[11] As the armed forces concentrated on fighting the Marxist organizations, the Peronist right and the police confronted the Peronist left, and in particular a large paramilitary organization called the Montoneros.[12] The military stepped up their counter-insurgency in mid-1974, capturing, torturing and executing *guerrilleros*. The People's Revolutionary Army (ERP) announced the indiscriminate killing of military officers in reprisal. The death of an army captain and his three-year-old daughter in December 1974 left a lasting impression on the military, and convinced the high command that the time for more decisive action had arrived. In the many interviews with commanding officers of the military government which I conducted fifteen years later, there still emerged a tremendous fear, if not panic, that their families could have fallen victim to these reprisals. The death of General Cardozo, head of the federal police, who was killed in 1976 by a bomb placed under his bed by his daughter's classmate, was a terrifying example of this fear. Rear-Admiral Horácio Mayorga recalled how he was ordered to change residence every fifteen days after he retired from the navy in 1974:

> What you Europeans will never understand is why the anti-subversive war was
> so unbearable for us. You are talking to a typical admiral. They tried to kidnap
> my daughter. They went to look for her at her school. They fired at the guards
> in front of my house, and they let me know in Puerto Belgrano that my maid
> had been picked up at the Bible class in the church next door by a *guerrillero*
> from the ERP in order to place a bomb [under my bed], just as had happened
> to Cardozo.[13]

The belligerence of the parties in conflict overshadowed the calls for moderation coming from prominent members in society on both sides of the political divide. A public discourse emerged in revolutionary pamphlets in which the military were called exploiters, worms, vermin, and parasites of the people, while the revolutionaries were described in the national newspapers as savages, subversives, terrorists, nihilists, nomads of cruelty, and drifters of destruction. The use of derogatory terms served to dehumanize the enemy and define oneself as supremely human, notwithstanding the violence that this humanity entailed. These terms set an irreconcilable tone that reached its height in a call to arms. The incensed vocabulary objectified the opponent, who became little more than a dangerous obstacle that stood in the way of a glorious future. The parties that contributed to the volatile atmosphere of the years immediately preceding the *coup d'état* of 1976, framed their violent acts in a discourse of war with apocalyptic overtones. The combination of a bellicose discourse, violent acts, antagonistic ideologies and a fear of each other's military potential formed the complex context within which enemies were named and targets defined. In 1975, the armed conflict had culminated in the hostile opposition of two parties, with the combined armed forces and police on one side, and on the other side a loose alliance of revolutionary groups with the ERP and Montoneros as the principal exponents. Both sides were determined to fight it out till the end.

The Structure of Enmity in the 1970s

The Argentine armed forces and the revolutionary organizations have been portrayed by some political analysts and actors as two demons who were involved in a voracious dialectic of mutual destruction entirely disengaged from the wider political and historical context.[14] The human rights activist Graciela Fernández Meijide makes the following observation:

> In this society they always try to divide things into two, into two positions. Thus, you have the theory of the two demons, the two pavements (*veredas*), and the two parties (*bandas*). This is for me all very Manichaean, totally Manichaean, and it doesn't help at all the development of a third position which would certainly comprise the majority of Argentines.[15]

Fernández Meijide points at the Manichaean aspect of Argentine culture, which continues to create new conflicts and oppositions without resolving previous ones. For this reason, it would be a simplification to characterize the complex political situation in Argentina during the 1970s as only an armed conflict between the military and the revolutionaries. The Argentine revolutionary organizations were certainly not the equivalent of the Italian Red Brigades or the German Red Army Faction which operated in a political vacuum, far from the concerns of the Italian and German working class. Rather the Argentine revolutionaries operated in a general climate of popular commotion. 'The violence from above generates the violence from below', was a popular slogan at the time. Tensions took place in factories, universities, parishes, army barracks and on the streets of the major industrial cities. The military denounced communist agitation and foreign infiltration, while the revolutionary organizations pointed at the exploitation of the working class by imperialist world powers and the national bourgeoisie as the causes of violence. These broad denunciations comprised the threat perception to the cultural constructs that each party tried to impose with violence on Argentine society.

An analysis of the public discourse shows that the threat perception remained the same during the 1970s – communism versus capitalist imperialism – but that the operational target changed from year to year according to shifting political forces.[16] Enemies come into existence when the fear about a perceived threat is channelled into violent action towards a specific target. The threat was seen as geo-political but the enemy was identified as domestic, not so much as a fifth column collaborating with a foreign power, but more as an internal enemy coopted by an ideology that served foreign interests, either capitalist or communist. The notion of a domestic enemy dominated the selection of targets, turned virtually everybody into a potential suspect, and pulled the conflict into a shadowy struggle about national culture and identity. This situation brings to mind Ernesto Sábato's *On Heroes and Tombs*, that mesmerizing account of paranoia and conspiracy: 'Everyone was mistrustful of everyone else, people spoke different languages, hearts did not beat as one (as happens during certain national wars, certain collective triumphs); they were two nations in the same country, and those nations were mortal enemies; they eyed each other grimly, there was rancor between them.'[17] The rancour of the revolutionary organizations was bred from a class-hatred that found its outlet in paramilitary actions. The revolutionary Peronist organizations, of which the Montoneros had become the most powerful, and the Marxist guerrilla organizations, especially the PRT-ERP, had virtually the same threat perception: 'Imperialism, monopolies, native oligarchies, active anti-Peronists [*gorilas activas*], the traitors of the [popular] Front and the [Peronist] Movement, and the remainder of the pro-imperialist clique.'[18] Everyone was a threat who was not considered to be on the side of the people, because 'where the people are not, there are only the antipeople'.[19] The People's Revolutionary Army (ERP) and the Montoneros regarded themselves as the incarnation of the Argentine people, and both considered imperialism and capitalism as the causes of Argentina's economic dependence in the world. The two organizations pursued other political ends, but their ideological differences would become relevant only after the present situation had been changed. Both groups tried to achieve their respective goals by attacking multinational corporations, banks, major national industries and the police. The Montoneros refrained during 1973 and 1974 from assaults on the military, focusing on the Peronist right instead, but they joined the ERP in 1975 in attacking the, as they called it, praetorian guard of the ruling class.

In late-1975 the Montoneros began to attack army bases, and naval and air force installations. This coordination of military actions between the two revolutionary organizations was, in the eyes of the military, a decisive but fatal step that called for all-out repression.

The foundation for the systematic assault on the revolutionary left was laid in February 1975, when a secret decree ordered the army to annihilate the small encampments of the Marxist insurgents in Tucumán. With considerable historical dramatism, the campaign was called Operation Independence. Operation Independence was a tactical breakthrough. The commander, General Vilas, argued that the most effective way to eradicate the guerrillas was not just to attack them in the hills and woods of Tucumán, but in particular to isolate the combatants from the people who offered them support.[20] Commander General Vilas reversed Mao Zedong's dictum that the guerrilla fighter had to operate like a fish in the water. This repressive tactic consisted of killing the fish by draining the water. Special task forces (*grupos de tarea*) raided houses and abducted suspects, while regular, uniformed counter-insurgency units combed the sparsely populated rural areas. This tactic proved so successful that it was employed in the rest of the country one year later.

The new counter-insurgency strategy transformed the theatre of operations into a diffuse environment of suspicion, where any person might be accused of collaborating with the enemy. The boundary between friend and foe was shifting dramatically. Torture was the judge that decided the fate of people, and fear was the punishment meted out to all alike.

The hills of Tucumán were soon replaced by the streets of Buenos Aires, Córdoba, Rosário and La Plata as the repression was secretly extended in October 1975 to 'annihilate the operations of subversive elements in the entire territory of the country'.[21] The decree called for a coherent plan of action with clear targets that allowed the army to organize the provisional undercover actions that had been carried out since at least late-1974. The confrontation had polarized into two opposing parties with on one side the combined security forces of police and armed forces, and on the other side a loose alliance of revolutionary guerrilla organizations. These two opponents were by no means of equal strength, but both went into the fight with the conviction that they would be victorious.

This division into two hostile camps characterizes most armed conflicts, according to Scarry: '[The] participants enter into a structure that is a self-cancelling duality. They enter into a formal duality, but one understood by all to be temporary and intolerable.'[22] Each party tries to out-injure its opponent, so that the victorious can impose their conditions on the defeated. Hostile parties should not be defined narrowly in terms of commanders and combatants, but each side tries to draw the rest of society into the conflict. The physical, political and ideological support of the great mass of people – many of whom would prefer simply to carry on with their lives – can be decisive for the final victory. Nobody remains untouched by the violence, as even those who succeed in avoiding any active incorporation can become victims. Societies that fracture along hostile rifts, as was the case in Argentina during the 1970s, deny all grounds for neutrality.

The guerrilla organizations regarded an enemy–foe division in Argentine society as the inevitable outcome of their revolutionary struggle. There was no legitimate middle ground between the two opposed parties: 'The sharpening of the repression and the beginning of a generalized civil war will polarize the camps and eliminate intermediary positions.'[23] Political violence was intended to accelerate the polarization of Argentine society. The armed forces also believed that the violent confrontation was unavoidable.

Important as Scarry's definition of war as a self-cancelling duality is in understanding the clash of opposing cultural constructs, this structure of enmity is a construct in itself. This social construction of enmity becomes visible in the anxieties about the presence of undecidables. Undecidables challenge existing and utopian cultural constructs by adhering to none, and undermine the inevitability of the structure of enmity. The many Argentines who did not want to become involved in the incipient civil war that was waged during the 1970s worried the parties in conflict considerably.

Enemy, Friend and Indifferent

The Argentine guerrilla organizations viewed the human rights organizations with ambiguity. They were praised for bringing the human and civil rights violations of the government forces to public attention, but were regarded privately as bourgeois institutions that failed to see the need for justified revolutionary violence. For instance, the journalist-writer Osvaldo Bayer called fellow-intellectuals to account. Bayer argued that the military were successful in their harsh repression because most Argentines applauded them with enthusiasm, guarded an accessory silence or waged a 'constructive' opposition by maintaining a dialogue with the dictatorship. He denounced the 'neutralist line' of certain politicians and intellectuals who declared that they were 'against violence from whatever brand' and were eager to show that they were free from 'subversive or communist ideas'.[24] Former president Raúl Alfonsín and the writer Ernesto Sábato were mentioned as notable examples of those despicable neutrals. The voices of moderation and dialogue who wished to bring the hostilities to a halt could, apparently, not be tolerated by the parties in conflict.

The official government discourse also departed from a belief in an inevitable polarization of Argentine society. Whereas in 1975 the armed combatants were still targeted as the principal enemy, in 1976 the military began to include so-called ideologues and sympathizers. General Vilas, who had left Tucumán and was stationed in the Patagonian province of Bahia Blanca, declared in August 1976: 'The fight against subversion [...] has been carried on until now against the visible head, the subversive delinquent, but not against the ideologue who generates, forms, and molds this new class of delinquents.'[25]

The targets were now to be found at both the armed and the ideological fronts. Military doctrine, which was influenced considerably by the counter-insurgency practices of the French during the wars of independence in Algeria and Indo-China, taught the Argentine military that guerrilla warfare was always waged on these two fronts. A 1967 text stated that 'Although it is true that the objective of the subversion is the mind of man, it is no less true that for its conquest it uses both weapons and ideas. As a consequence, there are two camps in which the subversion develops itself: the mental battle and the armed battle.'[26] The military were aware that this much more inclusive enemy definition implied a considerable adjustment of public opinion which still viewed war as the confrontation of two regular armies. Members of the military junta emphasized over and again during 1976, 1977 and 1978 that 'not only he who attacks with a bomb, a gun, or carries out a kidnapping is an aggressor, but also he who on the level of ideas wants to change our way of life'.[27] By 1977, ideologues were said to be even more dangerous than combatants: 'I am much more concerned about an ideologue than a combatant; the combatant is dangerous because he is destructive, because his bomb may end many lives. But the ideologue is the one who poisons, who robs children, who destroys the family, and who may create chaos.'[28]

Who were considered ideologues and who sympathizers? Did they mean the political strategists of the guerrilla organizations or the editors of clandestine papers such as *El Combatiente, Estrella Roja* or *Evita Montonera* who, with their vitriolic pens, tried to incite the Argentine people to a popular uprising? Jaime Swart, a minister of the Buenos Aires provincial government, specified that the ideologues were 'politicians, priests, journalists, and professors from all levels of education'.[29] Everyone who was involved in any sort of political activism, everyone who called publicly for social justice and respect for civil and human rights, could be branded as an ideologue. Sympathizers were all those who felt some affinity for the utopian ideals of the revolutionary left. An overwhelming majority of the 10,000–30,000 'disappeared' of the years of repression were labelled as ideologues and sympathizers, many of whom never brandished a weapon or participated in any armed assault. The military regarded them as dangerous because they were considered responsible for spreading subversive ideas, distributing illegal pamphlets, providing shelter and assistance to *guerrilleros*, or were believed to pertain to the large pool of people from which the guerrilla organizations drew their recruits.

All those who did not openly profess to be on the side of the military were regarded as supporting the enemy: 'The enemy are not only the terrorists, but the enemies of the Republic are also the impatient, those who place sectorial interests above the country, the frightened, and the indifferent.'[30] This incorporation of the entire Argentine nation into the conflict went even so far that General Ibérico Saint-Jean, the governor of the province of Buenos Aires, declared in May 1976: 'First we will kill all the subversives; then we will kill their collaborators; then [...] their sympathizers, then [...] those who remain indifferent; and finally we will kill the timid.'[31]

This lumping together of the indifferent, the frightened and the timid with enemy combatants, ideologues and collaborators was a brutal attempt to impose the structure of enmity on a large segment of Argentine society that fell outside the self-cancelling duality. In the eyes of the combatants, the indifferent refused to commit themselves to the armed contest, while the frightened and timid were fleeing from the open hostility to a self-absorbed private world. The indifferent, the timid and the frightened did not constitute a military or political threat but a conceptual and moral threat, a threat to the oppositional meaning of enmity and the partisan morality it entailed. They showed that the violence was not inevitable, but a product of human choice and making. Whereas the enemy became defined and definable through political violence, the indifferent escaped the logic of difference and became unclassifiable. They had become, in Douglas's terms, 'anomalies' and in Derrida's terminology, 'undecidables' who undermined the taken for granted opposition of enemy and friend.[32] Bauman observes in this connection:

> They are that 'third element' which should not be. The true hybrids, the monsters: not just unclassified, but unclassifiable. They therefore do not question this one [friend–foe] opposition here and now: they question oppositions as such, the very principle of the opposition, the plausibility of dichotomy it suggests. They unmask the brittle artificiality of division – they destroy the world.[33]

The indifferent undermined through their aloofness a duality that had been proclaimed as fundamental to society and, even more threatening, undermined the moral hierarchy of good versus evil that was implied by the opposition of enemy and friend.

Derrida argues that dichotomies, such as life and death, good and evil, culture and nature, soul and body, male and female, speech and writing, master and servant, and inside and outside, are all hierarchized cultural constructions in which the former pole is treated as being superior to the latter. Against these dichotomies, Derrida places so-called undecidables with contradictory meanings whose signified meanings can be derived only from their syntactical relations. Undecidables have 'false' properties that resist their inclusion in binary oppositions, yet without constituting a separate third term. Instead, they disorganize these dichotomies by inhabiting them.[34] Building on Freud's pathbreaking interpretation of *das Unheimliche* (the uncanny), Derrida draws attention to other words with antithetical meanings. For example, the Greek word *pharmakon* means poison, venom and spell, but also remedy, medicine and philtre. Its ambivalence is comparable to the English word drug which in colloquial speech refers both to a beneficial medicine and a harmful narcotic. Similarly, the German noun *Gift* means both poison and gift or present.[35]

Derrida's lexical deconstruction of the Greek word *pharmakon* leads him to the word *pharmakos* which means wizard, magician, poisoner and scapegoat. The wizard is the lord of the occult who lives between darkness and light, on the border of reality and imagination. He can cure and he can poison. The scapegoat also lives at the margins of society. The scapegoat is the incarnation of the *pharmakon*: 'Beneficial in so far as he cures – and for that, venerated and cared for – harmful insofar as he incarnates the powers of evil – and for that, feared and treated with caution.'[36] In ancient Greece, slaves, criminals, paupers and the disfigured were used as scapegoats. Outcasts and marginals in Athens were kept at public expense to be sacrificed as scapegoats when the city was overtaken by plagues, famines and droughts.[37] The scapegoat was the innocent victim whose death was supposed to restore the natural and social order. 'Scapegoat indicates both the innocence of the victims, the collective polarization in opposition to them, and the collective end result of that polarization', states Girard.[38] The frightened common people are not blamed for the violence itself but, being neither friend nor foe, are accused of placing themselves outside the established oppositional structure, upsetting the partitioning of society in hostile camps by unmasking it as a social construction, and threatening the social (dis)order by their ambivalence and indeterminacy: 'Difference that exists outside the system is terrifying because it reveals the truth of the system, its relativity, its fragility, and its morality.'[39] One might very well argue that Argentina's indifferent were used as scapegoats for the political conflict, were it not that they were not persecuted to restore a peaceful order but to maintain a polarized order of destruction.

Undecidables and the Uncanny

By considering undecidables as enemies of Argentine society, it became increasingly difficult for the warring parties during the mid-1970s to tell friend from foe, and even to discover whether their own bellicose selves had not become subverted. The enemy had become so diffuse that the Argentine armed forces became uncertain about their own identity, and began to define themselves through the contours of their opponent. Oneself was everything that the enemy was not. Brigadier-General Agosti proclaimed in 1978: 'Now we recognize our enemies. We know how they act and we know their objectives. We have proven that they are fundamentally different from us, some in their behavior, others conceptually and ideologically. When we have doubts about our own identity, we can find it by analyzing the identity of our enemy.'[40] The enemy had advanced to the perimeters of the self. The enemy was not just the one who attacked or subverted society, the one who infiltrated and poisoned one's family, but the enemy was the negation of the self. A self which could only be protected from total collapse by making a united stand. The people had to become a standing force against the subversion in which 'every citizen [is] dressed, in the inmost of his heart, in the combat uniform that the gravity of the hour demands from us all'.[41]

The Marxist revolutionary organizations also began to have doubts about their identity as the conflict progressed and the number of casualties increased. The losses were attributed to a faltering loyalty, ideological purity and the suspicious class background of members and leaders. The Marxist PRT-ERP promoted members of undisputable working-class origins to commanding positions. Identity became defined as a self shaped by working-class parents and matured through revolutionary struggle.

The Peronist Montoneros were equally concerned about their identity. They tried to instill its members with a revolutionary spirit, and instituted tribunals to enforce the political doctrine. One notable case is the fate of Tulio Valenzuela, a Montonero officer who was captured by the Argentine army in 1978. In order to save the lives of his wife and himself, he pretended to go along with a plan to assassinate Mario Firmenich, the First Commander of the Montoneros. Valenzuela was to lead an infiltrator to Firmenich's hideout in Mexico. Once in Mexico, Valenzuela escaped from his captors, warned Firmenich about the plot, and prevented the liquidation. But the Montonero commanders wondered about Valenzuela. Who is he? Is he a loyal member who against all odds thwarted the decapitation of the movement or is he a turncoat? On whose side does he stand? Valenzuela was court-martialled and convicted of treason. He was not executed, because of obvious extenuating circumstances, but degraded to second lieutenant and ordered to provide self-criticism. Valenzuela criticized himself for his arrogance in believing that he could singlehandedly combat the enemy from within, for violating the revolutionary doctrine, and for trying to reconcile his personal interests with the interests of the revolutionary movement. Demonstrating his loyalty to the guerrilla organization in a near-suicidal mission, he entered Argentina with false documents to continue the resistance against the dictatorship. Soon, he was caught and killed.[42]

In the eyes of the military and the guerrilla, society had to be placed ahead of the self if both were to survive. A self could be protected from total collapse only if society would make a united stand, either on the left or on the right. Every man and woman had to be mobilized in this war and be incorporated in the national forces of defence or, according to the guerrilla leaders, into a popular militia. If such national union could be achieved by either party, then the opponent would be facing an invincible force.

The discourse of enmity was a narrative about difference. This narrative emerged from opposed cultural conceptions about self and society, from opposed conceptions about how to organize Argentina, its political institutions and national identity. Violence became the idiom to achieve the society which both parties, in their messianism and utopianism, believed the Argentine people intensely desired. This narrative had to be sustained during the armed contest, not only to justify the use of force, but also to impel the parties to action, sharpen their political views, and maintain the desire to kill fellow human beings defined as the negation of one's own existence.

The German political philosopher Carl Schmitt, an avowed Nazi, defined the enemy as the Other who is existentially so different that serious conflicts with him or her cannot be arbitrated by an impartial third party. He wrote that 'War sprouts from enmity because it is the existential negation of another being'.[43] This conception of the enemy as the negation of self may lead to the fatal conclusion that therefore enmity is intrinsic to society, and that all its enemies should be eliminated to guarantee the survival of society.

The presence of an undecidable majority in Argentina, which seemed indifferent to the political conflict, heightened anxiety about possible defeat. The bellicose enemy could at least be dealt with since its self was the diametrical opposite of one's own realization in the world. The indifferent and human rights activists, instead, sowed chaos in the paradoxal order of enmity and, as Langer has said: '[Man] can adapt himself somehow to anything his imagination can cope with; but he cannot deal with Chaos. Because his characteristic function and highest asset is conception, his greatest fright is to meet what he cannot construe – the "uncanny," as it is popularly called.'[44] The undecidables were not for one party and against another. They were neither different nor the same. They were familiar, yet strange. They not only threatened the antagonistic structure of enemy and friend, but manifested an ambiguous and obscure self. This indeterminacy and strangeness made them evoke a feeling which Langer calls the uncanny, *das Unheimliche*.

Unheimlich means terrible, gruesome, fearful and strange. Some of its many meanings make it coincide with its opposite *das Heimliche*. *Heimlich* means homely, intimate, familiar and private, but also hidden, secret and concealed. *Das Unheimliche* 'is that class of the frightening which leads back to what is known of old and long familiar'.[45] In the same sense, undecidables provoke feelings of anxiety, strangeness and uncanniness because they reveal what is supposed to remain hidden, namely that social structures, whether structures of enmity or structures of order, are cultural constructions.

Julia Kristeva has argued that the stranger provokes feelings of uncanniness because he or she is the incarnation of our hidden self: 'The other is my [own] unconscious.'[46] Undecidables are so frightening and provoke such contempt because people project on them the darker side of their own unconscious. The undecidable does not demarcate the self from its inversion, and appears not to choose between good or bad. He or she seems to erase the boundaries of a moral universe, undermines people's faith in absolute truth, ethics and justice, and thus seems to be a stranger to society.

Violence and Morality

Being an undecidable does not necessarily entail passivity in the face of political violence, because such a position cannot suspend questions of morality. On the contrary, questions of morality can become more urgent in times of conflict because routine social codes and practices with their embedded morality have been abandoned. Most civilians will try to carry on with their lives in times of violence by bowing to the conditions imposed on them. They may have their private sympathies in a conflict but do not feel sufficiently committed to become actively involved. They are the uncommitted undecidables whom the Argentine military denounced as the frightened, the timid and the indifferent. Their inclusion among the enemy reveals an unconscious apprehension about an opposition proclaimed as fundamental. The indifferent occupied an unclassifiable position. They challenged the taken for granted opposition of enemy and foe by undermining its inevitability.

However, undecidables may also fight the conditions that society tries to impose on them. In Argentina, some undecidables became so troubled by the violence that they became actively involved in human rights organizations at great personal risk. These brave men and women became vocal undecidables who chose to stand between two fires. They condemned the violence as senseless and demanded that the human and civil rights of the citizens were to be respected.

Social conflicts and human suffering are the inevitabilities of life, but they remain of human making and unmaking. The decision to be an undecidable in a violent conflict does not make people into bystanders, but implicates them in the violence by challenging the totalizing destruction of difference in a society pervaded by fear. Fear was sowed by the military and the revolutionaries, but the combatants were not free of fear themselves. The undecidables aroused feelings of anxiety and uncanniness which threatened to undermine the unquestioned use of violence in the bosom of Argentine society. The majority of the civilian population was criticized for being unpatriotic, while human rights activists were accused of sabotaging a just war. They reminded the parties in conflict that social interaction, including violence, has always a moral dimension and that even enmity is a social construction. These demystifications provoked such profound feelings of uncanniness among the parties in conflict because they did not confirm their fundamental difference but revealed their common basis.

Notes and References

The research in Argentina on which this chapter is based was carried out between April 1989 and July 1991, and made possible by grants from the National Science Foundation and the Harry Frank Guggenheim Foundation.

1. See Derrida, *Disseminations*; Derrida, *Positions*.

2. See Scarry, *The Body in Pain*, p. 137.

3. The political violence of the 1970s or, more narrowly, the military rule of Argentina between 1976 and 1983, has been described with a confusing array of names that each betray different imputed causes, conditions and consequences. The military have used terms such as dirty war, anti-revolutionary war, fight against the subversion, and the Process of National Reorganization. Human rights groups talk about state terror, repression and military dictatorship. Former revolutionary organizations employ terms used by human rights groups, but also talk about civil war, war of liberation and anti-imperialist struggle. Whether the violence of the 1970s is described with the term anti-revolutionary war, civil war, or state terror is important for these groups because each designation implies a different moral and historical judgement that may turn patriots into oppressors, victims into ideologues, and heroes into subversives.

4. Author's interview with General Díaz Bessone on 12 June 1989.

5. See Crassweller, *Perón and the Enigmas*; James, *Resistence and Integration*; Munck, *Argentina*; Page, *Perón: A Biography*.

6. See Mattini, *Hombres y mujeres*; Santucho, *Los ultimos Guevaristas*; Seoane, *Todo o nada*.

7. Hannah Arendt's critique of ideology (Arendt, *Origins of Totalitarianism*, p. 469) applies here as much to the revolutionaries as to the military leaders who justified the 1976 *coup d'état* as a new beginning: 'Ideologies pretend to know the mysteries of the whole historical process – the secrets of the past, the intricacies of the future – because of the logic inherent in their respective ideas. Ideologies are never interested in the miracle of being. They are historical, concerned with becoming and perishing, with the rise and fall of cultures, even if they try to explain history by some "law of nature".'

8. Author's interview with former ERP member Pedro Cazes Camarero, on 29 May 1991.

9. *El Combatiente* 6 (93), 1973, p. 4.

10. See Robben, 'Deadly alliance'.

11. See Marín, *Los hechos armados*, pp. 110, 114.

12. See Gasparini, *Montoneros* and Giussani, *Montoneros* for critical inside perspectives of the Montoneros. See Díaz Bessone, *Guerra revolucionaria* and Orsolini, *Montoneros*, for military standpoints. Gillespie, *Soldiers of Perón*, offers an outsider's view.

13. Author's interview with Rear-Admiral Horácio Mayorga on 3 October 1990.

14. See Schiller et al., *Hubo dos terrorismos?*

15. Author's interview with Graciela Fernández Meijide on 16 May 1990.

16. Perelli, 'Military's perception', confuses threat perception with enemy definition in an otherwise interesting article about the military as political actors. Pion-Berlin (*Ideology*, pp. 5–7) argues that the Argentine military's violent response to the counter-insurgency was not based on an objective assessment of the real threat, but on preconceived notions about a supposed threat.

17. Sábato, *On Heroes and Tombs*, p. 177.

18. *El Descamisado* 1 (45), 1974, p. 17.

19. Ibid.

20. See FAMUS, *Operación Independencia*, and CJE, *Ejército de hoy*, for accounts of the fighting written from the point of view of the armed forces.

21. Poder Ejecutivo Nacional, Decreto 2770–72, 6 October 1975.

22. Scarry, *The Body in Pain*, p. 87.

23. *El Combatiente* 9 (221), 1976, p. 11.

24. Bayer, 'Pequeño recordatório', pp. 203, 208.

25. *La Nación*, 5 August 1976.

26. Masi, 'Lucha contra la subversión', p. 38.

27. General Videla, quoted in *La Nación*, 18 December 1977.

28. General Chasseing, quoted in *La Nación*, 19 September 1978.

29. Quoted in *La Nación*, 12 December 1976.

30. Admiral Massera, quoted in *La Nación*, 4 December 1976.

31. General Ibérico Saint-Jean, quoted in Simpson and Bennett, *The Disappeared*, p. 66.

32. See Douglas, *Purity and Danger*, Derrida, *Disseminations*.

33. Bauman, 'Modernity and ambivalence', pp. 148–9.

34. See Derrida, *Disseminations*, pp. 97, 221; Derrida, *Positions*, p. 43.

35. See Mauss, *The Gift*, pp. 59–62.

36. Derrida, *Disseminations*, p. 133.

37. Frazer, *Golden Bough*, pp. 670–2.

38. Girard, *The Scapegoat*, p. 39.

39. Ibid., p. 21.

40. Agosti, *Discursos*, pp. 66–8.

41. Admiral Massera, quoted in *La Nación*, 4 March 1977.

42. See Bonasso, *Recuerdo de la muerte*, pp. 185–99, 217–27; Gasparini, *Montoneros*, pp. 219–20.

43. See Carl Schmitt, *Der Begriff des Politischen*, pp. 27, 33. See also Schmitz, *Freund–Feind Theorie*.

44. Langer, *Philosophy*, p. 233.

45. Freud, 'The uncanny', p. 220.

46. Kristeva, *Etrangers*, p. 271.

SEVEN

From the Banality of Violence to Real Terror: the Case of Colombia

DANIEL PÉCAUT

Since 1980, Colombia has again seen intense violence. The national murder rate is one of the highest in the world, regularly exceeding 70 per 100,000 inhabitants. In certain towns and regions, the rate is as high as 400 per 100,000 inhabitants. Between 1980 and 1995 the estimated number of murder victims rose to more than 300,000.[1] Killings of more than five people are numerous; between 1988 and 1993 alone, there were almost 900 such incidents, resulting in 5,000 deaths.[2] A range of other indicators tends to confirm this trend. Thousands of trade unionists and political activists have been assassinated. One political party, the Patriotic Union (UP, Unión Patriotica) was decimated by killings and almost wiped off the political map. The number of officially recorded kidnappings increased from 1,000 in 1990 to a record of 1,717 in 1991. In all, more than half a million people have been forced to flee their home regions. In large swathes of the country, a huge variety of blackmail and crime rackets have become commonplace.

A similar type of violence is translated into localized forms of terror in many different rural and urban areas. This is particularly the case in areas like the Magdalena Medio or Uraba, where several armed groups are competing for the same territory.[3] The civilian population is subjected to the rule of silence in these areas, and massacres, civilian flight, thuggery, atrocities, fear and suspicion continue to be the rule. Moreover, the years 1987–93 have been marked by an increase in both random and targeted terrorism caused by drug traffickers and their shady allies.

Given this state of affairs, it is certainly surprising that the situation has not provoked more response from public opinion in Colombia and internationally. Certain events, such as the killings of prominent political figures, or some particularly bloody massacre, have without doubt had a considerable impact. Yet this kind of after-effect is only fleeting, and there is little evidence that the overall situation is giving rise to the kind of anger provoked by atrocities in Argentina, El Salvador or Guatemala.

Several factors may account for this relative lack of response, this silence. In this chapter, I will emphasize one of them: the banality or ordinariness of the violence which tends to obscure the existence of situations of terror. I have no intention, in talking of the 'banality of violence', of using the idea of a 'culture of violence', a notion often used by Colombian analysts. Whenever culture is invoked as an explanatory framework, and even more so in the case of violence, it is likely to reflect a somewhat lazy attitude, and to assume a tautological aspect as well. It is certainly the case that violent events have a long history in Colombia. During the contemporary period, the memory of the Violencia of the 1950s remains with people, and is often invoked as a justification by those who continue to practise violence in the present. Nevertheless, we cannot ignore new elements of the current violence. Its triviality or ordinariness relate to a number of factors specific to current events: in particular, the extremely heterogeneous nature of the violence prevents it from coalescing along a *single* axis of conflict. Among these peculiarities are: the lack of connection with pre-existing forms of group identity; the networks of control established; the many opportunities opened up; and a compatibility with the formal rule of law within the state. Thus, both continuity and discontinuity are apparent in this transition from everyday, banal violence to terror. In this chapter I intend to show how the marked continuities in the forms of violence led that violence to be perceived as given, rather than something new. No single coherent intellectual or political framework or category is able to explain this violence, even less to make any sense of it.

I do not intend to cover once again the context in which the present violence originally erupted.[4] Rather, in the first section I will deal with the inter-relations between the varying and multiple forms of violence in existence. The next section will explore various aspects of the banality of this violence, and in a third section I consider the specific conditions that accompanied the transition to a situation of terror. In the final section, I examine why terror, otherwise very real, has not been given a history nor indeed been met with broad moral indignation.[5]

Connecting Types of Violence

As already indicated, violent events in the Colombian context are particularly varied and diverse. They include armed confrontation between guerrillas and troops; operations by paramilitary and drug traffickers; protection rackets by urban militias; 'social cleansing' operations; political assassinations; organized and petty crime; and youth inter-gang warfare, brawls, vendettas and score settling. All these types of violence have contributed, in differing proportions, to the explosion in the number of homicides.

Political violence appears to account for only a minor share of the overall total number of homicides in Colombia. Research conducted in 1987 suggested that such killings were responsible for only 7 per cent of all victims.[6] But in reality, how is one to define the boundary between political and other forms of violence? It could be claimed that drug traffickers are not by nature political. Yet surely they do become political actors when they intervene in judicial procedures and electoral processes through means of corruption, and when *a fortiori* they force the state to buckle under pressure through massive resort to terror? Conversely, guerrillas are more obviously political actors, but again, how political are they really when they practise protection rackets and kidnappings on a large scale, and even resort to the services of organized crime and hired killers in order to achieve their goals? In many cases, the everyday violence, which takes the form of foul killings, settling of accounts and revenge killings, can be said to have a political dimension, to the extent that it too may express a sense of social anger, and may result from the weaknesses of the police and judiciary.

Is such an inflexible distinction between organized and disorganized violence not arguable? Groups like the guerrillas and drug traffickers are only relatively cohesive. There are numerous guerrilla groups, for example, each with its own multiple allegiances. Within one such guerrilla organization, FARC (Fuerzas Armadas Revolucionarias de Colombia), there are more than sixty groups that are far from united in terms of their approaches and strategies. Even at the height of their power, the well-known 'cartels' of Medellín, Cali, Bogotá and the Atlantic Coast were in reality little more than loose coalitions of various small groups.[7] Now that the cartels have been partially dismantled, these small groups have even greater autonomy than in the past. In the case of the paramilitary and the urban militias, although quite highly centralized, department-wide groups have recently started to be created. These groups have usually been even more unstable than in the case of the cartels, and they also have stronger ties with the criminal community. In the same way, criminality itself is not the product of a few scattered individuals or gangs, but of huge organizations, with the many consequences this implies. Just one example of this is that for some time the police, with great skill and expertise, were controlling the market in stolen cars.

Corruption affects all organizations and sectors of society, and this makes it almost impossible to make hard and fast distinctions between the various protagonists of violence. Statistical empirical evidence tends to suggest that there might be a correlation between the existence of 'organized' violent groups, including the guerrillas, and the increase in 'unorganized' violence. One of the reasons why the boundaries between political and non-political violence, organized and unorganized crime are becoming more and more porous is that all the armed protagonists have acquired the potential to control the key economic and productive sectors of the national economy.

The expansion of the drug economy – marijuana in the 1970s, cocaine since 1975, and presently heroin – has played a crucial part in shifting the stakes of violence. Production of cocaine and heroin has become particularly entrenched in regions where the FARC has become established or recently installed itself. Guerrilla warfare has formed a kind of protective covering, behind which drug trafficking, the growing of drug-related crops, and laboratory work, have been carried out without much risk of incursions by the armed forces. In return for this effective protection, the FARC enjoyed a financial godsend, obtained mainly from taxes on farmers as well as drug distributors. By the late 1980s, this enabled this particular guerrilla movement to double its number of fronts and increase its strength. It was this that largely explains the increase in poppy cultivation since the start of the 1990s.

The struggle soon extended beyond control of the drug trade to most primary production. Another organization, the ELN (Ejercito de Liberación Nacional), almost wiped out in the 1970s, rose again out of the ashes largely due to the control it exercises over the key petroleum-producing regions and the financial claw-backs it could impose. The same process took place in other mining areas, including centres of nickel and coal production, as well as in areas of commercial agriculture, such as banana production in Uraba, African palm cultivation or cattle ranching. Protection rackets and kidnappings became widespread, and even coffee-producing areas, which had remained relatively free from organized violence, experienced a take-over by drug traffickers and guerrillas, while also experiencing disturbingly high levels of petty, disorganized crime. The heavy concentration of vigilante groups in the emerald-producing areas has kept guerrillas at bay, but not the violence itself.[8] Generally speaking, guerrilla activity and violent crime in the country, both organized and disorganized, tend to coincide with areas of primary production.[9]

The guerrillas' strategy of controlling centres of economic activity as a matter of priority has transformed relations between all the armed groups. A certain degree of cooperation between guerrillas and drug traffickers is essential in areas where drugs are cultivated and processed. This also requires the implicit complicity of other local forces, including the military, the police and politicians. Transactions between guerrillas and drug traffickers are obviously not entirely free of conflict. This was shown in the break-down of a tacit agreement between the FARC and the traffickers, which resulted in a ruthless confrontation between the FARC and the paramilitary groups established by Gonzalo Rodriguez Gacha.[10] Such disputes can also break out between guerrillas and the armed forces in cases where the latter demand excessive bribes.[11]

Except in cocaine-producing areas, where they may be forced to cooperate, the interests of the guerrilla groups and drug gangs generally conflict. As the drug traffickers invest in land and livestock (and estimates suggest that they have already acquired more than 5 million hectares of the best land), like any other large land-owners, they become targets for the guerrilla groups whose goal is to impose revolutionary taxes and requisitions of property on such land-owners. In areas where this situation exists, there is systematic confrontation between the two groups. Transactions in other parts of the country, where there are other bases for generating wealth, involve both relations of cooperation and conflict. Nowhere have the guerrilla forces paralysed production, which suggests they are keen to preserve their sources of funding. They may even provide protection for companies and land-owners who keep up to date with the 'taxes' imposed on them. Other forms of interaction include the process of corruption of the political class by drug traffickers, and pressures exerted on government by guerrilla groups.[12] In this way, the framework for such strategic interactions is redefined, based on a highly diverse and flexible set of conditions.

Overall, this situation produces a fragmentation of Colombia's national territory in response to the relative strength of the various actors involved. The reorganization of the national territory, which results from the interactions between the armed protagonists, takes place along the lines of the mainly invisible boundaries established between areas controlled by one or other of these groups. By virtue of being under the hold of such groups and being the scene of their rivalries, regions such as Uraba and the lower Cauca valley have acquired particular identities.

It follows that violence seems to have taken on a distinctly prosaic character. There is little room in such conflict for political ideologies or differences in beliefs. Admittedly, guerrilla groups remain as actors in the political arena; their military presence ensures that this will remain the case, since it enables them to put in a token appearance in half the municipalities of the country, even in the outskirts of Bogotá itself.[13] Nevertheless, the political credibility of these groups has become minimal. Their prestige has diminished steadily since 1985, and public opinion has become more and more exasperated with their struggle, which seems to consist of a series of threats, and does not seem to lead anywhere in the longer term. Long before the end of the Cold War, these guerrilla groups had lost the means to express their aspirations for a better future. Their silence suggests that they believe their actions are sufficient indication of what they wanted, and what they stand for. Organized violence, on the other hand, has never inspired much political debate. Even in areas where such groups are well placed and have substantial influence, they have been reluctant to take part in elections. This is no doubt partly because of the climate of terror and violence, but it may also have something to do with fears that they may not gain much support from their presumed supporters.[14] There is still a difference between organized and random violence, but the two forms of violence have entered into a reciprocal relationship that has resulted in a situation of generalized violence. This generalized violence affects social and interpersonal relations, changing the workings both of institutions and of established values, and shuts out anything external, not leaving any space for the intervention of third parties. The interaction between various forms of violence creates its own logic, its own modes of conflict and systems of transaction. This violence is not based on class divisions or other collective forms of social identity.

The social tensions remain, and are to be found in all regions of the country. They are perhaps more marked today than they have ever been. At one time the coffee economy was able to ensure the Colombian regime's stability quite effectively, but coffee production now appears to be in a permanent state of crisis and long-term decline. The rest of the agricultural sector has not fared much better, particularly since the unprepared trade liberalization of 1991 exposed all domestic products to foreign competition. For the past two years urban unemployment has risen steadily, and salaries have stagnated or even fallen in real terms. With the end of the drugs boom in the economy, the government has also been forced to undertake austerity measures. All these factors aggravate the underlying tendency for conflict. Organized social groups are becoming rare and continue to disintegrate for reasons that can be found in other countries, but also in response to the widespread violence. Social actors are either manipulated by armed protagonists or simply swept along by the violence. The banana plantations of Uraba are an example of a situation where intense social unrest has not been translated into any public action by trade unions or other social groups. For a long time, repression of trade unions was so severe that they remained very weak. Officially, their powers of negotiation and representation were greatly enhanced after 1985, when they concluded a series of agreements that were among the most favourable for any pressure group in Colombia. In reality, however, trade unions are completely dominated by the two guerrilla movements based in the Uraba region. They are likely to suffer both from repercussions of internecine struggles between the two guerrilla groups and the use of terror by the paramilitary.[15]

Cultural identities are even more vulnerable than social movements. It is fair to say that cultural identities have always been fairly fragile in a country of inter-mixing and migration such as Colombia. Even so, perceptible differences can no doubt be said to exist between regional cultures. Although such cultural differences may give rise to a number of prejudices, they have very little bearing on the violence. Perhaps the only exception is in regions with a sizeable indigenous population, notably the Cauca; in these areas a particular guerrilla organization emerged, known as the Quintin Lame. Yet it is hard to be certain that this represents a form of identity politics, and is not simply the convenient and clever use of a cultural identity theme for other ends. In other parts of Colombia, political and partisan identities, which can be traced back to the nineteenth century, strengthened by the Violencia of the 1950s, have been remarkably stable, and are now the only lasting forms of identity available for many people. It is apparent that these forms of identity are strongly entrenched. However, the actual form taken by such identities depends on the type of relationship established with local government and other local social forces, since such identities take the form of allegiances that can be transferred with ease from one leader or one clan to another. Even such partisan allegiances may not necessarily prevent the formation of a local network of power based on armed groups. This task of infiltration is made even easier by the crisis taking place within the traditional party system.

Everyday Violence: Individual Careers and the Logic of Protection

The notion of generalized violence also implies that, at least initially, violence is not viewed as war, or as something catastrophic. Nor is it viewed as the consequences of individual acts of deviance. Like any other normalized process, violence under these conditions appears to offer a number of opportunities, including prospects for compromise, and to entail its own standards and regulations. The ordinariness of such violence lies not only in the low profile kept by the main leaders, but also has a lot to do with the lack of novelty characteristic of most political interactions, and with the lack of any imagined novel future.

Until fairly recently, violence has not noticeably disrupted the market economy.[16] Colombia can pride itself on having survived the 'lost decade' of the 1980s better than most other Latin American countries, including even Chile. The rapid growth of the drug economy did create many distortions, but also made it possible to avoid balance of payments deficits. Because of the violence, markets were not 'free' in the usual sense, but subject to relations of force, and many business contracts were not legally binding. Yet this situation was not entirely new since, even beforehand, the precariousness of the state had already encouraged the growth of illegal activities, including contraband, political protection rackets and clientelism, all of which do interfere with the normal workings of the economy.[17] Violence did, of course, generate extra transaction costs, but these were compensated for by the huge increase in available capital. Traditional land-owners might be persuaded to sell their land to drug traffickers, and generally do so at a very good price. When large industrialists or mine-owners were the victims of protection rackets, they were able to pass the costs on to consumers. Such growth and the inability of the state to provide even a minimum level of protection, have encouraged people to adopt a 'free rider' strategy, and to avoid the risk of becoming involved in any collective social action or political protest.[18]

Quite surprisingly, until recently, even the thousands of kidnappings carried out by all the armed groups did not lead to any mass protest. Instead, the potential victims resort to ever more sophisticated systems of self-protection, including taking out protection contracts as a form of insurance. Such individual strategies appear a more logical response than symbolic forms of protest. Furthermore, kidnappings have become so numerous that they are regarded as routine, and no longer come as a surprise. Even though many kidnappings come to a tragic end, they are regarded as simply another dimension of the violence. Everyone is forced to recognize the possibility that this may happen to them also. For example, one politician, who was kidnapped, held for several months by the FARC and forced to pay a large ransom, later concluded an alliance with the Union Patriotica (UP) during elections, even though the UP was supported by the FARC.

Moreover, a number of new opportunities arise out of the prevalence of illegality and violence, and these are obvious from the wide range of economic activities associated with the drug economy. It is estimated that more than one million people live directly or indirectly on the proceeds from this industry, and that many more subscribe to the notions of social mobility that go along with it. Of course, it does not follow that everyone benefits from the proceeds of the illegal economy and from the mechanisms of violence. A number of recent studies have suggested that violence is linked to prosperity, since the incidence of violence coincides with wealth-producing areas of the country. This is rather a simplistic assertion, since it does not take into account the many deprived and impoverished people who become involved in the violence, but are not invited to share in the spoils. The sizeable financial resources controlled by guerrilla groups have led other commentators to conclude that the violence could be seen as an unfair form of income redistribution. All the indications suggest that, on the contrary, owing to the violence, social inequality is now starting to increase, having declined somewhat between 1978 and 1985. The economy of violence does also have its social outcasts. Nevertheless, a career in violence offers opportunities that are particularly attractive to youth.

In many respects, a career in violence can appear as simply one of many on offer within the vast informal sector. Average incomes in the informal sector are estimated by one economist to have risen by 10.5 per cent per annum between 1984 and 1992, compared with an annual increase of only 3.1 per cent in the formal sector. Educational qualifications are less and less likely to confer any advantage. At the same time, the rewards for criminal activities increased threefold between 1980 and 1993. It is therefore not surprising that a growing proportion of young people give up their schooling in order to embark on illegal activities. Given the ineffectiveness of the criminal justice system, crimes can be committed with almost total impunity. For example, only one out of every three reported murders is ever investigated, and in only four of every hundred recorded murders is a conviction secured. The incentives for trying one's luck in the criminal world are all the greater because of the obvious success of a number of important criminal entrepreneurs. A career in subversion can also appear quite attractive. The 1980 Penal Code lowered the recommended sentence for political murders, as compared with ordinary homicides, to between three and six years.[19]

Joining the guerrilla forces or paramilitary groups is a career like any other. Not only do both these kinds of groups provide an income and a means of living; they also provide access to higher status, expressed in symbolic form through the uniforms and weapons of the organization concerned. Above all, through such organizations, the individual can become part of a large unit. The dislocation of family structures, and the social disruption, make it all the more attractive to take part in groups that have a set code of conduct and discipline. For young men of fifteen years of age or younger, the authority of their commanders replaces the failed authority of their own fathers. The same is true of the urban militias that bring together youth from a particular district. Entry into the guerrillas or the paramilitary can often be an alternative option to conscription into military service. In many families, children find themselves divided between the army, guerrilla groups and the other armed organizations.

Career patterns are thus far from being completely straightforward. During more than twenty years of violence, there have been a number of changes. The transition from being involved in drug trafficking to becoming part of a paramilitary group, or slipping into criminal activities of various kind has become a smooth one. Career paths of *guerrilleros* can be equally complex. Some may operate with drug traffickers for a period; while there are also many who return to civilian life, as well as those who change camps to join the paramilitary. The latter case is not unusual, and is the most interesting of all. A significant proportion of the leaders and members of the para-military actually originated from guerrilla groups. In some cases, such shifts in allegiance take place once a particular region falls under the control of the paramilitary; in other cases, individual circumstances, implicit or explicit threat of punishment, and inter-guerrilla rivalries can prompt such a switch in loyalties. Within each locale, this kind of redeployment of individuals simply serves to prolong and accentuate the phase of terror. The sheer diversity of these interchanging career paths, suggests that the everyday nature of violence itself results in a tendency of individuals to circulate between illegal, para-legal and legal activities. The same process of slippage occurs at the elite level in the widespread use of corruption.

In other regimes, the mere presence of an armed group at the local level does not always suggest the existence of violent confrontation, since some-times the motivation is one of protection. In his book on the Sicilian mafia,[20] Gambetta argues that these groups can be seen as a system of protection, making it possible for transactions to be based on relations of trust in a situation of overall distrust. Within limits, and in certain cases, this kind of analysis could equally be applied to the case of armed networks in Colombia, particularly those that exert their control over particular, territorially bounded areas. There are many places where the inhabitants, fearing the rise of unorganized violence, have been willing to call in protectors capable of imposing a sense of law and order.

This situation emerged particularly in areas of drug production. At the start of the 1980s, the movement of settlers into such areas, attracted by the prospects of quick profits, was translated into a rapid rise in murder rates. Given these conditions, the arrival of the FARC was well received. The

FARC, at the same time, satisfied the desire for law and order, and protected the interests of agricultural producers, to some extent compensating for the effective absence of state structures. The FARC did this by imposing a regulatory code of its own, by defining conditions for access to land;[21] by ensuring that some arable land continued to be allocated to food crops; by controlling all trade with drug traffickers; and by providing protection against military attacks. Guerrilla groups, however, are not the only social actors to provide this type of protection. In the Magdalena Medio region, paramilitary groups that ousted the FARC in mid-1985 carried out the same function for those who had been able to remain in the area rather than flee. In the outskirts of many towns, which are subjected to the arbitrary violence of the *sicarios* and other delinquent groups, popular militias fulfilled the same role by providing local surveillance.

Access to employment is often conditional on allegiance to one or other of the networks that control the local territory. This works in the manner of a union closed shop. In Uraba, for example, one particular banana *finca* is regarded as the private property of the FARC, and another the private property of the EPL. The same is true of the gold mines, of most cattle ranches, and of industrial firms located in towns controlled by the guerrillas or the paramilitary. Anyone employed in these sectors is expected to agree to the norms of their own network. The ELN's repeated sabotage of oil pipelines, for example, was also a way of creating work: the workforce employed to clean up the oil spillages is chosen in advance by the ELN.

Accepting protection does not automatically imply any ideological affinity with the protectors. A whole range of relationships can exist, from active participation by auxiliaries, such as militias armed with light weapons or open and covert civilian sympathizers, to straightforward sympathy and passive forms of acquiescence. In areas where armed protagonists have been installed for some time, as in the case of the guerrilla groups in some regions, habits are formed and the population often comes to view the external world in a hostile light. Even though all must submit to the constraints of their 'protectors', many are able to see this relationship as principally an instrumental one. Individuals' accommodation strategies differ, but it is not unusual for them to undertake a rational calculation that takes into account both the advantages conferred by the armed groups' continued presence in the area, as well as the cost of their own obligatory obedience to such groups' rules. If such an assessment proves negative, the consequence may be a transfer of allegiance from one protector to another; this has been the case in Magdalena Medio region, referred to earlier.

The nature of 'protection' does not rule out individual strategies of accommodation and adaptation, but does prohibit any form of autonomous collective action. I have already mentioned the weakening of all categories of social actors. This is the case even for traditional forms of social solidarity. The inhabitants of settlement zones were used to cooperating among them-

selves in order to carry out basic public works and construction. The *juntas de acción comunal* were clearly prestigious institutions. These kinds of collective action are tending to disappear, since those who would have taken the initiative for such organizing may be forced to join the ranks of the armed forces; alternately they expose themselves to retaliation. The state of public works, even in areas where financial resources are plentiful, is thus surprising. More and more frequently, the *juntas de acción comunal* simply come under the direct control of the armed groups. Admittedly, in some cases, regions that have been under 'protection' do experience the launching of forms of collective mass mobilization. There were enormous peasant marches in 1987–88, for example. These marches were sponsored by the guerrilla groups; in the first instance by the ELN, and in the second, more recent, case by the FARC. Participation in these marches, however, has been anything but voluntary. Peasant farmers no doubt join such marches spontaneously when they believe they will serve to promote their own interests. Nevertheless, their enthusiasm wanes when the marches continue one after the other, with the suffering and personal risks implied; their continued participation can become more a matter of constraint than desire.

This system of mobilization is not altogether new or unknown. Traditional political parties behaved in a similar fashion in many municipalities of Colombia. The clans and factions which held power often coerced the inhabitants into displaying their allegiance to them. This was often the price people were forced to pay to get access to resources, or even to have some peace, or avoid being forced to flee. A number of authors have referred to the existence of an 'armed clientelism', in order to emphasize the continuity with previous forms of clientelism. The major difference between these forms of 'coerced mobilization' remains that of the degree of integration or otherwise into the official structures of political life.

In some ways, the division of the country under the control of the armed groups and their power networks can be seen as an ordinary, banal situation. The logic of protection, though, cannot be regarded as if it were purely and simply a response to demand that put into place a mechanism for ensuring trust. In Gambetta's analysis, many specialists in the Sicilian mafia have pointed out that the 'supply' or offer of protection is undoubtedly more significant than the 'demand' for it. Moreover, this 'supply' is expressed through the use of violence, and instead of putting an end to a situation of distrust simply continues to feed unease.[22] This is even more so in the Colombian case, where the networks have no traditional foundation, and are, moreover, in a situation of competition with one another.

The logic of protection takes place against a backdrop of generalized violence and the interaction of the various armed protagonists. The notion of the 'supply' of protection, and the violence that it implies, is at least as important as that of 'demand'. Generalized acceptance of guerrilla control in the drug-growing areas is far from being the norm. In many cases, the

imposition of protection does not arise from any kind of local demand or felt need for such protection. When one 'protector' replaces another in a particular area, there is no consultation of the local people. The multiplicity of the armed networks implies that boundaries between them are complex and fluid. For example, such boundaries rarely divide clearly distinguishable regions from each other; rather, they cross whole districts, towns and neighbourhoods. Barrancabermeja, a major town, and one of the centres of petroleum refining, is divided in this way into neighbourhoods controlled by the paramilitary, the ELN and the FARC, among others. Divisions can even run between the blocks of flats and built-up areas of a single town. In Medellín or in Bogotá, where the control of each group may be confined to a micro-area, this is the situation. In Uraba the *fincas* are separated from each other by virtue of the group to which they are affiliated. Territoriality is, thus, completely tied up with the activities of the armed protagonists. Indeed, territorial control sometimes provides the basis for the subsequent accumulation of power, including military power. This is often the way in which the urban militias have established themselves. Exercising control over a particular neighbour-hood or housing area, urban militias were able to use this as a base for reconnaissance and for establishing connections and undertaking transactions with other armed groups. In every case, the counterpart of armed protection is the transformation of the land into a patchwork of micro-territories, each placed under the control of a particular organization.

The kind of violence inherent in this form of territoriality can remain banal and ordinary. Not much is needed, however, to tip the scales and transform such violence into terror.

The Practices of Terror

As with violence itself, it is useful to distinguish between two different kinds of terror. The first has no territorial basis, whereas the second makes explicit reference to a particular territorial area. The first form of the war has nothing to do with the logic of protection; the second is a perverted expression of that logic. I will mainly be focusing on analysing the latter type of terror, but will first briefly explore the former type.

Drug traffickers, via the intermediation of the paramilitary groups, often put into place a territorially based form of terror. Yet, on the other hand, the large-scale terror campaign conducted from 1987 until 1993, which had the most dramatic repercussion of all, had nothing to do with the territorial issue. Rather, this terror campaign aimed to destabilize the state, and thus create disarray in public opinion in order to force a renouncement of extradition measures. This was the main purpose of assassination attempts on major figures, political leaders, magistrates, and even of the random attacks through car bombs or by other means.[23] Recourse to such methods was undoubtedly made easier by the increasing canalization of violence. From as

early as 1984, it was possible for the cartel of Medellín to kill a minister of justice without causing any lasting outrage. Nor did this action prevent certain prominent figures from undertaking discrete negotiations with this cartel shortly afterwards. In addition, this case expressed another new shift. For the first time an armed group undertook violence that was deliberately intended to destabilize the state itself. Nothing similar had ever occurred in the previous long history of violence in Colombia. Key figures were assassinated, like Gaitán in 1948, and others were forced into exile,[24] but none of the earlier protagonists of violence had aimed to attack the very operation of the state itself. Besides, for a long time the guerrilla groups boasted that they were opposed to any terrorism. A sort of taboo had been broken, and as a result the whole realm of violence was redefined.

The terror used against the militants of the Unión Patriotica and other trade unions and political activists is not properly territorial either. Its main objective is purely political. First and foremost, it is a case of an alliance between drug traffickers, the military and local political leaders attempting to eliminate an opposition force rooted in the ever-changing guerrilla scene. There are admittedly other motives for the drug traffickers, including loosening the influence of guerrilla groups in the areas under their control. However, the systematic practice of a deterritorialized type of political terror is certainly a major departure from the previously established forms of violence.

The peasantry hold the military themselves responsible for creating much of the terror. This general accusation cannot be accounted for simply by the numerous excesses that the military commit in their routine operations. It is certainly significant that for many individuals this may be their sole point of contact with the state, and this state may well not behave as they might have expected it to. This can be related to the fact that the military tend to undertake only occasional military incursions; do not establish their presence territorially; and make very little effort to create networks of protection. The fairly bureaucratic mode of operation of the army, which involves the constant movement of its troops, does not make it possible for the armed forces to become familiar with particular groups of local inhabitants. The army often strikes blindly, lumping together peasants and guerrillas when it suits their purposes to do so, but when they withdraw they leave the field wide open, once again, to guerrilla groups. Individuals under these conditions, have no room for manoeuvre whatsoever. Moreover, the military includes the paramilitary, to whom the armed forces delegate most of the tasks of large-scale massacres, as well as the job of territorial control. In comparison to the military, the urban police forces have an even worse reputation. During operations in the 'war' against the Medellín cartel, they behaved little differently from the army in the rural areas, brutally bursting in on neighbourhoods where those suspected of harbouring the *sicarios* lived, and often killing and torturing at random. There is little doubt that such abuses of power by the forces of law and order lie behind the tendency of the population to tolerate

the demands and excesses of other armed groups, so long as they do not exceed what is considered tolerable.

Let us move on to the other kind of terror, that which is tied in with the inter-relations between networks and their bases of territorial control. The complementary relationship between protection and violence has already been mentioned. Even in the absence of any disputes between armed protagonists, however, it is possible for banal, everyday violence to be transformed into terror.

The degeneration of armed protagonists results from the continuation of violence, and in many cases expresses itself in more than mere bribery and corruption. This can also be the case for the drug traffick – in its final stages the Medellín cartel became embroiled in frequent internal settling of scores. Guerrilla groups and the paramilitary have also been unable to avoid such bouts of rough justice. Every guerrilla fighter has experienced episodes of violent bloodletting. From the 1970s onwards, Fabio Vásquez Castao, leader of the ELN, set a precedent by gunning down most of the university graduates who had joined his organization. The FARC has been able to keep more guarded about such purges. Nevertheless, such killings were both numerous and constant, and were directly carried out by the central secretariat, or the local bloc, front-line commanders. It is known, for example, that Braulio Herrera, who was given the task of recovering control over the Magdalena Medio in the late 1980s, undertook so many executions that he was eventually sent out of the country. More recently, during fighting with the paramilitary in Uraba, one FARC commander gave orders to shoot any man not fighting ferociously enough. The most disturbing and sinister case, however, was in 1987, when two leaders of the Ricardo Franco front (a dissident off-shoot of the FARC, which had for some time been close to M19) personally executed almost every one of their troops in Tacueyo, around two hundred men, on the grounds that they could be infiltrated by secret agents. This massacre provoked such an outrage that it influenced the decision of M19 to start negotiations with the government, and also contributed to the guerrillas' loss of credibility.

Although terror can, and does, operate within the armed groups them-selves, it affects civilian populations even more. The indiscriminate demands of the FARC faction, entrenched around Puerto Boyaca in the early 1980s, imposed exorbitant taxes and kidnaps for ransom on even the poorest people. It was this that led most of the local population to defect to the paramilitary and submit to the paramilitary's protection, even though it was based on fear and the practice of denouncement. The existence of informers ready to denounce any 'suspects' is implied in the very notion of a protection network. Having become used to the rule of silence, the population at large learns to trust no one. Simply crossing the boundaries between rival protection net-works, even for ordinary business purposes, can lead to accusations of betrayal.

Insecurity can augment a situation of terror. The case of the switching of allegiances in the region of Puerto Boyaca has been previously discussed. There are also deserters who change camp. This practice has become a common enough experience to lead local populations to distrust the claims of even the most apparently solid and well-established networks. In such cases, deserters may well take with them information that permits merciless revenge, in the event that the zone is forced to switch allegiance. In this respect, detailed information is available on the small village of La India in Santander, a *corregimiento* (small municipality) of Cimitarra.[25] The FARC was in power in this area for a long time, and imposed its protection, not without committing some excesses. When desertions to the paramilitary started to take place, the commander retaliated by punishing the civilian population. Some time later, however, he too deserted and joined the paramilitary forces. Situations such as these encourage relations of distrust not only towards the network, but also towards one's neighbours.

A situation of terror becomes even more obvious when territorial conflict takes place between various protagonists. 'Protection' can become a means of waging war, and 'frontiers' can become the site of indiscriminate conflicts and confrontations. It is no coincidence that terror is most entrenched and chronic in the Uraba region. All the armed groups maintain a presence in the region because, besides being a centre of banana production, it is also strategically located on the border with Panama. This means that much of the drug and arms trade passes through the port of Turbo and along other local trade routes. At one time it was possible for trading to be the main priority for the rivalling armed groups. For some time, the FARC, the militias, the drug traffickers, the paramilitary and their leader Fidel Castao (a former member of the Medellín cartel before he turned himself into Pablo Escobar's number one enemy), kept to a sort of *modus vivendi* within the port of Turbo itself. This did not prevent the various groups from simultaneously fighting, in parallel to this, for control along axes of conflict that changed with time.

In the early 1980s, the banana plantation owners carried out a wholesale campaign of attrition against workers' organizations. Two guerrilla organizations installed in Uraba came into conflict between 1985 and 1987. Trade unions also became involved as each guerrilla group tried to extend its sphere of influence. From 1987 onwards, pushed by drug traffickers and the military, paramilitary groups started to unleash their violence. The considerable means at their disposal were demonstrated by a series of massacres, mostly of EPL members, which were carried out the following year. The EPL finally laid down arms in 1991, after which time the FARC and a dissident core of EPL have tried to extend its control over the territory previously controlled by the EPL. Massacres took place in quick succession, sometimes, as in August 1995, at the rate of one or more per week, and many EPL veterans took up arms once again, this time allying themselves with the military and the paramilitary. From 1995 onwards, a broad paramilitary offensive, taking the

name Uraba and Cordoba Self-Defence Association, reconquered the entire region, ousted the FARC (who were obliged to take refuge in the mountains) and expelled thousands of people from the area.

Such criss-crossing, shifting axes of conflict and alliance find expression in a series of atrocities. The paramilitary are undoubtedly responsible for more of these than any other armed group. But all armed groups resort to terror and none has a monopoly on the frequent and violent massacres which are often carried out for simple revenge. All groups are capable of resorting to using *sicarios* in order to carry out assassinations and escape detection. Shifts in the military situation tend to encourage defections, which in turn heighten feelings of insecurity. During their offensive of 1996, the paramilitary killed numerous forces aligned with the guerrillas, while others were encouraged to join their own ranks by offering them wages twice those offered by guerrilla groups. Dozens of guerrillas left their own organizations. This made it easy to attack with considerable precision. In this way, killers quite commonly arrive in a particular neighbourhood with a ready-made list of the names of 'condemned' individuals. This does not prevent them from carrying out killings at random as well. As has been noted, the networks take the form of concentric layers of affiliated members. In addition, the killers do not always distinguish between militants and civilians who simply happen to live in places where militants are found. In fact, the use of terror is precisely intended to intimidate the population as a whole.

The intensity of the terror in Uraba is not just a matter of massacres and other such horrors. It has to do with patchwork patterns of rivalry which result from the very interspersed nature of territories controlled by various armed groups. Neighbouring *fincas*, different parts of the same village, or even members of a single family, may depend on different networks. This creates a situation of generalized distrust, even between relatives. The 'rule of silence' no longer needs to be imposed by the networks, but is taken on by individuals as a security measure in their daily interactions with each other. There is very little room for manoeuvre for such individuals, who adopt a 'see no evil, hear no evil' approach. The forced removal of the inhabitants of entire villages and neighbourhoods shows that the enemy can be very broadly defined indeed. In other areas, the population has the potential to place itself under the control of a new protector. The paramilitary are not without local support. Land-owners and the urban petty bourgeoisie are not the only ones who are secretly satisfied at the expulsion of the guerrilla groups and their allies. The same feeling extends to a significant number of ordinary people, who are tired of the demands of such groups and of their endless fighting.

The Uraba region is unusual because of the internecine war between the guerrilla groups, and also because none of the protagonists of violence can afford to lose his foothold in this highly strategic area. The mixture of terror and protection which operates in the area is more typical, however, with the

same combination found in Magdalena Medio and other regions of the country as well. In an urban setting, it is common for militia groups to transform themselves into gangs, and to become involved in blackmail and crime. They usually claim to be attacking adjacent neighbourhoods, while protecting their own. In fact, the result is much the same in both cases: a situation of daily terror.

In order to prevent the population from contemplating any resistance, recourse to terror is accompanied by the staging of situations of horror. For some time, the use of more sophisticated weapons put an end to the ritualistic and painstaking mutilation of bodies which characterized the Violencia in the 1950s. The symbolism of mass killings owes much to North American and Mexican television series. Indeed, the training of the *sicarios* of Medellín involved imitating the actions of protagonists of such television series. In this context, practices from the previous era, such as the issuing of progressively stronger threats, and the pre-announcement of deaths through blacklists and other warning signs, remain as relics of the past. The recent terror, however, especially that of the paramilitary groups, has marked a return to these former patterns. Dismembered bodies are routinely displayed in public places as a warning to would-be enemies.

There is nowhere to turn to for those whose lives are ruled by this terror. No protection is offered by the public authorities. Indeed, the forces of law and order play a key role in perpetrating acts of terror, and there is a remarkable lack of justice, as we have shown. In this context the prohibition on collective actions becomes even more marked than it would be in relation to the armed networks. A group of mayors affiliated to the UP, who in principle had the support of the FARC, have made efforts to provide support services for the local population. In practice, they are threatened both by the paramilitary and by the demands and armed intervention of the FARC. Almost this entire group of mayors has been killed. The FARC has often appeared sceptical of these elected politicians' claim to favour peace, allowing them to be 'martyred'. There are, however, a number of cases of local leaders who have tried to mobilize the population against the violence, and have managed to gain recognition of their neutrality by armed groups. Until now, such initiatives have inevitably been short-lived. In 1987 the leaders of La India, a village mentioned earlier, attempted to rise to this challenge, with the support of sections of the church, and asked the paramilitary and the guerrilla groups to respect their territory's neutrality. With the assassination of these leaders in 1990 and many people in the area, the rule of fear was re-established. As a result of an agreement between all the main political parties, including the communists, a woman mayor, Gloria Cuartas, was elected in Apartado, the capital of Uraba, in 1995. Her election was based on a broad-based consensus against the terror. The outcome was that terror was increased; the paramilitary showed their total indifference to the mayor by committing a particularly barbaric act,[27] the communists denounced the cross-

party agreement, and the eventual result was that terror increased rather than being reduced. In Aguachica, a municipality in Cesar, a similar attempt to establish a neutral status was launched on the basis of international moral support. But the activities of the paramilitary groups have extended to this region, and today both assassinations and massacres have started to take place in Aguachica.

Terror can be interpreted as a further step in the wider process of the de-institutionalization of violence. It is no accident that more mention is made in this analysis of the role of the paramilitary than of the military proper. The military themselves have repeatedly demonstrated their operational in-competence. A five-fold increase in the budget for the military in the past few years has not been translated into a greater level of military efficiency. Even in the rare event of disciplinary procedures being used against senior officers, following evidence of atrocities or support for the paramilitary, there has emerged a problem, referred to among upper ranks of the military as 'the Procurator syndrome'; this often encourages a kind of 'wait and see' attitude. This syndrome does not prevent, and may even encourage, the more efficient paramilitary forces to continue their underground operations.

The military are not alone in leaving the work of combating the guerrillas to private agents. A broad and implicit consensus around this issue has emerged since 1995, and particularly includes cattle-farming associations and some political movements. This whole situation has been aggravated by the decline in the authority of governmental organizations and the resulting discrediting of all public institutions.

Silent Terror

The diffusion of terror should mean the end of an ordinary, banal quality to the violence. Those affected by violence are faced with experiences of an intolerable nature. Acts of the worst cruelty and barbarity form an integral part of the rational pursuit of strategic goals by the various protagonists. However, these acts also constitute a kind of excess that bypasses this rationality. This can be all the more puzzling since no reference is made to antagonism articulated to notions of 'ideality' (*idéalités*),[28] which in turn are embedded in the mundane nature of the violence, and attacking any idea of social relations or a common humanity. It is, therefore, far from certain that the advent of terror necessarily means the end of the banality of violence. In this final section, the reasons why this might be so will be explained.

The first reason is the broader institutional context that incorporates two aspects which contribute simultaneously to the invisibility of the terror. On the one hand, institutional regulations have suffered from the effects of the violence. The inefficiency of the law and the criminal justice system, which has already been mentioned, is integral to the banalization of terror, but is not the only factor. As the criminal justice system has become subject to the

rules of bargaining, legal and juridical norms have lost their regulatory function. The system of reducing sentences, introduced in 1991, soon resulted in a subtle form of compromise with the drug traffickers, and the often derisory sentences imposed on these individuals, at least for some time,[29] contributed to an overall sense of impotence. In 1993 the penal code was revised in agreement with the drug traffickers' legal representatives. More generally, the corruption of the political class up to the highest levels shows that the rules of informality and illegality are the norm in public institutions. From this it can be deduced that these institutions are implicated in this whole matter of violence.

On the other hand, Colombia still insists on claiming for itself the status of a country governed by the rule of law. The 1991 constitution went a long way in extending and consolidating mechanisms needed for the protection of democratic politics. Human rights protection organizations are incorporated into all the public authority institutions, including the military. Although the military have considerable room for manoeuvre in their choice of tactics and strategies, they cannot escape their subordination to the public authorities.[30] As has already been mentioned, there has been occasional disciplining of high-level army officers; a massive purge of the police force has also been conducted. Over the past two years, the activities of the *Fiscalia* have at the very least served to undermine the social acceptability of drug traffickers and have brought to light the extent of political corruption in the country. The constitutional court has made some legal objections to the declaration of a state of emergency. It might appear as if this type of measure was unusual in Latin American countries, the undertaking to wage a war against 'subversion' notwithstanding. Both the government and the media are prohibited from using the term 'war' in any of their communications. Since 1982, government talks with the guerrilla representatives have taken place several times, and besides leading the M19, the ELP and Quintin Lame to accept a cease-fire and laying down of arms, at the very least these talks also led to a loss of political credibility on the part of guerrilla groups which continued to use arms. Public opinion is consistently against undertaking a frontal attack on guerrillas and other armed groups. Sometimes this reflects the desire for a mediated, peaceful solution, but more often it is based on fear at the prospect of a military show-down, and the consequences for civil liberties. This sense of a 'formal' respect for the rule of law cannot prevent the violence from continuing. On the contrary, the door is thereby sometimes opened to a wider extension of the logic of violence, since 'order' and 'violence' come to be seen as inseparably connected.[31] Above all, such a situation has the effect of limiting the visibility of both the violence and the terror, which both come to be seen as unavoidable pockets of lawlessness.

The second reason why terror does not end the banality, or everyday nature, of the violence is that the terror cannot be understood simply in terms of friendly or hostile relations. In some areas and during certain periods,

such a situation may undoubtedly exist. Confrontations between guerrillas and the paramilitary certainly take the form of a pitiless all-out war which interrupts normal business transactions. Such conflicts also express a wider problem of social polarization. In other regions, however, such interactions between the various armed groups continue. They are indeed implied by the continuing functioning of the drug economy. The profitability of this economic sector may be declining, with internal prices having suffered from the effects of the disorganization of drug networks following the arrest of numerous cartel leaders, as well as the diversion of the traffic to other countries, particularly to Mexico. Yet the available statistics suggest no fall in the acreage devoted to growing coca, and also suggest an increase in the acreage devoted to poppy growing. The FARC is very much involved in these trends. In fact, coca growing has been under their control and it was among the small-scale peasantry, traditionally highly susceptible to the influence of the guerrillas, that heroin production has emerged. The multifaceted game thus continues, with the traffickers and FARC being associates in one place and enemies in another. Even terror does not bring into doubt the prosaic nature of the violence. A number of hidden interests lie behind the intervention of the paramilitary. After recapturing invaded lands, terror easily pays for itself, to the extent that the price of land and of businesses in such regions increases markedly thereafter.

Relations of emnity and association, although they may exist locally, generally do not draw a line between the armed protagonists and their supporters. In areas subject to terror, the population is undoubtedly trapped between two opposing sides. For the most part, however, these two sides are not easily distinguished in political terms. Political points of distinction have lost practically all meaning for these people. Electoral abstention rates, which have now reached 80 per cent, are an indication of this. In trying to mobilize the population, without claiming to have their full support, and by repeatedly refusing to put forward candidates reasonably sympathetic to themselves, but instead supporting candidates from traditional parties (if only to bring them under their own control), the guerrillas show their awareness of the declining value attached to political life. In many respects, we are dealing with a society in which many of the institutional aspects of modern politics are in the process of disappearing. In some respects, there remain traces of nineteenth-century politics, based on collective identities and the interaction of clienteles.[32] The only difference is that in many areas collective identities and clientelistic relations are now simply based on coercion. Local conflicts and power relations are a reality which structures the society. They make no reference to any imagined realities, nor do they depict political conflict as something irremediable and unavoidable.

The third reason why the violence may remain banal, despite the advent of terror, has to do with memories of violence in previous periods, especially the period of the Violencia from 1946 to 1964. There are contradictory

strands within the collective memory of these events. In the first place, there is the memory of a civil war between two established parties, whose relations corresponded to a love–hate imagery. Given the horrors that this conflict brought with it, it has left its mark in the form of present opposition to any resumption of an all-out confrontation. At the same time, this collective memory has no socially recognized form. With the agreement of 1958 which officially ended the conflict, installing the Frente Nacional government, a heavy veil was drawn over the preceding events. The most that was officially admitted was that a certain brand of barbarity had flourished. Indeed, the idea of barbarity was employed to acquit the elites of the vital role they played in the violence, instead attributing it almost wholly to the supposed immaturity of the working class and peasantry. The latter were left with only the bitter after-taste of humiliation and defeat. They had fought one another for the Others (i.e. the elites) within a framework that tied them to the Others. The working class and the peasantry had provided almost all the victims of fighting, only to find afterwards that they themselves were put in the dock in place of the accused. Their experience was part of a senseless history. It remained in a state of 'infrahistory', a hidden history never able to be openly expressed.

It is no accident that there are three different memories of La Violencia, each of which bears hardly any resemblance to any other. The first way in which this memory is expressed is in opposition to the two political parties. This explanation makes it possible to disregard all other factors involved, including socio-economic interests, and also serves to obscure the sub-ordination of the working class and peasantry to the elites. Party-based positions have lost some of their importance, since the suffering of the time now appears somewhat arcane. The second way in which these memories are expressed is through individuals' accounts, which form no part of any wider collective reconstruction of the period of La Violencia. This situation results from the fragmented and localized nature of these individual experiences. However, it also illustrates that a wider explanatory framework for the events, into which particular points of view could, at least partially, be incorporated, has failed to emerge. Instead, there are only the individuals' separate accounts, which are embedded within the empirical details of the events themselves. The third kind of memory of the period is through a mythical reworking of its significance, which is the only way that shared experiences can ever take shape. The victims, in this sense, emphasize the continuity of the violence, which they claim has 'always existed'. According to this account, the violence of 1946 was an extension of that of 1932–33, which, in turn, was a con-tinuation of the violence of the Thousand Day War (1899–1902), and all this, in turn, perpetuated the violence of nineteenth-century civil wars. La Violencia thus comes to be perceived as a freak occurrence, or a disaster akin to natural disasters. Everything that has affected the victims since that time – migrations, changing work patterns and changing values – is attributed

to the violence of that period. In this account, violence has taken on the features of a myth.

This fragmented recollection of the past plays a role in structuring the perception of present-day events. There is still a tangible sense of the humiliations suffered in the past. It can be found in the anger of working-class and peasant youth involved in the present violence in one way or another. This anger pushes them to take up the thread of earlier events, both in order to achieve a different final result, and to push further along the hidden paths of the infra-history of the past. Their distrust of the state and of political leaders is based on longstanding feelings of resentment. Despite this, old-fashioned partisan political divisions continue to influence the consciousness of a large part of the population. There remains a notice-able fragmentation of opinions. Collective forms of action are ruled out by the violence, and this forces people to turn in on themselves, a negative individualization which also has to do with the long legacy of the dissolution of social ties. In this context, mythical representations of the past lose none of their potency or appeal. If anything, the idea that present violence is no different from that of the past, and the idea that society is essentially based on relations of force, are now more widely accepted than ever.

This kind of recollection can contribute to the process of the *banalization* of violence, making violence appear as if it had always existed in more or less its present forms, and forming part of the very nature of things. This makes it more difficult to determine what is novel in the current situation and thus to make sense of what is actually taking place. Such confusion is common to all parts of Colombia; not just those regions that have been recently settled, and have barely come under state control, if at all, but also in the major towns and in other regions which have been fully integrated into the commercial economy for some time. One noteworthy illustration which can be presented is that of the small town of Trujillo, in the north of the department of Valle, located close to one of the main transport routes and near a key centre of coffee production.[33] No other case can better illustrate both the continuities and discontinuities which characterize violent phenomena in Colombia.

The municipality of Trujillo was founded in 1931 and at first was controlled by liberal cliques who ensured that the majority of the settlers belonged to the Liberal party, even to the extent of recruiting members from among the prison population. The earliest social conflicts arose when a piece of land, thought to be publicly owned, was claimed by a notable who based his claim on property titles dating back to the colonial era. From 1942 onwards the conservative leaders sought to establish a network of clientelistic relationships. The years of La Violencia gave them the opportunity they needed to achieve this, and incidents of massacre and terror made it possible to 'conservatize' the whole town. Most former inhabitants were either forced to flee or to join the Conservative party. The lands 'abandoned' were bought up by one

of the local conservative leaders at a pittance. He thereby accumulated both fortune and the power to maintain his position as the undisputed large local land-owner, going on later to play a role in departmental- and national-level politics. Although 90 per cent of the local electorate continued to support the conservatives at this time, violence remained the norm, and came to be associated with factionalist in-fighting among conservative politicians. Using a strategy of constant terror, this local land-owner was able to maintain his position of dominance. On occasion he himself even killed opposition members, or employed hired killers to eliminate them, thereby obliging opposition supporters to flee and keeping tight control over the area. In spite of such misdeeds, in 1978 this individual was feted by the national leaders of the party. However, from 1980 onwards the powers behind new forms of violence started to make an appearance within the municipality of Trujillo. An ELN front was implanted in the area and gained the support of a large number of the peasants. At the same time, a powerful drug trafficker, already installed in a neighbouring municipality, started to accumulate land.

The successors of the large land-owner have employed all available means in order to maintain their secure foothold within the area. There was a military presence and one local priest also strived to maintain the *modus vivendi*. Fear became an ever-present reality, however, and everyone in the area became aware that terror could strike at any time. Three incidents, however, finally brought about a dramatic shift in the local situation. A dissident offshoot of the M19 arrived in the area in 1990, claiming to be holding drug traffickers to ransom. At the same time, the ELN organized a peasant march to Playa de Trujillo in which the peasants were forced to take part. Finally, in early 1991 a member of the Colombian army was killed in an ambush. In the days that followed, all the 'suspects' were shot dead one by one by the military, and by paramilitary groups linked to the drug traffickers. There were to be more than 120 dead, including the local priest as a consequence of military and paramilitary action. These facts were covered up for some time, but eventually came to light. For the first time, the state was obliged to accept responsibility for the situation.

A number of general observations can be made on the basis of this example:

1. There are clearly important differences between the goals of violence and the actors involved in different decades, whether in the 1930s, the 1950s, the 1960s or the 1990s. Episodes of violence none the less recur with sufficient regularity to produce an overall impression of continuity. The absence of any clear markers or historical turning point complicates the social construction of memory and its insertion within a historical sequence of events.

2. Overt violence has clearly come to form an integral part of all power relations in Colombian society. Such relations of violence cut across

existing institutions. By 1978, the Frente Nacional government having been in power for twenty years, the killings organized by a local leader were not even seen as violating the rule of law.

3. Even the minimal level of civil rights already secured is in jeopardy. Complex procedures are involved in obtaining title to land, for example, and the violence has the effect of limiting the scope of such legislation to those with the most firmly established land titles, such as the peasant farmers in coffee-growing areas. The result for other peasants is a permanently insecure state of daily existence.

4. Political citizenship is just as fragile as civil rights; there is nothing to protect it. The same is true for collective forms of identity, which are subject to the control of the various networks, and have become totally heterogeneous. There is little basic difference between local people's relations with a land-owner, with guerrilla groups, or indeed with any other group.

5. Even though it is terror that hits the headlines, the transition from ordinary violence to terror takes place fairly smoothly, without any major discontinuities. The massacre of 1991 happened to be officially recognized, but this was an exception. More usually, such incidents are regarded as falling outside the scope of any solidly constructed sequence of events.

6. In a municipality like Trujillo, it has become problematic to speak of violence in terms of boundaries, even invisible ones. The inhabitants are permanently trapped in the interactions of the various armed protagonists.

7. The terror at the local level certainly forms part of the wider phenomenon of terror at the national level. Yet this wider environment has little meaning for those immersed in the daily reality of the terror. This represents a further explanation as to why the terror cannot comfortably be incorporated into a wider sequence of historical events. The representation of the terror remains an elusive goal.

Conclusion

Among the main themes I have sought to highlight are: the banality of violence, and the impossible task of constructing a meaningful picture of terror. Of the numerous corollaries of these themes, I would again mention two: the fragmentation of the sense of the individual, and the disjointedness of public opinion.

This investigation has spoken of the individual's experience of violence and terror, but to which individual are we referring? All individuals find themselves at the meeting-point between various conflicting pressures. The individual is at one and the same time enclosed within networks of control, committed to a strategy of survival, sceptical in the face of public institutions, but also seeking 'state assistance'. There is no synthesis between these various pressures. As a result even the constancy of the individual's identity in time

should not be taken for granted.[34] It is not surprising that the only expression of a constant identity is in an account of things that leads the individual passively from one situation to the next.

The situation regarding public opinion is little better. There is a public response to events when there is an important symbolic dimension. But even these events are soon forgotten, as they follow each other in quick succession. Public feeling has suffered from a relapse. Except at times of drama, there are hardly any signs of public disquiet. Public opinion on a whole range of issues (including the drug trade), and policies towards the guerrilla groups, violence and corruption, either do not take shape at all, or change with circumstances (which amounts to much the same thing), going from one set of demands to another, from total support for negotiations to demands for the use of force. The same is true, *a fortiori*, in relation to the terror. Those who form public opinion in this respect are rarely exposed to it. The sequence of mass killings in Uraba are a dim recollection. Whereas the first such incidents caused an impact, as they have increased they have been reduced to the 'news in brief' section of newspaper. The penetration of violence into the towns increases the degree of disorder and undermines all traditional points of reference. The lack of response to the advances of the paramilitary and their trail of horrors, which is taking place at present, demonstrates the extent of this disorder and disorientation.

As we have seen, violence becomes a way of operating that undermines the basis for all established social institutions. Although the state's legal existence continues, it has little if any control over the course of events. The intervention of the United States forcibly introduced a third party in the local conflicts, making all local armed groups appear like members of a community of delinquents. The use of ultimatums undoubtedly has its limits as well: it can provide a different perception of the situation, but it often amounts to introducing yet another protagonist into the conflict. Besides their position of military power, it is not clear that the United States can claim to be identified with the rule of law, even less impose it on Colombians, whatever the deficiencies of their existing laws.

Notes and References

1. This figure was obtained by adding together official homicides from official police statistics. See Policia Nacional, *Criminalidad 1995* (Bogotá). From these figures, it can be suggested that this approximates the 'normal' situation in Colombia. Even in the 1960s, the homicide rate was rarely less than 15 per 100,000.

2. See Uribe and Vásquez, *Enterrar y Callar*.

3. The number of deaths in Uraba varies between 1,500 and 3,000, according to estimates.

4. The reader should refer to the books of the Comisión de Estudios sobre la Violencia, including Deas and Gaitán Daza, *Colombia, Violencia y Democracia; Dos Ensayos Especulativos*. The reader can also refer to the two volumes of the publication *Controversia*, entitled *Un país en construcción*. See also Pécaut, 'Présent, passé, futur de la violence'.

5. On the notion of *mise en intrigue*, see Ricoeur, *Temps et récités*.

6. According to estimates presented by Deas and Gaitán Daza, *Colombia, violencia y democracia*. This figure has subsequently been repeated frequently, though without any in-depth confirmation of its accuracy.

7. See Bétancourt and García, 'Colombie: les mafias de la drogue'.

8. Depending on conditions, emeralds constitute the second or third most important export of the country. For centuries, emerald-producing areas have been plagued by chronic problems of violence. Many of the country's most renowned bandits came from these areas. Mines are currently leased to private companies under contract, but most exports are contraband. This combination of legal and illegal activities in an area near Bogotá, yet relatively isolated, means the area plays a key role in strategies of violence. Gonzalo Rodriguez Gacha, a close associate of Pablo Escobar, came from this region. In the late 1980s a feud for control over the area between two rival camps resulted in several thousand deaths.

9. See Echandia, 'Colombie: dimensions économiques'.

10. The FARC was able to destroy the paramilitary groups installed in Putumayo, a department with a strategic role in drug-related activities. However, in other regions, and notably in Magdalena Medio, Rodriguez Gacha's paramilitary were able to eliminate col-laborators and allies of the FARC, including the militants of the UP.

11. It is certainly not a coincidence that the most murderous ambushes of the military by guerrilla groups took place in Putumayo and Caqueta, key centres of cocaine production, along with Guaviare.

12. In recent years guerrilla groups have tried to gain control over local investments by trying to bring the mayors, of whatever political persuasion, under their influence.

13. For an analysis from the point of view of a military strategist, see Rangel Suarez, 'Colombia: la guerra irregular'.

14. In many areas under guerrilla control, political lists with an allegiance to these groups have been obtaining a progressively smaller share of the vote over the past ten years or so. To attribute this solely to the terror would be to ignore the elecorate's mistrust of these somewhat ambiguous political parties. The guerrillas take advantage of this problem by supporting candidates from the traditional parties, and exercising tight control over them once they are elected.

15. For an account of social relations in Uraba, see Martin, *Desarrollo económico*, Botero, *Uraba: Colonización*, García, *Urabá, región, actores y conflicto*.

16. See Thoumi, *Economía, Política y Narcotráfico*.

17. This is the line of argument of Edgar Reveiz in his book *Democratizar para Sobrevivir*.

18. Bejarano, 'Democracia', offers a good illustration of this problem.

19. This information is taken from two studies by Rubio, *Homicidios* and *Capital social*.

20. See Gambetta, *Sicilian Mafia*.

21. Even the FARC is subject to the laws of capitalist accumulation. In certain depart-ments, and notably in Guaviare, a category has emerged of the cultivation of cocaine on large land-holdings, and these now account for a significant share of total production.

22. See Catanzaro, 'La mafia'.

23. These means included the blowing up of an airplane in mid-flight.

24. After 1950, this was certainly true for some key leaders of the Liberal party.

25. See García, *Hijos de la violencia*.

26. See Uribe, *Matar, rematar y contramatar*.

27. The barbaric act referred to involved the decapitation of a very young child in front of Gloria Cuartas and local schoolchildren.

28. This kind of conflict (around *idéalités*) is central to the thinking of Balibar in his

'Violence: idéalité et cruauté'. For him, it is important to establish a connection between the expression of ideals and violence itself.

29. Leaders of the Medellín cartel, like the Ochoa brothers, were given sentences of only two years. A key figure in the cartel of the northern Cauca Valley, who was suspected of having carried out several mass killings, was given a jail sentence of only three years initially, later increased to six. In late 1996, faced with the prospect of the 'de-certification' of Colombia by the United States, the government and the Congress increased these sentences and took steps to requisition the assets of drug traffickers. In the short term, the latter measure is unlikely to have much impact, given the sophisticated system of placing these assets in the names of various 'straw men' in order to disguise their true value.

30. Some authors view the Colombian military as enjoying almost complete 'autonomy'. One is Leal Buitrago, *El oficio de la guerra*. Although the term 'autonomy' somewhat lacks clarity, it is necessary to distinguish between military forces with the capacity to impose their own social programme on the civil authorities (as for example in the case of the military in Argentina or Brazil), and straightforward operational autonomy. The military have been largely unable to affirm themselves in political life, having long been considered with social disdain by the elite groups who were imprisoned within the civilianist tradition. The military's geo-political training is limited to that available in military academies and their budget, which was very low for a long time, must be approved by the National Congress. The counterpart to this was that the civilian elites left them free to carry out their military operations. This was a poisoned chalice, since without any clear political agenda, the military acted without any sense of purpose, reacting to events as they arose on a daily basis. Reference to 'national security' is purely rhetorical. None of the military leaders appears to have elaborated any clear conception of what this security means.

31. I refer the reader to my own study, *L'Ordre et la violence*.

32. See Guerra, *Le Mexique*, Demélas, *L'Invention politique*.

33. The account which follows relies heavily on the excellent study of Leon Atehortua Cruz, *El Poder y la sangre*.

34. On this theme, see Ricoeur, *Soi-même comme Autre*.

PART III

Peaceful Democratic Transitions?
Prospects and Problems

EIGHT

Collective Memories, Fears and Consensus: the Political Psychology of the Chilean Democratic Transition

PATRICIO SILVA

For many years now, Chile has been divided into two clearly defined countries that don't look at each other, don't touch each other, and don't know each other; but they sense and fear one another. The grave danger of this situation lies in the natural progression from fear to hate, and from hate to aggression – a progression which so often ends in the logic of war, as it did in September of 1973.[1]

The Chilean transition to democracy has been generally considered one of the most successful cases in the recent wave of democratization in Latin America. From a political perspective, the transfer of power from a military to an elected civilian government took place in an ordered manner, with a minimum of political turmoil and social dislocation. In addition, following the democratic restoration, a remarkable degree of political consensus has been achieved between the country's most important political forces.[2] Economically, Chile's performance has been repeatedly classified by international institutions as outstanding, in terms of growth and fiscal stability.[3] In the social field, the democratic governments have deployed huge and well-financed programmes to improve access for low-income groups to health, education and housing, with apparent success. The elimination of extreme poverty in the country has been declared as the nation's single major target; one which is expected to be achieved within the next decade..

Behind this very promising scenario, however, a substantial and very painful learning process can be perceived in which a series of psychological and emotional factors have contributed to shape a distinctive set of political attitudes and behaviour among the country's key actors. It can be said that Chilean society as a whole is still traumatized by its recent political history. However, this national trauma is many-faceted, being dependent on the

political and ideological orientation of the persons involved. For right-wing sectors, the memories of the radicalization of social conflict, the strikes, the street violence, the shortages of food and consumer goods, and the real or imaginary communist threat under the Unidad Popular government, have had a deep psychological impact. It would be almost impossible for an outsider to understand their conspicuous, uncritical and passionate support for the military government, if the political effects of this trauma are not properly taken into account. On the other hand, the unforgettable memories of Tuesday 11 September 1973 still produce intense sadness and bitterness among those who enthusiastically supported the Allende government. All previous certainties about the 'irreversibility' of the 'socialist process' were mercilessly destroyed in one fell swoop. In addition to this, the subsequent physical persecution, maltreatment and torture, labour uncertainty, ideological oppression and, for many, the hard experience of exile, deeply shocked the Chilean Left.

This chapter aims to provide an analysis of the main components of the existing political fears in Chile in order to assess the ways in which this psychological factor has influenced the attitudes and behaviour of the major political actors during the democratic transition. In my opinion, the almost obsessive search for agreements and consensus between the democratic coalition and the opposition – which, in fact, have been crucial to the success of the democratization process – reveals the existence of deep-seated apprehension on both sides, that is not only the product of past experiences but also of the many uncertainties normally generated by transitional processes. I certainly do not pretend to reduce the Chilean democratic transition to the logic of fear, as it is obvious that this process has been conditioned by numerous political, institutional, economic and cultural factors.[4] I just want to emphasize the role played by psychological factors in regime changes; until now this has not received sufficient attention in the study of the Chilean democratic transition.

In the first part of the chapter, I assess the collective memories, which exist for several sectors of Chilean society, about the past democratic experience that abruptly ended with the military coup. I will focus on two aspects of the fear that resulted from the crisis of Chile's political system in the early 1970s: the 'perception of threat', and the 'demand for authority'. In addition, I will refer to the difficult and painful discussion within the Chilean Left about the causes of the débâcle of the Allende experience. In the second part of the chapter, I mention the main mechanisms utilized by the former military government to preserve the sense of fear among the population, in order to use it both as a source of legitimacy among its supporters, and as an instrument of deterrence against its adversaries. In the third section I analyse the political behaviour of the supporters of the military regime in the years preceding the democratic restoration, when their memories and fears of the past conditioned their positioning *vis-à-vis* Pinochet and the

democratic forces. In the final part of the chapter, I describe the efforts by the democratically elected governments to eliminate the anxieties and to create confidence among business groups, the armed forces, and the right-wing political parties about their ability to rule the country and their objectives in doing so.

The Lasting Memories of the Past

In his seminal study on the emergence of bureaucratic-authoritarian (BA) regimes in the southern cone, O'Donnell pays particular attention to the profound economic and political crises which preceded the military take-over in Brazil (1964) and Argentina (1966).[5] His interpretation was later applied to the coups in Chile (1973), Uruguay (1973) and, again, in Argentina (1976). Previous to the military intervention, these countries indeed con-fronted a situation of generalized social and political conflict which was accompanied by a severe economic and fiscal crisis. This situation generated a profound 'perception of threat' among the economic elites, perceiving the crisis as a menace to the existing economic and political order. As O'Donnell indicates:

> The greater the threat level, the greater the polarization and visibility of the class content of the conflicts that precede implantation of a BA. This, in turn, tends to produce a stronger cohesion among the dominant classes, to prompt a more complete subordination of most middle sectors to them, and to provoke a more obvious and drastic defeat of the popular sector and its allies. This can be specified in several ways. First, a higher threat level lends more weight, within the armed forces, to the 'hard-line' groups not preoccupied [...] with the immediate achievement of 'social integration'. Second, and closely connected, a higher threat level leads to a greater willingness to apply and to support a more systematic repression for the attainment of the political deactivation of the popular sector and for the subordination of its class organizations, especi-ally the unions.[6]

This perception of threat constitutes a key factor in understanding the generation of a coup coalition in Chile which eventually led to the *coup d'état* of September 1973. However, the repercussions of this factor go much further. First, the perception of threat was not exclusively confined to the dominant groups in society, as this was also shared by the middle classes and even by some segments of the popular sectors. And second, this perception not only forms a major factor for the understanding of the military coup, but also for the understanding of the political behaviour displayed by Pinochet's supporters during his regime in general, and the transition period in particular. In other words, the perception of threat becomes a historical experience which for a long time continues to produce and reproduce both loyalties and distrust, impeding in this manner the generation of a nation-wide consensus.

THE THREAT OF THE OTHER When one looks back at the final days of the former Chilean democracy, one finds an extremely divided, over-ideologized and polarized nation, where a left-wing government was firmly determined to establish socialism in the country while a broad opposition furiously resisted it by all means.[7] In comparison with other cases in the region, both the level of pre-coup crisis and the perception of threat were extremely high in Chile. As Remmer states, 'Nowhere in the Southern Cone has the perception of crisis been more widely generalized or the "threat from below" more palpable than in Chile.'[8]

In contrast to those other southern cone countries, the threat in Chile came not only from certain groups of the population, but also from the government itself which explicitly attempted to change the existing socio-political and economic order. Furthermore, the threat to the economic elites was not merely the product of fear of possible damage to their interests; this had already occurred as a result of the expropriation of land, companies and banks. It was their very survival as a class and the existence of capitalism as a system that was at stake. The battle between the Unidad Popular and the anti-Allende forces was particularly violent in the countryside, where the process of land expropriation generated a climate of total confrontation between land-owners and the peasantry.[9]

A fundamental actor in the fall of the Allende government was the middle class. Although, at the beginning, the Unidad Popular government counted on the support of a part of this large social group, the disenchantment of the middle class with the government was already evident by the end of 1971. The growing radicalization, mobilization and combativeness of the urban marginals clearly frightened the middle class who experienced this popular agitation as a veritable 'revolt of the masses'. In addition, the deep economic crisis and the subsequent shortages of food and consumer goods had created intense apprehensions among the more affluent as they saw their consumer patterns and lifestyle seriously threatened.[10]

Even more importantly, the perception of threat had been extended to the military, as they feared the establishment of a parallel military power, by the radicalized sectors of the Left. The military leaders also feared the infiltration of their institutions by left-wing agitators and a possible insurrection from within the ranks of the army and the navy. Finally, the armed forces were also very concerned with their own participation in the Unidad Popular government (after Allende had demanded their presence in the government in November 1972), as this could eventually lead to the politicization of military institutions.[11]

SOCIETAL SATURATION Looking from a broader sociological perspective, the country's general crisis produced a climate of collective insecurity among the entire population. From a Durkheimian perspective, Tironi states the problem in the following terms:

The effervescence, the destabilization of daily life, the faintness of the limit between individual and mass, cannot be but transitory. In the long-run, it inevitably produces exhaustion and revulsion and, after a while, an unforeseeable reaction. In Chile, in 1973, broad sectors of society showed an unbearable fatigue. Due to the lack of channels that could ritualise the effervescence, permitting society to regain its unity and routine, Chilean society became desperate, leading to a many-sided demand for authority. From the political point of view, indeed, the Chilean situation seemed without an outlet [...] In mid-1973 many people began to look for an outlet, no matter which, for this distressing psychological situation. Obviously, those outlets were extra-constitutional.[12]

On the one hand, radicalised left-wing sectors demanded from Allende a *mano dura* against the seditious opposition in order to re-establish his presidential authority. On the other hand, the opposition adopted a clearly putchist strategy directed towards the violent overthrow of the government by the military in order to put an end to what was seen as an anarchist situation, and to re-establish the principle of authority. At the end, there was no place in Chile for moderates supporting a negotiated solution between the major political forces in order to avoid the collapse of Chilean democracy.

The Allende government and its final débâcle bring bad memories to both its former adversaries and supporters, as it actually represents the failure of Chilean society as a whole. This is particularly true for the Left which, following the coup, initiated a long and painful debate to ascertain the causes of Allende's fall. This debate evolved into a veritable collective therapy. The first essays on this subject (mainly party reports produced in exile) had a strong over-ideologized and recriminatory character as leftist political parties blamed each other for the tragedy. To the outside world, the left-wing parties referred to the coup as a *derrota* (defeat), to stress the militaristic nature of Allende's fall, in an attempt to present the military as a *diabulus ex machina* which unexpectedly interrupted the consolidation of socialism in Chile. With the passing of time, however, a process of demystification and secularization of the Unidad Popular experience took place: the errors and deficiencies of the Allende government were put at the centre of the analysis. At a certain point, some political leaders openly began to talk about the *fracaso* (failure) of the Unidad Popular experiment, stressing by this the coalition's own responsibility for the débâcle.[13] Many left-wing political leaders saw the coup not only in terms of collective shortcomings, but also as a personal failure. The traumatic experience of the change had taught a painful lesson to many Chileans. The day the military dictatorship comes to an end, the repetition of such errors which led to this collective failure must be avoided at all costs. The deep mark left by this experience repeatedly came to the surface in the words and thoughts of left-wing leaders during the transition period and after the restoration of democracy in 1990.[14]

As we shall see in the following sections, the fear of a repetition of the economic and political crisis of the pre-coup period conditioned the political behaviour of most of the country's political actors, and remains a potent force even now.

The Institutionalization of Fear

Following the *coup d'état*, the military began with the brutal repression of all the political and social sectors which had supported the deposed Unidad Popular government. Latin America had never before experienced such a wave of repression following a military take-over. Many thousands of Chileans were imprisoned, tortured and killed by the security forces. The unprecedented degree of violence used by the armed forces generated a deep sense of terror among ex-supporters of the Unidad Popular government.[15]

PROTECTION FROM INSECURITY In an attempt to legitimize the military take-over, the new authorities began an extensive news media campaign against the former government, which was blamed for the social and political turmoil of the previous years.[16] As Constable and Valenzuela recall:

> Official propaganda stressed the violence and chaos of the Allende years and depicted the coup as a glorious act of liberation. One brochure showed people waiting in bread lines while Allende stashed whisky and pornography in private hideaways. Another book contrasted scenes of Chile past and present, with hyperbolic captions. Yesterday there was scarcity, 'chaos, ambulances, violence'; today there was order, plenty, and 'a new morality'.[17]

In this manner, the new military government presented itself as the sole guarantor of order, citizens' security and authority. This is what Samuel Valenzuela has called the 'inverse legitimation' of the military government. It was an attempt to validate the new regime, and even to garner support for it, by pointing to real or exaggerated faults of the previous one.[18] And indeed, the offer of order, after a period of fervent changes and social mobilizations, was welcomed at the outset by many Chileans as an alternative to the previous period of polarization and social confrontation. In this context, a dictatorship was considered a 'lesser evil' in comparison to the uncertainties and fear produced by the Unidad Popular government.[19]

Although the military used its supposed ability to provide security to the citizenry as one of its main sources of legitimation, in fact the new authorities consciously generated fear and insecurity among the population through several mechanisms. In this way the government tried to convince Chileans that the existence and continuation of an authoritarian regime were necessary to deal adequately with persistent threats from the past. Instead of trying to normalize the political situation as soon as possible, the armed forces sought the institutionalization of the initial state of emergency, by giving the 'com-

munist threat' a permanent character within national life. The idea was that the enemy had lost a battle but not the war and was waiting for the right time to strike at the nation again. As a consequence the country was officially maintained under a *estado de guerra* (state of war) for one year, followed by two more years of *estado de sitio* (state of alert). Still later this situation of institutionalized emergency was consolidated in a *estado de conmoción nacional* (state of national commotion). For many years, a curfew was applied in the country's largest cities to maintain the sensation of abnormality and threat among the population.[20] In order to activate Chilean patriotism and support for the government, 'international communism', personified by Cuba and the Soviet Union, was identified as the country's greatest threat. According to the government, these countries could never forgive Chile for having ended communist domination in the country and, therefore, would surely lay in wait for a new chance to pounce.

In June 1974 Pinochet created the Dirección Nacional de Inteligencia (DINA), to coordinate the repressive activities of the security services of the several branches of the armed forces. DINA's remit was almost unlimited, operating virtually without restraint in the repression of dissidents. It was responsible for most of the cases of those people who 'disappeared' during the military government's time in power. DINA rapidly became Pinochet's main instrument for consolidating his personal rule. As Arriagada indicates:

It would be difficult to exaggerate the degree to which control of DINA concentrated power in the hands of the Chief of State. From mid-1974 [...] DINA was the backbone of the regime; no agency in Chile had greater impact on national life. The President's absolute authority over DINA effectively dispelled any pretence of equality between him and those who, in the months immediately following the coup, had been his peers.[21]

In 1977, following broad international condemnation and severe criticism from the Chilean Catholic Church, DINA was replaced by the Central Nacional de Inteligencia (CNI) in an attempt to 'legalize' repression. It is important to stress that both DINA and CNI were engaged in the task of maintaining fears among the population. As Garretón points out, following the creation of DINA:

Repression became more selective, combining covert acts of murder or kidnapping with spectacular actions which, witnessed by the whole population, were designed to instill fear [...] [T]he CNI followed DINA in almost all its methods [...] Between 1977 and 1980, while the political model was being defined, the repression was more targeted, instilling fear and breaking morale. Massive detentions, internal deportations, expulsions, and tortures predominated, although there were also some executions, carried out on the pretext of confronting armed resistance.[22]

Pinochet himself systematically referred to the dangers confronting the

nation. In a comprehensive study of his discourse, Munizaga indicates that the incitement of fear constituted a recurrent theme in Pinochet's public speeches. As she points out:

> The discourse of Pinochet is directed to enhance insecurity and to promote fear [...] Insecurity, fear and anxiety – which represent permanent and profound ingredients in the life of men and society; feelings, which accompany the uncertainties of any process of economic growth and social change – are the pillars upon which the military government pretends to sustain a government which aspires to obtain unconditioned adhesion of the ruled.[23]

BETWEEN GRATITUDE AND FEAR Fear was also a determining factor in the attitudes adopted by Chilean entrepreneurs toward the military government. Industrial and agrarian entrepreneurs were the groups most willing to accept the sacrifices demanded by the government's plan to restructure the economy along free market principles. Regaining security over their properties and dismantling industrial unions and the peasant movement was sufficient for them to express their trust in and optimism about the measures adopted by the military junta. Notwithstanding the evident risks of the new economic policy (reduction of tariffs, elimination of state protection, etcetera), Chilean entrepreneurs accepted the new economic model without reservation.[24] This attitude was not only the product of their gratitude towards the armed forces who liberated them from a 'Castroist regime', but also of their fears of a future recovery of left-wing forces and their possible return to power. As Stepan points out:

> The persistence of fear with the upper bourgeoisie was an important element in the bourgeoisie's willingness to accept individual policies that hurt the upper class [...] but were seen to be the necessary cost of protecting its overall interests. It is impossible to understand the passivity of the industrial faction of the bourgeoisie in Chile (a passivity, that, of course, increased the policy autonomy of the state) outside the context of fear.[25]

The unconditional withdrawal of the entrepreneurial class from the political and economic management of the country led to the unexpected formation of a new structure of decision-making, centred round a civil neo-liberal technocracy (the so-called 'Chicago Boys'), who often showed complete disregard for the entrepreneurs' views.[26] When, after a couple of years, entrepreneurial organizations timidly began to criticize some aspects of economic policy, they always tried to hold on to the distinction between the civil neo-liberal technocracy and the military rulers. Each time they protested against a particular economic measure, they explicitly directed their criticism to the Chicago Boys, while simultaneously expressing their support for the 'government of the armed forces'. However, this duality in their discourse did not yield results. The alliance between the military and the neo-liberal

technocrats had become very close and the former displayed no inclination whatsoever to interfere in the formulation and implementation of economic policy.[27] As Constable and Valenzuela point out:

> Businessmen responded deferentially to any criticism emanating from the new rulers. The freshness of their trauma kept them loyal to their liberators, and even the most prominent businessmen were reluctant to offend the military, for fear of being labeled dissidents or traitors. Despite their high-profile role in opposing Allende, business leaders found they had little personal influence on military officials or their high-powered economic aides.[28]

CONSUMERISM AND APATHY The application, during the years 1975–77, of the painful economic and financial measures by the 'Chicago Boys' (elimination of state personnel, cuts in salaries and tariffs, elimination of subsidies, price increases, etcetera) was accompanied by increased levels of repression by the security agencies in order to prevent any manifestations of discontent among the population. However, with the passing of time, the disappearance of the threat of 'subversion' eliminated one of the important justifications for the repression needed to maintain political control of the popular sector. The decline of fear posed a difficult problem for the government as they had to find new sources of legitimacy to retain support. As Kaufman notes, all the southern cone's military regimes faced this problem at a certain point in their rule:

> Declining fear is a secular feature of bureaucratic-authoritarian rule, or at least that this fear cannot persist indefinitely with the same salience and intensity that it acquired during the crisis period itself. It is likely to diminish most rapidly among middle-sector forces which risk less and can gain more than their military and capitalist allies from a relaxation of authoritarian controls. As a degree of 'normality' is restored to the daily rhythms of social life, a sense of security may also increase among at least some sectors of the military and capitalist establishment itself.[29]

In the late 1970s, the military government indeed reoriented its search for legitimation from the 'communist threat' towards the promises of the new neo-liberal model, as the Chilean economy began to show strong signs of recovery after years of recession. In 1978, for instance, the rate of inflation reached historically low levels, the fiscal deficit disappeared, the balance of payments displayed a growing surplus, and the economy in general showed a vigorous dynamism.[30] The military government clearly understood the importance of consumption in politics. Indeed, consumerism became a key aspect of the regime's attempt to increase its legitimacy and to consolidate authoritarian rule in the country. As noted before, the anti-Allende propaganda following the coup stressed the scarcity issue. This was, indeed, one of the most traumatic and hated memories surviving from the Unidad Popular

period, especially for the upper and middle classes. In the late 1970s, the media played a strategic role in fostering a further expansion of mass consumption in the country. In the period 1978–81, Chile experienced a 'consumption boom' as almost all consumer goods produced in developed countries became accessible to the upper and middle classes. As a result of the expansion of consumer credit, even parts of the popular sector obtained some access to the 'pleasures' of the developed world by, purchasing foreign products that symbolized modernity. In fact, the military government wanted to replace 'citizens' by 'consumers'. In this way, consumerism became a surrogate for political freedom and participation.[31] However, the high levels of consumption achieved by the upper and middle classes during the military government created a new source of fear among these social groups, which was not directly related to the past. They became afraid of losing their *present* standard of living, which was in many respects much higher than they had ever experienced prior to the Allende years.

In the long run, fear led to apathy, moral indifference and finally to apoliticism. Brunner talks about the *generación del conformismo*, who accepted the social atomization and individualism produced by the market and who feared politics for the uncertainties it brings along.[32] As we shall see in the following section, the uncertainties produced by political contest played an important role in the reactivation of fears during the democratic transition.

Transition to Uncertainty

The emphasis on economic growth and stability as major sources of legitimacy for the regime was a major weakness. In contrast to less distinct ideological concepts, as traditionally used by populist regimes, the goverment's economic objectives and promises were easier to measure. They had been reduced to very precise variables: high GNP growth, low rate of inflation, expansion of exports, and so forth.

For this reason, by the late 1970s, some left-wing circles assumed that the military government would fall if an economic crisis broke out. However, this economistic understanding of social reality overlooked at least two important factors. First, the Chilean population was not willing to bring down the military government, even in the event of an economic crisis, in the absence of an acceptable political alternative. And second, any major economic crisis would engender not only discontent among the upper and middle classes, but also social agitation and probably political mobilization among the popular sectors. The latter would lead to the intransigency of the dominant groups as the 'threat from below' would bring back the old fears of the early 1970s. The political situation in Chile during the early 1980s served to confirm the above, as I will argue below.

THE REAWAKENING OF CIVIL SOCIETY   The sudden collapse, in March

1981, of a leading financial group resulted in a speculative wave which provoked, in its turn, a general panic within entrepreneurial circles. This signalled the start of a severe economic crisis. In the following months, many financial institutions (the so-called *financieras*) and enterprises went into bankruptcy, production levels decreased dramatically, and unemployment jumped to critical levels. By the end of that year, the GNP had declined by 14 per cent.[33] The outbreak of this economic crisis led to the 'resurrection' of party politics in the country. After almost a decade, the outlawed political parties began gradually to re-establish their activities in an increasingly open manner, while the military government, showing clear signs of weakness, searched for some formula to tackle the new political situation.[34] A mass protest against the government, held on 11 May 1983, marked the reactivation of Chilean civil society. After that historical demonstration, several 'days of national protest' were organized on a monthly basis in Chile's major cities, demanding the restoration of democracy. At the beginning, the protest movement succeeded in mobilizing not only the popular sectors, but also an important part of the urban middle classes who had become apprehensive as a result of the economic downturn.

The 'days of national protest', however, soon gained an unexpectedly radical character, as the democratic opposition parties proved unable to channel and to guide the actions of the masses. This was particularly the case in the shantytowns surrounding Santiago where the protests against the government acquired almost insurrectional dimensions. Radical segments of the opposition, such as the Communist party and the Movement of the Revolutionary Left (MIR), actively supported the violent actions of the *pobladores* that they had chosen as a strategy of 'popular insurrection' to bring down the dictatorship. The government responded to this challenge with massive military operations in the shantytowns, which led to the death of dozens of *pobladores*. This demonstration of military power deeply shocked shantytown dwellers, as it resembled the methods used by the military forces following the 1973 coup.[35]

As Tironi points out, 'the violence which broke out as a result of the protests of 1983 and 1984 automatically revived the images of the traumatic crisis of 1973 in the collective memory'.[36] The military government used the mass media craftfully to drive home the image of *pobladores'* violence in order to revive middle-class fears of chaos and insurrection. At the end of 1984, the protests, which had previously taken place in Santiago's middle-class neighbourhoods, virtually disappeared. Both the 'threat from below' and the strong recovery experienced by the Chilean economy since mid-1984, calmed middle-class protests, enabling Pinochet to regain control of the situation.

The democratic opposition learned important lessons from the 'days of protest' that proved decisive for the subsequent political strategy to end military rule in the country. In the first place, the protests had shown that

mass mobilization would not bring down the dictatorship, which was still too strong and could count on considerable support among the general population. After this experience, the democratic opposition parties chose a top-down approach, aimed at achieving agreement at the highest political levels rather than political mobilization at the grassroots level. Secondly, the use of promoting violence proved to be counter-productive because it provided legitimacy to the military's use of repression. It also rekindled the fear of a reversion to old forms of confrontation. The mass protests also highlighted the fact that the goal of forming a united front against Pinochet was unrealistic: left-wing extremism had clearly chosen a violent and armed path, while the rest of the opposition movement had opted for a political solution. Thirdly, it became clear that the first priority for the democratic opposition was to put into place, as soon as possible, a coalition of parties which could offer a moderate and credible alternative to the military regime. And finally, it was very unlikely that the military government was prepared to depart from its institutional agenda, contained in the 1980 constitution. This implied that sooner or later the democratic opposition had to accept the validity of this controversial constitution, and use the narrow political space left to it by this piece of authoritarian legislation.

IDEOLOGICAL RENOVATION   It would be wrong, however, to explain the willingness of the opposition forces to develop a moderate political strategy solely on the basis of the lessons drawn from the protests. This experience, rather, provided a catalyst for the move towards the long and difficult process of rapprochement between Christian Democrats and socialists. I shall briefly discuss the main aspects of this process, for it has been strongly influenced by the traumatic experience of the coup and the repression which followed.

As I have already noted, the first task facing the Chilean Left, after the coup, was to deal with its own responsibility for the final débâcle of Unidad Popular. Equally complex were the discussions, in exile, about the significance of dictatorship and democracy in the light of the coup experience and Pinochet's authoritarian rule. The brutality of the military coup and the atrocities perpetrated by the military deeply marked the conscience of left-wing parties and their followers. This was not without ideological consequences. The disappearance of fundamental human rights and the benefits of citizenship were something which practically no Chilean had ever experienced before. When left-wing militants fought for the establishment of a dictatorship of the proletariat in Chile, very few among them had ever really thought about the real content and practical implications of the term 'dictatorship'. After September 1973, Chileans learned the bitter lesson of what it really meant to live under a dictatorship. The military regime led many Chileans, at home and abroad, to adopt a firm anti-authoritarian stance. Although, initially, this was a direct reaction to the Pinochet regime, it soon generated a substantial reformulation of attitudes towards fundamental issues

such as liberty, democracy, dictatorship, pluralism and tolerance. The restoration of democracy became the key demand of the Chilean opposition. For many, it had become clear that this demand for democracy could not be used just to get rid of Pinochet. Hence, many socialists abandoned their traditional position of considering democracy as merely an instrument to achieve power. Instead, they started to consider it as an end in itself. As a result of this so-called 'renovation' process, Chilean socialists began to look at democracy, as Arrate put it, as 'the space and limit of political action'.[37]

At the beginning of the 1980s, many socialist leaders began to see the creation of a centre-left alliance with the Christian Democrats as the only way to form a broad, strong and stable government which could count on an electoral majority. They also realized that such an alliance could be possible only if its political objectives were limited to the restoration of democracy (the main common goal). This meant that socialist demands which could jeopardize the alliance had to be avoided.[38] Within the Christian Democratic party (PDC) a similar process of 'ideological renovation' took place at that time. This gave rise to self-criticism on issues such as the party's decision to rule alone during the Frei government (1964–70), for not having exhausted all possibilities of dialogue with the Unidad Popular government to prevent the breakdown of the democratic system and for its involvement in the fall of Allende. The PDC also came to the conclusion that an alliance with the moderate sectors of the Chilean socialists was feasible and desirable in order to encourage the Left to follow the democratic path.[39]

THE 1988 PLEBISCITE AND ITS AFTERMATH The 1980 constitution established that, in 1988, a plebiscite should take place, by which Chileans would have to decide whether they did or did not want an extension of Pinochet's rule for another eight years. When the new constitution was adopted in 1980, the Chilean economy was booming and the regime's self-confidence and triumphalism were at their zenith. The government had expected that, by 1988, Chile would enjoy a high degree of economic prosperity and, hence, the population would enthusiastically support the continuation of military rule.[40] No one could have expected that within a year the neo-liberal model would face a severe crisis, and the military government would have to deal with a growing political opposition.

In August 1983 Christian Democrats, socialists and other small political parties formed the Alianza Democratica (AD), a centre-left alliance, with the aim of becoming the foundation of a future democratic government. Exactly two year later, following a successful mediation by the Catholic church, a 'National Accord for the Transition to a Full Democracy' was signed by the majority of the opposition forces, including elements of the Right. However, it was the approach of the plebiscite itself (scheduled for 5 October 1988) which mobilized the democratic forces for this historical trial of strength between the military government and the opposition. Paradoxically, the fact

that there was just one candidate (Pinochet) and that people could only say 'yes' or 'no' facilitated unity among the democratic opposition forces around a single common issue: a no-vote against Pinochet. This led to the formation of the 'Comando por el No', in February 1988, which united most of the opposition groups, with the exception of the communists who rejected the idea of participating in a plebiscite organized by the military rulers.

In the months leading to the October plebiscite, the fear of change and uncertainty increased significantly in the general population. The opposition forces of the past were also afraid of Pinochet's reaction should the no-campaign succeed. They were concerned that he could use the pretext of fraud to ignore his defeat or, even worse, he might reinstate the high levels of repression which had existed in the past.

Television played a fundamental role in the campaigns of both government and opposition and their trial of strength was played out as an 'electronic event'. In order to give some credibility to the contest, the military government permitted the opposition forces, for the first time in fifteen years, to communicate freely with the Chilean people through a daily fifteen-minute television 'spot', for three weeks prior to the plebiscite. Most analysts agree this was fundamental to the victory of the opposition in that historic referendum.[41]

As Hirmas indicates, fear played a key role in the official television campaign for the 'yes' vote while the opposition campaign was aimed at alleviating the people's fear of the consequences of a successful no-campaign.[42] Pinochet had for years repeatedly declared that there was no viable alternative to his rule by using the slogan 'me or chaos'. While the yes-campaign was extremely negative and based on the past, the no-campaign was focused on hope, optimism and reconciliation. Advertisements for the yes-campaign alternated scenes of a bright, prosperous Chile with grim footage of food lines and violence under Allende. One horrific 're-creation' featured a mother and child fleeing from a mob brandishing clubs and red banners: '"If we return to the past, the first innocent victim could be in your family", the announcer warned as the camera froze on smashing glass and the woman's silent scream.'[43] These images stood in sharp contrast to the opposition's advertisements, which were superior in technical quality and content. The creative, upbeat 'no' segments captured the nation's imagination. Each night, a kaleidoscope of Chileans, from bus drivers to ballerinas, kept time to the theme song 'Joy is Coming'. The message was an optimistic, simple appeal for dignity and democracy, and Patricio Bañados, a prominent newscaster who had quit state TV to protest censorship, urged: 'Without hatred, without fear, vote No.' Constable and Valenzuela categorically conclude: 'The government had lost the control of the truth, and the opposition had run away with it.'[44]

The triumph of the opposition demonstrated that an important section of the Chilean population had freed itself from the fear which had previously proved so powerful and had opted for democratic restoration. The democratic

opposition parties had obtained the people's confidence on the clear understanding that they did not want to go back to the past. Following the
plebiscite, the eleven parties constituting the Comando por el No decided to
establish the Concertación de Partidos por la Democracia, an electoral
coalition to contest the general elections scheduled for December 1989. The
fact that no chaos or violence followed the plebiscite, and that the opposition
adopted a reconciliatory attitude towards the defeated regime, convinced
many people that the Concertación coalition was trustworthy and that December 1989 could be the beginning of a peaceful transition to democracy in
the country.

Fears, Trust and Consensus

Following the Concertación's victory in the December 1989 general election,
Chile began a new chapter in its political history. Optimism and relief
flourished where, only a few years earlier, it would have been inconceivable
that the Pinochet regime could end by peaceful means. There was a sense that
the country now had a unique chance to build a modern democracy on the
basis of a sound economic system.

One of the most remarkable aspects of this new Chilean democracy has
been the readiness shown by both government and opposition to reach
comprehensive agreements and compromises on economic, political and social
matters. As Tulchin and Varas correctly assess:

> After seventeen years of military dictatorship, Chilean political leaders all across
> the political spectrum began to put an end to a long tradition of bitter con-
> frontations, and slowly to value more and more democratic stability through
> compromise. An important modernization of political life occurred under the
> authoritarian regime. It consisted of a more pragmatic, nonideological approach
> to political issues and a consensual commitment to the maintenance of
> democratic rules of the game. The trauma of the military coup and its long
> and bloody aftermath were powerful incentives for all political sectors not to
> recreate the same conditions that produced the breakdown of democracy.[45]

The democratic government, and particularly President Patricio Aylwin
himself, was extremely cautious at each step it took in order not to jeopardize
the delicate political stability the country had achieved following his installation in March 1990.

It is true that Chile, in contrast to other countries in the region, had
inaugurated democratic rule under quite auspicious circumstances. For many
years, the country's economy had steadily grown while the financial situation
was relatively sound. On the other hand, O'Donnell and Schmitter argue that
countries which have previously had a long experience of democracy, and
hence with the workings and routines of its institutions, possess significant
advantages over those countries which have to shape a democratic order for

the first time.[46] Both Chilean politicians and the general public felt comfortable and familiar with the re-establishment of the democratic rituals. They experienced them as a 'return to the nation's roots'. However, in the particular case of Chile, the bad memories of the period leading to the collapse of the old democratic system, persisted. As Valenzuela indicates:

> Such cases of reconsolidation of democracy are [...] hampered by returning images of the crisis that led to their breakdown, which opponents of the democratic process will usually attempt to emphasize. Successful redemocratizations therefore require a deliberate effort on the part of the democratizing elites to avoid resurrecting symbols, images, conducts, and political programs associated with the conflicts leading to prior breakdown.[47]

As mentioned before, one of the most painful memories of the pre-coup period was the effect of the economic crisis (hyper-inflation, food shortages, etcetera). One of the greatest concerns about the new democratic era was the question of whether the Aylwin government would be able to maintain the economic and financial stability inherited from the military government. There was a particular fear of the attitude unions would take *vis-à-vis* the government and the entrepreneurs, now that they were free to use their rights (including strikes) to demand improvements in salaries and working conditions. The government, however, was resolute in its avowed aim of managing the economy successfully. The Concertación coalition wanted to destroy the myth that authoritarian governments are better than democratic ones at promoting economic growth and development. If the Aylwin government succeeded in showing its ability to provide even higher levels of social and economic development, it would not only legitimize democratic rule, but would also weaken the fear lurking among many Chileans that there could be a return to the past. The intensive energy expended by finance minister Alejandro Foxley and his team to ensure the continuation of economic prosperity is incomprehensible if due consideration is not given to the collective memories of the past. As Oppenheim indicates:

> Chileans remembered well the turbulent and chaotic days that had preceded that fall of Salvador Allende, along with the violence that ensued. The country had suffered a collective trauma. As a result, Chileans were extremely sensitive to situations that they thought might recreate previous crises. For example, many Chileans associated inflation and economic dislocation with the Allende government; consequently, the Aylwin government made the day-to-day management and stability of the economy a major priority.[48]

The Aylwin government developed a new practice of regular consultations with opposition parties, entrepreneurial organizations and trade unions to obtain broad political and social support for its economic policy. This practice, which has been continued by the government of Eduardo Frei Jr, has clearly helped to reduce the traditionally high levels of distrust in Chilean politics.

This *política de acuerdos*, as it has been called, made possible, among other things, increased taxes to finance social programmes, an increased minimum wage and improvements to labour legislation.[49] The consensus between government, opposition and entrepreneurs with respect to economic policy is undeniably related to the fact that the Concertación government continued with the application of neo-liberal policies.[50] Indeed, the Aylwin and Frei governments have accepted important economic postulates introduced by the 'Chicago Boys', such as the subsidiary role of the state in economic activities; the re-assessment of the role played by foreign capital and the domestic, private sector in economic development; the adoption of market mechanisms and efficiency criteria as the main instruments for the allocation of resources; the need to keep public finances healthy, and to consolidate macro-economic stability. In this manner, right-wing parties and entrepreneurial circles were, in general, satisfied with the economic course pursued by the civilian governments. Furthermore, they were also very reluctant to adopt a more oppositional stance against the government, fearing that this would lead to a strengthening of the more radical sectors within the Concertación which, in turn, would lead to a partial or complete abandonment of neo-liberal economic policies.

The Concertación government realized, however, that political stability would not be achieved by simply guaranteeing financial stability and economic growth. Something also had to be done to improve the living conditions of millions of Chileans who had been excluded from the fruits of economic growth. The poverty issue, however, had to be dealt with in a very cautious way, since government initiatives to combat poverty could be seen by right-wing circles as a disguised attempt to pursue populist or even socialist objectives. The Concertación governments have consciously depoliticized the social question in Chile to prevent any radicalization or confrontation on this issue. In contrast to the pre-coup period, social inequalities are not now perceived in extreme ideological terms, but are considered from the perspective of modernization. The common ground of government and opposition is that a country like Chile, which is experiencing a substantial process of growth and modernization, simply cannot afford to leave large segments of the population in extreme poverty. Extreme poverty is seen as not only ethically deplorable, but also technically unacceptable within the country's overall development strategy. Therefore, social justice is presented as the efficient elimination of poverty. In this way, the principle of social justice has been linked to the goals of economic efficiency and political stability.

The country's good economic performance under democratic rule has shown many Chileans that the fear of an economic crisis following the restoration of democracy was unfounded. There is widespread trust and confidence in the strength of the Chilean economy and its future perspectives. In short, during the past few years, the fear of a return to political radicalization, violence and economic crisis has been virtually eliminated. Some had

hoped this would, in turn, be sufficient to bury the past. However, for many, the pain and suffering of the past could not be buried as long as the country did not properly deal with the legacy of the horrors of the authoritarian period.

THE CONTEMPORANEITY OF THE PAST: THE QUESTION OF HUMAN RIGHTS Although during the past few years Chileans have managed to build a solid consensus on several fundamental issues, such as the pattern of development and the commitment to democracy, they still continue to be extremely divided about the causes and the significance of the crisis of the previous democratic system. As Tironi points out, it is not just a question of wounds – as wounds eventually heal – but also a lack of a common interpretation of history. Conventionally, the evocation of a common past nurtures the collective feeling of being part of a national community. In the Chilean case, however, the past still constitutes a latent source of conflict for the population.[51] It is for this reason that, following the restoration of democracy, the Chilean people almost instinctively restrained themselves from referring to the past, as this would make the objective of national reconciliation more difficult to attain.

Being the last country in the southern cone to restore democratic rule, Chile was in a position to evaluate the pros and cons of the ways the neighbouring countries dealt with the issue of human rights violations under the military regimes. The choices of doing nothing (Brazil), or bringing the question to a referendum (Uruguay), or passing a 'full-stop law' (Argentina), were not open to Chile, because the socialists within the governing Concertación coalition and important segments of the population were not willing to leave crimes unpunished. The Aylwin government had to act extremely cautiously on this matter because of the specific nature of the Chilean transition. This made it very difficult to find an adequate solution for the human rights problem, without having a negative impact on military–civil relations and, indeed, on support for the government among different segments of the population. One part of the population, including the armed forces and the social sectors which supported their authoritarian rule, still held to the thesis that, after 11 September 1973, Chile was in a 'state of internal war'. Hence, all that occurred during those years was the unavoidable result of the war waged by the armed forces against subversive groups. The other part of Chile – including the Concertación parties, the left-wing movement, human rights organizations and the rest of the population – considered the armed forces responsible for the systematic violation of the most elementary human rights.

Contrary to other countries in the region, the Chilean military returned to the barracks with full confidence and a certain mood of triumph. They thought that they had proved their competence and reliability by having implemented a clear political agenda as well as by respecting its outcome: the

loss of the 1988 referendum and the 1989 elections. Moreover, they were also proud of having modernized the Chilean economy and society. They were confident that the democratic authorities could not bring them to justice; in 1978, Pinochet had passed an amnesty law covering all past crimes. Most of the flagrant human rights violations that occurred during the Pinochet regime (including the notorious 'disappearances') took place between 1973 and 1978 and the Chilean Supreme Court had already confirmed the validity of the 1978 amnesty law.

One of the first decisions adopted by President Aylwin was to use his prerogative to set free most political prisoners. Those who were convicted by military tribunals for grave offences (assassination of military personnel and civilians) obtained a new trial in the civil courts. The next step was to establish what really happened to the victims of the military government. For this purpose, the Aylwin government announced, in April 1990, the formation of the 'Commission for Truth and Reconciliation', in order to investigate all the cases of human rights violations culminating in death. This commission was chaired by Raúl Rettig, a prestigious legal expert, and was composed of a group of experienced jurists from different political backgrounds. The armed forces expressed their discontent with this investigation as they considered it a breach of the 1978 amnesty law. The government rejected this objection by arguing that the Rettig Commission was not judging anyone, but just trying to establish the truth. On 4 March 1991 President Aylwin addressed the nation in an historic television broadcast, during which he informed the Chilean people about the main findings of the Rettig Commission. The commission concluded, among other thing that 2,279 persons had been killed, victims of human rights violations. Aylwin ended his address by asking the families of the victims for forgiveness in the name of the entire Chilean nation.[52]

A test case for the return of the armed forces to the rule of law has been the so-called Letelier case. In September 1976, Orlando Letelier, former minister of foreign affairs under Allende and a prominent leader of the Chilean opposition in exile, was murdered by a car bomb in a street in the centre of Washington, DC. The criminal investigation found a trail leading directly to the head of the Chilean intelligence agency (DINA), Colonel Manuel Contreras. The United States demanded the extradition of Contreras, but Pinochet rejected this request. The Letelier case has since remained a major obstacle for a complete normalization of diplomatic relations between the USA and Chile. The pressure from Washington on Chile was such that Pinochet was forced to exclude the Letelier case from the 1978 amnesty law. Following the restoration of democracy, the government gave high priority to the solution of this case. Although it could not interfere directly in the normal course of justice, the government put pressure on the Supreme Court to make an extra effort to bring the guilty persons to trial. In September 1991, a judge called for the arrest of General Manuel Contreras and his

associate General Pedro Espinoza. At the beginning of 1993 they were brought to trial, but they were later released on bail.

During 1993, the human rights issue began to wane. Some sectors of the population considered the publication of the Rettig Commission's findings and the Contreras trial as sufficient. As a result, the government of Aylwin's succesor, President Eduardo Frei Jr, decided that the question of human rights was no longer central to the political agenda. Frei's major concerns have been directed at the elimination of the remnants of authoritarianism (certain parts of the constitution, the composition of the senate, the autonomy of the army and so on), and at the internationalization of the Chilean economy, through possible participation in arrangements such as NAFTA, Mercosur, APEC (Asia Pacific Economic Cooperation) and so on.

Despite the country's good economic performance and clear improvements in the situation of the poorest people during the 1990s, the issues of the past remained alive in the minds of the Chilean population. This has resurfaced dramatically since June 1995, following the Supreme Court's final sentencing of Contreras and Espinoza to seven years in prison. The announcement of this verdict reactivated the national discussion about the legacy of repression and human rights violations, bringing to the surface the deep psychological wounds originated by the political experiences of the last twenty-five years. It has also produced a significant deterioration in relations between the government and the armed forces, as the latter fear that this verdict will be the beginning of a wave of trials and imprisonment of military men.

In an unprecedented act of defiance, Contreras ignored the sentence and declared that he would never go to prison. To avoid his detention by the police, he sought refuge in a military hospital in southern Chile under the pretext that he required medical attention. For a while, both the judicial system and the government proved unable to bring him to prison, while the army continued to show its support for its former comrade. In the end, Contreras abandoned his resistance and was imprisoned. This event put the government in a difficult position as it demonstrated that the armed forces still do not recognize the authority of the democratic government and the rule of law. The increasing tensions, in the mid-1990s, have reawakened the fundamental split within civil society. Right-wing politicians argue that the adoption of a kind of 'full-stop law' has become imperative because otherwise Chile will remain divided about the past. The Concertación government decided, in August 1995, to send three new proposals to parliament, aiming to put an end to the human rights question and the transitional process.[53] However, this has damaged the consensus between the government and the opposition, as the latter have become divided on this issue, putting in danger their support for the government's proposal. Chile is now confronted with the difficult task of facing its past and finding lasting solutions for its human rights question; a problem which can no longer be avoided.

Concluding Remarks

The Chilean democratic transition shows that economic prosperity, social improvements and political stability are not, by themselves, sufficient to bury traumatic memories of repression and violence. The healing of political traumas, which remain in both segments of Chilean society, has been rather slow, painful and partial, as they were spontaneously or deliberately reactivated at critical moments during the transition period. Paradoxically, the generation of a 'balance of fear' between both parts of Chilean society seems to have facilitated the achievement of working agreements and consensus between the country's main political leaders in order to avoid a situation of open confrontation. However, consensus achieved on the basis of fear can never provide a firm basis for long-term political stability.

While the current Chilean *clase política* talks with an impressive sense of realism and technocratic rationality about how to deal with the economic and social challenges of the present and the near-future, almost no one can hide his or her emotions when the subject of past repression and violence is debated. The old saying that the past lives on in the present is painfully true in present-day Chile, where the goal of national reconciliation is mixed with fear, distrust and hate which dates back to the Unidad Popular government and the Pinochet dictatorship. The healing of the collective traumas within Chilean society will depend, to a large extent, on the seriousness of the effort by politicians, intellectuals, spiritual leaders and teachers to reconcile the existence of two totally opposed versions of the country's recent political history which keep alive the threat of future confrontation.

Postscript

This chapter had been written some time before the detention of General Augusto Pinochet in London on 16 October 1998. Because of the enormous political importance of this event, I will briefly examine its repercussions for the issues analysed in this chapter.[54]

It is no exaggeration to state that the news of General Pinochet's detention in London caused a political earthquake in Chile. Since that day the relative consensus that had characterized the Chilean democratic transition has been seriously damaged. While Pinochet's opponents made every effort to express their satisfaction with this 'present coming from heaven', his supporters were deeply shocked by this 'awful news' coming from Britain. Almost instantaneously, the old split between *pinochetistas* and *anti-pinochetistas*, which many had thought to be already part of the past, re-emerged with full vigour. Since then both groups have forcefully been defending their opposite versions of the causes of the 1973 military coup, blaming each other for it. It is clear that Pinochet's detention has led to a revitalization of these different readings of the past and the role of General Pinochet in the country's recent political history.

One of the most remarkable direct results of Pinochet's detention has been the reunification of the Chilean Right. Since the restoration of democratic rule in 1990, the Right had been divided into two antagonistic fronts. On the one hand, the Unión Democrática Independiente (UDI), representing the hard core of *pinochetismo*, consistently defended the former military government and launched an intransigent opposition to the Concertación governments. On the other hand, Renovación Nacional (RN), representing the more moderate and democratically oriented sectors of the Right, gradually started to distance itself from the *pinochetista* camp from the early 1990s onward. For instance, Renovación Nacional constituted a very constructive opposition during the Aylwin government, supporting on various occasions the adoption of legislation aimed at the strengthening of democratic rule in the country. Since the restoration of democracy, both parties have been fighting bitterly with each other to secure support from the conservative electorate.

Following Pinochet's arrest, however, the rival sectors spontaneously closed ranks around the general's defence. At the same time, they started an aggressive rhetoric against the left-wing sectors, similar to that used by the Right during the 1988 referendum. The first reaction of Pinochet's supporters was to blame the Concertación government and particularly the Left for what had happened. Without any evidence, they alleged that both the government and the Left must have sent the wrong signals to Europe, namely that Chile would be pleased if legal action was taken against the former dictator. Later, however, right-wing sectors began to make a distinction with regard to the Concertación government between the Christian Democrats and the socialists, concentrating their criticism on the latter. According to the conservatives, the detention of Senator Pinochet was proving that the ideological renovation of Chilean socialists has been a fake and that revenge, not reconciliation had been their main driving force. The right-wing sectors also revived the old idea, put about during the military government, that Chile was a victim of 'international communism'. Pinochet's detention was presented as an act of aggression against the country by 'international socialism', as part of a malicious plot by a conspiracy of social democratic governments in Western Europe.

These right-wing reactions were very emotional; no sign of concern has been shown with respect to their repercussions for the country's political stability. On the contrary, some right-wing leaders called in covert terms on the armed forces to take a more firm attitude on Pinochet's detention, showing to both the Chilean government and Europe that the military were still capable of acting politically in response to this kind of event. The armed forces in fact have repeatedly declared their full support for their former commander-in-chief. At the same time, however, the military institutions have maintained a calm and subordinated attitude *vis-à-vis* the government, openly backing the latter's legal and diplomatic efforts to get Pinochet back to Chile.

Another important consequence of Pinochet's detention has been the re-opening of the national debate on the issue of human rights abuses during the military government. The radical Left and many human rights groups immediately organized large public campaigns and demanded, through the mass media, the re-opening of many legal cases against military men who had participated in gross human rights violations during the dictatorship. They argued that the Concertación's goal to achieve reconciliation within the Chilean nation had failed because the human rights question had not been treated satisfactorily by the Aylwin and Frei governments. In their opinion, Chile was now paying the price for its attempt to cover up the past. This suggests that if Pinochet was allowed to return to Chile, the pressure within Chile to bring him and others responsible for human rights violations to justice would increase dramatically, having an unpredictable impact on the country's political stability.

The arrest of General Pinochet has also generated serious tensions within the Concertación coalition itself, leading to uncertainty as to its future. From the outset President Frei adopted a formal constitutional stance, defending the senator's alleged immunity since he travelled with a Chilean diplomatic passport. Frei saw the arrest as an affront by Britain against Chilean national sovereignty. This official position caused a serious controversy within the Concertación coalition as several socialists leaders, including some members of parliament, welcomed the detention of Senator Pinochet and his possible extradition to Spain. These growing tensions between Christian democrats and socialists have been further sharpened by the upcoming presidential elections of December 1999. The Concertación had still not decided who would be its joint candidate and both the Christian Democratic and Socialist parties claimed that the next Chilean president should come from their own ranks. Opinion polls showed that the socialist candidate, Ricardo Lagos, was far more popular than the Christian Democratic candidate, Andrés Zaldívar. For this reason, Zaldívar's supporters attempted to use the socialists' alleged lack of loyalty towards the Frei government as evidence for Lagos' un-suitability to lead the coalition during the next elections.

These tensions within the government coalition have been aggravated as a result of attempts by right-wing sectors to provoke further divisions between both coalition partners. They hoped that the Concertación coalition would disintegrate prior to the 1999 elections, so that the road to the presidency would be blocked for the socialist Ricardo Lagos. The Right has also invited the Christian Democratic party, in covert terms, to form a large centre-right coalition. After a while, however, these attempts by the Right to divide the Concertación proved counter-productive. It led the coalition members to realize that they could not afford to throw away their sustained efforts, involving many years of hard work, to constitute a stable government of Christian democrats and socialists.

Despite this rather pessimistic scenario regarding the reconciliation in Chile

generated by the arrest of Pinochet in London, there are some auspicious elements which need to be mentioned. For instance, the division among Chileans around the Pinochet affair has not resulted in direct violent confrontations between the two opposing camps. Almost all of the street demonstrations, whether in favour or against Pinochet, that have taken place since October 1998 instinctively avoided violent clashes with their opponents. The Pinochet supporters have concentrated their protests in the well-to-do neighbourhoods of Santiago and systematically avoided the city centre where clashes with anti-Pinochet forces could be expected. In addition, their main targets have not been left-wing organizations or the like but the embassies of Great Britain and Spain. On the other hand, many people who welcomed Pinochet's detention consciously decided not to celebrate this event openly, either out of fear of a reactionary backlash or just to avoid further polarization of the political situation. In addition, both the fanatic *pinochetistas* who were furiously burning British and Spanish flags and the radical left-wing activists who forcefully demonstrated against Pinochet, represent only a small minority of the Chilean population. As many opinion polls conducted during this episode have demonstrated, the large majority maintained a calm and sometimes even indifferent position towards the detention of Pinochet. Furthermore, people's political preferences seemed not to have been changing as a result of the event. Most people seemed to be much more concerned with the negative impact of the Asian financial crisis on the Chilean economy, and particularly with the preservation of their jobs. In my opinion, many Chileans abstained from voicing strong opinions and hence from contributing to further polarization out of fear for the prospect of a possibly combined political and economic crisis in the country.

To date (January 1999), Pinochet has been continuing his legal battle in the British courts to avoid extradition to Spain and to obtain permission to return to Chile. Whatever the Law Lords' final verdict, Chile will continue to face the figure of General Pinochet and his traumatic legacy. Therefore, the political past will give cause for division among Chileans for a considerable time in the future.

Notes and References

1. Politzer, *Fear in Chile*, p. xiv.
2. See Allamand, *Centroderecha*; Foxley, *Economía política*.
3. See Bosworth et al., *Chilean Economy*.
4. See Drake and Jaksic, *Struggle for Democracy*.
5. O'Donnell, *Modernization*.
6. O'Donnell, 'Reflections', p. 7.
7. See Garretón and Moulian, *Unidad Popular*.
8. Remmer, *Military Rule*, p. 116.
9. See Silva, 'The state, politics and the peasant unions'.
10. See Vylder, *Allende's Chile*. In this respect, the press, which was mainly in the hands

of the opposition forces, did play a decisive role in generating and strengthening the fears of the middle class (see also Dooner, *Periodismo y política*).

11. Valenzuela, *Breakdown of Democratic Regimes*, pp. 98–103.

12. Tironi, *Autoritarismo*, pp. 125–6.

13. See Garretón, 'Political evolution'; Silva, 'Social democracy'.

14. In an interview, the minister secretary general of the government during the Aylwin administration, Enrique Correa, a leading figure within the Chilean Socialist party, expressed this feeling in an unambiguous way: 'We have made many concessions, but it is thanks to these concessions that we have built the democracy we have today [...] We have constructed a political and economic order which will be very stable. And the contributions of the socialists will remain related to that success, in the same way we remain related to the failure of the early 1970s. The socialists of the future will be the inheritors of that success, and not of the failure of the past.' *El Mercurio*, 2 February 1992.

15. Politzer, *Fear in Chile*, reproduces the life histories of several Chileans whose own words show the deep fear generated by the military dictatorship.

16. In another attempt to legitimate the coup and to scare the population, the military government announced the existence of a so-called 'Plan Z' by which the deposed government was supposed to have planned the assassination of key opposition leaders, influential members of the business world, the military high command, and their families. Although no convincing evidence for the existence of that plan was provided, many Chileans were more than inclined to believe any accusation against the Allende government.

17. Constable and Valenzuela, *Nation of Enemies*.

18. Valenzuela, 'Democratic consolidation', pp. 78–9.

19. Lechner, *Patios interiores*, p. 102.

20. See Tapia, *Terrorismo de Estado*.

21. Arriagada, *Pinochet*, pp. 18–19.

22. Garretón, 'Political evolution'.

23. Munizaga, *Discurso público*, pp. 19–20.

24. Campero, *Gremios empresariales*; and Campero, 'Entrepreneurs'.

25. Stepan, 'State power', p. 321.

26. See Silva, 'Technocrats and politics'.

27. See Moulian and Vergara, 'Estado, ideología y políticas'.

28. Constable and Valenzuela, *Nation of Enemies*, p. 202.

29. Kaufman, 'Liberalization and democratization', p. 93.

30. See Edwards and Cox-Edwards, *Monetarism and Liberalization*.

31. See Silva, 'Modernization, consumerism and politics'.

32. Brunner, 'Cultura política'.

33. See Angell, 'Chile since 1958', pp. 189ff.

34. See Valenzuela, *Military Rule*; Cavarozzi and Garretón, *Muerte y resurrección*.

35. Martínez, 'Miedo al estado'; Salazar, *Violencia política*.

36. Tironi, *Autoritarismo*, p. 181.

37. Arrate, *Fuerza democrática*, p. 234.

38. Walker, 'Nuevo socialismo'; Silva, 'Social democracy'.

39. See Huneeus, 'Partidos políticos'. Christian Democratic leaders such as Alejandro Foxley started in those years to talk about the need to draw up a 'national project', although he realized it would not be easy as a result of the many fears dividing the Chilean people. As he notes: 'the traumatic experience of the last years has left too many wounds. It impedes some people's ability to forget in order to be able to deal with the requirements of the future. It blocks others because of fear and uncertainty about what is to come. It makes it more difficult for society as a whole to take on a collective rational stance: to take

the decision to live together in peace and to jointly build up a country.' Foxley, *Democracia estable*, p. 35.

40. In those years, Professor Arnold Harberger, one of the main intellectual mentors of the 'Chicago Boys', proclaimed: 'One can predict in ten years Chileans will enjoy a standard of living similar to that of Spain, which has a domestic product at the moment about double Chile's, while in 20 years Chileans will possibly be enjoying the same standards of living as Holland' (quoted in O'Brien and Roddick, *Chile*, p. 68).

41. See Angell, 'Chile since 1958', p. 194; Constable and Valenzuela, *Nation of Enemies*, p. 307; Portales and Sunkel, *Política en pantalla*, p. 108.

42. Hirmas, *Franja*, p. 110.

43. Constable and Valenzuela, *Nation of Enemies*, p. 305.

44. Ibid., p. 307.

45. Tulchin and Varas, *Dictatorship to Democracy*, p. 4. As Alejandro Foxley, minister of finance in the Aylwin government, noted: 'Today we experience an exceptional historical occasion: we devote ourselves to a new experience of social peace, of a constructive mood of optimism; conditions which imposed themselves almost for the sake of survival, after having lived a lengthy period in a deeply divided and unstable society. This moment must be used and be projected into the future' (Foxley, *Economía política*, p. 120).

46. See O'Donnell and Schmitter, *Transitions: Tentative Conclusions*, pp. 21–3.

47. Valenzuela, 'Democratic consolidation', p. 79.

48. Oppenheim, *Politics in Chile*, p. 207.

49. Foxley, *Economía política*; Cortázar, *Política laboral*.

50. Petras and Leiva, *Democracy and Poverty*.

51. Tironi, *Liberalismo real*, pp. 147–8.

52. See Oppenheim, *Politics in Chile*, pp. 210–22.

53. See for a description of the content of those proposals, *Latin American Weekly Report*, 31 August 1995, WR-95-33, p. 388.

54. The author resided in Chile in November and December 1998 and closely followed the day-to-day events related to the Pinochet affair.

NINE

Shadows of Violence and Political Transition in Brazil: from Military Rule to Democratic Governance

KEES KOONINGS

Among those countries in South America that have passed through the so-called 'democratic transition' during the past fifteen years, Brazil stands out because of the gradualism of the process, its long duration, and the concomitant high degree of continuity from military rule through to the full restoration of civil democracy. So, while few will doubt that the Brazilian political system has now acquired a substantially democratic form and content (including almost all of the ideal typical civil and political citizenship rights), still, many observers highlight the difficulties of democratic consolidation despite the apparent success of the transition.

One of the reasons for this state of affairs has been the hybrid nature of the Brazilian military dictatorship itself between 1964 and 1985, and the ensuing characteristics and determinants of the democratic transition which occurred roughly from the mid-1970s to the late 1980s. Throughout this period, political institutions were adapted to democratic rules and procedures on a step-by-step basis. The main social and political actors who had been involved in the politics of authoritarianism remained in the centre of power after 1985, although trade unionism, social movements, and left-wing political parties were gradually accepted into civil society and the political arena from about 1982 onwards. Moreover, the process was put under considerable strain by the persistence of economic instability and the growing pressure exerted by a variety of social demands. The result, in the mid-1990s, has been that of a consolidated democracy facing a number of problems, such as the half-completed institutional reform of the state, a political culture that may often be at odds with democratic transparency, and a legacy of social problems that may erupt into a new phase of polarization and open conflict. Especially the latter kind of problem forms the background to much of the violence that plagues present-day Brazil. It is my contention that, in the case of

Brazil, it is not so much the legacy of past repression and political violence that may pose a threat to the consolidation of legitimate democracy, but rather the near-endemic nature of peculiar forms and pockets of social violence today. In so far as this problem relates to the Brazilian state, an important dimension of current violence results from difficulties in upholding the effective rule of law in the country. The Brazilian transition has, till now, mainly addressed the political and institutional aspects of restoring democracy; the wider conditions for democratic legitimacy (that is to say, social justice, rule of law and effective overall citizenship) remain uncertain.

It is the purpose of this chapter to review the legacy of military rule, the nature, scope and limits of the democratic transition, and the physiognomy of present-day conflicts and violence. First I will discuss the origins and the consequences of Brazilian militarism, in order to explain how and why this resulted in a military-dominated authoritarian regime that was driven by the logic of a pervasive but low-intensity 'battle' against domestic opponents, especially between 1968 and 1979. Then I will review the transition process as it unfolded after 1974. The problems affecting this process not only stemmed from the persistence of military tutelage, but also from the complexities of the Brazilian political system and the monumental tasks it faced after the restoration of civil rule. The final part of the chapter focuses on the contemporary manifestations of social conflict and violence in Brazil. I will raise the issue of the relevance of current forms of violence and insecurity for the prospects of consolidating democracy and upholding the rule of law.

The Rise and Demise of Military Authoritarianism

THE MILITARISATION OF POLITICS The roots of the military regime of 1964–85, and the political violence it perpetrated, can be found in the gradual development of an interventionist military institution that started as early as 1889, when the army overthrew the monarchy and sent Emperor Pedro II into exile in Portugal. Throughout the twentieth century, the Brazilian military became an active player on the national political stage. The armed forces turned into what has been labelled a 'quasi-party'. The aim of this military 'party' was to influence or take part in government on behalf of a project of national development and 'greatness'.[1] After the proclamation of the republic the army adopted the task of modernizing the nation, often in defiance of the dominant regional oligarchies.[2] With the army-led overthrow of Emperor Pedro II in 1889, the military took over – for all intents and purposes – the role of moderating power (*poder moderador*) that until then had accrued to the emperor. This role assigned to the military the task of guaranteeing the integrity of the nation and its constitutional order against all threats, external and internal, and to intervene for that purpose if necessary. During the Old Republic (1889–1930), military interventions took place mostly

at the behest of the civilian elites, especially in order to suppress local or regional rebellions.

Military involvement in politics underwent significant changes after 1930, notably under the Estado Novo (1937–45) and again after 1950. The armed campaign mounted by Getúlio Vargas to overthrow the government in 1930 relied on the support of important segments of the federal army, especially those linked to the *tenente* (lieutenants') movement of the 1920s.[3] From then until 1964, the military effectively wielded their tutelary prerogatives, based on the notion of moderating power. It is noteworthy that in several instances (1937, 1945, 1955) military interventions were as much a response to demands aired by certain civil political factions, as actions inspired by the logic of military political reasoning itself. Still, the contours of a more autonomous military approach to national political affairs started to emerge when the notion of 'national security' was introduced in the 1934 constitution. During the Estado Novo, the military developed views on the relationship between economic development – especially industrialization – and external security and military strength. As a consequence, the military firmly supported the industrialization efforts sponsored by the Vargas regime.[4] By then, the armed forces consolidated the idea that they had a legitimate stake in national economic development, in public administration and, hence, in politics.

After 1950, the political orientation of the military gradually acquired a new dimension. Immediately after World War II the armed forces seemed to adhere to liberal democratic principles when they forced Vargas to step down and to put an end to the Estado Novo dictatorship. But the foundation of the Escola Superior de Guerra (Superior War College, ESG) in 1949 and the return of Vargas to the presidency – this time as an elected populist in 1950 – pushed the military slowly but steadily towards a more authoritarian orientation. During the 1950s, the concept of 'national security' was further developed into a comprehensive doctrine to guide the internal political strategy of the armed forces. This process has been amply documented,[5] but for the purpose of our discussion, it is important to note its consequence in sharpening the political orientation of the military. The core element of this was the fusion of military and political objectives and strategies in relation to internal affairs. The goal of national development and the task of efficient public administration were regarded as crucial for national security, since the latter rested necessarily on the full capacity to mobilize the economic, political and 'moral' resources of the nation.[6] At the same time, this vital interest was seen as being threatened by the increasing radicalization of populist and left-wing sectors. Thus, the concept of the 'internal enemy' was construed not just to designate armed subversive or guerrilla opposition (which was virtually absent prior to 1964), but for anybody opposing conservative–capitalist modernization, the stability of the state, and the integrity of its embodiment – the armed forces. Eventually, this orientation led to the military intervention of March 1964, when the government of president João Goulart was seen

as having fallen definitely under the influence of radicals, to the extent that the government itself crossed the boundaries of legality as defined by the military. Under the 1946 constitution, this gave the armed forces the right and even the moral obligation to intervene.

It is important to note that it was not anti-communism *per se* that triggered the coup. Only when 'radicalism' seemed to have invaded the upper echelons of the government, during the opening months of 1964, penetrating even the armed forces, did the interventionist faction within the army manage to muster sufficient support among high-ranking officers to make a coup possible. General Gustavo Moraes Rego Reis, a junior colonel at the time of the coup, stated in 1992 that one of the decisive moments was the participation of President Goulart in the mass demonstration for basic reforms in front of the Central do Brasil railway station in March 1964 in Rio de Janeiro: 'I stood at a hundred meters from the stage where Jango [João Goulart] stood, there in front of the Central. If he only would not have appeared [...] An anticommunist declaration by Jango, a call in favor of discipline against subversion and lack of discipline that was already present within the Armed Forces would have kept him in office longer.'[7] General Ivan de Sousa Mendes, who became head of the national intelligence service in the Sarney administration in 1985, recalled: 'It was not only the military hierarchy, no. It was the very republican hierarchy that was at stake. The respect for the vested authorities. All that would have been turned upside down.'[8]

For many military officers, fear of a communist threat was not primarily inspired by the conservative ideological position prevailing within the armed forces, but rather by the notion that communist radicalization would put the integrity of the armed forces, and hence the nation, in jeopardy. The memory of the role of the communist military in the 1935 uprising of the communist Aliança Libertadora Nacional (National Liberating Alliance, ALN) further nurtured these fears. In turn, many civilians, linked to the anti-populist UDN and to the business community, called for an intervention. Their expectation was that a 'classic' moderator-style coup would open the way for the installation of an anti-populist civil government. However, between 1964 and 1967, the decision of the generals to intervene eventually matured into the installation of long-term military rule that was used to reform the state in order to pursue both the objectives of national development and the elimination of internal enemies.[9]

THE CONSOLIDATION OF MILITARY RULE Between 1964 and 1969, the Brazilian military took a series of steps to ensure their political control and to set the stage for the elimination of their opponents. The outstanding features of the results of this course of action were – for the purpose of the present discussion – twofold. In the first place, military control over the government and the public administration was achieved not by abolishing the existing democratic politico-institutional framework, but by purging and

amending it, as well as by adding parallel militarized components to it. In terms of the democratic transition set in motion in the mid-1970s, this meant that the military could try to control the transition by using existing institutional mechanisms that were under their control. Secondly, a comprehensive security apparatus was set up that was fully integrated into the militarized state, yet at the same time endowed with a high degree of *de facto* autonomy. Furthermore, as I will discuss below, the repressive apparatus took on enormous proportions, totally incommensurable with the actual scope of the threat posed by the (armed) opposition against the regime.[10]

For the military that took power in 1964 the first worry was to establish a legitimate foundation for their intervention, not only in terms of the prevailing political doctrine of the armed forces themselves, but also in terms of the existing political and institutional order. Legality was broken for the purpose of rescuing the legal order; democracy was suspended for the sake of its survival. (This line of reasoning would prove to be recurrent among the institutional military dictatorships in South America after 1964.) In Brazil, the military introduced the artifact of the *ato institucional* (institutional act), executive decrees given the status of a constitutional amendment. These acts were used, especially in the period from 1964 to 1970, to put the political arena under firm military control and to allow for the ousting of political opponents. The first institutional act legitimized the *coup d'état* as a necessary and therefore self-legitimizing 'Revolution' to avert the threat of communist radicalization. The second and third ones, issued in 1965 and 1966, curtailed the powers of Congress and changed the party system and the electoral agenda. They were a direct response to the electoral gains registered by the opponents of the military regime. Direct presidential and gubernatorial elections were substituted by elections in federal and state electoral colleges. The existing political parties were abolished and replaced by two new parties: a regime-supporting party, named the Aliança Renovadora Nacional (National Renovative Alliance, ARENA) and a moderate opposition party, called the Movimento Democrático Brasileiro (Brazilian Democratic Movement, MDB). Early in 1967, the regime pressed Congress into accepting a set of amendments to the 1946 constitution that sanctioned most of the decrees issued since 1964. Most significantly, these constitutional modifications incorporated the tenets of the national security doctrine into Brazil's political and legal system.

The sharpening of authoritarianism in the late 1960s followed a short period of relative political opening endorsed by Castello Branco and his successor Costa e Silva. During 1968, however, social and political resistance to the military regime grew. In that year, students and factory workers mounted large-scale protest meetings and strikes while politicians from the legal and illegal opposition tried to set up a broad anti-authoritarian alliance named the Frente Ampla (Broad Front). This alliance united politicians of different persuasions, ranging from conservatives Carlos Lacerda and Magalhães Pinto

to former presidents Juscelino Kubitschek and João Goulart, and the radical populist Leonel Brizola. The Frente Ampla inspired a more assertive stance adopted by Congress against the arbitrariness displayed by the military power-holders. The regime reacted by persecuting student and union leaders, suspending the rights of opposition politicians, and by outlawing the activities of the Frente Ampla.

These challenges to the military regime led to a new round of the militarization of politics. By the end of 1968, the construction of the tutelary system was completed after the promulgation of the fifth institutional act (AI 5). This act gave the executive, hence the military, almost unlimited power to curtail Congress, to suspend political rights, and to prosecute political adversaries without *habeas corpus* and under military law. The latter provision was further specified by the National Security Law of 1969, which widened considerably the definition of activities considered to be crimes against national· security.[11] As a result, an elaborate quasi-legal structure was put into place which allowed the military to step up its repressive actions against perceived 'internal enemies'. From 1969 onward, the military regime entered its most violent phase, first under the interim junta which briefly replaced Costa e Silva during his illness, and then under the presidency of General Emílio Médici (1969–74), selected by the generals to succeed Costa e Silva.

VIOLENCE AND REPRESSION UNDER MILITARY RULE By 1969, a legal structure had been set up to formalize and justify repression (or, from the military point of view, the war being waged against an internal enemy). To put this into practice, an elaborate edifice of anti-subversive agencies was constructed. In the Brazilian case, the repressive apparatus was quite out of proportion to the real size of the armed opposition against the regime. It was not only large but also bureaucratically complex and intertwined; it was not even transparent to the military power-holders themselves. The mentor of the regime and founder of the Serviço Nacional de Informações (National Intelligence Service, SNI), General Golbery do Couto e Silva, used to refer to it as a 'monster' or a 'black hole'. Military testimonies confirm the lack of clarity, the hierarchical confusion, and sometimes even the internal con-frontations embedded in the structure of the security apparatus.[12]

The essence of this system was the combination of intelligence and operational counter-insurgency capacity. In 1964, the SNI was set up to provide the executive with overall information pertaining to 'national security'. The SNI resided directly under the presidency and the Conselho Nacional de Segurança (National Security Counsel, CSN) and supervised security and intelligence units in ministries, public agencies and state companies. In addition, the SNI fielded its own paid agents and also counted on a large number of paid and unpaid informants.[13]

In 1967, the three armed services themselves started to enhance their

independent intelligence capacity. The most important was the Centro de Informações do Exército (Centre of Army Intelligence, CIE). This new agency was allowed to operate separately from both the SNI and the conventional 'E₂' intelligence sections of the regular army units, and it reported directly to the minister of the army in the cabinet. Two years later an operational anti-subversive capacity was developed (under the supervision of the regional army commanders and the CIE), first in São Paulo where the Operação Bandeirantes (OBAN) took over the fight against the (armed) opposition from the regular state police and army forces. It was under the direct military command of the Second Army and received funds from the *paulista* business community. OBAN was licensed to carry out covert operations, including arrests and interrogations, against suspects of subversive activities. In 1970, the counter-insurgency apparatus was consolidated when the so-called Destacamentos de Operação de Informações (Operational Intelligence Units, DOI were formed). These units were autonomous and consisted of personnel from all branches of the armed forces, the police forces, the fire brigades, and so on. Operational supervision was carried out by the Centros de Operações de Defesa Interna (Operational Centres for Internal Defence, CODI), in order to bypass hierarchy and communication bottlenecks between the different branches of the security apparatus. Formal command of the DOI-CODI system resided with the regional army commanders.

The result of all this was that, by 1970, a complex security apparatus was set up that was formally controlled by the army command hierarchy, but at the same time wielded considerable operational autonomy and involved personnel and resources from various branches of the security forces. An estimated 20,000 people were directly employed by the different security and intelligence agencies; an unknown number acted as informants.[14] The size of the repressive apparatus was the result of a pre-emptive expansion in view of the perceived threat of an armed opposition to the regime. Its *modus operandi* was largely uncontrolled and arbitrary, in violation not only of prevailing legislation but also of the directives that were supposed to guide the counter-insurgency operations themselves. Thus, between 1968 and 1974, a climate of fear was created as a result of the perceived omnipresence of the system and the arbitrary nature of its operations. This climate of fear went beyond the actual scope of repression within the country.[15]

The armed opposition in Brazil never even remotely attained the scale of its southern cone counterparts (especially the Tupamaros in Uruguay and the Montoneros in Argentina), let alone the opposition armies active in Central America in the 1970s and 1980s. The Brazilian armed opposition was small, fragmented and short-lived. In all, probably no more than a few hundred men and women were involved in various efforts to mount armed resistance against the military regime. It was doomed to failure from the outset not only because of the military superiority of the Brazilian army, but also due

to the lack of unity and clarity of purpose within the ranks of the radical opposition itself.[16]

There were basically three kinds of armed oppositionary activities.[17] First, there were the efforts by the radical populist opponents of the military to set up a strategy of armed resistance with the help of anti-regime elements within the armed forces. Leonel Brizola, a former politician of the Partido Trabalhista Brasileiro (Brazilian Labour Party, PTB), ex-governor of Rio Grande do Sul and former congressman, planned armed actions from his Uruguayan place of exile using funds supplied by Fidel Castro. Related to this scheme, the actions of the Movimento Nacional Revolucionário (National Revolutionary Movement, MNR) between 1965 and 1967 – initiated by former military officers who were fired because of their loyalty to the Goulart government – were short-lived. Likewise, similar operations by nationalist militant movements such as the Movimento Revolucionário (MR)-21 and MR-26 were rapidly repressed by the security forces of the regime. In 1968, Brizola abandoned the option of armed resistance and adhered to the Frente Ampla opposition front that advocated a democratic alternative to the military regime.[18]

Secondly, small dissident factions that split from the Partido Comunista Brasileiro (Brazilian Communist Party, PCB) in the course of the 1960s responded to the intensification of authoritarianism and repression after the promulgation of the AI 5 with 'revolutionary violence'. Their basic strategy was to set up an urban guerrilla group in preparation for revolutionary *focos* in rural areas. These actions were strongly inspired by Cuban revolutionary doctrine and by the activities of Che Guevara in Bolivia in 1967. Especially during 1968, 1969, and 1970, groups like the Ação Nacional Libertadora (National Liberating Action, ALN) led by former PCB-leader Carlos Marighella, and the Vanguarda Popular Revolucionária (Revolutionary Popular Vanguard, VPR) led by former army captain Carlos Lamarca, engaged in bank assaults to raise funds, and in a series of kidnappings of foreign diplomats in order to exchange them for imprisoned left-wing militants. The series of kidnappings began with the spectacular capture of the US ambassador, Charles Burke Elbrick, on 4 September 1969. In the following months, the kidnappings of the Japanese consul in São Paulo, and the German and Swiss ambassadors took place. All these diplomats were subsequently released in exchange for imprisoned leftist militants. Soon, however, the security forces managed to clamp down on the principal urban guerrilla groups. Leaders like Marighella and Lamarca were chased down, captured and killed. Others were disappeared.

The third type of armed resistance against the military regime was inspired by the Chinese revolutionary model of the 'prolonged people's war' by which rural guerrilla fighting would eventually lead to the surrounding and conquest of the cities. This strategy was espoused by the Maoist Partido Comunista do Brasil (Communist Party of Brazil, PCdoB) that had split from the PCB in 1962. From 1966 onwards, the PCdoB set up a guerrilla infrastructure in the Araguaia river region in the Amazonian state of Para. The effort was

quite modest, however, and never amounted to more than eighty to ninety guerrilla fighters. In 1972, the intelligence agencies of the regime discovered the group and a massive counter-insurgency campaign, involving an entire army division, was unleashed on it. Still, fighting went on for almost two years and, in the process, arbitrary repression was unleashed against the region's rural population.

The various efforts at putting up armed struggle against the military were a reaction to intensified repression after 1968. In turn, the armed actions led to the further expansion of the security apparatus directed against the 'internal enemy'. Covert operations, detentions and torture in clandestine interrogation centres became routine practice, especially after the founding of OBAN and the DOI units. Despite the relatively limited scale of the armed opposition, counter-insurgency violence was heavy-handed and often brutal. Widespread institutional torture occurred, yet at the same time the higher level commanders could pledge their ignorance and, in some cases, their formal rejection of these methods.[19] The military were convinced that they faced a severe internal security threat posed by an unseen enemy which warranted every type of retaliation. This notion has remained unchallenged among Brazilian military officers up to this day. For instance, in 1992, General Leônidas Pires Gonçalves, operational commander during the 1970s and later the minister of the army in the civilian Sarney government (1985–90), made the following observation: 'I think the operations of the DOI-CODI were very good. And if they are so badly criticised today, we owe that to the enemies who are within the media, because 95 per cent of the actions of DOI-CODI were to defend this country [...] That was a fight. That was war.'[20]

Médici himself, in a rare interview given to *Veja* magazine in 1984, said that he was forced to employ the army in counter-insurgency operations because the police were not up to the task. He recalled saying to his minister of the army, General Orlando Geisel (Ernesto Geisel's brother):

'But only our men die? Then when you invade an *aparelho* [an urban guerrilla hideout], you'll have to go in firing machine guns. We are in a war, and we cannot sacrifice our men.' Even today [addressing the interviewer] there is no doubt that it was a war, after which it was possible to restore peace to Brazil. I got rid of terrorism in this country. If we would not have accepted that it was a war, if we would not have acted drastically, we would have terrorism until today.[21]

The notion of war was not only employed by the military but also by members of the guerrilla groups. Members of the latter did not hesitate to use random violence themselves. The only survivor of the *comandantes* of the ALN, Carlos Eugenio Paz, described in an interview in 1996 his involvement in bank assaults – one of the methods employed to raise money to set up *foco*-type guerrilla operations in the backlands:

Often you were firing a machine gun to escape from a police encirclement and you could not know if you had hit anyone, and even less, if you had killed anyone. But when I killed, it was always to survive [...] The logic in which we lived, at that time, was the logic of violence, of war, and there does not exist a clean war.[22]

In addition, not only the (known) perpetrators of armed opposition were targeted; repression was also unleashed against a wide range of political and social organizations, and against individuals considered to be threats to national security. In effect, the consequences of repression in Brazil in terms of generating an overall climate of arbitrariness and fear went well beyond the actual size of the armed opposition or the amount of violence needed to repress it. At the same time, many Brazilians were either unaware of state terrorism or chose to turn a blind eye. The years of the most brutal operations of the regime coincided with the so-called economic 'miracle'; support for the Médici government, especially among the middle class, was substantial. In addition, the top brass of the military hierarchy always denied that 'extraordinary' amounts of violence were employed, or that systematic violations of human rights took place. Excesses were either denied or justified with the 'war'; in the best of cases, they were regarded as the lamentable actions of a few low-ranking officers and soldiers.

It is noteworthy that, in the course of this process, the security agencies became increasingly autonomous and arbitrary in their *modus operandi*. As Stepan notes, the pace of repression was stepped up even after 1974, when the military themselves claimed the final victory over the armed rural and urban opposition.[23] The intense political polarization of the late 1960s and early 1970s had led to the subsequent strengthening of the so-called 'hard-liners' within the regime. The latter used the anti-subversive strategy to legitimize the closure of the political system and the abuse of human and civil rights by referring to the 'state of war' that Brazil was experiencing at the time. This contributed to the evolution of the security forces into what Stepan called 'the army's relatively autonomous repressive apparatus'.[24] This issue proved to be an important factor in the problems faced by the gradual regime-led transition to democracy after 1974.

THE LOGIC OF CONTROLLED FEAR: THE DEMOCRATIC TRANSITION AND THE MILITARY To accept an extrication from politics and a return to democracy is difficult for a military that have been involved in grim anti-subversive repression, for two reasons. On the one hand, the logic of war underlying the repression may have convinced the military that their continuation in power is necessary in order to keep the internal enemy at bay. On the other hand, involvement in human rights violations may have instilled a fear of reprisal among the military themselves upon being replaced by a civil government. The political strategists among the Brazilian military

who came to the fore in 1974 were aware of these dilemmas. They sought a strategy that could provide the military with a gradual and legitimate way out while, at the same time, giving the armed forces sufficient control over the democratization process. So, a transition from above, such as took place in Brazil, gives rise to a variety of fears. As Kaufman argues, the waning of fear for the 'subversion' of order allowed authoritarian regimes to initiate or to go along with liberalization, and to return to a form of *normalidade política*.[25] The civil opposition, having shed the principle of revolutionary struggle and having accepted, in principle, the terms of the transition agenda, face the constant fear of *retrocesso* or authoritarian backlash. The protagonists of the regime develop new fears, at least in the Brazilian case: on the one hand, they fear the reaction of the hardliners and the security apparatus and the pernicious consequences this may have for the integrity of the military corporation; on the other hand, the return to civil rule, possibly with opponents to the former regime in power, may create a process of holding the military accountable for state terrorism – a situation the armed forces, as a political actor, will try to avoid even at considerable costs.

In view of dilemmas such as these, Médici's successor, President Ernesto Geisel (1974–79), adhered to the notion of a *democracia forte* (strong democracy), which meant a limited return to civil liberties by granting some political influence to parties and civil society. Geisel's transition strategy was meant to allow for greater interest representation within the political arena in view of increasingly complex economic and social problems, thus enhancing the long-run legitimacy of military rule while controlling the more obscure sides of the authoritarian situation.[26] To achieve this goal, the regime allowed for gradual liberalization within the existing institutional framework, including amendments to the authoritarian legal artefacts. The latter were deemed necessary to allow the military to act as guardians of order and stability, with a virtual right of veto within the political system. From this point of departure, the *distensão* ('decompression') process (as Geisel's strategy was called) faced danger from two sides: on the one hand, the possibility that the civil political opposition would try to use the space opened up by the regime to speed up the democratic transition and to go beyond the limits of the *democracia forte*; on the other hand, the resistance likely to be put up by the hard-nosed authoritarians within the regime, principally those linked to the security complex.

Since Brazilian militarism after 1964 had preserved, at least nominally, some of the institutions of formal democracy (namely elections, parties and legislative bodies), the transition set in motion in this way was not only regime-led but also, as Lamounier points out, election-driven.[27] One of the first consequences that could be noted was the unexpected victory of the oppositionary party MDB in the 1974 elections for the National Congress. In the following years, the electoral advance of the MDB continued (through the 1976 municipal and the 1978 congressional elections) while at the same

time oppositionary forces gained ground within society. Trade unions, the church, legal organizations (such as the Order of Brazilian Lawyers, OAB), the student movement, grassroots organizations, and even the domestic industrialists became active in criticizing or denouncing the military regime. Towards the end of the 1970s, the rise of new and massive forms of trade union militancy gave a further impetus to the anti-regime mobilization.[28]

Under the Geisel presidency, the regime tended to react to the opposition's gains with repressive initiatives, such as curbing the political space of the opposition by the use of *ad hoc* exceptional legislation.[29] Geisel refused to abolish the legal artefacts of the repression years, such as the AI 5, the National Security Law, and the authoritarian constitutional amendments passed by the junta in 1969 during the illness of Costa e Silva. Geisel merely deactivated these artefacts temporarily, to be re-used in times of 'crisis' – meaning undue political headway made by the opposition or 'irresponsible' agitation by popular organizations and leaders.[30] In retrospect, Geisel commented upon this strategy as follows:

> It was my idea, really, to avoid the use of the AI 5 whenever possible. But then appeared the lack of understanding of the opposition. I demonstrated, in speeches and public acts […] that I wanted to normalize the country's situation, to end press censorship, etc. They thought that was weakness and decided to launch an attack. So they forced me to react. If I wouldn't have reacted, my power clearly would have been weakened and then a series of projects that I wanted to realise, including the *abertura*, perhaps would have been impossible.[31]

Geisel's successor, General João Figueiredo, was committed formally to *abertura*, a political 'opening' aimed at restoring full democracy, provided that gradualism was observed and order maintained. In essence, the transition strategy of the Figueiredo administration failed; its objective was to hand over power in 1985 (in the usual controlled way) to yet another (military) candidate of the regime's party (ARENA, later PDS, see below).The implicit aim was to secure control over the executive until at least the early 1990s. This strategy was thwarted, however, by a combination of factors. The basic one was the tremendous acceleration of the mobilization and political activation of (civil) society, a process that was nurtured by a widespread discontent with political arbitrariness and the lack of respect for civil rights. Additional factors complicating the position of the military regime were to be found in growing economic difficulties, and sharpening conflicts within the regime itself.

The growing dissatisfaction became manifest in the continued progress made by the opposition parties in the elections of 1982.[32] In that year, political parties which had previously been granted somewhat broader organizational freedom, disputed open elections for state governors for the first time since the mid-1960s, together with legislative elections on the federal and state levels. The opposition, represented by the recently formed PMDB, PP, PDT,

and PT,[33] almost secured a majority in Congress against the PDS (ARENA's successor party) and won key state governments, among which were São Paulo, Rio de Janeiro, Minas Gerais and Pernambuco. This result was crucial for the construction of a viable political alternative to the military regime. The careful negotiation of an electoral alliance for the 1985 presidential succession was accompanied by the intensification of social mobilization. This reached its apogee in 1984 during the massive demonstrations in favour of direct presidential elections (diretas já). As one social sector after another rallied behind the opposition banner (including the urban middle classes and the business elites), the political result was that the 1985 election of the new president by the Electoral College (Congress plus a number of state legislation deputies) showed a majority for PMDB's candidate Tancredo Neves. During the months leading up to this indirect election, the opposition parties PMDB and Partido da Frente Liberal (Liberal Front Party, PFL, a split-off from the PDS) formed the Aliança Democrática (Democratic Alliance, AD) to boost Tancredo's candidacy and to come to an arrangement with the military.

The military, that is to say the Geisel and Figueiredo administrations, had to balance stick and carrot; the authoritarian safeguards were seen as necessary but could be used only if, at the same time, a minimum of progress was made on the transition front. Brazilian politics from 1974 onwards became a drawn-out transition towards democracy that hovered between these juxtaposed positions. Although the process was initiated and regulated by the military themselves, in the end, the opposition alliance succeeded in breaking through the limits envisaged by the military power-holders. Throughout the course of the transition, however, authoritarians within the regime and the military apparatus tried to erect barriers to the restoration of civil democratic rule. Geisel constantly had to find a balance between his project of disentsão and the resistance of the military authoritarians. As Geisel himself put it in retrospect: 'That is to say, I had to fight at two fronts: against the communists and against those who fought the communists.'[34] This came out clearly in the apparently contradictory actions taken by his government: gradual liberaliza-tion and a certain concern for the uncontrolled violations of human rights within the security apparatus, yet at the same time the endorsement of authoritarian backlashes such as the Lei Falcão and the April Package. On balance, the strategy of distensão prevailed despite attempts by military hard-liners to slow down or to revert the transition.

These hardliners were active on two levels. On the one hand, the pro-tagonists of the so-called intelligence community continued the arbitrary repression of perceived opponents throughout the 1970s. As is argued by Alves, the ambivalence of the situation in which political liberalization went hand in hand with continued waves of repression against 'communist sub-versives' led to considerable uncertainty.[35] The most notorious of the cases of repression was the arrest and subsequent death of the journalist Vladimir Herzog on the DOI's São Paulo premises, in October 1975. By and large, the

wanton repression backfired, not only because it considerably strengthened the peaceful civil opposition against the regime, but also because it made the gradualists among the leading military officers more aware of the institutional dangers facing the military, and hence the need to press on with the transition. Therefore, commanders formally responsible for units in which human rights violations occurred sometimes faced sanctions following official military investigations, despite the resistance put up by the hardliners.[36] The most serious challenge to Geisel's strategy was posed by the attempt to launch his minister of war, General Silvio Frota, as a candidate for the 1979 presidential succession. Frota's bid was supported (or even engineered) by leading members of the operational security forces who opposed the *distensão* and sought an intensification of authoritarianism and 'anti-subversive' repression. Geisel responded with the dismissal of Frota in October 1977.

At the same time, social protest against arbitrary repression was growing and was proving increasingly difficult to ignore. For Geisel and his successor, Figueiredo, it was clear that the problem of repression and human rights had to be solved in order to preserve control over the transition process. In 1979, an amnesty law was agreed between the Figueiredo government and the opposition. It was a compromise between the regime and the opposition: political prisoners would be released (when not charged with 'blood crimes'), and persons fired or exiled for political reasons could re-assume their positions or return to the country. Former members of 'illegal' organizations were even allowed to enter political life. At the same time, the law granted a general pardon for all military and security personnel involved in the repression.[37] The year before, in 1978, the infamous AI 5 was revoked under the Geisel government.

Though formally adopting the goal of full democratization of political life during his term, Figueiredo proved, in the end, to be a victim of the antagonism between the moderate and the hardline factions within the regime. Figueiredo, himself a former head of the SNI, included alleged authoritarians such as generals Walter Pires and Octávio Medeiros in his cabinet. At the same time, General Golbery do Couto e Silva stayed on as head of the civil household of the presidency. With Medeiros as minister of the SNI, the influence of the intelligence service over policy issues and the political strategy of the regime increased. In fact, it was expected that General Medeiros, head of the SNI, would be selected as Figueiredo's successor.[38]

The 'Riocentro' scandal in 1981, in which a bomb killed the sergeant and injured the captain sent out to place the device at a music festival in Rio de Janeiro, effectively discredited the political aspirations of the intelligence sectors; but the affair also severely weakened the position of Figueiredo because of his refusal to mount a full-fledged investigation into the matter.[39] The Riocentro bombing attempt also marked the end of right-wing subversion against the *abertura*. The initiative within the transition passed to the opposition, which gradually increased its support both from the public and from

among representatives of the governing party.[40] During the voting in April 1984 over a constitutional amendment presented by PMDB congressman Dante de Oliveira to re-establish direct elections for the presidency, the military sealed off the federal capital Brasília. They feared that announced demonstrations might disturb the 'proper' climate for the voting; that is, they might put congressmen from the governing PDS party under pressure to vote for the amendment. The hardliner General Newton Cruz, former head of the Central Agency of the SNI in Brasília and at that time in charge of the Planalto Military Command, put tanks in the streets and personally went out on Brasília's avenues, battering upon the hoods of cars that turned out in massive numbers on the streets to offer a horn-blowing support to the amendment in defiance of the arrogant military show of force.

General Golbery do Couto e Silva assumed a clearly more moderate position when asked to comment on these massive appeals to restore full democracy:

> The people certainly want the direct elections. To vote is a strong desire of society, for many reasons: tradition, the natural wish to participate, and even the attraction of the civic festival alongside other interests, some of which are hard to confess. The direct elections offer advantages but also many drawbacks and risks [...] The principal risks reside in untruthful demagogy, in reckless opportunism, in irresponsible charisma, and in the exploitation of the good faith and the naïveté of the people.[41]

Clearly a certain sensitivity for the issue of popular sovereignty can be noted, but also fear for a breakdown of order if irresponsible or opportunistic characters abuse political freedom. Implicitly, the statement shows that military guidance and controlled rules of the game could not be forfeited despite the re-democratization sought by the *abertura* process.

More covertly, hardline generals made a desperate last attempt, in September–October 1984, to block the imminent victory of the opposition candidate of the PMDB, Tancredo Neves, in the indirect elections of January 1985. Generals within the government, notably Pires and Medeiros, were reported to have supported the idea of a new military intervention, *uma virada de mesa* (a turning of the table), justified by the 'crisis' caused by the failure of the regime to control the succession process. Part of the manoeuvre consisted of spreading false information about links between Tancredo and the PCB. The alleged aim was to force the cancellation of the succession process and the prorogation of Figueiredo's presidency. The political astuteness of Tancredo and his political allies in defusing the crisis, coupled with the resistance to the intended coup put up by legalist commanders within the upper echelons of the armed forces, prevented the coup from actually happening in September 1984. This allowed the indirect elections of January 1985 to proceed. Tancredo Neves won with a comfortable majority against PDS-candidate Paulo Maluf. Subsequently, the drama of Tancredo Neves's

sudden illness unfolded. On the eve of his inauguration in March 1985, he was hospitalized and his vice-president-elect, José Sarney, the former ARENA president who had switched sides in 1984, took office ad interim. Tancredo never left the hospital; he died in April 1985 and Sarney became the official head of the first post-military government, called the New Republic.[42]

The Military and Politics after 1985

After the restoration of civil government in 1985, two issues continued to be relevant regarding the role of the military within the process of democratic consolidation. The first one refers to the problem of 'tutelary power' held by the armed forces vis-à-vis political society; this was of major importance, especially during the New Republic. The second issue is that of the legacy of human rights violations committed by the security forces during the years of the dictatorship; this issue has had, up till now, almost no impact on democratic consolidation.

THE TUTELAGE PROBLEM Despite the restoration of civilian rule in 1985, powerful mechanisms for the political influence of the military were preserved. Especially under the New Republic, the military wielded what has commonly been called 'tutelary power'.[43] Throughout the Sarney administration, the armed forces exerted pressure on the civilian government through their presence and policy-setting role within the government, and through public or private manifestations and threats. The military maintained at least six top-level officers as ministers within the government (army, navy, air force, intelligence, joint chiefs of staff, military house), and they interfered with a number of political issues, among which were the land reform and labour issues. The army and SNI ministers were especially influential in the intra-government policy-setting process, and were also actively putting pressure on Congress and public opinion through admonitions and public statements.

The influence of the military had not been called into question by Tancredo Neves, on the eve of his election by the Electoral College, in respect for the decision of the leading generals not to support the coup staged against his ascendancy in 1984.[44] The continuing military influence was also the result of the political weakness of the Sarney government. Sarney himself enjoyed little popular support due to his background as a former leading ARENA politician, the way he attained the presidency through the mechanisms of the military regime, the fact that he was the 'stand-in' for the capable and respected Tancredo Neves, and his lack of success in dealing with the country's economic and social problems. Sarney had serious problems establishing an effective congressional base. Most of the time, the largest party in the governmental coalition, the PMDB, acted as the de facto opposition under the leadership of Ulysses Guimarães, the president of Congress. To compensate for this, the Sarney government gravitated towards the military

in search of political support. In turn, the military reasoned that Sarney, with his political roots in supporting the government during the period of military rule, could be expected to pay heed to the military's points of view.

In addition, the structures of intelligence and influence-peddling set up by the military during the dictatorship (CSN, SNI, CIE, etcetera) were preserved with full vigour. It has been argued that as a consequence of the increasing complexity of the economic, social and political problems faced by the Sarney government, the attributions of the SNI and the CSN were expanded to include labour issues, the land question, foreign policy, the arms industry and administrative corruption.[45] For instance, General Ivan de Souza Mendes, head of the SNI with the status of cabinet minister in the Sarney government, observed in relation to the interest displayed by the service for the numerous strikes that were taking place between 1985 and 1990:

> We always received information, but the objective was to follow the strikes only from the point of view of state security. The strikes should not represent a threat to the stability of the government nor, for that matter, to the security of the state itself. The SNI had to worry about those facts and follow them closely.[46]

The most conspicuous of the issues raised by the military under the New Republic had to do with the formulation of the role of the military under the new constitution.[47] Traditionally, Brazil's republican constitutions ascribed to the armed forces the role of guardians of the constitutional order. In August 1986, General Leônidas Pires Gonçalves, minister of the army, made it clear in an address on the occasion of the Day of the Soldier, that the armed forces would not accept any alteration of this provision in the new constitution that was to be drafted. His argument echoed the well-known identification of the military with the nation and its fundamental priorities, this time for the sake of protecting Brazil's fragile democracy:

> To guarantee the constitutional powers, law and order means to secure the full functioning of the executive, legislative and judiciary powers, to have the prevailing legal provisions obeyed, and to preserve harmony within the Nation [... This is] a mission that will be carried out by the Armed Forces in cases of extreme necessity, and only after other legal instruments are exhausted [...] Not to foresee this would mean a weakening of the government of the Union, and an elimination of her capacity to intervene decisively would imply changing the Armed Forces [...] to mere spectators of chaos and disorder, whenever they occur.[48]

After the November 1986 congressional elections, the Constitutional Assembly started to debate the drafting of a new constitution, and many favoured the elimination of this constitutional prerogative that, in the past, had served to legitimate military interventions. For the military, the preservation of this provision was vital. Not only did they take recourse to

conventional and legitimate opinion-forming and lobbying, but they also threatened a *retrocesso* (a return to authoritarianism) in case the new constitution would not recognize the established role of the armed forces. This role defined the military as the protectors of the constitutional order and its three branches of power, including the right and obligation to intervene at the invitation of either one of these powers. The constitution that eventually emerged in October 1988 did indeed express the role of the armed forces in precisely these terms. Furthermore, the traditional presence of the military in the cabinet (with the three armed forces branch ministries) was not reduced. Since then, the issue has not been raised again, even when in 1993 the Brazilian people were asked by referendum to reconsider the country's governmental system.

From 1990 onwards, a number of institutional aspects of militarism were removed. The constitution of 1988 had provided for the abolishment of the CSN and its replacement by a Conselho da República (Council of the Republic) and a Conselho de Defesa Nacional (National Defence Council, CDN). Just before the end of his term, however, Sarney had decreed the formation of a Secretaria Asesora de Defesa Nacional (Advisory Secretariat on National Defence, SADEN) to replace the CSN. President Fernando Collor, however, abolished both SADEN and the SNI immediately upon taking office in March 1990. Instead, a Secretaria de Assuntos Estratégicos (Secretariat for Strategic Issues, SAE) was set up and brought under greater (but not yet complete) civil control. The military expressed regret over the elimination of the nation's intelligence capacity, but acknowledged at the same time that part of the former SNI personnel and operations continued as such, albeit informally. In addition, the intelligence capacity of the three armed forces took on greater significance.[49]

Since 1990, the military has, by and large, adopted a lower profile with regard to the political process and crucial policy issues. Fernando Collor, the first directly elected president since 1960, could use the legitimacy obtained through his victory at the ballot to scale down the political ambitions of the military, if not out of conviction then at least for reasons of convenience. At the same time, the armed forces were oriented towards a larger measure of 'old professionalism': institutional and technological modernization, external defence (e.g. along the Calha Norte flank of the Amazon region) and international peace-keeping operations (e.g. in Angola and Mozambique). Possibly the gradual rise of neo-liberal orientations in economic policy-making also did not match well with the traditional statist and interventionist outlook of the Brazilian military. It was also clear to the military that the growing complexities of governing Brazilian society and politics would not be handled well by a return to authoritarian rule.

Hunter argues that the increasing significance of electoral politics started to work against the preservation of important military prerogatives from 1990 onwards. She notes that civilian politicians gave priority to adopting

positions that would be in line with popular preferences rather than with those of the men in uniform. Civil politicians showed increasing ability to work the Council of the Republic and the CDN in order to reduce military influence on overall government strategy. As Hunter demonstrates, military influence in important areas such as public finance, labour issues and Amazon policy was effectively contested due to the opportunities and imperatives provided by the logic of democratic politics.[50]

At the same time, the armed forces seemed to advance in the direction of incorporating the support for democracy as a corporate value. The military were explicit in stating their support for a constitutional solution to the 1992 and 1993 corruption crises. Likewise, they opted for more subtle and covert ways of manifesting their view on political matters, which tended to become more trivial. It has been reported, for instance, that the minister of the army urged Fernando Henrique Cardoso, then minister of finance in the Franco government, to restrain the erratic behaviour of President Franco after the *calcinha* affair during the 1994 Carnival.[51] The principal focus of military political agitation in the 1990s was the size of the military budget and the level of officers' salaries, but even these issues may keep alive political activism among the military. On the other hand, large areas of military prerogatives, such as its institutional autonomy, its complete control over defence matters, and its internal guardianship, have as yet not been dealt with. The point has not been reached where the opinion and the positioning of the armed forces can be safely seen as irrelevant to the question of democracy in Brazil.

THE LEGACY OF REPRESSION AND THE HUMAN RIGHTS ISSUE If we consider the legacy of repression and human rights violations that took place under the military governments (especially between 1968 and 1976), it is clear that up till now this has not been a major issue in Brazilian politics, unlike in Argentina and Chile. A number of reasons can be cited. In the first place, and in absolute terms only, the scope and intensity of state terror, armed conflict and human rights abuse was limited when compared with Chile, Argentina and maybe even Uruguay. The 1984 report from the Bishops Conference on torture, assassination and disappearance documents some 125 cases of vanished political opponents.[52] As we saw, the most significant military campaign against subversion was waged in the early 1970s in the Araguaia-Tocantins area of the eastern Amazon, where fewer than 100 guerrilla fighters were easily eliminated by some 20,000 troops. As I mentioned earlier, torture was widespread and systematic, committed through an elaborate system of secret bureaux supervised by the intelligence community. But in proportion to the size of the Brazilian population, it was limited. This is not to deny the gravity of repression in Brazil, but it can explain why, even before the final stage of the military regime, the amnesty law was passed with the opposition's overall consent, which extended not only to opponents of the regime but also to 'possible' human rights violations committed by

the security forces themselves. Since then, a number of individual cases have been brought before the judiciary authorities through private initiative, but the military did not allow these cases to be tried in the military justice system. Armed forces spokesmen continued to defend the 'patriotism' of the 'anti-subversive' actions perpetrated during the 1960s and 1970s.

Recently, after the start of the Cardoso administration, the issue of the pension rights of the officers that were loyal to the pre-coup civilian government of Goulart and who were suspended or fired as a consequence, was raised again. Gradually, the military turned towards the acceptance of the legitimacy of their (or their kin's) claims to pension rights. The issue is subtle, since such recognition would imply the illegitimate nature of their dismissal and thereby the illegitimate nature of the 1964 intervention itself. A second issue that has been raised in recent years concerns the claims for recognition and financial compensation put forward by relatives of the disappeared. The Cardoso government chose not to ignore the issue, despite forceful opposition put up by the military. Already in 1994, still during the Franco administration, minister of war Zenildo Lucena rejected all responsibility for the disappeared because they were either subversives who were killed 'in battle' in ways not known to the armed forces, or had become army informants and hence received new identities. By mid-1995, the Cardoso government prepared a bill that would recognize a disappeared as 'dead'; financial compensation for relatives was considered since it was the state that had been responsible for their fate. Under this law, a Special Committee for the Dead and the Disappeared was set up, and some 136 cases were recognized.[53]

The military maintained their opposition against this form of dealing with the legacy of repression. They felt that the 1979 amnesty law should be seen as the final solution to the problem, arguing that the use of force during the anti-subversive struggle was justified. In addition, the military feared that investigations into the fate of the disappeared would reveal a number of sensitive issues that could be unfavourable to the military's current position. Partly as a result of military pressure, it was stipulated that only relatives of those that had disappeared from prisons or police stations would receive recognition and compensation. José Gregori, a legal consultant to the ministry of justice at the time, and who later would become head of the national human rights secretariat installed by Cardoso, observed: 'We did the minimum the families need and the maximum the military would accept.'[54]

In sum, the 1964 coup continues to be seen by the military as having been a necessary and perfectly legitimate intervention: a revolution to save the country from communism. The military, therefore, continue to oppose even balanced and careful official efforts to deal with the wounds left by past arbitrariness. Hence, no process of national guilt assessment, systematic persecution of human rights abuse, or reconciliation and truth, have, up till now, been desired, supported or sought either by the military or by the major civilian political forces.

Political and Institutional Dimensions of the New Democracy

CIVILIAN POLITICS AFTER 1985   The New Republic (1985–90) can be seen as the final stage of the Brazilian transition. Not only was a full restoration of civil democratic institutions and practices envisaged, but visible progress in tackling the huge economic and social problems was also expected by the public. It was clear that dealing with the so-called 'social debt' would be crucial for the long-term success of democratic consolidation.[55] Before the indirect elections in January 1985, but after the defeat of the vote calling for direct presidential elections (in April 1984), AD-candidate Tancredo Neves toured the country to drum up support for his presidency and the modest reform programme he advocated. Tancredo pretended to address the major economic and social problems with moderation, on the basis of an explicit social 'pact' between the principal social forces. Sarney did not prove capable of constructing such a social pact. The main social sectors, notably business and organized labour, were wary of his government's intentions and were not prepared to accept distributional losses in exchange for uncertain economic and social policies. One of the first major reform initiatives, the land reform, met with failure due to governmental indecisiveness, juridical complications, and the threat from the land-owners to react with violence.[56]

As the New Republic drew on, it became increasingly clear that its performance would be mainly measured against the degree of success of its economic policies. The intricate question was how to stabilize the economy (addressing the foreign debt and controlling inflation) while at the same time revitalizing economic growth and dealing with extreme social inequalities. Soon, inflation became the core issue. The New Republic witnessed a number of efforts to control inflation, most of them based on a heterodox set of approaches and none of them successful. Stabilization policies were subordinated to the political considerations of President Sarney and his dwindling group of supporters. This was illustrated by the fate of the most ambitious of the stabilization plans: the Cruzado plan of 1986. This plan froze prices and wages in such a way that wage-earning consumers experienced a considerable rise in purchasing power. The (temporary) result was an enormous boost in President Sarney's popularity and a landslide victory for the PMDB in the crucial November 1986 elections. Soon after these elections, the Cruzado plan caved in under the pressures of its in-built flaws (overheated internal demand, producers' strikes and rampant black-marketeering to avoid the price freeze). Sarney's approval rate fell with the plan, never to recover again.[57]

The 1986 congressional elections were of vital importance for the consolidation of democracy, in view of the constitutional powers bestowed upon the new Congress. The debates over the new constitution dominated most of 1987 and 1988, with a high level of involvement of sectors and groups from Brazilian society.[58] In the end, the process yielded an elaborate

constitution in which a large number of claims and priorities were in-corporated. As a result, the new constitution was unbalanced and left a number of issues unresolved. Its overall tone was nationalist, statist and reformist, its principal merits being the full restoration of formal civil liberties and full political democracy, and the incorporation of some social issues. Much had to be put into practice, however, through subsequent ordinary legislation, which proved to be a cumbersome affair.

It was, however, the economy that raised the anxiety of the population and, more than anything else, eroded the position of the government of the New Republic. Sarney's popularity and legitimacy dwindled in the face of erratic economic growth and rampant inflation. The inability of a number of successive finance ministers to address inflation led to widespread mistrust of the government and of politics at large. The manifestations of political opportunism (seen by many as cynicism) among many politicians further contributed to the demise of the New Republic. At the same time, political preference among the population moved towards either popular candidacies from the Left (mainly PT) or to right-wing neo-populists who attacked the New Republic and its shortcomings. This was clearly shown by the campaign and the results of the presidential election in 1989.

The 1989 election was contested in two rounds, as stipulated by the new constitution. Initially, conventional left-wing candidates like old-time populist Leone Brizola and PT-leader Luis Inácio 'Lula' da Silva led the polls. But out of the blue, the candidacy of Fernando Collor de Mello rocketed during the 1989 electoral year. Collor espoused a liberal–populist discourse, promising to end the vices of the existing political system (mainly corruption and clientelism) and to 'modernize' Brazil through an unspecified mixture of economic liberalization and social reform. It was widely held that the real success of the Collor candidacy was engineered by the coverage of his candidacy by the powerful Globo media group. As Collor rose in the polls, most centre-right groups rallied behind his candidacy, especially between the first and second turns. The second turn was a show-down between Collor and Lula. Collor won by fewer than 10 percentage points.

The election of Collor, and the runner-up result of Lula, clearly showed a broad desire for change. None of the parties or politicians linked to the military regime or to the New Republic managed to obtain significant support during the first electoral round in October 1989. Collor, more than Lula, managed to appeal to a broad spectrum of voters: elite, middle-class, and even the workers and the poor. They were attracted by the discourse of 'change' and 'cleaning the stable', set in a carefully nurtured 'anti-political' imagery of the young and handsome candidate. Edified by electoral legitimacy, Collor was sworn in in March 1990, and he was determined to make changes. His performance did not match his pretensions, however. Although the modernization of the economy was set into motion, with rather substantial trade liberalization and a first round of privatization, social reform was absent

and the all-important stabilization plans failed to control what had by then become hyperinflation. Popular mistrust of Collor was immediately fuelled for his first stabilization plan included large-scale confiscation of private saving deposits. But Collor's biggest problem was Congress. Although convincingly elected president, Collor did not have an expressive political party. For his candidacy, he had used the empty hull of an obscure party (the Partido da Renovação Nacional – Party of National Renovation, PRN) with only a few seats in Congress. The large parties were, for the most part, hostile to Collor and his schemes, which aimed at bypassing existing political hierarchies and loyalties, and threatened the interests of various groups and sectors represented by these parties. The congressional elections of 1990, less than a year after the start of the Collor administration, reinforced the larger parties and deepened the anti-Collor bias of the legislature. Especially the PMDB and the PFL forced political concessions from the government in return for support for executive initiatives and plans.

The demise of Collor was as sudden as his rise. In June 1992, he still enjoyed world-wide attention and the presence of a large number of foreign political leaders during the United Nations Conference on the Environment and Development (UNCED) held in Rio de Janeiro. By that time, the first rumours of irregular presidential conduct appeared in the press. These hints soon developed into the unravelling of a major scheme of corruption, fuelled by the press, denounced by popular protests, and eagerly picked up by a congressional inquiry commission that set itself to the task of finding out the truth. The result was an indictment of Collor and his suspension awaiting an impeachment procedure. In December 1992, Collor formally resigned. The most important aspect of this 'Collorgate' drama was not so much the case itself, nor the dismissal of a president, but the fact that the affair was handled within the limits of constitutional procedures. Both the general public and the military showed sufficient faith in the democratic institutions to await and accept the outcome of the congressional inquiries.

Collor's resignation brought his vice-president, Itamar Franco, to the presidency. This hitherto unexpressive politician set himself to the task of engineering a broader support base in Congress. Already hostile to Collor when he was vice-president, Franco put most of the liberalization reforms on hold, since he was more inclined towards the conventional nationalist/statist approach of economic development than towards deregulation and global integration. Franco especially singled out the financial sector as culprits, since they benefited hugely from the ever-rising rate of inflation. Franco managed a more sympathetic attitude towards Congress by including politicians from a broad party spectrum in his government. Congress, however, was soon turned towards itself: 1993 witnessed the eruption of yet another corruption scandal, this time involving a number of influential Congress members who had taken fees from construction companies while members of the powerful budget commission.

Economic success came only towards the end of Franco's term and was crucial for the election of Fernando Henrique Cardoso to the presidency in October 1994. Cardoso had accepted, early in 1993, the post of minister of foreign affairs in the Franco government, but a few months later he was persuaded to move to the finance ministry. During late 1993 and the first half of 1994, Cardoso and his team carefully designed a stabilization plan that led to the introduction of a new currency, the real, in July 1994.[59] The apparent success, manifest in a steep drop in inflation, paved the way for Cardoso's successful bid for the presidency. The real package brought him popular trust, and a political alliance forged with the PFL and part of the PMDB brought him the necessary support in Congress. This support was needed for the ambitious reform programme envisaged by the Cardoso government. The reforms included the elimination of constitutional obstacles for economic liberalization and the privatization of major state-owned companies. Furthermore, fiscal and social security reforms should solve the federal government's huge financial problems. The end of public sector job stability was targeted as a condition for downsizing the state apparatus.

The Cardoso reform agenda progressed slowly but steadily during his first term in office. Opposition to the reforms came mainly from the PT and from organized groups in society, such as the trade unions and the movement of landless rural workers, who felt threatened by the 'onslaught of neo-liberalism'. Among business sectors and the middle classes, the Cardoso government enjoyed a fair amount of support. Early in 1997, Cardoso managed to have another constitutional amendment accepted which allowed for the immediate re-election of heads of the executive at all three levels of government: president, governor and mayor.

Despite the fact that the possibility of re-election added complexities to the already cumbersome game of welding political alliances in support of the Cardoso administration, the re-election of the president in the 1998 presidential elections proved unprecedentedly easy. With a clear majority of the votes obtained already during the first round of the elections, in October 1998, Cardoso left the runner-up candidate, Lula, clearly behind. The third most voted candidate was Ciro Gomes, a former political ally of Cardoso (and in fact his succesor as finance minister during the final months of the Itamar Franco presidency, in 1994). This shows that the 1998 elections confirmed the political hegemony at the federal level of the social–liberal coalition that supported the Cardoso administration.[60]

At the same time, oppositionary forces made some headway at the state level. In the politically important state of Rio Grande do Sul, Cardoso's ally, Antônio Britto, lost out to the Workers Party's candidate Olívio Dutra in the second round of the elections for state governor. Likewise, in Minas Gerais, Itamar Franco won the governorship in the second round, auguring a critical position *vis-à-vis* the Cardoso administration. These politicians represented various strands of left-wing or populist opposition against Cardoso's reform

agenda. The pressure on this agenda was clearly increased by the subsequent eruption of a financial crisis, in January 1999. Widely seen as part of the global chain of financial upheaval that had started in East Asia in 1997 and hit Russia in 1998, this crisis forced the real to devalue sharply, thereby bringing in fear for renewed inflation. Furthermore, the recession that most observers expected to result from the devaluation and the implementation of the IMF-sponsored adjustments to back up the US$ 40 billion relief package, was likely to aggravate the already existing problems of unemployment and poverty. This may well put the support for the Cardoso administration to the test, through increasing popular mobilization and a reshuffling of political allegiances in view of the upcoming municipal elections in the year 2000.

DEMOCRATIC CONSOLIDATION: A PROVISIONAL BALANCE   The restoration of democratic politics in Brazil since 1985 has progressed to a considerable extent, but at the same time it was not free from complications. Already from 1979 onwards, basic civil and political rights were progressively restored. In 1982, direct elections for state governors were held for the first time since 1965, along with fairly open elections for state legislatures and Congress. This was followed by the restoration of civilian government in 1985, with the explicit aim of returning to full democracy within five years. In 1985 and 1986, elections for major city governments and councils, and for a full congressional renewal, were held. Subsequent state and federal legislative elections took place in 1990, 1994 and 1998, municipal elections in 1988, 1992 and 1996, and of course, direct presidential elections in 1989, 1994 and 1998.

The groundwork was laid by the enacting of the new constitution, finished in October 1988. This constitution restored direct presidential elections, confirmed full freedom of party organization and collective action within civil society, and gave greater power to Congress and to the state and municipal levels of government. The vote was extended to illiterates and youngsters from sixteen to eighteen years of age, the formal position of Indians was improved, and provisions against gender and ethnic discrimination were included.[61]

Nevertheless, the constitution left some unfinished business. The first issue to be mentioned was the reconsideration of the political regime itself. The Brazilian people would be allowed to decide in a referendum whether Brazil should be a presidential or parliamentary republic, or even return to the constitutional monarchy abolished in 1889. In April 1993, a huge majority of the electorate voted in favour of the maintenance of the *status quo*, i.e. a federal republic based on presidentialism.[62]

Other flaws in the political system remained unresolved, however. The party system is notoriously fluid and unstable; the electoral regime favoured small, more backward and generally conservative states in the northeast over the more populous and urban-industrial states of the southeast and south.[63]

In general, Brazil's political institutions are not so much fragile as subject to continuous change (at least until 1995), to the extent that Lamounier speaks of a 'hyperactive paralysis syndrome' among politicians and parties: a continuous search for institutional reform as the solution to political dilemmas despite the fact that party fragmentation makes such reforms unfeasible.[64] The constitutional amendment to allow for presidential (and other chief executives') re-election was the latest example of the permanent drive to change political institutions. In addition, although the 1988 constitution ruled out the typical instrument of arbitrary rule, the *decreto-lei*, it introduced something similar: the provisory measure (*medida provisória*), which has been used in order to force policy initiatives of the executive past Congress.

As far as political practice is concerned, a number of contradictory trends have been emerging. On the one hand, a basic democratic consensus has been gradually solidified among the major political groupings, in the sense that political strategies, alliances and conflicts have been charted within the confines of institutional rules. Elections are essentially free and fair, and, due to mandatory voting, massively attended. The extension of the vote to illiterates and persons aged sixteen to eighteen has increased the Brazilian electorate to 78 million citizens in the 1994 presidential and congressional elections.[65] Elections in Brazil since 1985 have been basically competitive and fair. Candidates and campaigning have been reasonably respectful of electoral legislation, and have never approached the vulgar personalism currently fashionable in US elections. For instance, during the 1989 presidential campaign, the Electoral Court barred the irregular candidacy of a popular media magnate and talk-show host who was pushed forward by the Sarney government in order to waylay the rise of Fernando Collor in the opinion polls. It has been especially significant that the two major institutional crises of the Collor/Franco term (1990–94), that is to say, the corruption affair involving Collor himself and the 1993 corruption scandal involving a group of Congress members, have been dealt with in basically constitutional terms, and without interference from the military.

On the other hand, the political process has been characterized, on all levels, by personalism and clientelism, a certain degree of elitism, various forms of corruption, and generally weak links between parties and society at large (with the possible exception of the PT). Patronage was rampant during the New Republic and used to cement congressional alliances in favour of the particular ambitions of President Sarney, notably to secure his five-year term in office. The (party) political process underlying the constitutional debates showed a number of what could be considered 'imperfections'. Positioning with regard to the main issues to be dealt with provoked constant reshuffling of alliances and loyalties within and among congressional factions and individual members. Especially, the government exerted itself in using clientelism and favouritism in order to influence majorities on specific issues (such as the length of the presidential term in office). Congressional alliances

were shaped more by personal deals and loyalties than by party programmes and coherence.[66] After 1990, this phenomenon might have declined somewhat, although Collor tried to use clientelism in an effort to avert his impeachment in 1992. Even Cardoso did not manage to remain totally aloof from clientelistic practices for his agenda of substantial administrative and political reforms, and to win his shot at a second term. Particularly, patronage at all levels, ranging from local politics to the forging of voting alliances in Congress, has remained important. A main reason for this is the pervasiveness of personalism, already referred to, in combination with the endemic fluidity of the party structure. This is enhanced by the continuing political clout of the northeast, where such practices are at the core of party politics; for instance, the very influential *cacique* from the PFL of Bahia, Antônio Carlos Magalhães, has been involved in practically every important political scheme since 1985. Yet, under Cardoso, the social-liberal alliance of Cardoso's own party, the Partido Social Democrático Brasileiro (Brazilian Social Democratic Party, PSDB), the PFL and part of the PMDB, in which important political forces from São Paulo, the northeast (Bahia, Pernambuco, Ceara), Minas Gerais and the wealthy southern states (Paraná, Santa Catarina and Rio Grande do Sul) are united, appeared sufficiently solid to underscore his reform agenda. On the regional and local level, a wide variety of political situations has emerged, ranging from conventional regional oligarchies and local bossism to progressive regional alliances (such as in Ceara and Rio Grande do Sul) and the participatory politics of PT municipal governments in important cities such as Porto Alegre.

In terms of the socio-political foundations of democratic consensus, it can be observed that most social groups and classes appeared committed to democratic procedures.[67] The business elites and the large land-owners are well represented in various congressional factions. Especially the so-called 'new right' (neo-liberal politicians of the Partido Liberal, small- and medium-sized business, and the large land-owners of the Rural Democratic Union, UDR, which, in fact, ceased to exist in 1995) has been integrated into the democratic and civil polity, and seems to keep authoritarian inclinations at arm's length.[68] The middle classes, the working class, and even parts of the urban and rural poor have managed to increase their access to the public domain through trade unions and all kinds of voluntary civic associations. The level of political organization and mobilization of Brazilian society is considered to be high, though to a large extent dissociated from the daily business of party politics. The trade union movement has recently been weakened due to the ongoing economic crisis, informalization and liberalization.[69] The rural poor, especially the landless peasants and their movement, maintained links with the PT but hover between peaceful actions and more radical and violent initiatives, such as the occupation of rural estates and confrontations with the state police. I'll return to this problem in the next section.

To sum up, then, by and large institutional democracy (and the basic civil

and political rights) seems firmly in place, with some shortcomings. Political praxis and political culture have become increasingly congruent with democracy, but, at the same time, a number of peculiarities such as personalism, clientelism and *ad hoc* shifting of party loyalties remain at odds with what one would call 'mature' democracy.

The Current Threat of Violence

One of the great paradoxes of the Brazilian transition is that the end of authoritarian rule and the restoration of democracy did little to diminish the problems of violence, arbitrariness and insecurity within society. On the contrary, although it is virtually impossible to substantiate, it may be claimed that with democracy the levels and extent of social violence have been increasing. This may well be a matter of perception: those in Brazil who tend to express *saudade* (melancholic longing) with respect to the years of 'law and order' under the military obviously forget that the military themselves were one of the prime perpetrators of arbitrary violence. In addition, the increase in ordinary crime started long before the recent return to democracy and may even have received an important boost under the dictatorship.

Be that as it may, what is significant for the purpose of this chapter is that the perception of violence and insecurity has certainly become more intense during the past ten to fifteen years. This can probably be explained by the fact that it was exactly the return to democracy that had heightened expectations of improvement in security and the rule of law. To this, one may add the apparently more 'pluriform' nature of social violence and conflict. Brazil, in fact, presents the most telling case of the 'new violence' that affects Latin American societies in the post-authoritarian period. It is no longer just the left-wing radicals, or the poor – who have always been subjected to different forms of (state) violence – who are facing the threat of violence and insecurity. Especially since the mid-1980s, violence has turned into a common option for land-owners, shopkeepers, law enforcement officers, criminal gangs, drug lords and, in some places, backland politicians.

It is open to debate whether the current wave of social conflicts and violence threatens the long-term viability of democracy in Brazil. At any rate, its impact appears to be much greater than the legacy of past repression in casting doubt on the state's ability to uphold citizenship rights and the rule of law. The apprehensions concerning social conflicts and various forms of violence today stand in sharp contrast to the relative overall indifference with regard to terror and violence from the past. So, as the institutional and political dimensions of democracy now appear to be firmly established in Brazil, ongoing violence and problems in the field of human rights continue to call into question the quality of Brazilian democracy *vis-à-vis* many of its citizens. I review briefly the main manifestations of the problem in two areas: violence and social conflicts, and crime and law enforcement.

SOCIAL CONFLICTS AND VIOLENCE At the heart of the matter lies, of course, the deeply engrained pattern of social inequality and exclusion within Brazilian society. This refers not only to the problem of widespread poverty, but to the overall syndrome of systematic exclusion from formal livelihood resources (land, work, wages), from public welfare schemes, from political participation, and even from the nation as a collective social and cultural construct. This exclusion is based on various combinations of class and ethnic divisions, and is further complicated by the persistent significance of personal ties that can determine whether one is 'in' or 'out' in terms of effective citizenship.[70]

In a direct sense, what is at stake is the issue of 'social citizenship'. In the long run, poverty and exclusion work against democratic consensus and stability.[71] They not only bring 'structural violence' that operates through the day-to-day hardships produced by inequity and deprivation;[72] they also fuel outbursts of violent conflict.

The role of violence in social conflicts, and even in everyday life and culture, has, of course, a long history in Brazil. Colonial society was founded upon coercion, in the form of the crucial institution of slavery. In nineteenth-century Brazil, the repression of social protest and regional revolts was added to the spectre of violence.[73] Up till the present day, the handling of opposing interests between different groups or actors often involves the use of violence, usually by the more powerful of the parties involved. Endemic violence prevailed especially in the more peripheral rural areas.[74] As a rule, private elites could count on compliance or active involvement of representatives of the state. Violence perpetrated either by private parties or by the so-called 'forces of the law' has been brought to bear against social activists such as landless peasants occupying an estate, metal-workers on strike, indigenous communities, or gold miners (garimpeiros) being expelled from their site. Especially on the Amazon frontier, daily violence is endemic and testifies to the incapacity of the state to uphold a legitimate and peaceful internal order. This may well contribute to a general climate in which violence is seen as a normal option when pursuing interests or resolving conflicts. In particular, certain segments of the elite, such as land-owners faced with landless squatters, or shopkeepers annoyed by street children, resort to violence on a routine basis.

During the New Republic, it was mainly labour strikes that provoked repressive reactions on the part of the authorities. I have already discussed the vivid interest in labour issues displayed by the SNI. Still, organized labour enjoyed far greater room for action under the New Republic than during the years of military rule. Trade unionists felt that the time had come to demand compensation for the rapid income deterioration experienced by wage earners prior to 1985. The result was an impressive strike wave during the years of the Sarney government. In some conspicuous cases, strikes were met with repressive violence by the authorities. In March 1987, the army and the navy

were deployed to end massive strikes by port workers and oil-refinery workers. In November 1988, a strike at the state-owned steel plant at Volta Redonda, in the state of Rio de Janeiro, was violently repressed by the army, resulting in three casualties and two dozen wounded.[75]

After 1990, the principal social movement to attract violent reactions was the landless movement (Movimento dos Trabalhadores Rurais Sem-Terra, MST). While the armed forces were kept at arm's length, the task of controlling and repressing the movement fell upon the military police, who in Brazil are responsible for the standard police tasks of law enforcement and the maintenance of public order, under the command of the state governors. The movement started in the early 1980s in Rio Grande do Sul and was greatly invigorated during the short period in which the Sarney government tried to enact a land reform. Under the New Republic, the land issue provoked the formation of private armed groups against the MST by the large land-owners, organized in the UDR and paid for through cattle auctions under its auspices. During the 1990s, the MST stepped up its militancy and resorted to occupying holdings belonging to large land-owners or to the state but considered 'unproductive' and therefore eligible for expropriation.[76] The MST has been operating on the delicate divide between institutional strategies, maintaining certain links with the PT, the Central Única dos Trabalhadores (Unified Labour Central, CUT), civic protest (such as the peasant march on Brasília in April 1997), and forceful occupation of land which, when successful, was followed by efforts at community development on the holdings.[77] The land occupations and other militant actions often led to violent confrontations, especially with the military police sent in to handle the situation, but also with gunmen hired by the land-owners.

During the Cardoso government, these kinds of confrontations became more frequent. Although Cardoso made efforts to implement the land reform he had promised during the 1994 electoral campaign, MST leaders felt the reform was not progressing fast enough while rural social problems were at the same time becoming more severe. The MST did not reject the notion of dialogue in itself, but land invasions and militant actions were seen as necessary to induce the government to speed up land reform and to abandon 'neo-liberalism' – the principal ideological and political 'opponent' of the MST. In August 1997, MST leader João Pedro Stedile referred to the April 1997 march on Brasília and to the Chiapas rebellion in Mexico in the following terms:

> With the march, we forced the government to change tactics. Until then they adopted a policy of isolating the MST. That has stopped. Now the government talks and hits afterward. It is a policy of beating and prose [...] Chiapas played an important historical role by showing to the world that neoliberalism had failed in Mexico. Before, the elites inside and outside Brazil presented that country as a model, but now nobody talks about that anymore. In a certain way, Chiapas was the fall of the Berlin Wall for international finance capital.[78]

By the mid-1990s, the use of force by MST members became more frequent, but the reaction of the forces of order was almost always disproportionate. In July 1995, the military police engaged in a violent eviction of an 'isolated' group of *sem-terra* (landless rural workers) who had occupied an estate near Corumbiara, Rondônia, resulting in nine rural activists and three policemen killed. The military police were reported to have tortured those taken into custody.[79] Less than a year later, the killing of nineteen and the wounding of fifty-one squatters by the military police of the state of Para caused a general uproar. In an action designed to remove 1,500 *sem-terra* who had put up a road block near the municipality of Eldorado do Carajás in protest at the slow pace of the land reform, some 268 policemen armed with rifles and machine guns encircled the protesters and fired deliberately into the crowd, sometimes at point-blank range. The action followed failed negotiations and increasing impatience on the side of the authorities.[80] With respect to the rural question, the government seems to be caught between *sem-terra* militancy, and the powerful congressional faction which represents the large land-owners and tries to prevent a more rapid modernization of social relations in the countryside. At the same time, the outbursts of violence against rural protesters or squatters seriously call into question the effectiveness of the rule of law in Brazil.

THE NEW WAR: CRIME AGAINST SOCIETY In urban Brazil, the problems of violence and fear are equally related to the problem of upholding the rule of law. In the cities, the issue of criminal violence has been prominent during the past ten or fifteen years. For analysts, urban violence in Brazil may be an expression of 'class domination and resistance' in the context of a highly exclusionary form of capitalism; or it might mean an impediment to the extension of citizenship to the poor and the excluded.[81] To ordinary people it soon assumed the proportions of a collective psychosis. The most unsettling aspect of the problems of crime and insecurity is not just the apparent incapacity of the state to guarantee the safety of its citizens, nor the periodic deliberate violation of the rights of the poor strata of the population by the police forces, but the active compliance of a large number of law-enforcement agents (maybe even entire units) with everyday wanton violence related to organized crime. It is true that this problem is especially salient in Rio de Janeiro and the many reports on urban violence, organized crime and police arbitrariness in this metropolis are not necessarily representative of Brazil as a whole. Still, this problem is also manifest in many of the other major cities in Brazil, and the situation in Rio certainly contributes to a general sense of fear within the country which is shared by both middle-class urbanites and the urban poor, especially the *favelados* (shantytown dwellers). However, the way in which both broad categories experience the 'urban war' is quite different and reflects the fundamental social separation that runs through Brazil's urban society.

Urban crime and crime-related violence have a long history in Brazil, not just in Rio de Janeiro but in all major Brazilian cities. Drug-related organized crime has clearly been on the increase since the late 1970s, when Brazil – especially Rio – became a transit route for cocaine from the Andean countries to the European markets, and a growing consumer market itself.[82] The rise of numerous cocaine trafficking groups in the *favelas* (shantytowns) of Rio de Janeiro, each headed by a local drug lord, brought with it the rapid proliferation of sophisticated weaponry among gang members in the *favelas*. At the same time, criminal activities, especially kidnapping and drug trafficking, took on an increasingly organized form. In the course of the 1990s, violence between the drug gangs and the police in Rio de Janeiro took on the contours of a civil war. Not only did this lead to a marked increase in the levels of violence and a generalized sense of fear among the city's population, but it also blurred to a significant extent the distinction between 'official' and 'criminal' order and violence.

In the first place, the rise of drug-related criminal activities prompted the police to step up their already established habit of employing indiscriminate violence against *favela* inhabitants during so-called *blitz* operations against drug gangs and drug barons. Such operational methods are, in part, engrained in long-standing police practices and are further stimulated by pressure from politicians and middle-class public opinion to deal with the problem of crime and lawlessness. Secondly, this leads to a situation in which the poor *favela* inhabitants live in a permanent state of fear of being caught in the violence among rival gangs, or between the criminals and the official guardians of law and order. This in turn gave the organized drug gangs in the *favelas* opportunities to offer alternative structures for security and order in the shantytowns. Leeds has documented the role of gang leaders in imposing their control by using various combinations of services and threats, giving rise to a parallel power structure in the poor neighbourhoods controlled by the crime leaders and their heavily armed retinues. In some cases, such as in the notorious *favela* of Roçinha, these practices expanded to adjacent upper-middle-class neighbourhoods when well-to-do inhabitants also turned to gang leaders, seeking order and a certain measure of safety.

Finally, in Rio de Janeiro in particular, numerous members of the civil and military police force have been involved in criminal activities such as assassinations, kidnapping and drug trafficking. This became manifest in the aftermath of the most infamous of the explosions of violence in the 1990s: the killing of twenty-one inhabitants of the *favela* Vicário Geral on 30 August 1993. Immediately, it was widely suspected that members of the civil and military police forces had formed the group of heavily armed and masked gunmen that carried out the killings.[83] The investigations led to a number of declarations involving police officers in extortion rackets and in the cocaine trade. It was increasingly felt that the Rio police were unable to live up to their tasks. Bleak scenarios were drawn up (for instance by the Escola Superior

de Guerra) in which it was envisioned that, in some near future, the city would be ruled by mobsters and their private armies such that 'The constituted powers [...] will have to ask for the involvement of the Armed Forces, to take on the difficult task of confronting this horde of bandits, of neutralizing them, and even of destroying them so that Law and Order can be maintained.'[84]

One year later, in November 1994, the state and federal authorities decided to launch a federal intervention in Rio de Janeiro by sending army units into the *favelas* to deal with the drug gangs. The intervention, dubbed Operação Rio, echoed an earlier brief experience of deploying federal troops to maintain order during the UNCED conference in 1992. Operação Rio was carried out until mid-1995 without having any long-term effects on crime fighting or the reduction of violence. It contributed only to the confusion as to the way in which the problem of law enforcement should be handled: by a duly reformed police force under the control of democratic local governments, or by the military?

Summing up this brief and by no means exhaustive overview of the current situation in Brazil, it can be observed that, although the escalation of violence and the ensuing disappearance of effective democratic governance in Rio de Janeiro represent an extreme case, it is clear that the problems of violence, fear and insecurity have not been adequately addressed in Brazil, especially as concerns the poor and excluded segments of society.[85] This casts a shadow over the advance of democracy that the country has been struggling to bring about during the past two decades. Recent reports on the situation of human rights in Brazil confirm the paradox of a worsening record of effective rule of law despite the consolidation of political democracy in the country.[86] In Brazil, the democratic transition has ended the systematic disregard of individual freedom and human rights by the government; but it has also led to more diffuse and maybe widespread forms of violence and human rights violations, whereby it is no longer the opponents of an authoritarian regime, but instead a fragmented set of actors (some of them state-related) who appear both as perpetrators and victims of a new kind of violence that seems to have become endemic.[87]

Conclusion

Brazil's military regime was the first in a cycle of authoritarian governments that introduced repression and state terror as a systematic and doctrinal feature of rule in Latin America. However, the Brazilian dictatorship preserved a curiously hybrid nature in which part of the formally democratic institutional structure was preserved to underpin the 'legality' of military rule. Compared with its southern cone neighbours, the scale and extent of repressive violence under Brazil's military governments was limited, but this was to a large extent offset by the large size and pervasiveness of the regime's

security apparatus. The growing autonomy and uncontrollability of this apparatus was one of the reasons the regime itself decided to adopt a course of gradual liberalization from the mid-1970s onwards. The preservation of a certain degree of civil institutionality gave the military the possibility of controlling the transition to a considerable extent, and of securing a substantial portion of its institutional and political prerogatives after the return to civil government in 1985. By adhering to the transition rules set by the regime while at the same time building up effective political alliances and a strong societal support base, the opposition to the regime was able to assume governmental power against the preference of the military, thereby ending a regime that used arbitrariness as one of its basic resources.

After 1985, the process of democratic consolidation has been successful on a number of counts, especially with regard to the full restoration of individual and political liberties and the nature of electoral policies. On the other hand, persisting flaws in the party system and political culture, added to continuing uncertainties as to the final institutional make-up of the Brazilian political system, have contributed to a permanent sense of uneasiness as to the viability of democratic politics, at least until 1995. With the advent of the Cardoso government, political stability has improved significantly, and the adoption of an ambitious reform agenda augurs favourably for the long-term prospects of political democracy, despite the difficulties of putting the reforms into practice.

Towards the end of the twentieth century, the principal shadows that are cast over democratic governance in Brazil are not caused by the legacy of past repression, as in the case of countries like Argentina, Chile, El Salvador and Guatemala. Instead, they stem from the combined problems of poverty and social exclusion, on the one hand, and the spread of everyday violence and the practical failure of the rule of law, on the other. This double syndrome continues to undermine effective citizenship for substantial portions of the Brazilian population. Any future test of the success of democratic politics in Brazil will necessarily involve the way this fundamental trauma of insecurity is being tackled.

Notes and References

1. See Andrade, 'Brazil: the military in politics'; Rouquié, *Military*. For a discussion of the historical formation of military political doctrine see Hayes, *Armed Nation*.

2. The Old Republic (1889–1930) was marked by the supremacy of regional elites linked to land-ownership and the local and state-level political machines. These oligarchies tended to distrust the federal army, giving preference to the regional paramilitary forces they controlled. The army, in turn, gradually developed an anti-oligarchic stance, either cloaked in a conservative modernization discourse or in a leftist-reformist one. See Hayes, *Armed Nation*; Quartim de Moraes, *Esquerda militar.*

3. See Figueiredo, *Militares e a revolução.*

4. See Hilton, 'Armed Forces and industrialists'.

5. See Alves, *Estado e oposição*; Dreifuss, *1964*; Hayes, *Armed Nation*; Stepan, *Military in Politics*; Stepan, 'New professionalism'.

6. See Couto e Silva, *Geopolítica do Brasil*.

7. Interview reported in D'Araujo et al., *Visões do golpe*, p. 40.

8. Ibid., p. 143.

9. The first military president after the coup, Marshal Humberto Castello Branco, was inclined to return to 'normality' after he had served out the original presidential term of Jânio Quadros (assumed by Goulart after Quadros resignation in 1961). Pressed by the growing strength of the political and societal opposition, and by the hardliners within the military, Castello accepted the continuation of the generals at the apex of power. See Velasco e Cruz and Martins, 'De Castello a Figueiredo'; Alves, *Estado e oposição*, pp. 87-95.

10. The best account of the formation of the repressive apparatus is provided by Alves, *Estado e oposição*; see also Stepan, *Rethinking Military Politics*, especially pp. 25-9.

11. See for a comprehensive discussion Alves, *Estado e oposição*, chs 3, 5 and 6.

12. See D'Araujo et al., *Os anos de chumbo*.

13. See Stepan, *Rethinking Military Politics*, especially ch. 2.

14. See Zagorski, *Democracy vs. National Security*, p. 99. Rizzo de Oliveira, 'Aparelho militar', p. 58, states that by the mid-1980s the SNI 'represents a legacy consisting of an intelligence structure that permeates all levels and functions of the state, penetrates society, has real budgets that are secretive and not submitted to any control outside of the executive itself and employs 300 thousand agents.' According to General Octávio Medeiros, minister-head of the SNI in the Figueiredo government, the SNI employed no more than 3,000, including the staff of the National Intelligence School (Escola Nacional de Informações, ENI); see the interview with Medeiros in *Veja*, 9 July 1997.

15. The Brasil Nunca Mais project, carried out under the auspices of the São Paulo Archdiocese, made an effort to present a complete report of the repressive apparatus, its methods, its targets, and the results of imprisonment, torture, death and disappearance. I return to these issues below. See Archdiocese de São Paulo, *Torture in Brazil*.

16. The Brazilian Communist Party (PCB), until the mid-1960s the most important party to the left of *trabalhismo* populism, always advocated a peaceful transition to socialism, passing through the stage of 'national bourgeois democracy'. Its leader, Luis Carlos Prestes, who was a former *tenente*, later commander of the guerrilla group known as the Prestes column that was active in the 1920s, and later one of the leaders of the 1935 communist uprising organized by the National Liberation Alliance (ALN), never endorsed the views of younger militants who supported a violent revolution inspired by the Chinese, Cuban and Algerian revolutionary regimes.

17. See Alves, *Estado e oposição*, ch. 6; Mir, *Revolução impossível*; Quartim de Moraes, *Dictatorship and Armed Struggle*; Archdiocese de São Paulo, *Torture in Brazil*, chs 9-12.

18. See Mir, *Revolução Impossível*, pp. 165ff.; Archdiocese de São Paulo, *Torture in Brazil*, pp. 99-100.

19. See the testimonies by leading military officers in D'Araujo et al., *Os anos de chumbo*.

20. Quoted from his testimony in ibid., p. 254.

21. Quoted from an interview in *Veja*, no. 819, 16 May 1984, p. 15.

22. Quoted from an interview with Carlos Eugenio Paz in *Veja*, no. 1455, 31 July 1996, p. 8.

23. Stepan, *Rethinking Military Politics*, p. 28.

24. Ibid.

25. See Kaufman, 'Liberalization and democratization'.

26. See Stepan, *Rethinking Military Politics*, ch. 3.

27. See Lamounier, 'Authoritarian Brazil revisited'.

28. See for overviews of the growing opposition from various social sectors: Tavares de Almeida, 'Novas tendências'; Tavares de Almeida, 'Difícil caminho'; Cardoso, 'Papel dos empresários'; Cava, '"People's church"'; Diniz, 'Empresariado e a nova conjuntura'; Diniz, 'Empresariado e transição política'; Martins, '"Liberalization" of authoritarian rule'.

29. Such as the Lei Falcão which restricted access of the opposition to free television and radio airtime, and the so-called April Package of 1977 which tampered with the electoral game by, among other things, introducing appointed senators (senadores biônicos) and increased the influence of the northeastern states in the Electoral College.

30. Velasco e Cruz and Martins, 'Castello a Figueiredo', pp. 45–6.

31. Quoted from General Geisel's statement in D'Araujo and Castro, Ernesto Geisel, pp. 389–90.

32. See Fleischer, Distensão.

33. The party reform was the result of legislation introduced during the opening stages of the Figueiredo government. ARENA, the party that supported the military regime, was changed into the Partido Democrático Social (Democratic Social Party, PDS). The MDB was split – this was the main objective of the regime – into the Partido do Movimento Democrático Brasileiro (PMDB), the Partido Popular (PP), and the Partido Democrático Trabalhista (Democratic Labour Party, PDT), incorporating the former populist current led by Leonel Brizola. In addition, the Partido dos Trabalhadores (Workers' Party, PT), the new party formed by the trade union militants at the end of the 1970s, was legalized.

34. Quoted from General Geisel's statement in D'Araujo and Castro, Ernesto Geisel, p. 369.

35. See Alves, Estado e oposição, p. 200.

36. See D'Araujo et al., Volta aos quartéis, p. 33. See also the statements of General Gustavo Morais Rego Reis in the same volume, pp. 65–7.

37. See Alves, Estado e oposição, pp. 268–9.

38. In a recent interview, General Medeiros declared that he himself never aspired to be a presidential candidate but that the suggestion was made to him by Figueiredo's (civilian) vice-president, Aureliano Chaves. See the interview with Medeiros in Veja, 9 July 1997.

39. As a result, Golbery do Couto e Silva resigned as minister of the civil cabinet, since he had insisted upon an official inquiry.

40. An important reason for the defection of PDS members of Congress was the expectation that the controversial former governor of São Paulo, Paulo Maluf, would be selected by the PDS convention as the party's candidate to succeed Figueiredo in the indirect elections of January 1985.

41. Interview with Golbery do Couto e Silva in Veja, no. 819, 16 May 1984, p. 9.

42. In Brazil's political historiography, Tancredo de Almeida Neves is listed, however, as one of the nation's presidentes, despite the fact that he had not been able to assume office formally. His illness and death provoked intense popular passion, and led to a climate of combined expectations and anxieties already at the outset of the return to civilian rule.

43. See especially Rizzo de Oliveira, 'Aparelho militar'; also Góes, 'Militares e política', pp. 234ff.

44. Rizzo de Oliveira, 'Aparelho militar', pp. 75–6.

45. Góes, 'Militares e política', p. 236.

46. General Ivan de Souza Mendes, in D'Araujo et al., Volta aos quartéis, p. 157.

47. See Quartim de Moraes, 'Função das Forças Armadas'; Rizzo de Oliveira, 'Constituinte'. The congress that was elected in November 1986 was given the task of drawing up a completely new constitution. While this process went on (from November 1986 to October 1988), the joint Congress, i.e. the Senate and the Chamber of Deputies, acted as a constitutional assembly (Assembleia Constituinte, in short, the Constituinte).

48. General Leônidas Pires Gonçalves, quoted in *Senhor*, no. 185, 1 September 1986, p. 26.

49. See Hunter, *Eroding Military Influence*, pp. 60-9; see also the statements of General Leônidas Pires Gonçalves and General Ivan de Souza Mendes, in D'Araujo et al., *Volta aos quartéis*.

50. See Hunter, *Eroding Military Influence*.

51. This hilarious 'affair' – receiving a kind of smug international attention mainly through CNN broadcasting – involved (unmarried) President Itamar Franco inviting a not unattractive female dancer in the 1994 Carnival *desfile* up to his *camarote*. Unlike all television-watchers in Brazil, the president was unaware of the fact that the lady (who according to evil tongues was nothing more than a prostitute) had no underwear. See for the military's dissatisfaction, that may even have reached the point of considering (and then rapidly rejecting) an intervention against the Franco government: Dimenstein and De Souza, *História real*, pp. 139-43.

52. This report was published under the title *Brasil: Nunca Mais* by the Vozes publishing house in 1984. See the English translation, cited in this chapter: Archdiocese de São Paulo, *Torture in Brazil*.

53. See reports in *Veja*, nos 1392 (17 May 1995), 1403 (2 August 1995), 1406 (23 August 1995) and 1407 (30 August 1995).

54. See *Veja*, no. 1403, 2 August 1995, p. 20.

55. See Lamounier, 'Brazil: inequality against democracy'.

56. See for the initial stages of the New Republic Diniz et al., *Modernização*; Corrêa Leite Cardoso, 'Movimentos populares'; Sola, *Estado da transição*; Sorj, 'Reforma agrária'; Tavares de Almeida, 'Difícil caminho'.

57. For the Cruzado plan and its aftermath see Sola, 'Heterodox shock'.

58. See Bruneau, 'Brazil's political transition'.

59. See for an account of the political genesis of the real plan Dimenstein and De Souza, *História real*.

60. Cardoso won the presidential election in the first round, in October 1998, with 53 per cent of the valid votes. Lula obtained close to 32 per cent, while Ciro Gomes came out third with less than 11 per cent. The remaining candidates were inexpressive in terms of votes and peripheral in terms of political position. Number four was the excentric medical doctor and conservative populist Enéas, with only 2 per cent. All the major political figures of the post-1985 period were absent, either because they lacked support or because they participated in elections for governorships or senate post in view of the generally expected victory of Cardoso. For an overview of election results see the Tribunal Supremo Eleitoral (Electoral Supreme Court), at www.tse.gov.br (April 1999).

61. Bruneau, 'Brazil's political transition', pp. 267-77.

62. See for an analysis of the Brazilian debate on the form of government, with an implicit preference for a parliamentary system, Lamounier, 'Brazil: toward parliamentarism?'

63. See Schneider, *Brazil: Politics and Culture*, p. 131.

64. Lamounier, 'Brazil: inequality against democracy', p. 160. For a further elaboration of this notion see Lamounier, 'Brazil: the hyperactive paralysis syndrome'.

65. See Santos et al., *Que Brasil é este?*

66. See Campello de Souza, 'Brazilian "New Republic"', pp. 370ff.

67. See for instance the statements of leading figures collected in DaMatta et al., *Brasileiro: Cidadão?* In 1993, 60 per cent of Brazilians expressed a preference for democracy as a system of government, despite the various setbacks of the preceding years; see Moisés, *Brasileiros e a Democracia*, p. 264.

68. See Campello de Souza, 'Contemporary faces'.

69. See Costa, *Tendências*, for an overview of recent developments within the Brazilian labour movement.

70. See DaMatta, *Casa e a rua*, pp. 71ff; also DaMatta, *Carnavais*, ch. 4.

71. See Lamounier, 'Brazil: inequality against democracy'.

72. This becomes painfully real in the lives of the utterly poor, as in the northeast, dramatically analysed by Scheper-Hughes, *Death without Weeping*.

73. See Oliven, *Violência e cultura*, p. 13.

74. See Foweraker, *Struggle for Land*, for an analysis of the long history of violence on the Brazilian agrarian frontier. See *IstoÉ*, no. 1233, 19 May 1993, for a report on the 'war' between gunmen and squatters and their defenders in the Bico do Papagaio region, notorious for its rural violence since the early 1980s; over 1,000 people were killed between 1982 and 1992.

75. See Hunter, *Eroding Military Influence*, pp. 89–90.

76. See Navarro, *Política*.

77. See the reports in *Veja*, no. 1491, 16 April 1997, especially 'A longa marcha' ('The long march'), pp. 34–5, 'Condenados a luta' ('Condemned to struggle'), pp. 36–41, and 'O radical da tradição' ('The radical of tradition'), pp. 46–8, portraying MST leader João Pedro Stedile.

78. Quoted from an interview to *Veja*, no. 1507, 6 August 1997, pp. 12–13.

79. See *Veja*, no. 1405, 16 August 1995, pp. 37–8.

80. See the detailed report in *Veja*, no. 1441, 24 April 1996 ('Sangue em Eldorado'), pp. 34–9.

81. See Oliven, *Violência e cultura*; also Paixão, 'Crime'.

82. Leeds, 'Cocaine and parallel politics', pp. 54–8.

83. See *IstoÉ*, no. 1249, 8 September 1993, especially the report 'Extermínio em gotas'. See also Leeds, 'Cocaine and parallel politics', pp. 65–6, and Ventura, *Cidade partida*.

84. Quoted from an unpublished ESG document in *IstoÉ*, no. 1249, 8 September 1993, pp. 34–5.

85. See Pinheiro, 'Democracies without citizenship'.

86. See for instance US Department of State, *Brazil Country Report on Human Rights Practices for 1996* (Bureau of Democracy, Human Rights, and Labor, January 1997). This report is generally favourable about the institutional dimensions of civil rights and political democracy, but is critical of human rights related problems in fields such as arbitrary police violence, death squads, street children, child labour, compulsory labour, domestic violence against women, and violence against indigenous populations. Official recognition of the human rights problem by the Cardoso government has resulted in a comprehensive national human rights programme. A major area of attention in this programme is formed by the issues of police violence, police competence and reform of the judiciary system. One short-term line of action proposed in the programme is 'a draft law that regulates the use of firearms and ammunition by police officers *off duty* and increasing control during active duty hours'. See Programa Nacional de Direitos Humanos summarized on the Internet, www.mj.gov.br/pndh (1997) (emphasis added).

87. See for this notion Panizza and Barahona de Brito, 'Politics of human rights in Brazil'.

TEN

The Transition under Fire: Rethinking Contemporary Mexican Politics

WIL PANSTERS

What have the doctors said? Rather than to cure some illnesses, you have to learn to live with them, they say [...] For the rest, the organism of Mr. President has a frightening capacity to recover and the crises even offer you an emotional catharsis.[1]

During his last address to the nation in 1928, President Plutarco Elías Calles declared that the era of the *caudillos* had come to an end and that the era of institutional politics had begun. He thereby referred to the assassination of President Elect Obregón earlier that year and the subsequent efforts to found the Partido Nacional Revolucionario, precursor of the current ruling party Partido Revolucionario Institucional (Institutional Revolutionary Party, PRI). It was the elite's answer to an imminent crisis: unite the members of the revolutionary family, who in previous years had proved to be 'a quarrelsome and fractious fraternity', and prevent a renewed outbreak of violence around presidential succession as had occurred in 1919, 1923 and 1927.[2] It was also an attempt to bring provincial bosses, *caciques* and political movements into the fold of the central government. The elite settlement pressed ahead energetically against the will of certain factions, thereby provoking a short-lived military revolt in early 1929, and managed to diminish substantially the risks of personal ambitions and rivalries, and their concomitant forms of praetorian violence in the decades that followed.

Sixty years on from the Calles declaration, in December 1988, President Salinas de Gortari proudly suggested that the era of the one-party system was virtually over. Subsequently, he layed out an ambitious programme for economic liberalization, political modernization and reform of the state. At the same time, Mexico's political opposition had emerged combative and strengthened from the fraudulent elections of July 1988. In particular the coalition that had maintained the candidacy of Cuauhtémoc Cárdenas (later transformed in the Partido de Revolución Democrática or Party of the

Democratic Revolution, PRD), was imbued with, if not certain of, the coming of an imminent rupture in the political process.

This critical conjuncture marked the birth of a discourse of change and movement.[3] The ruling elite gathered behind the discourse of modernization that encompassed further economic liberalization, reform of the state, reform of the ruling party and a reorientation of state–civil society relations. The left-wing opposition, sometimes in tune with the centre-right opposition of the Partido de Acción Nacional (National Action Party, PAN), was fighting for the consolidation of its newly acquired strength. The discourse that structured its outlook and political agenda was that of democratization or (social) democratic rupture, defeat of the PRI, and a reorientation of socio-economic policies. The discourses of modernization and democratization are articulated by the discourse of transition. Dependent on the ideological position towards the causes, consequences and possible choices surrounding the political situation at the end of 1988, both discourses postulate the need for change and transition: either from a model of statist populism towards a model of market-led pluralism, or from a model of authoritarianism and neo-liberal economics towards a model of democratic reform and a more equitable distribution of resources.

As in the case of events which occurred when Calles' idea of a great turning point invaded political discourse, the discourses of modernization, democratization and transition have become the markers of public and academic debate. The discourse of modernization and modernity had such profound effects during the apparently remote heydays of *salinismo*, that one of Mexico's most renowned spokesman on culture and politics, Carlos Monsiváis, ironically observed in 1992 that: 'Modernity [...] is now the shining star, the only goal [...] The national future depends on modernity, and nobody doubts it.'[4] Additionally, the fact that there is an absence of any real discussion of the inevitability of imminent modernity is significant.

In recent years, Mexico has witnessed strong attempts by politicians, intellectuals and journalists alike – all those who can be earmarked as the 'primary definers' of public debate – to convert the idea of modernization and transition to an inevitable and undisputed fact. Take for example the observation made by that other respected spokesman of Mexican cultural life, Hector Aguilar Camín: 'Even to those most inclined to yield in front of *the hard facts of history*, it is evident today that Mexico has embarked decisively upon the course of this paradigm of modernity.'[5] 'Hard facts' can be found in the characteristics of Mexican civil society – modern, participatory, educated – and its relations with the state, all of which is underpinned by economic policies (NAFTA, privatization, export-oriented industrialization). Only a few years have passed since these words were printed, and it has become clear that modernization in Mexico has (also) meant violent political infighting, armed rural rebellion and economic crisis.

Also similar to the conjuncture almost seventy years ago should be the

warning not to mix historical fact and political interpretation. In this chapter I will first briefly describe the main characteristics of Mexican authoritarianism – the starting point for an alleged process of 'transition' – and the problems it has encountered in recent years. Then I will investigate the nature and the degree to which a process of transition can be discerned in Mexico. Although several issues have been put forward as being significant for an analysis of such a process, here I will look at the important political actors, their strategies and options in relation to the issues of electoral outcomes, electoral legislation and corporatism. In order to deepen our understanding of the factors that influence the functioning of the Mexican political system, I will cross the boundaries of much of the transition literature, criticize its institutional bias and look at the cultural and practical dimensions of politics. In the final part of this chapter, I will relate this perspective to an analysis of contemporary developments that have shown a notorious increase of violence.

The Pillars of Mexican Authoritarianism

Most authors would agree that the institutional and inclusive nature of the authoritarian regime that emerged from the revolutionary fray is its foremost character.[6] The basic principles of the formal political and juridical framework of the Mexican regime are enshrined in the constitution adopted in 1917. The constitution contains both liberal principles that protect individual *political* rights and principles that enable strong state interventionism. The first principle makes a case for popular electoral sovereignty that is materialized in periodic elections at all levels of the state. The electoral agenda has effectively been maintained in Mexico ever since the constitution was put into effect.[7] The revolutionary principle of no re-election, that expressed the popular rejection of the deformation of the liberal constitution of 1857 during the Porfiriato, has also been held intact.[8] The tenacity with which the principle of no re-election has been maintained has the obvious advantage of elite circulation. The rotation of different political factions has assured the system a certain amount of vitality to the degree that it has mobilized energies and opened up opportunities for those who seek access to political circles. In the first decades after the armed phase of the revolution, this principle meant that members from hitherto subordinated classes could climb to the upper echelons of the post-revolutionary state.[9] This degree of political institutionalization and constitutionalism sharply contrasts with the frequent elimination of constitutional guarantees under authoritarian military governments in other parts of Latin America. It has also provided a barrier against what Whitehead calls 'manifestations of pebliscitarian instability' in periods of transition.[10]

The space reserved for popular sovereignty has from its very inception been minimized by the expanding force of state interventionism. The constitutional articles that provided for state intervention were a response to the

social agenda of the revolution and have ever since constituted a powerful source of legitimacy. For decades the ideology of the revolution has effectively marked the boundaries of public debate, thereby limiting the emergence of alternative political discourses. This ideology acted as a unifying force and formed the basis of an exclusive claim to political power, thereby hampering the development of ideological pluralism. In order to materialize constitutional *social* rights (most importantly, in the areas of land, labour and education) the state acquired crucial influence over the country's resources and the authority to redistribute them. The profound land distribution programme, particularly during the presidency of Lazaro Cárdenas in the second half of the 1930s, is a telling example of how a huge, federally controlled bureaucracy organized and supervised land reform.

Peasants who benefited from the land reform were organized in corporatist organizations that were organically linked to the revolutionary party. The strengthening of the bargaining position of the labour movement is equally connected to its institutional linkages to the regime and the revolutionary party. However, the organizational incorporation of peasants, workers and diversified popular groups simultaneously turned them into subordinated recipients of governmental policies. As long as these incorporative mechanisms were linked to policies of reform and distribution that also sought political and cultural emancipation, albeit paternalistically, the government was able to enjoy support from below. But when these reformist policies were increasingly abandoned, what had started as a process of popular empowerment was transformed into an instrument of control. Active citizenship was thereby severely curtailed.

As one of the pillars of Mexican authoritarianism, the corporatist pact that emerged in the 1920s and 1930s, and was consolidated in the 1940s, also accounts for its inclusionary character and helps to explain the system's longevity. Despite the fact that corporatism has functioned as a control mechanism, it has also effectively operated as a mechanism of mediation. Half a century ago the corporatist organizations represented most social groups and their interests. They organized the distribution of the benefits of economic growth. In return, the organizations were responsible for converting these benefits into support for the system at large (both electorally and organizationally). The very success with which these organizations fulfilled their role effectively reduced the role of elections to a ritual in legitimizing the regime.[11] The strength of the PRI was also based on the purposeful dis-articulation of the opposition (i.e. on the lack of viable alternative electoral options).

If the organized masses came to play a subordinated role within the revolutionary party, the latter was to occupy a position that was dependent on the executive. The consolidation of an extremely powerful presidentialist system, which rests on both constitutional and meta-constitutional prerogatives, is intimately related to the construction of an organized popular base.

This is because it created hierarchical links between the presidency and the popular masses, organizationally mediated by the ruling party. This system emerged in the wake of the conflictive displacement of territorially based power blocs in the 1920s and 1930s by political groups that were structured along the lines of social class (corporatism).[12] Although executive power has always held the upper hand over the ruling party, this tendency has been accentuated in recent years. The rise to power of an administrative technocracy at the beginning of the 1980s has diminished the role of the party as an arena of political bargaining. The political predominance of the executive, a phenomenon that is reproduced at other levels of the administrative hierarchy (governors, municipal presidents), also applies to the legislative and judicial bodies. During most of the post-revolutionary period, these bodies, which should function as the most significant counter-weights to the power and eventual abuses of the executive, were controlled by the president and the party leadership through an extensive system of patronage.

Presidentialism seriously undermined the principle of federalism that is enshrined in the constitution. Formally, the *municipio libre* (free municipality) is the basis of the administrative hierarchy, while the federal states possess considerable degrees of autonomy, but in fact local actors and government agencies are dependent on both political decision-making and funding from higher administrative levels. Mexican federalism has been effectively neutralized by the tellurian forces of corporatism and presidentialism, crucial pillars of one of Latin America's most centralized political systems.[13] Despite suggestions to the contrary, recent policies of decentralization have not effectively altered this situation.[14] Political and administrative centralism was underpinned by the ideology of revolutionary nationalism that became a crucial force in the drive towards unity and the monopolization of political space. The exaltation of the *raza cósmica* (cosmic race) was connected with the unification of the revolutionary family and the exclusion of alternative political projects. The emphasis on 'Mexicanness' and nation-building was epitomized by the revolutionary party and especially by the centripetal force of the presidency. If the priviliged locus of the Mexican citizenry is the *municipio*, then *de facto* centralist organization of political power, and the subordination of the powers that should represent popular sovereignty (parliament) and guarantee individual and collective rights (judiciary), are serious impediments to the realization of the liberal principles of the constitution. In sum, pervasive presidentialism, state corporatism, accentuated centralism, the secondary role of elections as a source of political legitimacy, and discursive closure (all articulated by a dominant ruling party) have, generally speaking, constituted the cornerstones of Mexican authoritarianism.

In combination with sustained economic growth, these key political institutions were responsible for Mexico's postwar political stability. The ugliest side of authoritarianism, violent repression by the state, remained hidden most of the time, at least at the level of national politics (see also Chapter

5 in this volume). However, if considered necessary by the ruling elite, force was used without hesitation. The army and the police were deployed to break strikes, to evict peasants, and to repress student protest, among others. Violence was also used against the political opposition, mostly at the local level, and, notably, against dissidents within the PRI.

In this perspective on Mexican authoritarianism, the state colonized civil society to such an extent that it hampered the constitution of social actors with a capacity of political expression and representation of their own.[15] In the face of the powerful Leviathan, Mexican civil society appeared to be a fragile creature. According to Loaeza, the decisive autonomy of the state, relative to the subordinated and dependent position of civil society, forms the heart of Mexican authoritarianism.[16]

Authoritarianism and Change

The previous characterization of Mexican authoritarianism can be taken as a starting point for the discussion of developments and policies that have augmented the pressures on Mexico's authoritarianism and that have contributed to the ruptures in the system of mediation and representation.[17] The crucial paradox of Mexico's socio-political development, from the 1940s onwards, has been that the effective functioning of the system between approximately 1940 and 1970 has itself created the conditions for its increasing malfunctioning. The success of Mexico's model of import substitution development, which was critically conditioned by the political regime, had a profound impact on the country's social structure. The emergence of an urban middle class and a strongly entrenched bourgeoisie has altered the social landscape that originally gave rise to the political system under the rule of Lazaro Cárdenas. At that time Mexico was still a predominantly rural society, with some significant urban industrial pockets and with a recent memory of the civil strife that had ravaged the country.

The corporatist institutions that were built in the *cardenista* years corresponded roughly to the social structure, as did the consolidation of a strong, centralized presidential system that was a response to the threat of military uprisings and political fragmentation. However, the processes of industrialization and urbanization gave rise to a more sophisticated and diversified society. The political effects were recognized from an early stage. Already in 1946, President Avila Camacho added the popular sector to the PRI's internal organization and from this moment onwards its role within the party has only increased. The first to experience the effects of the changing relations of social and political forces was the peasant sector (the Confederación Nacional Campesina, CNC). When emphasis on development policies began to fall increasingly on industry and commercial and large-scale agriculture, *ejidatarios* and smallholders rapidly lost much of their bargaining power. Not suprisingly, organized labour benefited from the strengthening

of the urban and industrial segment. Socio-economic change also promoted higher levels of literacy and education and greater access to information and travelling.

After more than three decades of vigorous socio-economic development, it was clear to small and medium-scale entrepreneurs, professionals, the 'informally' employed and the unemployed that they did not find a place in the corporatist system of interest mediation.[18] All these developments crystallized most notably in the urban middle classes. The student movement of 1968 is generally seen as the first (violent) expression of the tensions that were building up between the country's increasingly diversified social forces and its political institutions. Because the students demanded recognition of their citizen rights and challenged the state's monopolization of public space, 1968 has been interpreted as the first sign of an emancipation of civil society. The regime responded with the political reform of 1977–78, that aimed to channel discontent to the electoral system. Former president Echeverría observed in those days that the reform strived to 'incorporate the majority of the citizens and social forces into the *institutional* political process.'[19]

The possibility that the political reform of the 1970s would gradually bear fruit, was thwarted by the outbreak of the 1982 economic crisis, which significantly sharpened social discontent. The social forces which had been fermenting during the previous several decades were politically articulated both outside and within the realm of the ruling party. Electoral competitiveness, albeit volatile and protest-oriented, increased considerably. A breakthrough was the victory of the PAN in major cities in the state of Chihuahua in 1983. Consequently, a more aggressive brand of *panismo* (PAN militancy) emerged throughout the north and managed to become highly influential at the national level. Politicians and commentators alike suggested that elections were becoming the only source of political legitimacy and sovereignty. This shift is exemplified by the recurrent post-electoral disputes – a quiet acceptance of official figures seems to be the exception nowadays – and also by the way the regime has been forced into far-reaching negotiations with the opposition about electoral reform during the Salinas administration. Moreover, the emphasis placed by the ruling elite on reforming the PRI, in order to perform better in elections, and the widespread presence of citizen committees that scrutinize the whole electoral process, sometimes assisted by foreign delegations, all point to the growing importance granted to elections. Moreover, the multiple reforms of the electoral legislation in recent years have diminished the margins of the ruling elite for manoeuvring and fraud. The 1994 presidential elections, and even more so the 1997 elections in which the PRI lost the national capital as well as its majority in the Chamber of Deputies, clearly provide proof for this assertion. Seen from this perspective, it should be concluded that increasing electoral competitiveness and electoral reform have contributed to a redefinition of the lop-sided relationship between state and civil society.

If the emancipation of the electoral arena is proof of the 'awakening' of civil society, popular reactions to the 1985 earthquakes have given further strength to this argument. The spontaneous birth of numerous self-help organizations in response to the disaster made the state look particularly ill-equipped and under-prepared to handle the situation, and gave an impetus to the idea that the acute problems could be resolved without state mediation.[20] Popular movements have arisen in every corner of society and many of them vindicate rights and press for more effective forms of political representation. Foweraker has recently argued that contemporary popular movements no longer reject the political system *per se*, but rather attempt to secure institutional recognition. For that purpose they construct linkages with the legal and institutional system of government, always in combination with direct action and mass mobilization.[21] Haber has argued that popular movements have been an ingredient in Mexico's changing political landscape and that their main role is that of government watchdogs.[22] These and other developments (to which I will turn in the next section) have challenged Mexico's authoritarian heritage in several ways and have opened up opportunities for further change. They also form the raw material from which the discourses of modernization and transition have been constructed.

Questioning the Mexican Transition

The controversial 1988 presidential elections are broadly seen as the most important political culmination of a long cycle of social and economic change. Urbanization, socio-economic and demographic differentiation, rising levels of education and the proliferation of modern means of communication (i.e. secular developments that profoundly transformed Mexico's social structure), finally invaded the political and electoral arena. Since these structural tendencies are viewed as irreversible, it seems likely that the political consequences, such as increasing electoral competitiveness and pluralism, will eventually end one-party rule and corporatist control. By the end of the 1980s 'many of the axiomatic, unshakable truths about the Mexican system' had been demolished.[23] Compared to other Latin American countries, where turbulent developments such as military coups and civil war had upset political and social relations, Mexico had long seemed a society free of dramatic turnabouts.[24] Authoritarian rule was entrenched and modulated. However, after 1988 dynamism was injected into Mexico's political imagery. A gradual or sudden collapse of the revolutionary elite, and the subsequent installation of a more democratic polity, became thinkable.

However, optimism about the feasibility of a democratic transition soon began to fade. This phenomenon of 'democratic disenchantment' has been noted, though for different reasons, more widely in Latin America, particularly in the southern cone.[25] In Mexico, it set in with the 1991 parliamentary elections, when the PRI recovered most of the terrain it had lost in 1988.

At the regional level, elections remained highly contested, leading to governments of the PAN in Baja California, Chihuahua, Guanajuato and Jalisco. Doubts about the expected demise of the PRI and, consequently, a transition towards a more democratic society began to emerge and infiltrated scholarly writing. From the beginning of the 1990s onwards, the idea of transition became qualified by numerous adjectives. The doubts were linked to certain characteristics of the Mexican political system and government policies aimed at containing the risk of a regime breakdown through pre-emptive reform.

Several commentators have felt obliged to elucidate the Mexican 'transition' with the help of concepts that express ambivalence and uncertainty. More than ten years after Enrique Krauze pleaded for the installation of a 'democracy without adjectives', most commentators today are driven to 'adjectivate' the Mexican transition.[26] Neil Harvey analysed the situation in terms of a 'difficult transition' in which the forces unleashed by neo-liberal economic policies interact with neo-corporatist formulas of political representation.[27] In 1991 Sánchez Susarrey spoke of the 'uncertain transition' and two years later a book called *La transición interrumpida* (The Interrupted Transition) was published. In 1994, Whitehead listed the enormous institutional and cultural obstacles for authentic democratization inherent in the peculiar brand of authoritarianism, but concluded that a democratic rupture was possible. Jorge Javier Romero analysed the situation after the 1991 elections in terms of the *pantano de la transición* (the transition swamp). Post-1988 optimism has gradually been replaced by a much more careful interpretation of the possibilities and limitations of a democratic transition. Romero pointed to the weakness of the Mexican party system and critized the incapacity of the dissident coalition headed by Cauthémoc Cárdenas (later becoming the PRD) to transcend its radical anti-system position. This prevented the party from participating in a national debate about further political liberalization and democratization. As a consequence, the centre-left that had catapulted itself to the centre of the electoral arena in 1988 gradually lost terrain, while the PRI and the PAN embarked on a strategy of *concertación* (mutual arrangement). However, for Romero the consolidation of a strong centre-left party is a prerequisite for the consolidation of political pluralism.[28]

The argument that the centre-left opposition has refrained from participating in negotiations with the regime (at least until 1995) renders implicit support to the idea that the regime has indeed taken steps to create political spaces from which a process of transition could eventually be constructed. But how can such a hypothesis be tested? How can transition be measured? How does Mexico fit within the broader debate? O'Donnell and Schmitter have suggested that the arrival of democratic politics is usually preceded by a series of policies that enhance political liberalization.[29] One can think of policies aimed at the reform of the electoral process, the reorganization of the ruling party and the restructuring of corporatism. Seen from this perspective, events in recent years render some credibility to the interpretation

that Mexico is experiencing a process of liberalization. In the following sections I will further assess this claim.

Elections

In the electoral arena the Salinas regime demonstrated more tolerance towards the opposition than was to be imagined by many of its critics or even by its adherents. The recognition of the victory of the PAN in the gubernatorial elections of Baja California in 1989, and later in Chihuahua, provided a clear rupture with the past when the PRI was still driving a *carro completo*, a 'whole' or 'undamaged' car as the expression goes. President Zedillo has apparently continued this policy, as the repeat of the PAN victory in Baja California and its spectacular victories in the important states of Jalisco (with the country's second largest city Guadalajara), Nueva León (with the economic powerhouse Monterrey) and Querétaro prove. It has become clear that the PAN can make serious in-roads into the Mexican heartland.

There are two sides to this apparently clear move towards political pluralism that question the extent of its reach. The electoral victories of the PAN in provincial Mexico cannot be dissociated from political developments at the national level. Here, the Salinas administration was forced to negotiate with the PAN leadership – in itself a healthy element of democratic politics – about crucial policy issues. Long and difficult negotiations between the PAN and the PRI about electoral reform came to an end only when, at the beginning of 1989, an agreement was negotiated between the PAN leadership and the ministry of the interior (not in parliament). These negotiations led to a so-called 'letter of intent', in which the government subscribed to modifications in the electoral law that were in accordance with the wishes of the PAN. The PRI first denied the existence of this agreement, and in the ranks of the PAN it caused factional disputes.[30] It is generally believed that in return for *panista* parliamentary support for government policy initiatives, which were generally contested by the centre-left opposition, the government 'conceded' electoral victories after negotiations with the *panista* leadership. Thus, what appears to be a democratic opening is at the same time the result of corporate and elite bargaining. This claim can be substantiated by the outcry of local groups of *priístas* about what they perceived as acts of treason on the part of the national elite. In 1989, PRI members in Baja California felt that party president Luis Donaldo Colosio broke the (informal) party rules by recognizing the electoral victory of *panista* candidate Ernesto Ruffo for governor, while they had already announced the victory of the PRI.[31] The municipal president of Mérida (Yucatán) stepped down in 1993, a fortnight after he had taken up this position. In the midst of outcries of fraud and in a clear attempt to highlight Mexico's efforts towards demo-cratization on the eve of the official coming into force of NAFTA, it was decided in Mexico City-based government offices that PAN candidate Correa

Mena would become mayor. Local *priístas* were enraged by the decision and mounted a series of protest meetings.[32] The conquest of political spaces by the opposition was thus an 'elitist and negotiated' transition, that was ultimately geared towards the maintenance of the conditions and mechanisms that would enable the elite to remain in power nationally.[33]

Policies towards the opposition were not only subjected to elite bargaining but were also selective.[34] While the PAN was on speaking terms with Salinas, the PRD was confronted with old-fashioned strategies of the PRI and local and regional power groups. The cases of Michoacán and Guerrero, and more recently those of Nayarit, Chiapas and Tabasco, have clearly shown that the regime applies different criteria to different political opponents. This ambivalent situation renders support to the hypothesis that while some form of electoral legitimacy is being consolidated in certain Mexican regions, on the whole, electoral competition is still subject to political bargaining. During the Salinas presidency, the logic of legitimate electoral democracy, which presupposes the attainment of public office solely on the basis of votes cast by citizens, was still subordinated to the logic of bargaining between different political actors. It can be no surprise that the only opposition party that has been able to capitalize on its electoral performance was the one that was prepared to bargain in areas that were highly significant to the regime. This argument does not downplay the organizational and electoral efforts of the PAN, or the degree of popular support the party has obtained; neither does it over-rate the electoral performance and the size of the following of the PRD. It only states that behind the stage of oppositional access to power, unaccounted forms of political bargaining are taking place backstage, most likely in the offices of the minister of the interior in Mexico City.

The case of the electoral strife in San Luis Potosí in 1991 can further illustrate this point. Here neither the PAN nor the PRD held the upper hand, but an authentic regional political movement, the Frente Cívico Potosino, headed by Salvador Nava. The gubernatorial elections of 1991 in San Luis Potosí and the neighbouring state Guanajuato coincided with the important mid-term parliamentary elections. In San Luis Potosí elections pitted *priísta* Fausto Zapata against the aged and prestigious Nava, who had managed to build an exceptional coalition with the PRD, PAN and PDM. The elections were troubled by various forms of fraud, and voter registration was biased towards vested interests. San Luis Potosí provides a classic example of a state in which the major urban areas are dominated by the opposition, while the more backward rural areas, basically the Huasteca, deliver the votes to the PRI. As expected, the PRI-dominated areas received by far the highest levels of voter registration. Throughout the campaign the PRI used its proven tactics to influence the vote: complete domination of the local media, excessive funds for propaganda, accusations against the opposition of provoking violence, etcetera. Pre-electoral fraud was followed by an even bigger fraud during the elections themselves.[35] Nevertheless, the local press declared Zapata

winner even before the polls had closed. Although there existed ample evidence of fraud, Nava declined to enter the judicial jungle of the electoral bodies. Instead he organized a movement of civil resistance.

The tense situation in San Luis Potosí received an unexpected boost when the gubernatorial candidate of the PRI in the neighbouring state of Guanajuato resigned after equally fraudulent elections and a *panista* assumed the post *ad interim*. As the federal government proved willing or was forced to sacrifice its candidate in Guanajuato, expectations also rose in San Luis Potosí. Meetings were held, a silent march was undertaken, roads were blocked, and during the last address of the outgoing governor, female followers of Nava made themselves heard by battering on their kitchen utensils. At the same time others started a permanent meeting in front of the government palace. While Nava travelled back and forth to Mexico City and catapulted himself to a national platform, Zapata no longer appeared in public. During one of his visits Nava was offered a compromise: Zapata would become governor with Nava occupying an important position in his government or Nava would become governor with *priístas* in crucial positions. He refused.[36] When Zapata officially took the oath on 26 September 1991, in the presence of President Salinas, the aged and ill Nava embarked on the highly publicized March of Dignity to Mexico City. A group of women prevented Zapata from entering his office. The demand: Zapata was to resign. Less than two weeks later he did so. Nava suspended his march and returned to San Luis Potosí, where he was welcomed like a hero. That same day, *priísta* Gonzalo Martínez Corbalá flew to the *potosino* capital to take over the government. The situation in San Luis Potosí had been as competitive as in Guanajuato, and the different outcome can be explained only by a logic that is external to the regional relations of power. The presence of the PAN at the negotiating tables in Mexico City and the refusal of Nava to trade were of crucial importance in the decision to concede the interim governorship in Guanajuato to the PAN and in San Luis Potosí to the PRI. Had the logic of Guanajuato applied to San Luis Potosí as well, the interim government should have gone to the *navista* movement. It is obvious that this was not in the interest of the PRI or the PAN.[37]

The electoral process in Mexico has long been subject to sophisticated juridical *candados* (locks), which made it difficult for oppositional groups to participate, to register certain candidates, and to protest arbitrary decisions; in sum, to exercise their constitutional rights. It is, therefore, no surprise that the issue of reforming electoral legislation has been on the agenda of contending political forces for some time. Since the important political and electoral reform was launched in 1977, negotiations about, and adjustments to, electoral legislation have intensified. Despite some positive changes, the introduction of the 1986 Federal Electoral Code by President De la Madrid meant a reinforcement of executive control and ample guarantees for the ruling party to maintain a predominant influence on crucial aspects of the

electoral process. In many ways, the 1986 reform was a setback, compared to the political liberalization of 1977. Most notably, it sanctioned the constitutional character of the concept of governability, by which a party would receive the absolute majority in the Chamber of Deputies even though it had received less than 51 per cent of the votes. The significance of this reform, which was the legal framework of the 1988 presidential elections, can hardly be over-estimated. One analyst has maintained that without it Salinas would not have become president.[38] In the wake of these elections, preparations began for a reform that was adopted by parliament in 1990. Despite some advances, such as increased funding for parties and a further regulation of partisan access to the mass media, the Federal Code of Electoral Institutions and Procedures contained numerous clauses that safeguarded presidential and *priísta* control of the electoral process: the clause of governability was modified but not eliminated; members of the Federal Electoral Tribunal were to be elected from a list composed by the president; the Federal Electoral Institute was controlled by presidential appointees and *priísta* delegates; and polling station officers were chosen by district presidents, who themselves were dependent on a federally controlled bureaucratic apparatus. In the face of increasing electoral competition, the regime responded with what appeared to be a liberalization of the electoral legislation, but it actually boiled down to legislative sophistication aimed at strengthening 'the security mechanisms of the system in order to maintain control of the electoral results and guarantee the PRI the presidency and a majority in the Chamber of Deputies'.[39] In 1996, after twenty months of hard-edged negotiations, the Zedillo government and major opposition forces approved yet another electoral reform package. Among the most important elements of this package are the fact that future elections will no longer be organized by government officials but by citizens, and that the Federal Electoral Institute will be transferred from the ministry of the interior to the judicial branch. These new rules were successful during the 1997 parliamentary elections. Although progress has certainly been made in the area of electoral reform, there is another side to this process. Recently, Cansino has pointed to the paradoxical effects and functions of permanent institutional reformism. He rightly argued that while consolidated democratic political systems will adapt institutionally to a changing environment to improve its function (system output, efficiency), in societies where non-democratic practices pervade the system, such as Mexico, institutional reformism is primarily a mechanism for legitimation. Thus, instead of viewing continuous amendments to the legal and institutional aspects of the political system as an indication of genuine democratization, it is also the result of the need of unwilling elites to gain (temporary) consensus and legitimacy.[40]

Corporatism

Being a fundamental aspect of Mexico's authoritarian political system, the fate of the corporatist pact should be a good indication of the degree of the system's liberalization and democratization.[41] At the beginning of its *sexenio* (six-year presidential term), the Salinas administration put in motion a process by which corporatist influence within the PRI was diminished. The spectacular removal of two notoriously corrupt and powerful union *caciques* was certainly a bold step in that direction.[42] But when the administration came to reform the ruling party, which would have had long-term and institutional effects on the political role of organized labour in particular, boldness and vision were replaced by half-heartedness and pragmatism.

For many years the corporatist arrangement had fulfilled two essential functions: first, it organized (electoral) support for the ruling party in exchange for transmitting and distributing goods and services towards the popular masses, and second, it played a crucial role in assuring economic stability during the period of rapid industrialization, and especially during the economic crisis of the 1980s. At the end of the 1980s, it became painfully evident that the corporatist organizations were failing in both areas. The dominant elite responded with reform initiatives aimed at restructuring the relationships between the state, the corporatist sectors, the ruling party, the economy and the electoral arena. In 1989 the president of the PRI, Luis Donaldo Colosio, pointed out that in order to maintain the PRI's electoral force, the leadership could no longer depend (only) on the corporatist organizations. Instead, a more direct relationship should be established between the party and individual citizens.[43] Access to individual citizens was organized in a revamped version of the party's territorial structure. The Popular Sector of the PRI was the scene of the most important experiments, but in the end the project failed. After a few years of organizational change the Popular Sector, now called the Federación Nacional de Organizaciones y Ciudadanos (National Federation of Organizations and Citizens), had returned to the basic structure of 1988, albeit with a streamlined bureaucracy. Political practices had remained the same, but conflicts between modernizers and traditionalists within the party actually sharpened.[44]

Whereas experiments in the Popular Sector were largely oriented towards the issues of voting and gaining access to new constituencies, the labour sector was especially targeted in relation to the economy. The restructuring of the economy and industry, in particular, demanded greater efficiency, productivity and flexibility. Privatization and the breaking up of collective labour contracts have been among the most frequent consequences, clashing with the interests of the traditional corporatist bureaucracy.[45] If the ruling technocratic elite were to go ahead with their project of economic restructuring, it seemed imperative to limit labour's political leverage within the party. The reorganization of the corporatist sectors was discussed at the 14th

General Assembly of the PRI in 1990. It became clear that the labour sector would not simply step aside in the face of organizational innovations. The CTM threatened to boycott the meeting if it could only count on 8 per cent of the assembly's delegates, as was originally proposed. The bargaining power of the labour union proved strong enough almost to double the amount of its delegates. The assembly ended with organizational ambivalence and hybridity. The old corporatist pillars *and* the new territorial organizational units came to exist side by side. All this had little to do with transition and democratization. In his analysis of the relationship between Salinas and the ruling party, Hernández Rodríguez has convincingly shown that the rhetoric of modernization and democratization of the PRI was in fact subordinated to the overall objective of bringing the party completely under the command of an elite that has an increasingly functional relationship with the party.[46]

The diminishing role of the traditional corporatist organizations in the broader political landscape (as a result of malfunctioning and political intervention from above), was balanced by trends of neo-corporatist restructuring during the Salinas years. In industry and services, a new form of unionism has emerged that has been welcomed by the government. With a greater amount of autonomy these unions, exemplified by those of the telephone workers and the electricians, focus on negotiations about salaries, fringe benefits and working conditions in relation to increasing productivity.[47] This variant of neo-corporatism combines a pragmatic stance towards basic union rights with a 'willingness to ally with capital in a joint quest for higher productivity and quality [which] earned it recognition as a valid interlocutor in proposals concerning these issues'.[48] Although outside the realm of labour relations, Craske has portrayed the Programa Nacional de Solidaridad (PRONASOL) as a variant of neo-corporatism. She argued that PRONASOL, while focusing on new issues like urban services, regional development, women and schools, reinforced the centralism of corporatist sectors and reproduced their hierarchical organizational structures. Her study of popular neighbourhoods in Guadalajara concluded that PRONASOL 'has done little to break away from the traditional PRI practices of clientelism, arbitrariness and the lack of the clear rule of law'.[49]

The Temporal Horizon

In accordance with the ideas put forward by O'Donnell and Schmitter, changes in the electoral arena, modifications of the electoral legislation and the restructuring of corporatist arrangements could be interpreted as building blocks of a process of transition.[50] As such, the dramatic presidential elections in July 1988, which brought Salinas de Gortari to power, are frequently seen as the starting point of this process. But 1988 did not constitute a rupture comparable to the moments when the generals retreated from power in South America, nor can it be compared to the dramatic events by which civil

wars came to an end in Central America. In Spain the starting point of the transition was the death of the *caudillo* and in the Philippines the beginning was marked by the overthrow of a dictatorship. In the case of Mexico, there is no agreement about temporal delimitation. According to Cisneros this is not just an academic matter, because it has an immediate bearing on our understanding of the phenomenon of political liberalization and transition.[51] Fortunately, Mexico's recent political process possesses other options for situating the onset of liberalization. In an article written a few years before the spectacular 1988 elections, Kevin Middlebrook traced the onset of the process of political liberalization to the 1977–78 political reform initiative of the López Portillo government. This reform facilitated the registration of opposition parties and, generally speaking, expanded the channels for political mobilization and representation. The political reform was the government's and the ruling party's response to a series of challenges that undermined the efficiency and legitimacy of the PRI. Although the overall effects of this process of political liberalization were limited, Middlebrook observed that 'it marked an important departure in Mexican politics'.[52]

In what sometimes appears to have become a frantic search for the establishment of a starting point of the supposed transition in Mexican politics, 1968 has frequently been put forward as a relevant turning point. It is argued that the student movement and its underlying middle-class support were the first openly to dispute the ruling party-state system. The demands for citizen participation and governmental accountability provoked a conflict about the political leadership of society. It was a movement that went much further than just the issues related solely to university autonomy; it made a broader case for effective citizenship. Although the agitated summer of 1968 ended in brutal repression, its longer-term effects are argued to be so profound that there exists 'a line of continuity between this experience [1968] and the electoral opening which, since July 1988, seeks to put an end to the hegemony of the official party'.[53] These effects range from the modification of values and behavioural practices, through a reorganization of class alliances within the ruling elite (favouring the urban middle classes to the detriment of traditional corporatist sectors), to the emergence of public opinion as a political factor. Others have emphasized that it was the violent suppression of the 1968 student movement that provoked the spreading of leadership and ideologies throughout society. In urban neighbourhoods and peasant communities, among teachers and workers, lay the seeds of a new political culture that prepared the ground for what eventually ended in the electoral uprising of 1988.[54] Although neither the political and symbolic importance of the events in 1968 nor their effects on subsequent developments should be under-estimated, it is open to debate whether the student movement was, indeed, the first expression of protest that combined a corporate identity (university autonomy) with mobilization in favour of the general demand of citizenship. It should not be too difficult to argue that the great labour

movements at the end of the 1950s also fought for a combination of corporate and political rights (participation in decision-making). They also did so with reference to the constitution and they too were brutally repressed. In the context of the polarizing effects of the Cuban revolution and adjustments in the country's power bloc, it could even be argued that the 1958–59 conjuncture constitutes a more important rupture than that of 1968.

If we take into consideration the variety of circumstances, feasible candidates for the onset of a process of political liberalization and subsequently a transition could be 1988, 1978, 1968 and maybe even 1958.[55] But where does all this lead us? Wouldn't it be more appropriate to view the entire period as a continuous phase of transformations with identifiable conjunctures of political crises, or, as Cisneros has done, political cycles?[56] The concept of transition is formulated by O'Donnell and Schmitter as a period 'delimited on the one side, by the launching of the process of dissolution of an authoritarian regime and, on the other, by the installation of some form of democracy, the return to some form of authoritarian rule, or the emergence of a revolutionary alternative'. Stated in these terms, the concept seems to possess little real meaning when applied to the Mexican case.[57] The question should perhaps be why decades of crisis followed by policies of political liberalization and opening have *not* (yet) been able to consolidate a democratic order. I would like to suggest that the difficulties of determining the timing and rhythm of the transition are related to the ambivalent nature of Mexico's political system itself. It thus seems necessary to look at the Mexican political system from another perspective.

The Universe of Primordial Loyalties

An emphasis on the institutional nature of Mexican authoritarianism tends to overlook the existence of other organizational principles that structure Mexican society and politics. The Mexican regime effectively undermines the workings of the *trias politica*, of administrative accountability, political checks and balances, electoral sovereignty, federalism, ideological pluralism and the development of citizenship. But if an analysis of Mexican authoritarianism focuses solely on the legal-institutional framework, it will not be able to understand the everyday operative rules of authoritarianism. Next to institutional *structure*, political *praxis* needs to be included in the analysis. Mexican presidentialism does not only rest on the ample powers granted to it by the constitution, but also, if not primarily, on the central position it occupies in the universe of personalistic, informal relationships. The president stands at the top of a network of interlocking pyramidal *camarillas* (informal political groups) that extend his power into the different domains of the political and social system. *Camarillas* cross-cut institutional, ideological, social and sectoral barriers and are welded together by personal loyalties. Their informal character hides them largely from the public eye and accounts for much of the fluidity

and adaptability of Mexican politics. The presidential clique or *camarilla* articulates the leaders of a wide range of subordinated *camarillas* that represent political and social actors, such as party leadership, union bureaucracy, entre-preneurial groups and intellectuals. The legal prerogatives of the president to appoint collaborators to crucial positions in the administration is thus com-plemented and extended by discrete prerogatives that make him the centre of a universe of personal loyalties that reaches beyond the formal areas of presidential authority.

Two weeks after Ernesto Zedillo had assumed the presidency, I arrived at the remote village of Tancanhuitz in the Huasteca Potosina to carry out some interviews. I visited the local branch of the Instituto Nacional Indigenista, whose director had promised to help me with contacting possible informants. Aware of the possible effects of a presidential turnover, I asked her whether she enjoyed living in Tancanhuitz. She responded positively but quickly added that several weeks before she had handed in her resignation, thereby sticking to the informal rule by which every non-unionized employee of a government institution is expected to resign when there is a presidential turnover. If Zedillo would maintain the general director of the Instituto Nacional Indigen-ista, so would the head of the San Luis Potosí office, and so the head of the delegation in Tancanhuitz would have a good chance of retaining her position. If, however, the new president appointed a new general director, it would cause a wave of new appointments down the administrative hierarchy into the most remote areas of Mexico and her letter of resignation would be accepted.

The significance of the informal rules that surround the Mexican presid-ency thus becomes painfully clear during the conjuncture of the presidential succession, not only at the lower levels of the administrative pyramid, but particularly at the very apex. The presidential succession of 1993–94 was accompanied from the very beginning by a series of unprecedented incidents that publicly demonstrated the merciless sanctions that go with breaking the informal rules of the game. When the leaders of the PRI officially announced (after Salinas had decided) that Luis Donaldo Colosio would be the PRI presidential candidate, there came an end to several months of tension. However, contrary to previous experiences, his major opponent, Manuel Camacho Solís, did not publicly and unequivocally announce his support for Colosio. Instead, he waited a few days before appearing in public and then declared that he indeed had seriously participated in the presidential race. He thereby clearly broke the rule of the *cargada*, the unanimous expression of support for the candidate by his former rivals and the party's sectors. A few weeks later, the armed rebellion in Chiapas broke out and Camacho Solís was soon appointed by the president as the official spokesman and negotiator for the government. As a consequence it was Camacho and not Colosio who monopolized the mass media, thereby creating serious problems for the latter's campaign managers. When Colosio was murdered a few months later, the tensions between Camacho and the party establishment had risen to un-

precedented heights. At Colosio's burial, Camacho was almost physically attacked by a crowd of enraged *priístas*. Rumours about his involvement in the murder and even in the rebellion in Chiapas abounded. Because he had purposefully broken the informal rules of the power game, and attempted to survive the loss of the presidential bid, the death of Colosio meant the political death of Camacho.[58]

The articulation of power-brokers through sophisticated personalistic networks is one of the main factors that can explain the lack of the independence of the legislative and judicial bodies, a crucial element of Mexican authoritarianism. Crucial positions in these bodies (magistrates, leader of the parliamentary majority, presidents of important congressional committees) are likely to be occupied by individuals that are either appointed directly by the president or through the mediation of the ruling party. In both cases they belong to the inner circle of the 'revolutionary family'. The metaphor of the 'family' is relevant here because it refers to a universe in which political relations are regulated by kinship (fictive or not), friendship and personal relationships.[59] Personal loyalty to the leader of the *camarilla* or to the president himself, and not (necessarily) impersonal bureaucratic performance, constitutes the heart of these relationships. That does not mean that bureaucratic or administrative performance is irrelevant, but only that it is a function of complying with personal loyalties. An efficient administrator is somebody who carries out a task delegated to him by his superior, without causing political problems for his superior and his *camarilla* or faction. If the successful completion of such a task would occasionally require the bending of bureaucratic rules or even twisting the law, the administrator can count on the protection from his superior. Relationships of personal loyalty are thus ultimately based on reciprocity and trust (*confianza*), an assumption of shared reliablity that enables people to engage in relations of exchange under uncertain, changing and vulnerable circumstances.[60]

If *camarillas* are an important vehicle for regime cohesion at the level of the elites, the mechanism that links them to the lower orders of the social hierarchy, down to the factory floor, the *ejido* and the marketplace, is that of clientelism and brokerage. As an exchange mechanism between actors of different hierarchical standing, clientelism or patronage has been operating in Mexico under highly diverse circumstances, both historically and socially. Whether the exchange took place between a bureaucrat of the Departamento Agrario and poor peasants in the 1930s, between squatters in Chalco and a district officer of the ruling party, or between a university director and students, they were all lop-sided relationships of reciprocity. Individuals that participate in such networks are thus able to obtain certain benefits or resources that could otherwise be withheld from them. Their bargaining position in political space and their access to resources, is constructed in terms of (instrumental) friendships and mutual obligations. Pertaining to a group becomes a valued asset. An unconnected individual, an individual with

no friends is a *don nadie* ('Mr Nobody'). In a country such as Mexico, with highly centralized political power, the proximity to power is a crucial variable for any would-be group leader or patron. The ruling party and the bureaucracy have since long been the most important routes to get there.

In the case of Mexico, the phenomenon of clientelism is inextricably linked to the *cacique*, the strongman whose characteristically informal, personalistic and often arbitrary rule is buttressed by a following. The *cacique* usually combines the threat of violence with some variant of 'private morality of obligations', graphically portrayed by the character of Lázaro Pizarro in Aguilar Camín's novel about an oil union *cacique*.[61] The *cacique* and the president are the political figures that condense the personalization of power and the ambivalences of the Mexican political system. *Caciquismo* has penetrated the institutional framework of the state but at the same time defies institutionalization.[62] *Caciquismo* and clientelism have been called the sinews of corporatism, and are thus crucial phenomena in the structure of state–society relations in Mexico.[63] They constitute mediating or exchange mechanisms, both between federal and regional or local power domains, and between different social groups (e.g. bureaucracy and peasants). For the nineteenth century this mediating mechanism has been described in terms of political cultural brokerage between the world of liberal *letrados* and the provincial world of traditional primordial loyalties that was not equipped to realize the conceptions of liberal ideology.[64] The effective concentration of political power and resources in the hands of the executive (nationally, regionally and locally) and the inclusive character of Mexican authoritarianism in the twentieth century, has reproduced the need for intermediaries in order to furnish linkages of the masses to the state. It has (re)created privileged points of transmission (brokerage) through which ordinary people gain access to resources.[65] The *cacique* strives to monopolize and defend such points, sometimes with the use of violence. He cultivates personal relationships with his following, and projects himself to the upper echelons of the hierarchy on the basis of a group following (i.e. a collective actor). To extract resources from the state, individuals engage in group-like, corporate and personalized relationships. Studying the electoral process, Guillén López has observed that processes of corporate and *caciquista* mediation and negotiation pertain to a political culture that recognizes the existence of a separate established power with which people negotiate. In contrast, liberal political culture presupposes a direct political relationship between the citizenry and the state. Power is then not an established, external entity but one that is determined and directed by the people through elections.[66]

Although this universe of primordial loyalties mainly applies to the state and to the ruling party PRI, its relevance is not limited to these domains. The personalistic logic does not pertain to specific political ideologies, parties or actors, but rather to political culture in general. Hence, it can come as no surprise that opposition parties and non-governmental organizations reproduce

similar practices.[67] The omnipresence of personalistic mediation has thus profound consequences for the constitution of citizenship and for the thinking about the transition.

Transition, Violence and Fear

The notion that the personalistic logic is part of the everyday functioning of the political system is something that is certainly not unique to Mexico. However, the fact that Mexico's authoritarian political system is so highly centralized, that power is so concentrated in the presidency to the detriment of counterveiling powers, and that the dominant organized groups are part of or linked to the ruling party, make Mexico particularly susceptible to the properties and dynamics of the personalistic logic. This has important consequences for the discourses of modernization and democratic transition. The institutionalist focus of these discourses is useful in pointing to legal-institutional change as a fundamental condition for constructing a more plural, open and democratic society. If, however, this is supposed to occur without taking into account *camarilla* politics, it is unlikely to achieve the objective of full-blown democratization. The effectiveness of institutional change and reform is as much conditioned by socio-economic processes as by the cultural codes that regulate the universe of primordial loyalties. The poverty of much of the current debates about transition resides precisely in the fact that it narrows the notion of democracy to the ambit, of elections and tends to measure 'the moral health of the nation purely in terms of whether the latest round of elections have been fair and "transparent".'[68]

Throughout much of the history of post-revolutionary Mexico, the workings of the political system, the economy and the cultural repertoire of personalism have managed to create some kind of stable (authoritarian) articulation. *Camarilla* politics penetrated the bureaucracy, but the rhythm of the electoral agenda and the principle of no re-election saw to it that there was a regular circulation of elites, although within the confines of the ruling party. The ideological latitude of the PRI permitted pendular swings in policy orientations, which ensured that different sectors and groups acquired political weight periodically. This prevented the ossification of the bureaucracy and explained the system's capacity to adapt to changing circumstances. The turnover of elites also created career options for promising politicians and bureaucrats. The centralization of political power in the presidency and the articulation of informal power groups across different institutions, organizations and regions, while hampering the development of an impersonal bureaucratic logic, did produce some form of societal cohesion and integration, absent in many other Latin American countries.[69] Sustained economic growth generated the spoils that were modestly distributed through the (corporatist) system. Due to these general conditions, the use of political violence could be expelled effectively from the higher echelons of the political

system. However, the stability and civilianization of national politics cannot be dissociated from enduring acts of violence on the lower levels of society. On the contrary, they are positively related. Local-level political violence has contributed to the overall stability and civility of the political system (see Chapter 5 in this volume).

In recent years, the articulation between institutional arrangements, economic developments and the universe of personalistic loyalties has suffered erosion. Economic crisis, drastic policy reorientations imposed from above and supported from without, institutional reform, and the proliferation of alternative political and socio-economic projects from below, have dramatically increased the strains on the overall system. Social, economic, political and cultural changes have unleashed forces that are difficult to channel through the old systems of checks and balances, and *pan y palo* (bread and stick). Rogelio Hernández has recently argued that the most important source of Mexico's instability resides in the fact that, while the traditional representational and mediating mechanisms have become dysfunctional, the electoral and party system possess insufficient strength to replace them. This is so, as I argued above, because the enduring monopoly of the ruling party prevented the development of a strong party system and of active and conscious citizenship. As a result, the electoral arena has become a channel of protest, instead of a platform of distinct political and programmatic options; it has become a source of pressure, instead of a solution for unchannelled tensions. No other institutional arrangements that can effectively represent societal and political interests have yet emerged.[70]

The combined result of neo-liberal economic adjustment, institutional malfunctioning, and the decomposition of personalistic networks and loyalties has been an increase in violence at *all* societal levels. The adoption of neo-liberal economic policies alienated sectors and political groups associated with the previous development model. PRONASOL has provoked tensions among different political groups (mostly within the PRI) about the distribution of government resources. Political and electoral reform has accelerated the diminishing effectiveness of local PRI leaders and increased the mobilization and awareness of oppositional groups and parties. During the Salinas administration various local and regional elections ended with serious outbursts of violence, as in Michoacán (1989), Guerrero (1989) and Chiapas (1994). The centre-left PRD suffered most from violent repression. The party itself claimed to have documented the murder of 292 activists between July 1988 and January 1995. The Comisión Nacional de Derechos Humanos confirmed official responsibility in 67 out of 140 cases of killings the PRD had reported.[71] The Salinas administration emphasized the elections as a source of legitimacy, both internally and externally, but they rather became a source of instability.[72]

While violence related to electoral conflicts seemed to be localized, the outbreak of the *zapatista* rebellion in Chiapas in January 1994 made violence

a national problem. In the context of this chapter it is not possible to go into the roots and background of this rebellion (see Chapter 4 in this volume). For our purpose it is sufficient to observe that the EZLN was the first organized and armed opposition movement in Mexico since the 1970s. The fighting between the EZLN and the army and the police was particularly fierce during the first weeks of the conflict. After the announcement of a cease-fire, open confrontations gave way to more hidden forms of violence in remote areas of the conflict zone. In June 1996 another armed guerilla movement, the Ejército Popular Revolucionario (Popular Revolutionary Army, EPR), appeared for the first time in public during a meeting in the state of Guerrero that commemorated the massacre of seventeen peasants a year earlier. Less than two months later the EPR made violent incursions into six different states, killing several people.[73] The regime responded with 'the full force of the state', leading to a militarization of a large part of the south-eastern states.[74]

A few months after the outbreak of the *zapatista* rebellion, another dramatic event shook Mexico. The assassination of the presidential candidate of the PRI, Luis Donaldo Colosio, on 23 March 1994 sent shock-waves through the entire political system. Most importantly, it created a feeling among members of the ruling elite and in society at large that violence could endanger institutional stability. Within the PRI the assassination caused great tensions because the alliances of personalistic groups that had just consolidated around Colosio's candidacy disintegrated rapidly. The nomination of Ernesto Zedillo as the party's new candidate demanded adjustments and led to sometimes fierce factional disputes at different levels of the political hierarchy.[75] Although one individual assassin was immediately arrested at the scene of the crime in Tijuana, rumours about a conspiracy quickly surfaced. At this critical conjuncture, everything seemed possible: from a resumption of armed conflict in Chiapas, and a breakaway movement from the PRI led by former presidential contender Manuel Camacho Solís, to a military coup and Salinas declaring a state of emergency that would enable him to postpone the elections. Although none of these scenarios happened, the events created a broadly shared sense of insecurity and fear. In June 1994 the *zapatista* leadership declared that the EZLN was not prepared to sign the provisional agreements with the government. These developments, and the general sense of insecurity and instability they generated, led to the recording of the presidential elections of August 1994 in history as 'the elections of fear'.

A month after the elections, the secretary general of the PRI, José Francisco Ruiz Massieu, was assassinated in the centre of Mexico City. In this case it was clear from the start that the murder was related to fierce factional disputes in the intransigent core (*núcleo duro*) of the ruling elite.[76] As such, the death of Ruiz Massieu is proof of the dysfunctional nature of the traditional channels of conflict regulation. Moreover, the increasingly fierce and violent nature of *camarilla* politics within the bureaucracy and the ruling

party undermined the credibility of the country's institutions. This effect was further aggravated by the fact that the judicial investigations of the Colosio and Ruiz Massieu cases developed into an arena of political infighting, imputations and corruption. Further assassinations and disappearances of people somehow related to these cases, the repeated dismissal of magistrates in charge of the investigations, and the dubious role played by members of the Salinas family have strengthened the popular view of Mexican politics as a corrupt and bloody soap opera, that can perhaps be ridiculed but not trusted.

Distrust in government institutions, especially in the area of law enforcement, was generalized when the December 1994 peso-crisis plunged the country into economic, social and moral disarray. The economic consequences for the great majority of Mexicans were dramatic. With political and corporatist organizations suffering the consequences of disorientation and discredit, and the law enforcement agencies unable to handle high-profile criminal and corruption cases, an extreme sense of frustration among the popular and middle classes about their economic fate and security produced a moral outrage about the ruling elite, especially the Salinas clan. Although it is generally argued that it is difficult to establish a causal relationship between economic crisis and violence, developments in Mexico in recent years have undoubtedly shown an increase of different forms of disorganized violence, particularly in the large cities. Armed assaults, robberies, kidnapping and many forms of petty crime have become familiar phenomena for many Mexicans. Incidents in which ordinary citizens take the law into their own hands have also increased, and appear to be the result of widespread anger, frustration and distrust in police officers and judges. Since 1993 around 250 cases of popular lynchings have ocurred. The seriousness of these events has recently been underlined by a member of the Supreme Court of Justice who made the startling declaration that 'it is a clear sign that there is no rule of law.'[77] More generally, these developments seem to validate the claim put forward by Zermeño that, as a result of different disordering processes, Mexico runs the risk of falling into a state of 'acute anomie, generalized disaffection with regard to social order, and the weakening or disappearance of basic social units', which can lead to outbursts of disorganized violence.[78] Do President Zedillo's calls to television companies to restrain the broadcast of an increasing number of television programmes that deal with violence perhaps reflect a deep-seated fear of an awakening of *México bronco* (untamed Mexico)?[79] There is little doubt that the Mexican situation is drifting away from what Torres-Rivas has identified as an important variable for the deepening of a transition: 'a legitimacy that is upheld by a broad faith in a mandate, a concept of obedience that the citizen absorbs and that leads to stable public institutions.'[80]

Finally, Mexico faces the problem of what appears to be a widening influence of drug cartels within the political system and society at large. In most major incidents of recent years, there have been rumours of the

involvement of drug dealers, drug-related corruption and violence including: the murder of Guadalajara's Archbishop Posada in 1991, the assassination of Colosio, the imprisonment of Raúl Salinas and the recent arrest of General Gutiérrez Rebollo, head of Mexico's drugs enforcement agency. On the ground level there have been shoot-outs between different drug gangs, between drug dealers and the police, and between different police forces. Although it is difficult to assess with some precision the impact of drug trafficking on Mexico's current political system, there can be little doubt that added to the sources of violence mentioned above, it constitutes a major challenge to institutional stability and transition.

Concluding Remarks

Mexican authoritarianism has always occupied a marginal or exceptional position in the broader debate about (bureaucratic) authoritarianism in Latin America. These models were originally elaborated against the background of developments in societies that differed substantially from the path taken by Mexico at the time. Thus, the question should be raised whether it is useful to stretch or modify a concept to such a degree that it may lose its original intention and analytical potential. True, the concept of authoritarianism has been succesfully absorbed in the wider academic discourse of the peculiarities of the Mexican political system. However, the potential of the concept of transition may well be much more limited. I have tried to argue that a process of political liberalization can be identified in Mexico, but that it is frought with contradictions, hidden agendas and ambivalences to such an extent that the usefulness of the concept of transition should be seriously questioned. Furthermore, I have pointed to the problem and arbitrariness of determining the starting point of the transition.

The discourses of transition and state-led modernization basically concentrate on reforming the institutional foundations of authoritarianism. The 'transition discourse' perceives institutional change as a vehicle for democratic rupture, and the 'modernization discourse' perceives it as a road to 'change without rupture'. The foregoing analysis suggested that such institutional approaches miss a crucial element of Mexican authoritarianism. A recognition of the importance of personalistic relationships and *camarilla* politics raises serious doubts about a conceptualization of transition that cannot incorporate factors driven by deep-seated cultural codes. It is perhaps because of the specificity of Mexico, where the monopolization of political space by a single though heterogeneous partisan force has been so notorious and enduring, that the force of the personal logic appears so prominent. It gives Mexican authoritarianism its particular ambiguity, that in its turn can explain much of the system's proven adaptability and capacity to survive, ironically alluded to in the quotation at the beginning of this chapter. Thinking about the Mexican case, Cansino suggested that the higher a system's organizational ambiguity,

the slower and more laborious will be change and eventual democratic transition.[81] However, primordial loyalties play a role in Latin American politics in general, and it therefore seems inevitable to incorporate them in the thinking about the fundamental elements of the discourse of transition, most notably the issue of citizenship.[82] This is why Hernández concluded that political actors should concentrate their efforts on stimulating learning processes that will contribute to the constitution of citizens.[83] In her stimulating analysis of popular groups in Argentina and Peru, Elizabeth Jelin focused on the painstaking task of constructing citizenship in a universe in which the forces of clientelism are (still) operating. An authentic transition requires the adoption of behaviour and beliefs that are consistent with the notion of democracy. It requires democratic learning processes among both the elites and the popular classes.[84]

The murder of president elect Alvaro Obregón in 1928 stood at the cradle of the revolutionary party. The institutional arrangements that emerged from this conjuncture were designed to ward off the danger that personal ambitions and praetorian violence would turn the revolution into 'a cradle of anarchy'.[85] In following decades the party structure, the corporatist pact and the presidential prerogatives were successful in curbing and regulating the volatility and risks of the forces of personalism. The universe of primordial loyalties was domesticated (not eliminated) by the institutional architecture of post-revolutionary Mexico. The murder of presidential candidate Luis Donaldo Colosio in 1994 may be a telling symbol of how the increasingly violent forces of *camarilla* politics are nowadays contributing to the collapse of the institutional arrangements. The sharpening of *camarilla* politics shades into the institutional framework and generates regime instability. The discretionary use of the law and the use of violence were always inherent to the logic of personalism, but today they tend to subvert the institutional framework. The disruption of important areas of the political and socio-economic system simultaneously fosters different forms of violence and undermines the mechanisms to counteract them. In a country like Chile, debates and policies concerning the transition need to incorporate the ways in which violence and fears associated with past regimes can be *mastered* (see Chapter 8 in this volume). In Mexico, processes oriented towards a reordering of political and institutional arrangements have *generated* new forms of violence and fear. In 1994 former presidential contender Manuel Camacho Solís described two options for stability in Mexico. One would imply the recognition of the basic problems, different evaluations, the participation of new political actors and the construction of new alliances. The other option, which more closely reflected the situation in Mexico at the time, implied, among other things, 'Maintaining fear in society so that in whatever change and movement it will discern a risk to its tranquility and patrimony. This is an option. It has functioned and may continue to function for some time, but how long, what for and to what consequences for Mexico?'[86]

Notes and References

1. The quotation is taken from Solis' short novel *El gran elector* (p. 15), where the author describes the conversations between a president who has been in power for more than sixty years and his personal secretary. (All quotations originally in Spanish in this chapter were translated by the editors.)

2. Knight, 'Mexico's elite settlement', p. 121.

3. In 1991 Fernando Pérez Correa wrote: 'In Mexico there is an open debate, under the auspices of the culture of change.' Quoted in Barros Horcasitas et al., *Transición*, p. 284.

4. Monsiváis, 'Duración de la eternidad', p. 39.

5. Camín, 'La obligación del mundo', p. 49 (emphasis added).

6. César Cansino has recently listed the variations in the definitions of Mexican authoritarianism. Generally speaking, Mexico is treated as an exceptional case. See Cansino, *Construir la democracia*, pp. 171–2.

7. Elections are held for virtually all official positions in Mexico, also outside the realm of the government.

8. When former President Salinas de Gortari appeared even to be flirting with possible re-election, it provoked an immediate and broad condemnation.

9. A fictional account of such a successful career can be found in Camp, *Memorias*. The account is based on Camp's extensive studies on the development of the Mexican political elite in the twentieth century.

10. Whitehead, 'The peculiarities of transition *a la mexicana*', p. 115.

11. See the perceptive article by Hernández Rodríguez, 'Difícil transición', pp. 238–40. Other scholars have maintained that it is difficult to accept that elections in earlier decades were mere rituals. See Molinar Horcasitas, *Tiempo de la legitimidad*. Evidence for this argument can also be found in studies on regional political processes. See e.g. Rubin, 'Popular mobilization'; Pansters, 'Citizens with dignity'.

12. As I have shown elsewhere, this process was not a zero-sum game. Territorially based power blocs have continued to play an important role in the functioning of the Mexican political system but since the end of the 1930s they have no longer been the only pivot of political power. See Pansters, *Politics and Power*.

13. For the historical development of federalism see the chapters on Mexico in Carmagnani, *Federalismos latinoamericanos*.

14. See Rodríguez, 'Politics of decentralization'.

15. See Bizberg, 'Crisis', p. 702.

16. Loaeza, 'México, 1968', p. 27.

17. Below I will analyse the political-cultural dimension that is missing from the foregoing characterization.

18. See Bizberg, 'Crisis'.

19. Quoted in Rodríguez Araujo, *Reforma política*, p. 56.

20. This and other examples of popular organization inspired some authors to suggest that civil society was really being organized from below. This was later questioned by Zermeño who rightly argued that most of these organizations did not have a lasting effect. See Zermeño, 'Crisis, neoliberalism and disorder'.

21. Foweraker, *Popular Movements*.

22. Haber, 'Cárdenas', p. 242.

23. Cornelius, 'Overview', p. 2.

24. An important exception should be made for the 1968 student rebellion.

25. Munck, 'After the transition'.

26. Krauze, *Democracia sin adjetivos*.

27. Harvey, 'Difficult transition'.

28. See *Nexos*, 176, August 1992, pp. 37–45.

29. See O'Donnell and Schmitter, *Transitions: Tentative Conclusions*.

30. Gómez and Bailey, 'Transición política', p. 83.

31. Guillén López, 'Baja California', pp. 162–3.

32. These observations are based on Demmers, *Friends and Bitter Enemies*.

33. Hurtado, 'Características', pp. 136–7.

34. See Meyer, *Segunda muerta*, p. 123.

35. A report of two independent organizations, which witnessed the elections at 750 polls, concluded that in more than half of the polls some kind of irregularity had occurred. Quoted in Aziz, 'San Luis Potosí', p. 13.

36. See Granados Chapa, *Nava sí, Zapata no!*, p. 168.

37. Shortly after this episode the relationships between the *navista* movement and the PAN deteriorated quickly. For a more detailed analysis of this conjuncture see Pansters, 'Citizens with dignity'.

38. Gómez Tagle, 'Electoral reform', p. 80. Another excellent and detailed analysis of the electoral reform of 1986 is Emilio Krieger, 'Derecho electoral'.

39. Gómez Tagle, 'Electoral reform', p. 86.

40. Cansino, *Construir la democracia*, pp. 191–2.

41. Hurtado, 'Características', p. 135.

42. The decision to remove the leaders did not respond to a democratizing project. The imprisonment of the oil-workers' leader Hernández Galicia was largely informed by his active opposition against Salinas' presidential candidacy.

43. Cornelius et al., *Mexico's Futures*, pp. 28–9.

44. Craske, 'Dismantling or retrenchment?'

45. The recent work of Ilán Bizberg is highly relevant; see his 'Crisis'; also 'El régimen político mexicano'; also 'Modernization and corporatism'.

46. Hernández Rodríguez, 'What to do with the PRI?'

47. Initiated by the leader of the telephone workers' union, some unions that were part of, yet more independent from, the more traditional corporatist arrangement, joined forces around this new union strategy and founded the Federación de Servicios y Bienes.

48. Garza Toledo, 'Restructuring', p. 214. See also Harvey, 'Difficult transition', pp. 19–23.

49. Craske, *Corporatism Revisited*, p. 42.

50. See O'Donnell and Schmitter, *Transitions: Tentative Conclusions*.

51. Cisneros, 'Modelos'.

52. Middlebrook, *Political Liberalization*, p. 31.

53. Loaeza, 'México, 1968', p. 16.

54. See for example Pérez Arce, 'Enduring struggle'.

55. After the election of Cárdenas as mayor of Mexico City, it may well be that some scholars will baptize 1997 as the 'true' starting point of the transition.

56. Cisneros, 'Modelos', pp. 75–6.

57. O'Donnell and Schmitter, *Transitions: Tentative Conclusions*, p. 6. Pérez Correa argues that in Mexico there is really no need for a (democratic) transition since a broad definition of democracy which applies to social, economic, cultural and political spheres would mean that Mexico has in fact been going through a prolonged process of 'gradual and sustained democratization'. See Pérez Correa, 'Reflexiones'. I hope to show later why I cannot subscribe to this interpretation.

58. For an interesting, though partial account of these events, see Márquez, *Por qué perdió Camacho*.

59. Developments during the last months of the regime of Salinas de Gortari, which involved his family, namely his brother Raú and his former brother-in-law, Ruiz Massieu, gave the metaphor of the 'revolutionary family' a new and banal meaning.

60. Roniger, *Hierarchy and Trust*, p. 10.

61. The first part of the definition is from Friedrich, 'Legitimacy of a cacique', p. 247; the second part is from Clapham, 'Clientelism', p. 5. The novel is Aguilar Camín's *Morir en el golfo*.

62. Knight, 'Historical continuities', p. 96.

63. See Foweraker, *Popular Movements*, p.16.

64. Guerra, *México*, p. 167.

65. For an interesting review of the different functions of a *cacique* as a broker see Peña, 'Poder local'.

66. Guillén López, 'Social basis', p. 255. See also his article 'Political culture'.

67. See Guillén López, 'Political culture'.

68. Craske, 'Dismantling or retrenchment?', p. 90.

69. The comparison between Mexico and Peru is interesting in this respect. See Mallon, *Peasant and Nation.*

70. See Hernández Rodríguez, 'Difícil transición', pp. 245-9.

71. Amnesty International, *Mexico. Human Rights in Rural Areas*, p. 33.

72. Gómez Tagle, 'Electoral violence'; also Hernández Rodríguez, 'Difícil transición', p. 254.

73. *La Jornada*, 29 August 1996.

74. Corro, 'Operativos militares'. See also César López, 'EPR reta'.

75. Elsewhere I have analysed the consequences of the murder of Colosio in the regional political arena of the state of San Luis Potosí. See Pansters, 'El hambre'.

76. The notion of *núcleo duro* comes from Zermeño, 'Intellectuals and the State'

77. The number and the quotation come from *Proceso*, 1036, 8 September 1996, p. 11.

78. Zermeño, 'Society and politics'.

79. See Puig and Vera, 'Petición'.

80. Torres-Rivas, 'Democracy', p. 49. Although political events in 1997 suggest a return to more civilized forms of political bargaining, it seems too early to amend the foregoing arguments.

81. Cansino, *Construir la democracia*, p. 179.

82. I have analysed this problem extensively in Pansters, 'Theorizing political culture'.

83. Hernández Rodríguez, 'Difícil transición', p. 257.

84. Jelin, 'Cómo construir ciudadanía?' Another interesting study is Fox, 'Difficult transition'.

85. *El Universal*, 22 August 1928, quoted in Knight, 'Mexico's elite settlement', p. 116.

86. Camacho Solís, *Cambio sin ruptura*, p. 21.

ELEVEN

A Loss of Purpose: Crisis and Transition in Cuba

GERT OOSTINDIE

I n Spain in 1994, a bitter Cuban exile told me his latest Castro joke. Fidel is performing as a *toreador*. The arena is packed. The crowd watch with bated breath as the enormous bull rushes at *el líder máximo*. In the nick of time he steps backwards, completely in control. As the bull rushes past him, Fidel leans forwards, his head inches from the bull's enormous head. The bull continues a few paces and then falls to the ground, dead. Consternation. 'Fidel, what did you do?' Fidel: 'I only whispered in his ear, *Socialismo o muerte.*'

I repeated this joke scores of times in Cuba. What fascinated me was not so much the hilarity, but the eagerness with which so many Cubans kept on explaining the punch line to me. Had I understood it properly? Faced with the choice between socialism or death – the motto with which Castro usually concludes his speeches – the bull preferred to die. *Así estamos.* That's what things have come to.

Cuba is in crisis, and Cuba is in transition. In this chapter, I aim to summarize the ingredients and depth of the present predicament and to discuss the direction and pace of the transitions under way. In addition, I present a number of observations regarding legacies from the present which a post-communist Cuba will again have to face. The chapter combines scholarly analysis with a more personal approach. I attempt to use my own experiences of and observations on the island to indicate some of the deeper layers of the current crisis, and to reflect on the applicability of this volume's emblematic title, *Societies of Fear*, to the Cuban case.

The Demise of the Revolution

For present purposes, the revolution's emergence, its initial achievements and failures, and its post-1989 collapse can be summarized succinctly.[1] Despite common assumptions, Cuba was one of the more developed countries in

Latin America before the 1959 revolution. However, its economy was completely dependent on sugar and on the USA, and the gulf between Havana and the impoverished countryside was enormous. The political history of the island, which had become independent under US tutelage around the turn of the century, was characterized by incompetence, corruption and violence. Cuba in the 1950s was undeniably ripe for change. Although the followers of Castro never constituted a mass movement, he was able to count on a large popularity after the 'triumph of the revolution' (jargon now rephrased as *el accidente* on Cuban streets). A more equitable distribution of wealth, diversification of the economy, clean politics and renunciation of US patronage were aims which could call up wide support in the country.

The balance of the revolution up to 1989 was two-sided, and usually involved weighing up differing elements. On the one hand, by regional criteria Cuba enjoyed a reasonable standard of living, fairly evenly distributed among the entire population as a result of the levelling out of what had been enormous economic and social inequalities. The regime guaranteed an impressive system of health-care and education. In addition, the position of women and of the Afro-Cuban population improved considerably, at least in public life. Finally, thanks to the new start which was made in 1959, Cuba was a source of inspiration in the region and much farther afield. This was reinforced by the ongoing conflict with the USA. The American embargo, no matter what its economic significance, helped to underline Cuba's stature as the proud David standing up to Goliath.

On the other hand, critics and opponents of the revolution focused primarily on the extreme concentration of power, the society's militarization, the limited civil rights, the repression of all political opposition, and the dependence on the Soviet bloc. The debate between supporters and opponents has often been marked by complete mutual incomprehension. More impartial observers, many of these located outside the Havana–Miami–Washington axis, tended to favour a point of view which simply juxtaposed the polar opposites enshrined in the two perspectives.

In the meantime, the relevance of discussing the achievements of the Cuban revolution in terms of this balance sheet had begun to be overtaken by events. By 1970 state policy, largely based on the Soviet model, had not brought about any genuine diversification of the economy. Sugar remained the main product, and dependence on the Eastern bloc was as strong as the subjection to the USA that it had replaced. The various economic policies which were implemented after 1959 were marked by inefficient production and distribution and a chronic shortage of consumer goods. Cuba had begun to experience negative economic growth during the period 1986–90, before the collapse of the Soviet bloc.

The termination of Eastern European protection for what had once been seen as a case for the Soviet model made the previous balance of pros and cons redundant. Within months, it became apparent to all but the revolution's

most staunch partisans that many of the achievements of the revolution had merely been financed by the Eastern bloc. The withdrawal of support exposed the glaring weakness and inefficiency of Cuba's planned economy. By 1995, the size of the economy was only half of what it had been in 1989, and in spite of the present, apparently impressive growth rates, the visible pace of recovery is, in reality, tantalizingly slow.

The Mid-1990s Crises

With the collapse of the Eastern bloc and the concomitant withdrawal of Soviet support to Cuba, a crisis that had already been smouldering on the island came into the open. Public discontent, certainly not a common phenomenon of the post-1959 era, became widespread. Growing impoverishment, frustration and demoralization led to a dramatic collapse in the legitimacy of the regime and of Fidel Castro himself. Although one could feel that something was brewing, it took a remarkably long time for the tensions to burst out. Until 1994, only a few incidents, mainly outside Havana, were reported. The riots that broke out in the capital on 5 August 1994, though rapidly quelled, were a novelty and an unmistakable signal. Once again the regime applied the 'safety valve' technique: coastal controls were suspended as they had been during the 1980 Mariel crisis, when more than 100,000 Cubans were allowed to leave the country. This time, over 30,000 refugees (*balseros*, or 'raftpeople') seized the opportunity to leave by sea on any available vessel.

In the following weeks, intensive US–Cuban negotiations led to an agreement in which Cuba committed itself to stop the exodus. The remaining 30,000 *balseros* interned in the US military base of Guantánamo on the southeastern coast of Cuba were allowed to leave for the USA. However, proclaiming them the last ones to arrive without a valid visa, Clinton abandoned the line of more than thirty-five years of Cold War diplomacy: Cuban refugees would no longer have the automatic status of political refugees. While some hoped that this agreement would initiate an era of more pragmatic US–Cuban relations, such expectations were not to be realized. Indeed the opposite was true as exemplified by a tightening of the embargo through the passing of the Helms–Burton act. After the shooting by the Cuban army of two small and unarmed aircraft belonging to the Cuban–American organization *Hermanos al Rescate*, the Clinton administration controlled this trend by reconstituting a harder line towards Cuba.

At the same time, both Latin America and the European Union have become increasingly upset by the intransigence and the political immobility of the Cuban regime. By 1996, these two blocs found their own policy of 'constructive dialogue' with Cuba frustrated by the regime's unwillingness to wed political reform to its economic liberalization. The Cuban position in international politics is once again characterized by isolation. Castro's eagerness to visit the Vatican in late 1996, and the ensuing 'hot news' of the

Pope's visit to Cuba in early 1998, only underline this isolation. The regime's enthusiasm about this potentially risky visit to the island demonstrates its own sense of being an outcast.

In reality, a decade after the fall of the Berlin Wall, Cuba is still caught between partial economic adjustments from above and growing dissatisfaction from below, hardly any political openings, and an isolated position in world politics.

Economic Decline

The post-1989 economic breakdown was devastating for Cuba. The cumulative destruction of the island's economic infrastructure; the collapse of the sugar industry and the failure of other sectors of the economy to pick up the slack; and, of course, the shrinking of per capita incomes to less than half of the modest levels attained in the mid-1980s – all have been extensively documented.

All over Cuba, the consequences were quickly felt. Cubans soon learned that following official guidelines led to a reduction in the amount of goods and services which people had long taken for granted. The disastrous food situation was a striking illustration of the failure of the planned economy. Cuba is one of the least densely populated and most fertile countries of the Caribbean. Nevertheless, both the volume and range of agricultural products available were minimal in the early 1990s. With the exception of Haiti, no country in the Caribbean failed as comprehensively in providing its people with food. The subsequent opening of peasant markets has helped to lessen the worst of the food crisis, even if the quantity and quality of supplies continued to be limited and expensive. Over the past several years, the regime has implemented a number of measures which would have been unthinkable a decade earlier, such as the far-reaching dollarization of the economy, the promotion of joint ventures with foreign corporations, and experiments with domestic 'capitalist' markets. For many reasons, it remains questionable whether these economic changes will inspire sufficient confidence in the foreign investors whom Cuba is so frenetically trying to woo, and whether they will provide a solution to, or at least a substantial alleviation of, the crisis in the relatively short term. There are signs, however, that the 'reforms' are having a limited success. In 1995, economic growth rates suggested a hesitant recovery, and by January 1997 the regime boasted prospects of a growth rate of nearly 8 per cent for the year ahead. Yet, whether the reforms and concomitant growth will be sufficient to ease popular discontent remains an open question.

The introduction of a parallel 'dollar economy' along with measures reminiscent of a market economy has inevitably led to the creation of a two-tier economy and a population of haves and have-nots. Those managing to operate in the 'capitalist' sector are much more successful. Few people still

entertain reservations about the need for more market-oriented activities, and there are very few who do not participate in the semi-illegal informal sector. Still, the growth of the dual economy is met with understandable resentment by those – still a majority – who have lost more and more in the post-1989 years without seeing anything take its place.

Who profits from the economic openings? Those who have access to dollars, either through relatives abroad, or through participating in the 'dollar economy' in Cuba. Every visitor to the island will be familiar with the wide range of legal, semi-legal and illegal services which are provided by individual Cubans working for the tourist dollar. Less conspicuous are state organizations, such as the Cuban army, which are currently active in these markets.

Dissidence and Repression

Unrest is growing behind the crumbling façade of socialist Cuba, and, as the events of 1994 revealed, it can suddenly erupt. There is, however, a more widespread change taking place. Never before have Cubans complained as openly about the regime as they do now. The country now faces the risk of a whole generation of young people turning their back on education, the state economy and many of its fundamental values. All this has severely undermined the legitimacy and strength of the regime.

In this respect, one needs to imagine the ideological effects of the economic crisis. The post-1989 *período especial* has been a training school for civil disobedience. As no one can survive without ignoring the letter and even spirit of Cuban law, every Cuban has now learned semi-clandestine behaviour which has significant implications. Socially, every citizen faces the problem of a sliding scale of values. Buying or selling an egg on the black market is as minor an offence as one may think of, yet for some undividuals it opens the door to potentially serious criminal behaviour. From the regime's perspective, the political implications of this behaviour are even more worrying. The necessity to sidestep the law demonstrates, in glaring terms, the regime's inability to help its citizens. At the same time, the act of actually breaking the law may help many Cubans develop a political awareness that the state's hold on the population is not omnipotent after all.

This has clearly been one of the lessons of the 1994 riots and the *balseros* crisis. The state's response to the black market has been pragmatic, legalizing and hence controlling and taxing citizens' activities rather than enforcing regulations which are now obsolete. Its reaction to political dissent, on the other hand, has been anything but flexible. Despite growing dissatisfaction with the lack of political liberty, the willingness of the government to liberalize political activity appears minimal. The totalitarian style remains supreme. There may not be excessive violence, as in so many other authoritarian regimes all over the world, yet the strict surveillance of all sorts of potentially independent institutions such as churches, universities and cultural

centres continues undiminished. The same applies to individuals seeking independent political parties or labour unions. There is no space whatsoever for the organization of opposition, as its would-be platform *Concilio Cubano* experienced when its public meeting was cancelled at the last moment, at the height of the *Hermanos al Rescate* crisis, in 1996.

The regime is suffering from a self-imposed dichotomy. On the one hand, there is the unwillingness to do away with a system which not only confers many privileges and considerable power to its elites, but with which large portions of the population have psychologically come to identify over the years. On the other hand, there is the fear among these very elites that, as soon as repression is seen to be decreasing and a genuine political opening emerges, the current leadership and the system that it represents will irrevocably fall. The recent history of the Eastern bloc suggests that this fear is quite justified.

The Crisis Within

There is a worrying social dimension to the economic decay of socialist Cuba. The ongoing collapse of the economy and the progressive betrayal of the high expectations nurtured by the revolution have incited a sense of despair and a concomitant social disintegration which will arguably haunt Cuba for a long time, no matter what the pace and ultimate character of the transition will be. Some observations regarding the illegal economy, a generational gap, gender, and racial relations illustrate the point.

First, the short-term successes of the new 'entrepreneurs' (from hookers and pimps to illegal taxi drivers and black marketeers) seem to confirm that the respectable long-term strategies of the past for achieving social success have been undermined. Further education and university degrees do not provide employment, or, if they do, only low-paid work. Participation in the civil service and party organs? Who still believes in them? Ever fewer people may mourn the erosion of the Communist Party and related institutions. All the same, it is certainly a problem for the future that the present protracted impasse has not only brought about an enormous demoralization, but that it can mean that many out of one or more generations of young people go to waste. Growing up among the ruins of communism, without a real picture of what to expect from a future capitalist society, leads many to drift along without any ambition. The cost to society is evident. The price that an individual has to pay may be even higher. A dramatic example is the *jineteras*, a Cuban euphemism for women working as prostitutes.

During the last few years, the regime has singled out tourism as the main growth sector of the economy, although it has done so reluctantly and with concern about the predictable spin-offs. Castro has often complained about the loss of the 'virginal purity' of the revolution.[2] He had good reason to do so. The still modest tourist boom inevitably involved the demonstrative

effect of relatively rich, mainly white, capitalist tourists; the exoticization of
the local culture; and the inevitable growth of illegality on the fringe. The
phenomenon of the *jineteras* must have confirmed Fidel's worst fears. Every
hotel, disco and beach which attracts tourists is crowded with a mass of
young women, and men, offering themselves for money. And there is little
doubt that not only Cuban state officials, but equally state organizations have
been benefiting from sex tourism.

Jineteras are a metaphor for decline. They do not regard themselves as
prostitutes. As Carmen claims: '*Estoy puteando, sí, pero no soy puta.*'[3] Making a
television documentary about these young women, we were able to interview
and film not only many *jineteras*, but some of their grandfathers as well, men
who had known Havana as a US brothel before the revolution and now saw
history repeating itself. The discussions, and particularly the confrontations
between the two generations, were often highly charged and moving. The
sad thing was that each of the two parties – for that is how it was in most
cases – had a tale to tell which was as convincing, or at least as understandable, as that of the other party.

> She: 'I'm broke / there's nothing to eat / we haven't got anything / I have to
> look after my kid.'
> He: 'Things aren't that bad / there's always an alternative / you're behaving
> like a prostitute / you're throwing away your dignity.'

And more such words. Spirited discussions marked not only by bitterness
but also by mutual concern and love – one of the reasons why they are so
sad. At one point, one wondered whether those families in which close
relatives had long since accepted the dealings of their daughters, granddaughters or sisters weren't even more depressing.

Why is the phenomenon of prostitution so distressing in Cuba? Sex-work
is a worldwide phenomenon. The young girls and women hanging around
Cuban hotels and discos are looking for clients for the same reasons as
women in cities like Bangkok, Lagos, Manila or Santo Domingo: not enough
money to go round, what they see as the lack of genuine alternatives, the
obligation to support relatives, and so on. What adds an extra painful
dimension to the presence of these *jineteras* in the streets of Havana is not
so much the phenomenon itself, nor the reasons behind it, but simply the
realization that history has come full circle. Today, the revolutionary refrain
of Havana under Batista as the brothel of the USA has become a sad
parody of itself.

How many times has Castro labelled 'old' Cuba as the whorehouse of the
USA during the thirty-five-plus years that he has been governing the island?
The revolution would not only offer the country a better future, but it would
also restore the dignity which the *pseudorepública* had lost. And now, in the
mid-1990s, Cuba is back to square one. No hotel is without its flood of
young prostitutes and randy tourists. All the bargaining in the hotel lobby,

less and less discreet and without exception pricey is intended less to bring this sector out of the sphere of illegality than to let a few other Cubans share in the proceeds. It is not that the phenomenon is unique. It is rather the awareness that the huge supply of *jineteras* makes it clear in the most tangible way possible that this is the end of an era. A dream shattered, and one doesn't need to have been a believer to experience its tragedy. A dream shattered, and to gain a better idea of what that feels like, one should simply talk to older Cubans, old enough to have lived under Castro's corrupt predecessor, Batista, who now see their granddaughters 'on the street'.

This semi-professional prostitution may be an extreme expression of the Cuban crisis. Yet in a wider sense, the mentality of making one's skills available as long as there is a dollar reward is not limited to the *jineteras*. Nor is the supply limited to physical goods or material services, such as the ones offered by clandestine taxi drivers, cigar vendors, and so on. Many others, such as artists and even Afro-Cuban religious specialists, cater for the dollar market too, often demonstrating a mentality which at times seems only different in degree rather than substance from the *jineteras'* cynical and desperate outlook.

'Che' Guevara used to prophesy that the New Man would be born, or rather produced, in Cuba. He was wrong. All the same, the awareness that so much is now being wasted is a reminder of the various achievements that were made. The decline is painfully visible, as is the loss of organized solidarity with the economically weak, especially old people; and there are many more dimensions. Women's emancipation is a case in point. The revolution's policy was primarily successful in public life – Cuban men discarded little of their *machismo* in their private lives – but at least that result was achieved. Now more and more Cuban women are finding that their partners are passing the responsibility for housekeeping and child-care on to their shoulders all too easily, and perhaps even more than they ever did in the past, while precisely now it is so extremely difficult to keep a household going.

Again, this is a problem of wider dimensions which was officially acknow-ledged even before the present crisis. The rectification campaign started in 1986 targeted the Cuban family as one of the areas in need of correction of 'negative tendencies'. To anyone studying Latin America and the Caribbean – or the 'inner-city crisis' in USA, or Caribbean minorities in Europe for that matter – the list of problems reads as a painfully familiar one. Teenage pregnancy, early marriages, a high divorce rate, single parent, female-headed households: the revolution apparently did not do much better than other social systems. By 1987, officials such as Vilma Espín, president of the Federación de Mujeres Cubanas (and spouse of Raúl Castro), were openly deploring the hedonism and lack of responsibility and revolutionary spirit of younger generations.[4]

One may doubt whether it makes much sense to think of *machismo* as a 'pre- revolutionary' rather than as a deeply engrained characteristic of Cuban

(and Latin American) society. Either way, the revolution has apparently not broken the spell. There are indications that, in the present situation, women bear an even heavier share of the crisis than men do. Many Cuban women certainly say so, and impressionistic evidence tends to support their case. Thus, for instance, it seems more than just a passing comment on the present predicament of Cuban women that among the 1994 *balseros*, single, young men were the largest category, many of them leaving spouse or girlfriend and children behind. Likewise, of the young *jineteras* working in Havana or the Varadero beaches, many have a child to support whose father is no longer of assistance, if ever he was.

The Resurgence of 'Race'

Race, long an official non-issue in Cuban society, is another sphere of life in which pre-revolutionary history and its legacies and revolutionary slogans and realities provide a worrying enigma. The post-1959 ideology has been one of colour blindness. Afro-Cuban emancipation has certainly been a constant in official government policy. Racial discrimination was formally abolished, and there has been an undeniable increase in the number of Afro-Cubans in schools and universities, in white-collar positions, and so on. There is strong evidence that the Afro-Cuban population benefited disproportionately from the revolution's redistribution of wealth and opportunities.

In itself, such successes need not reflect a particular interest in the fate of blacks; in his famous 1953 speech, 'La historia me absolverá', Castro did not even mention Afro-Cubans as a specific group. In fact, after the first months of 1959 the potentially explosive issue of racism was not allowed to surface in official discourse again until the mid-1980s.[5] Rather, the socio-economic emancipation of blacks reflects the revolution's programme to improve the lot of the lower classes, in which Afro-Cubans just 'happened' to be over-represented. At the same time, however, the leading positions remained almost exclusively in white hands, and among the elite there was no question of colour blindness, not in the public sphere, and much less so in intimate relations. It was always a matter of opinion whether improvement was really to be merely a question of time, as many hoped or promised. In fact, both exiled Afro-Cuban and African American intellectuals published bitter accounts of the persistence of racism in revolutionary Cuba.[6]

In the current deep crisis, the black population is more essential for Fidel's survival than it has ever been. There are no reliable statistics available, but it is realistic to estimate the proportion of Afro-Cubans at a near 60 per cent of the total population. This is a sharp increase over 1959, not least because most of the emigrants were white. In this context, it is not surprising that there has been a deliberate policy of courting the black population by labelling Cuba as *afrolatino*, of stressing the island's history of slavery, and of displaying more tolerance towards the Afro-Cuban culture than used to be the case.

This strategy has attempted to exercise a greater control over black Cubans at the same time.

The way the regime has handled Afro-Cuban religions is a telling case.[7] In line both with Marxist–Leninist orthodoxy and the policy to control every sphere of society, and with the traditional elite definition of Cuba as a western or even outright white nation, any attempt to promote an Afro-Cuban culture as distinct from what was defined as mainstream Cuban culture was prohibited or at least thwarted for most of the revolutionary period. In fact, in the early 1980s participation in Afro-Cuban religious cults could still be classified along with drug and child abuse and juvenile delinquency as 'pathological behaviour'. Starting in the mid-1980s, this policy was remarkably reversed. Afro-American religions such as *santería* became accepted ingredients of Cuban culture. For much of the revolutionary period, believers had encountered serious problems with the authorities for even the most discreet demonstration of their creed. Suddenly, the state began actively to court Afro-Cuban religious leaders. Today, *santeros* wear their paraphernalia openly in the streets, ceremonies are attended by quite numerous gatherings, in which whites seem to have a growing share, and Afro-Cuban religions have finally become legitimate subjects for research in scholarly institutions from Havana to Santiago de Cuba.

To some extent, this rather spectacular policy shift may reflect a growing need even within the ruling elite to find spiritual comfort in the present crisis; in fact, figures as highly placed as Raúl Castro are rumoured to be believers. Yet one may well speculate on more machiavellian motives for this sudden emancipation of Afro-Cuban religions. Trivial as it may seem, Afro-Cuban cults soon became a financially rewarding sideline for the emerging tourist industry. More importantly, as these religions proved impossible to eradicate, turning the wheel the other way was not only pragmatic but also extremely useful in order to secure Afro-Cuban support for the regime, and to suggest that the regime was indeed searching for ways to relax its control. Actually, from a perspective of *raison d'état*, it would be wiser to allow the proliferation of perhaps more escapist and outworldly oriented religions such as *santería* or *palo monte*, with their lack of national organization and hierarchy and their tenuous international links, than to tolerate the growth of the Catholic Church with its potentially subversive political impact. After all, in various Eastern European and Latin American transitions, the Catholic Church has played a crucial role.

Meanwhile, in spite of this feigned or real acceptance of Afro-Cuban culture, and in spite of the relative improvement in socio-economic position, black Cubans are still predominantly concentrated in the lower strata of the population. One may debate whether this demonstrates the revolution's unwillingness, or simply its incapacity, to break a deadlock dating back many decades and even centuries before 1959. For now, however, it is sufficient to conclude with the bitter irony that although the Afro-Cuban population has

made the most relative progress since 1959, this advance is quickly being annihilated by the present crisis. A major disadvantage confronting the Afro-Cuban population is that its share in dollar remittances sent by the predominantly white Cuban American community is very limited. The consequences are evident. Black youths in the major Cuban cities are now prominent in all branches of the illegal economy, not the least among the *jineteras*. The theme of race and racism is clearly among the hitherto taboo subjects now all too openly discussed again all over Cuba. At the same time, and certainly to the dismay of the regime, Afro-Cubans now figure prominently in the dissident circles, such as in the *Concilio Cubano*.

At the same time, it is the black Cubans who are understandably frightened by the prospect of a return of the predominantly white Cubans from Miami and the Florida coast. In the meantime, there seems to be something of a white backlash here and there in Cuba. Some identify black Cubans with the failed revolution, and one hears blatantly racist remarks in this respect. 'Because all the support has not got them any further,' they simply aren't up to it.' Others blame Afro-Cubans for an alleged disproportionate involvement with subversion and the illegal economy. These are plenty of different sticks to beat the same dog with – another explosive ingredient in any future Cuba.

The Crisis Within: Pain, Anger and Fear

Not surprisingly, then, emotions run high in contemporary Cuba, and in spite of frequent oblique incantations of a Cuban *calor humano* which would help Cubans through this period as it has through earlier crises, the emotional climate is bitter. Such bitterness need not be unidirectional. A painful and often angry awareness of the failure of the experiment may be shared by most Cubans, yet the target of such frustrations differs. Whereas many, and perhaps most, Cubans put the blame on the failure of Fidel's regime, there are still large numbers who hold the counter-forces – whether the USA, Cuban exiles, or the 'spoiled' younger generations – responsible for the crisis. Pain and anger therefore are potent ingredients in contemporary Cuban discourse, a potentially explosive cocktail indeed. Moreover, even if in less consistent fashion than used to be the case, anxiety over the state's unbroken capacity to clamp down on 'anti-social' behaviour lingers.

A couple of personal observations may help to elucidate both the significance of such emotions in today's Cuba and the puzzlement an outsider frequently feels in trying to account for these.

I'm photographing a completely decrepit building which once stood as a monument in the centre of Havana. A middle-aged woman laughs as she passes by and says: '*Chico, estás fotografiando las ruinas del socialismo*' ('Boy, you are taking pictures of the ruins of socialism'). One hears more remarks of this kind while taking such pictures of demolition sites: '*Así está toda Cuba, arruinada*' ('That's the way all of Cuba is like, ruined'). During the last few

years reporters have described the progressive decline of Cuba in a variety of ways. Anyone who knew Havana before the 1990s must be astonished at the ruination of the city, the empty shops, the shortage of food. Still, one wonders what is the more baffling indication of the new Cuban condition: the ruins and the poverty, or the openness with which Cubans now give voice to their desperation. In the early 1980s, too, there was decay to be seen, the standard of living was modest, and there were a lot of complaints about the lack of 'luxury' and the omnipresence of a state which many felt to be not so much hostile as *pesado* ('heavy'), irritating and annoying. But hardly anyone ever ventured to criticize anything in public.

All that has certainly changed, at least at a grassroots level. The 1994 *balsero* crisis was one dramatic episode when irony, sarcasm and subdued despair gave way to openly expressed bitterness and anger. These were weeks of dramatic scenes in and around Havana and other coastal towns, as well as on the open sea, where many people drowned, and many more agonized. There was outrage, misery, fierce discussions, and something closely resembling a collective psychosis: not only were people leaving, but now 'it' was bound to happen. But it remained unclear just what to await. Another riot, a rebellion, a clamp-down by the regime? How does one find out in a country where the news is almost by definition anecdotal, and in an atmosphere which came so close to hysteria at this time?

We were filming at the Cojímar beaches, just outside Havana, in August 1994, at the height of the *balsero* crisis. A rocky beach was covered with makeshift rafts, different ones every day. Those leaving, nervous, *macho*, explained in front of the whirring cameras of the world's press why they wanted to leave: '*¡Aquí es peor que en Haití!* ('Here it is worse than in Haiti').[8] Predominantly young adults, often men, were leaving their girlfriends and young children behind 'to go for them later'. The stay-at-homes and the curious always formed a large majority; the fury and openness of the discussions; the bitterness of both the *balseros* and the spectators, whether sympathetic or not; the aggression, including that towards one another; the eagerness to speak out.

Cojímar, June 1995: there is nothing left to recall last year's episode. It is as if none of it ever happened; and if you want to hear anything, it's better to do so indoors where people still do a lot of talking. The relatives and neighbours of the three *balsero* protagonists of our 1994 documentary tell us once more the rest of the story. All three were picked up by the US coast-guard and interned in Guantánamo. They did not get any further for many months. In desperation, one of them escaped from the base, was rescued from a minefield by the Cuban navy, and came back by bus to Havana. Bitter irony. All for nothing. He does not want to talk. The other two have just heard that they belong to the last group which will be allowed to go from Guantánamo to the USA. Very mixed feelings among those left behind. Their menfolk did not fly in vain, but they have been gone almost a year by

now, leaving their female and young relatives in an even greater predicament without them. And the prospects of ever being 'picked up' are very uncertain. Increasing financial demands are imposed by Cuba on those who leave. In the USA, the time when Cuban immigrants were invited in with open arms has passed, as has the time that a fresh Cuban immigrant would easily find reasonably paid work. The hopes of those left behind to meet again with their *balseros* are uncertain. We rate the chances even lower, but cannot bring ourselves to tell them.

Habana Vieja

And so Cuba is still on the ever-prolonged eve of something unknown. Havana: a city full of miniatures, which the visitor may find amusing or melancholic, but which many Cubans now find gloomy or aggressive.

One more impression. A shoe-shiner seated in the hallway of a dark flight of stairs in the old city centre. A common enough phenomenon in the countries surrounding Cuba, but a striking one here. Until recently such activities were not allowed: even on this scale, business was capitalism, after all. Now that it is permitted in the context of economic liberalization, many prospective entrepreneurs lack the necessary experience and spirit of enterprise – not to mention the trivial fact that they lack the requisite materials. Just try to get shoe polish in a country crippled by shortages of all kinds. For sale in dollars, like anything else, but how do you get hold of the dollars in the first place?

I decide to have my shoes polished, hoping at the same time, in vain, to shake off the man who has been following me for several *cuadras* in the hopes of getting his hands on some of my money. A feeling familiar to everyone who walks through cities with a good amount of beggars – in Havana, of course, a phenomenon of the last few years only. One feels guilty not giving anything, but not much better if one does; and now and then one simply feels fed up, especially if the beggar is truly aggressive and irritating. Such is the man following me now. Around thirty-five, and looking healthy enough. An 'anti-social element' in the language of the revolution, not because of his political views but because he does not seem to have a job and disgraces his country by definition as a beggar.

I try to start up a conversation with the shoe-shiner while he is polishing my shoes. It's tough going, he isn't very talkative. Emaciated, black, he must be around eighty. Looks pretty tough. All this time the beggar has not given up. He runs through the whole gamut of prayers and curses. It is hot, I have had more than enough, and I burst out: 'Why don't I give you anything? What have you done for me? What do you actually do all day? Why should foreigners give people like you a tip while you do nothing except bother us? Look, this man here is doing something for me, that's why I pay him. You're much younger, but all you do is complain.' And more of this kind of talk

of which I am not proud, but which certainly helps to let off steam. To my surprise, the shoe-shiner suddenly stops polishing and shakes me firmly by the hand without saying anything, gestures at the beggar to clear off – which he eventually does – and carries on with his work.

Now he starts to tell fragments of his life story. He worked when he was a young boy ('as a slave, really'), and never stopped working. Now he is eighty-three. The revolution made his life so much better, but the US blockade made it all more difficult every time. Racism was terrible before 1959, and disappeared afterwards. The revolution made one big mistake: spoiling the younger generation with free education and so on. 'Now they don't know you have to work to eat, and they choose the easy way: begging, prostitution.'

I listen with mixed feelings. The fact that the US embargo has long lost whatever justification it might once, if ever, have had is clear, but it is nonsense to suppose that the embargo explains why the Cuban economy has been in the doldrums for so long. Most people, both Cubans and foreign observers, agree that institutional racism was worse before the revolution than it is today, but does this mean that racism has disappeared? Nonsense. And I have more sympathy for the 'spoiled' Cuban youth. The present-day dissatisfaction is an expression of a deep frustration, a loss of confidence in a revolution which kept on making more promises than it was able, or sometimes even willing, to keep. But at the same time, how can one fail to sympathize with the old man's bitterness at the generation which has had it much easier than him, and who will not provide for him in his last years? How could one contradict him, what would be the point of reminding him of the obvious failure of Cuban communism to provide him with a reasonable retirement: the shabbiness of his old clothes, his incredible leanness, the fact that he still has to work for a few indispensable cents at his age?

Like the *jineteras*, the shoe-shiner too comes to symbolize the unfulfilled promises of the revolution; the shocking tragedy for the older generation, people who did believe, and who also gave a lot in the conviction that it would result in something better for all Cubans. The system has never functioned properly, only too often the leadership has been cynical, foolish or misleading; but still there was once confidence of some kind. For the Cubans who once believed – and perhaps still do, despite their better judgement – Cuba in 1997 is a worse drama than it is for the younger generation. After all, lots of young people never believed in the dream which now lies shattered for so many of the older generation.

The Regime's Staying Power

Presiding over this sad situation is a regime which has held power since the very beginnings of the revolution, and is therefore rightfully identified with whatever *el proceso* achieved, or failed to achieve. There are obvious analogies with Eastern Europe on the eve of the *Wende*. When the Eastern bloc

collapsed, it was generally supposed that Cuba would be the next domino. The bankruptcy of Eastern Europe had not only deprived the communist model of its credibility, but it had also stripped Cuba of its crucial economic benefactor. Why did these predictions fail to come true? Why did Castro remain in control while the system of fraternal regimes in the Eastern bloc collapsed like a house of cards?[9]

Several factors help to explain the remarkable resiliency of the regime. The visible gains of the revolution guaranteed the legitimacy of *el proceso revolucionario* for much longer than had been the case in Eastern Europe. Moreover, though socialism may not have been as popular among the Cuban population as was argued by the regime, it was certainly not seen, as it was in much of the Soviet bloc, as an imposition by an imperialist USSR. In Eastern Europe, this imposition tended to foster anti-communist nationalism. In Cuba, arguably, the opposite happened. Over three decades of US hardline policy only helped Castro to capitalize on Cuban nationalism for the regime's sake. Combined with the omnipresence of a large-scale system of control and repression, this encouraged a larger degree of complacency than was the case in Eastern Europe. This 'complacency' was encouraged by the fact that Cuba generally exported its dissidents and successfully prevented the emergence of an opposition organized around institutions such as trade unions or the church. Even geography helped: no bitter winters inspiring panic over expected shortages of calories and fuel, no domino effect in an isolated island at a large physical distance from its fraternal regimes.

Yet there is more. Many Cubans see the alternatives as undefined and obscure, if not alarming. While the Eastern European opposition was oriented towards Western Europe, the Cuban orientation towards the USA is ambivalent. Although Cubans are painfully aware of the enormous differences in prosperity and political freedom, there is also a certain apprehension about American life. The Cuban media have systematically highlighted the toughest aspects of US capitalism; besides, the expectation that the former welfare state provisions could be scrapped to a large extent under capitalism is not ill-founded. In addition, there is concern about an economic and political invasion by the Cuban Americans, who could completely overshadow the local population, taking control of business and government, claiming their former houses, and so on. As indicated above, the racial factor plays a part in all of this too. Even if the Afro-Cuban population is still predominantly represented among the lower echelons of society, black Cubans are understandably afraid that their position will deteriorate under American-style capitalism. Evidently, there are also very concrete stakes in maintaining the status quo. Officials fear a day of reckoning for their participation in the communist state. But in a wider sense, the prospect of a sudden breakdown of authority now evokes fear of anarchy.

This brings us to a crucial factor making Cuba socialism *sui generis*: Fidel. Much has been written on Castro's charisma, and even if his flamboyant style

has definitely deteriorated with age, just like the appeal of his revolution, there is no doubt that he still personifies the revolution and holds the key to Cuba's immediate future. Journalists continue reporting that Cubans hardly dare think about a Cuba without Fidel. One may well question the extent to which this once probably valid statement still holds true. Again, the Cuba of the 1990s is a country in which foreigners are continuously approached by Cubans not only practising 'anti-social' behaviour, but equally voicing strong opinions on *el barbudo*. The question may be less whether Cubans can imagine a Cuba without Castro, but rather to what degree they dare voice their views, whether in private or in public. Certainly, they do so far more openly than ever before. Yet there is always the apprehension, and occasionally indeed the sudden and unnerving affirmation, that a plain-clothes security official is listening and may act, or that there will be another clamp-down on the openings conceded so far. As long as he is still in charge, another type of question emerges. Castro may still hold the key to a smoother transition, but is he willing and able to use it? Here, the Cuban regime appears to be even more closed and enigmatic than were most of its Eastern European counterparts.

Castro's charisma, communism and *cubanidad* may indeed have been a potent potion in the past. Yet by now it is hard not to conclude that repression is the main explanation why the *¡abajo Fidel!* slogan is so seldom heard or read. In that sense, indeed, Cuba is as much a society of fear as one undermined by sabotage and illegality. Either way, of course, the fact remains that the immediate future still depends very much on what Castro will allow to happen.

Scenarios for a Transition

With the benefit of hindsight, the collapse of the Eastern European communist bloc was relatively easy to explain. Yet even in 1989, on the eve of the fall of the Berlin Wall, few specialists foresaw the astonishing direction and pace of the changes overtaking the Soviet bloc. This observation may serve to remind us of the perils of forecasting regime transitions in general, and of predicting the future trajectory of Cuba in particular.[10] This truism has certainly been experienced by the scholarly and journalistic communities – not to mention the Cuban population both on the island and abroad – infinitely charting and discussing the state of affairs on the island. As soon as the Soviet bloc collapsed, many observers started to predict the imminent fall of Fidel Castro's communist regime. Some of the best journalistic books published in the early 1990s were sold under such telling titles as *Castro's Final Hour* and *Fin de siècle à la Havane*.[11] Yet in 1997, Castro is still *el líder máximo* and, in spite of the prolonged crisis devastating the country, there is no firm evidence that he will soon cease to be so. At least, therefore, his final hour seems to be a remarkably long one.

Cubanology so far has been at a loss adequately to predict the outcome of

the Cuban crisis. Indeed, there is not one obvious encompassing scenario for the next few years. Scenarios vary from maintenance of the economic status quo with increased political repression, through the 'Chinese–Vietnamese' model of market socialism, to democratization and a complete break with the planned economy. Maintaining the economic status quo and stepping up repression is no longer a viable strategy and has accordingly been abandoned, despite Fidel Castro's initial lack of flexibility. The regime has definitely opted for a scenario of economic reforms without significant change to the political system, and particularly a refusal to tolerate any opposition.

What will be the result of this policy? The economic transition towards a free market and more capitalism is irreversible, as the regime consistently informs potential foreign investors. This is absolutely true, as there indeed is no alternative left. The question is only how long it will take for this to produce tangible and lasting results. For the time being the economic future of Cuba evokes the picture of a development that has come full circle. Not long ago, Cuban historian Manuel Moreno Fraginals, once a figurehead of Cuban Marxist historiography, now an exile in the USA, summed up his view of the future of Cuba quite graphically: *país capitalista y pobre*. One sees the point.

The political scenario, which will in its turn affect the pace of the economic transition, is more difficult to predict. Can one conceive of an ideal transition? Under the circumstances, the most realistic scenario still seems ongoing economic liberalization, which then might eventually be followed by a political opening. A preliminary question is, evidently, whether the economic reforms will pay off in time for the regime, a rather open question. Should the answer turn out to be positive, in this model a second-phase political transition might still be a receding horizon, as is evident in Vietnam and China. One would expect such a delay to cause more serious problems in Cuba than in these two Asian countries, simply because of the emphatically western orientation of the island in terms of its politico-cultural tradition and environment, and because of the weight of the exile community. In the end, we have to confront here once more the opaqueness of the power game, and particularly the crucial question of how Fidel Castro's position will evolve.

Among the more spectacular political scenarios are that of foreign intervention, an internal coup, or the death or withdrawal of Castro. The first two options are not very likely. Under 'normal' conditions, an intervention is practically excluded; no one takes this idea seriously apart from isolated Cuban radicals in Florida. It would undoubtedly be in vain and would lead to large-scale bloodshed, while foreign (US) interests no longer have much to gain from a bloody intervention in the current situation. An internal coup would have to be executed or supported by the army. This is not very likely either. The ministry of defence is led by Cuba's number two, Fidel's brother Raúl. The two brothers wield enormous power over the army, partly because they have constantly been on their guard – resorting to physical elimination

where necessary – against the rise of popular military leaders with possibly subversive ideas of their own, such as General Ochoa in the late 1980s. As for the party and the bureaucracy, there too the reformers can apparently operate only in an extremely cautious way, within the limits set by the commandment of absolute loyalty to their *líder máximo*.

Castro will obviously not live for ever. As long as his health permits, however, he will not be prepared to leave the fort; he repeatedly states that he cannot transfer the leadership at such a difficult time as the present, an argument that comes across persuasively in a *macho* culture. Castro will probably resign only if he is no longer able to rule, or if he is forced to go. That does not seem to be on the agenda for the time being.

Besides the scenario of a gradual transition, there is the possibility of a crash landing. New, more extensive riots, leading to a popular uprising, would force the army and the police to take sides. This would mean either heavy repression to regain control or the end of the regime. In the first case, even the option of external intervention might regain plausibility, evoking prospects of massive bloodshed. The latter case, regime collapse, would spell chaos and anarchy too, at least for a time – again, hardly an attractive scenario. One hopes that the USA will keep its distance, while less pockmarked parties such as Latin America and Europe may act as arbitrators.[12] All the same, it is more likely that the transition will primarily be an internal affair.

Finally, a word on the regional context. As the transition progresses, Cuba will return more and more to its natural habitat: the Caribbean, Latin America, Florida. Now that the Cold War is over, Cuba will come to be an entirely new and much more serious threat to the neighbouring areas. In economic terms, the island will be reinserted primarily into the US sphere of influence, though without giving up the links that have been reinforced with Latin America and the European Community during the last few years. The geopolitical situation may thus be slightly more in equilibrium than it was before 1959. Given its potential and scale, Cuba may completely outstrip the other Caribbean islands in the crucial economic sector of tourism. In addition, (temporary?) large-scale emigration and the problem of the illegal economy will come to affect other countries more than in the past – especially if there is a crash landing with a loss of internal order. A weak transition government could be the ideal breeding ground for the growth of Cuba as yet another Caribbean centre for narcotrafficking, money laundering, and other mafia-like practices. Both the USA and the smaller powers in the region will then look back with nostalgia on the time when Cuba was still Castro's Cuba, communist, and safely isolated.

Fin de Siècle

Cuba has long been the odd one out (or, depending on one's perspective, the odd one in) in Latin America. It continues to be so today, as its leadership

continues stubbornly to refuse to join the wave of democratization which
has swept the continent since the 1980s. Both for its domestic achievements
and for its lonely and in a sense heroic posture against the USA, Cuba has
long inspired enthusiasm and admiration throughout the Americas south of
the Río Grande. Cuba's internationalism, too, while provoking concern among
politicians of different leanings, served to boost the island's status as a major
power with a different agenda. Already prior to the collapse of the Soviet
bloc this reputation had become tarnished, even among the Latin American
and Caribbean Left.[13] In the post-Cold War era, little is left of a Cuban
model. Tales of economic catastrophe, the permanence of totalitarianism,
and massive discontent now dominate the imagery of the Cuban revolution.
As a point of reference and a model to emulate, Cuba has definitely lost
whatever significance it once had.

As Cuba has become ideologically ever more isolated and economically in
dire straits, the Cuban population continues to experience both economic
hardship and political repression. Yet does it really make sense to think of
Cuba as a 'Society of Fear', as this book's title proposes? One may want to
express reasonable doubt. There are no killing fields in Cuba, and it makes
only limited sense to compare Castro's Cuba to the slaughterhouses which
have disgraced the Latin American continent in the postwar years. Cuba, too,
has had its share of violence, of executions and disappearances, yet the
figures were less gruesome than in many other places.

On the other hand, the degree of totalitarianism which has characterized
the communist regime is probably unrivalled in modern Latin American
history. Within Cuba, the revolution has generated a sterile intellectual climate
in which only a few dare to volunteer creative ideas, and in which hardly
anybody gets away with dissident opinions.[14]

There are no independent labour unions, space to manoeuvre for churches
is extremely limited, academic institutions are fully controlled, neutral NGOs
do not exist, most dissidents have been deported or are harassed. The
authoritarian regime now nearing its fortieth anniversary has definitely not
produced conditions favourable to an early soft landing.

By repressing or exporting dissident organizations and individuals, the
revolution has undermined, if not destroyed, the basis for an early national
reconciliation. Abroad, there are the exile communities, the most vociferous
of these with a dubious reputation for tolerance and democracy. Their
abhorrence of reconciliation is not only dysfunctional but equally reminiscent
of Castro's own stubbornness. Credible mediators are hard to come by, and
Castro, the one who should allow them to start doing their work, is not
sending out any clear positive signals so far. For the moment, as the island
remains in the doldrums, and as long as there is no such thing as a 'post-
Castro' Cuba, one can only hope that Fidel, with his obsession with being
a Historical Character in capitals, will settle for a negotiated, gradual, but
significant, opening of his regime.

Meanwhile, Cuba suffers from an overly protracted *fin de siècle*. The post-1989 *período especial* has provided a detrimental training school. One senses uncertainty, regret, frustration, a loss of purpose and dignity. Many Cubans now drift along without much ambition. This is a waste of precisely what the Cuban revolution did supply for decades: relatively well-trained and motivated human capital, and, perhaps even more, a sense of solidarity and common destiny. Straying away from all this not only causes social disintegration and a loss of purpose today; it also threatens to usher in endemic anomie, criminality and anarchy, should the present repressive institutions collapse. The prospect is horrendous indeed.

The importance of a rapid and peaceful transition is obvious. The longer the current malaise continues, the more of whatever economic, educational and moral gains the revolution made will be lost. The longer the present decay and demoralization continue, the more likely a crash landing, and the more difficult the task of reconstruction and national reconciliation.

Postscript

The events of 1997 and 1998 have not given cause to alter the views expressed in this chapter. The Pope's visit to Cuba in January 1998 was an encounter between two old men, each trying hard to show the world his personal stamina and his unwavering faith in his own cause. It is difficult to establish which of the two succeeded the best. For Castro, the Pope's visit *per se* was useful in enhancing his own credibility in the world. Yet at the same time it demonstrated how desperately he needs to boost this credibility, both at home and abroad, and how enthusiastically many Cubans took this opportunity quietly to demonstrate perhaps not their longing for Catholicism but certainly their longing for fundamental changes in society.

In the winter of 1998, former Chilean dictator Pinochet was imprisoned in the United Kingdom. At the time of writing, it is not yet clear whether he will indeed be put on trial for the atrocities committed under his rule. Reactions to Pinochet's arrest have been mixed in Chile. International human rights organizations have welcomed a trial, stating that this is an important signal for dictators all over the world that they cannot get away for ever with their crimes. Laudable as this may be, there is a darker side to this story. If dictators can no longer be sure of the guarantees given for a negotiated transition, then why should they bother to cede power anyway? For Castro, stepping down has now become an even less attractive proposition. Many Cubans therefore, no matter how much they may welcome a possible trial of Pinochet, must nurture mixed feelings regarding the consequences for their own country. Thus, Cuba remains caught in a deadlock of tantalizingly slow change.

Notes and References

Apart from the Postscript written in January 1999, this chapter was completed in February 1997, and is based on both literature and printed sources and on various visits to the island. My personal experiences in Cuba date from 1981, 1985, and from five field trips in the period 1994–97. Fragments of this paper were published in the Dutch press and were used in two documentaries made for Dutch television. I would like to thank Patricio Silva and the editors for their useful comments on the earlier version.

1. More detailed overviews of the revolutionary period are presented in Eckstein, *Back from the Future*, Pérez-Stable, *Cuban Revolution*, and Bengelsdorf, *Problem of Democracy*. Admirable journalistic accounts of the situation in the early 1990s appear in Oppenheimer, *Castro's Final Hour*, and Fogel and Rosenthal, *Fin de Siècle*. Useful scholarly accounts on this period include Baloyra and Morris, *Conflict and Change*, Domínguez, *Cuba: Order and Revolution*, Mesa-Lago, *Cuba after the Cold War*, and Pérez-López, *Cuba at a Crossroads*.

2. E.g. *Granma*, 25 November 1993.

3. Literally: 'I'm playing the hooker, but I'm not a whore'.

4. Smith and Padula, 'Cuban family', p. 182. On Cuban youth culture, see also Fernández, 'Youth'.

5. See Moore, *Castro, the Blacks and Africa*, p. 28.

6. See particularly the book by the Afro-Cuban exile, Carlos Moore, *Castro, the Blacks and Africa*. Not surprisingly, his polemic position and work have provoked heated debate among pro- and anti-Castroites. In a short introduction to the book, Domínguez underscores several of Moore's points; his own views are more cautious, though (cf. Domínguez, *Cuba: Order and Revolution*, pp. 7–8, 224–7, 483–5). For a severe criticism, see Brock and Cunningham, 'Race'. Alejandro de la Fuente provides a thorough and cautious evaluation of the material advances made by the black Cubans during the revolution. See Fuente, 'Race and inequality'; cf. Knight, 'Ethnicity'.

7. Cf. the rhetorical use of the 'shared' past of slavery by Castro in his address to Nelson Mandela, in Matanzas (Mandela and Castro, *How Far We Slaves Have Come!*). On the political significance of the official recognition of Afro-Cuban religions, see Moore, *Castro, the Blacks and Africa*, pp. 343–5; Oppenheimer, *Castro's Final Hour*, pp. 337–55.

8. Untrue, to my mind; but what's the use in saying so, at that point?

9. For a systematic analysis of the relevance of the Eastern European experiences for Cuba, see the reader edited by Mesa-Lago, *Cuba after the Cold War*, particularly the contributions by Linden, 'Analogies', and Mesa-Lago and Fabian, 'Analogies'; see also Radu, 'Cuba's transition'.

10. Cf. O'Donnell, Schmitter and Whitehead, *Transitions: Comparative Perspectives*. For Cuba, see the literature mentioned in note 1; Schulz, *Cuba and the Future*, and Smith, 'Cuba's long reform'.

11. See Oppenheimer, *Castro's Final Hour*, Fogel and Rosenthal, *Fin de Siècle*.

12. See Oostindie and Silva, 'Europa en de Cubaanse crisis'.

13. See Borzutzky and Pérez-López, 'Impact of the collapse'.

14. Much has been written on the narrow limits of expression in revolutionary Cuba. A useful summary is provided by Dopico Black, 'Limits of expression'. Dissidents claim that the situation has anything but improved under the *período especial*.

TWELVE

Epilogue: Notes on Terror, Violence, Fear and Democracy

EDELBERTO TORRES-RIVAS

Democracy is not Irreversible

During the 1970s and 1980s, Latin American political life passed through one of those authoritarian cycles, to which the region appears to be fated, in its oscillating path between democracy and dictatorship. This was the third phase of such historically recurring moments since the end of World War II. Given the characteristics adopted by military dictatorships in Argentina, Bolivia, Brazil, Chile, El Salvador, Guatemala, Haiti, Nicaragua, Peru and Uruguay, in terms of the use of violence and fear, it may be stated that more than half of Latin American societies (forming 75 per cent of its overall population) have experienced various forms and degrees of political terror.

It can hardly be questioned that the nature of the violence unleashed during those years of military dictatorship was without parallel in any other moment of Latin American history. Dictatorships have been a recurrent element in the region, and up until now there is no evidence to suggest that, in the prevailing conditions, we shall not experience them again in the future, if the hypothesis of authoritarian cycles has any grounds in reality.

Even more than theory, history itself reminds us that a stable democracy is not an irreversible democracy, with elected governments now firmly established across the continent, and in which the prestige of democratic values reaches a hitherto unknown universality.

In the following pages, I offer several considerations regarding the Latin American political violence of the recent past. This chapter does not represent an analysis of the repressive state, but rather of the effects produced by the terrorist methods adopted by that state. The forms of public violence exercised during the 1970s and 1980s, must be regarded as a conscious policy applied by the state; one that justified itself in terms of the defence of the democratic system, as defined within the strategic framework of the United States' doctrine of national security, that the Latin American forces of 'order' made fully their own.

From a position of political power, from the state itself, society was punished in order to defend 'itself' from 'itself'. The search for order via the use of violence left society even more disorganized than before, paralysed cultural life for a significant period, undermined confidence at the inter-personal level, and left entire societies in a continuing state of fear.

Probably no other moment in history ever manifested this kind of double hypocrisy, and never has violence been unleashed in such proportions against the civilian population in general through torture, disappearances and deaths. In the same way, never before was death applied using the sinister pretext that, through state violence, the primary need of defending political demo-cracy was being achieved. Defending democracy in such a way, the military trampled it underfoot. No argument in favour of democracy can be used within this infernal vicious circle of terror and fear.

Since the transition to democracy originated in moments of erosion and crisis, and replacing authoritarian structures, the heritage of the immediate past is still there, and cannot be regarded as simply an experience to be held up as an example of past errors.

There is a warning to be made: not every definition of violence takes account of an essential fact, which is that not all members of society recognize the same acts as violent and, accordingly, such acts may be justified in different and even contradictory ways. There is an implicit subjectivity precisely because in this case we are dealing with a political perception and, besides, one with a background relativity since it corresponds to perceptions that are always culturally determined.

It is necessary, then, to conclude that, both theoretically and politically, the classification of a violent act must be made – always is made – from a normative point of view. If this point of view is made explicit, the passions involved can be better explained, even while being aware that one can never analyse dispassionately the phenomena related to death without the anger and sadness inspired by death itself.

Violence Has No Starting Point in History

It is not enough to remember that Latin American societies have experienced different moments in history in which violence has been offered as a method of government. It must also be borne in mind that the recourse to force is not merely inherent in the political order, but that at times it is the most immediate means of preserving that order. In the 1970s some phenomena emerged that acted as a stimulus to disobedience and discontent, manifesting themselves on a massive scale and tending towards rupture with the status quo, within a context of crisis; such expressions appear for the most diverse reasons and in different national contexts as the justification for the terror that, with or without good reasons, was unleashed.

Military, authoritarian governments are dictatorships of crisis, when the

deficiencies of the political system and disequilibrium in the market began to be felt. The decision to take over the state was not in order to deepen capitalism, since, without exception, the military governments proved incompetent in economic crisis management. It is also worth emphasizing that the subversive insurgencies of those years never really threatened the roots of the system. It was more an extremism of means than ends.[1]

The recourse to direct violence in political relations increased: between dominant and dominated classes; between the state and its political opposition; and as an expression of popular discontent against the state.[2] That led – in a loss of the sense of order – to a transformation of politics into war. In Argentina and Uruguay the breakdown of the political system led to the creation of a guerrilla left that responded to violence with violence. In Chile a project for reorganizing society, a pacific and civilized transition, was brutally drowned in blood and held back for a whole generation. In Central America, armed insurgency was a desperate response to decades of exclusion and manipulation of society by force, and so on.

In summary, it can be said that state terrorism was not a merely contingent phenomenon directly produced by popular insurgency; rather it arose out of a long-established tradition, was a response coherent with the continental security strategy forming part of the East–West conflict, clearly expresses a failure of the political order to manage crisis and was a rational option for the armed forces of the region, whose institutionalization was strengthened in opposition to a radically mobilized civil society. This being the case I believe that violence has no starting point in history.

The Ubiquity of Violence

Perhaps it is necessary to remember that the experiences of violence and fear have always been present, widespread and deep-rooted among the poor of Latin America. They are grounded in the uncertainty of daily life at levels that are already not sufficiently consciously expressed: in the absence or inadequacy of income; chronic deficiencies in diet and clothing; the experience of delapidated dwellings and poor health, leading to loss of hope for the future and the dilemma of whether to choose hunger or crime.

This is a form of structural repression originating within a world of extreme physical and moral poverty. It is what many specialists call structural violence, since it re-creates and reproduces itself in labour relations (and all the more so when jobs are in short supply), through the many forms of disguised unemployment, in educational segmentation, and in the inevitable impact of low income on these societies. It is a form of violence that manifests itself especially in the loss of the culturally acquired sense of respect for oneself and others, and thus in a feeling of indignity, impotence, loss of worth.

All this is a potent breeding ground for the generation of highly aggressive

personal behaviour. It is the sub-culture of poverty, in which frustration and fear produce permanently aggressive states of mind. It is the violence of the dispossessed that is turned inwards upon themselves, among equals, permanently and fatally. However, it is not with this kind of violence that I am concerned here.

The problem that interests me here is that of political violence and its lasting consequence, fear. This is the fear that takes hold of social collectives, although it generally takes on individual expression and different forms of adaptation to which the violence of the strongest almost always leads. It is a commonplace, when talking about social relations, to remember that force is implicit in their definition. This is even more the case when one begins to analyse the context of political relations which are, almost always and in an even greater degree, forms of asymmetric coercion, in the universe of the power relation between unequals.

As this has always been so, it may be recognized that modern society has done no more than disguise the handing over of power, in its most brutal form, to the legitimate authorities, that depend in the last resort on the possibility of using force. By definition, public authority reserves the right to use coercion in order to ensure that the other behaves in a way he or she may not wish to act; the existence of 'other wills' always implies a contradictory composition of force, a confrontation at some (not always clearly defined) place that broadens out when we are dealing with public spaces of power, in which both the predictable behaviour of the obedient citizen and the death-defying conduct of the rebel are possible outcomes.

The obedience of those who comply with the law, but with fear, is qualitatively different from that of the citizen who takes part in political meetings against the government, joins a politically very active union, and makes a legal denunciation of the misbehaviour of a government official without fear of reprisals. There is no need to refer here to the habits of those who pay their taxes on time, who vote with varying degrees of enthusiasm, and who deposit their rubbish carefully in the appropriate containers, separating the glass from the paper. These are examples of behaviour typical of a modern, integrated society, where a collective common sense exists regarding such conduct expected of the citizen. They are examples of a situation into which fear does not enter.

All this is normal day-to-day life in a political order where fear does not exist. In such cases there is a behaviour – active or not, rational, explicit or less conscious as the case may be – always expressing a legitimating procedure. In situations of dictatorship, order does not necessarily enjoy this free adherence of the obedient citizen. In such situations, the option of public violence appears as the first condition, in an effort to force the kind of active or passive behaviour necessary to uphold governability.[3]

The limits of public behaviour are thus enclosed in a field of multiple forces of varied significance. By this I wish to suggest that the causes of

rebellion and obedience belong on the same plane as the factors of violence that are used in favour of order, and using order as their pretext.

The history of power and its exercise is unequivocally associated with the use of public force, political violence and their most important effect: fear. Without a doubt, it is possible to live with fear in an anthropomorphic version of death. What remains to be discovered (since it is very close to our contemporary experience) is what kind of democratic life can be constructed with citizens who are frightened. Violence is the most important feature of dictatorship, but this does not rule out its presence in democracy.

State Terrorism

Violence is generally defined as a socially constructed and learned form of behaviour, aimed at producing physical or symbolic attacks on persons or the destruction of their property. State violence is, then, the use, tolerance or threat of force by agents of the state, or its representatives, carried out in an organized manner and expressing itself directly or obliquely, practically or symbolically.[4] The notion of force, which is used at times as a synonym for violence, is implicit and is understood in an even more general way, since by this term we refer to the actual or potential use of violence to force another to do what he or she otherwise would not do. For the purposes of this chapter, the terms are regarded as interchangeable.

When we talk about the violence that comes from all sides of society, we are referring particularly to state terrorism, on account of its omnipresence. We are thus moving towards other aspects of society than that of poverty: situations where the experience of fear is of another nature, since it affects other class groups, without, however, ceasing to affect the poor.

This contribution is concerned with the political violence applied by the state in many Latin American countries during the decades of the 1960s, 1970s, 1980s and 1990s. This state violence must be regarded as a socio-pathological phenomenon with the following characteristics: it is the massive utilization of the resources of force against particular socially defined groups; it is violence of a clearly illegal nature, both on account of the excessive nature of the procedures and the extent of its application; but above all because it is carried out with an avowedly ideological justification.

Violence is illegal to the extent that the state applying violence exceeds its legal capacity to do so. The limits are well understood when such acts take place in a democratic regime, with a full legal structure, with a clear categorization of criminal offences and established instruments for arriving at judgment and authority to punish. Generalized impunity is the most visible symptom of this illegality, although not the only one. The democratic regime is coming to be defined, in Latin America, basically as that which respects its own legality. State terrorism is the failure of that legality and is a direct expression of a profound crisis in the juridical system and its institutions.

I use the word ideological because violence is used to destroy or neutralize a political enemy. As happened in numerous instances from Argentina to Guatemala, state terror in its excess began by punishing an object targeted for strategic reasons determined by the 'theory' of internal security. However, the process of violence rapidly acquired a momentum of its own, flowing almost naturally along a course defined by purely ideological and emotional motivations.

This is what happens when criminal acts are justified by the state as actions against 'communism' or 'subversion', as punishment of 'traitors' or destruction of 'the enemy'. And so, in an ascending spiral, the authoritarian state unleashes a war on objectives ever more ill-defined, dealing blows against anodyne groups of society, as when its immoderation begins to affect the family and friends of the 'enemy', the 'neutral' citizen, and so on, until in the end the figure of the 'suspicious person' appears on all sides.

Political prejudices, intolerance towards the opposition and, in many cases, anti-communism as a reactionary prejudice, led in the past to sporadic, although brutal, violence; but the ideology and strategies of counter-insurgency and national security introduced a change of register and turned justifications of terror into an explicit ideological system (civil-military dictatorships used them in this way). Furthermore, one has to also recognize that violence, that is by definition sanguinary, was no longer irrational. The rationalization of the harm inflicted, the permanent menace, created the social conditions for fear and terror.

The structure of an authoritarian condition, life within a military dictatorship, like those experienced in Latin America in recent times, is founded upon the militarization of social life. The mere existence of the 'suspicious person' implies the existence of a structure of permanent surveillance. People spy on each other in order to report each other, and accuse in order to bring punishment upon the other. There can be no punishment without previous accusation and since the aim is punishment, surveillance is the first step. A vicious (and infernal) circle is thus constructed that does not, however, always begin with that implacable logic of watching–accusation–punishment. Sometimes people are punished without accusation, and accused without surveillance. And worse: watched over without motive, while everybody watches over everybody else.

In the realm of authoritarian arbitrariness suffered by many Latin American societies, we find the 'theory of the three circles' formulated by General Ibérico Saint Jean in Argentina in 1976. Saint Jean explained that the struggle against subversion could not restrict itself to the first circle – that of the subversives – but must advance into the second circle, formed of their sympathizers. How was one to define them? Based on what criteria? Finally, there were the suspicious persons, situated, unreflectingly, in the third circle, consisting of those who do not support directly or actively the anti-subversive struggle. According to the logic of 'he who is not with me is against me',

'they' must therefore fall into the same category as the enemy. They (those situated in the third circle) are suspect and must be punished. The legal order shrinks beside a greater universe, made politically arbitrary by the struggle against subversion.

The suspicious person may appear at any moment during this irresponsible flight into madness. He/she appears as part of a scenario marked by the imperious need for surveillance, by gratuitous accusations and, finally, by arbitrary punishment; an indeterminate situation in which the threat of violence is everywhere and directed from all sides. In this kind of situation, described in the following section, everyone is afraid. The double metaphor proposed by Garretón for differentiating the various feelings of danger – the fear of the dark room and the fear of the barking dog – helps to classify the quality of fear perceived.[5] The former implies an undifferentiated or total danger that may become concrete at any moment, a danger against which there is no easy rational response; the latter, on the other hand, is a fully identified danger against which one can choose a rational course of action.

The Trivialization of Horror

During the 1970s and 1980s, many Latin American societies have been societies in fear. In those societies, the state agents' repeated and massive use of force meant that citizens became accustomed to living under the threat of death, living with death itself and with the worst methods of dealing death. A politically insecure existence – a situation in which the condition of citizen is unpredictable in its durability, together with a certain perception of danger resulting from probable threats – ends up constituting a generalized socio-political syndrome that is not adequately described by the general term 'insecurity'. To this condition of insecurity resulting from direct threat, one must add the intimate reaction produced by the mere information received of deaths repeated on a massive scale, taking place in our midst. This is what I refer to as the trivialization of horror.

In daily life, large sections of the civil population during the years of the military dictatorships in Argentina, Colombia,[6] Guatemala, Haiti, Peru, Uruguay, in some parts of Brazil, Honduras and Mexico, and at certain moments in Bolivia, Nicaragua and Paraguay, repeatedly experienced state terror that finds its essence in a phenomenon that produces insecurity and pain in the greatest degree: that of the disappeared person on political grounds. The fear and insecurity produced by this phenomenon lead to lasting reactions, perhaps passive or neurotic adaptations, in response to the permanent presence of death. These are collective adaptations in situations where, for many years or throughout extensive regions, there has been a repeated experience of state terror leading to the violent death or disappearance of loved ones or acquaintances. This disappearance may take the form of people taken into custody, never to be seen again, or of those driven into exile or underground. One's

fellow man is, in these situations, of necessity someone known: a relation, a friend, a neighbour, a friend of a friend, or simply a familiar face that is suddenly noted by its absence in the neighbourhood or the workplace. In our Judeo-Christian culture, death is always a painful event: one we reject, and that moves us in various ways. Even natural death is a traumatic experience, since we do not accept it as a foreseeable fact of life. The death of our fellows takes us by surprise, produces rage, fear, and/or pain – the magnitude of which varies in proportion with our closeness to the victim – and these emotions find expression in different forms of interpersonal reaction.[7]

In the life experience of those whose daily life is far from politics – and not only for those who dare to take part in the game of active disobedience – it is traumatic to have to accustom oneself to living with extraordinary and abnormal conditions of pain and fear, insecurity and lack of confidence. It is what O'Donnell has called the 'normalization of the abnormal' and appears in those conditions where a climate of generalized uncertainty prevails: in other words, a climate that affects all levels of society.[8] It is a situation of illegality in the sense that the rules of the game are not known or, when they are known, are ignored by the officials of public order.

When political repression is stepped up, fear and anxiety become generalized and the situation is perceived as ever more a 'limit situation': one defined by the real danger personified in the disappeared people. The modality of the 'disappeared' is even more cruel than public assassination, since it raises the perception of danger by placing it in an imaginary world, unsure but probable, created by the possibility that the disappeared person is alive. While one suspects that the disappeared person may be dead, nobody knows the truth. Doubt, prolonged over time, is a highly productive way of sowing fear. Fear has come to stay.

The tools of repression and terror to which the population has become accustomed are many.[9] Police corps with different names proliferate. These are legal bodies that exceed the limits of the legitimate state and act illegally, that indulge in brutality in the exercise of their normal functions. They are authorized to carry out extraordinary initiatives. There are also illegal groups known generically as 'paramilitary groups', a name that reflects the function they carry out rather than their structure. Paramilitary groups are, then, military bodies, acting in the immunity afforded by generalized illegality and protected by the secrecy that surrounds their tasks of abduction and murder.

The activities of the repressive bodies increase with impunity; the police forces, the *escuadrones de la muerte*, or groups of thugs who operate as if they were private organizations, and other variations on the same theme, carry out assassinations, kidnappings, disappearances and force others to act in ways that affect large sections of society. None of this could be done without the open complicity of a section of civil society: the judicial powers, the establishment press, the employers' organizations. Nowadays generals do not act without lawyers, nor without other kinds of professionals. All this con-

firms the existence of a common repressive front, at times a broad front, and never, in our times, an isolated group.

The banalization of fear, a consequence of that permanent cohabitation with death, was not an end in itself, but a means. This exercise of contempt for the law, where rules were decided upon (and therefore rationalized) from within the centres of power, forms part of the mechanism of power, because the exercise of power in our times requires it. Political order, in this atrociously authoritarian culture, can be guaranteed only through recourse to violence. For this reason fear is a means of bringing order, it is a necessary element in political power, a necessary element for order as defined by that power. The psycho-social mechanisms that are set in motion in terrorized societies have not been comprehensively studied in our part of the world. Do we understand the negative and castrating effects of such mechanisms in a period in which the citizenry is undergoing a process of transition towards democracy?

Secrecy, on the other hand, always accompanies the policy of terror. The general result is the appearance of the suspicious person, of denunciations, mutual spying, surveillance, betrayal and punishment. In the reproduction of terror, those who betray also die. A strategy is developed by which everyone becomes an accomplice. In the end total silence is imposed. There is a double mechanism, nowadays, in the phenomenon of political violence: on the one hand, a demultiplication of effectiveness, increasing; and on the other, the dissolution of responsibility in its administration. The ritualization of violence progresses in different directions until it becomes accepted as a fact of the daily public and private lives of ordinary people: the terrorized citizen who knows only that he/she is still alive, but not the cause or reason of the death of the other. To inquire about a political murder is to become an accuser of power or an accomplice of its enemies. 'Fear' seeks at all costs to be apolitical.

The use of terror is only of political utility if its results are publicly known. This explains the trivialization of horror. Fear has at least two functions: to punish the victim, and to set an example to those around him/her. The various effects necessary for the establishment of the 'sense of order' needed by a dictatorship follow from this. One desired effect is to paralyse protest: terror leads to inactivity and its result is a retreat into personal isolation as an adaptive response. Another form of this is the personal evasion, the withdrawal into unproductivity, the 'interior exile' of the intellectual. Another effect of fear is to feed 'moral cowardice', complicity, which is another form of adaptation, this time not by omission but by action. In this situation one saves one's own life by collaborating with those who produce death.

All this shows that the natural instinct for survival is more powerful than the ethical sense of culpability. These societies have produced 'heroes' and 'deserters', 'traitors' and 'rebels', but also an overwhelming majority of citizens who became accustomed to terror and failed to react to it in a way that

might be expected in a democratic society. This, of course, was natural since democracy was the first thing to disappear.

To live in insecurity, with the sensation of a permanent threat, or close to pain and death, all contribute to the breakdown of basic solidarity, and commiseration with the suffering of others. There is no worse complicity than conscious, reasoned indifference. This climate also feeds other kinds of anti-social behaviour: vengeance via hired killers; taking justice into one's own hands; a generalized increase in crime, particularly collective juvenile delinquency, in the form of local gangs; and the bringing of the law and the legal system into contempt. In Latin America we are entering a new era, but new phenomena of violence are emerging in the increasing insecurity caused by common criminality, the illegal drug trade, '*guardias blancas*' and new forms of political repression.

Transitions with Fear

The history of the transitions towards the construction of political democracy that have been taking place over recent years is still, in many of the countries concerned, a chronicle of 'incomplete transitions'. Such incomplete transitions have been called 'transitions towards uncertainty', because the socio-political dynamics of the transition include no formal commitment to complete the construction of the political institutions satisfactorily within a particular period of time. It is not actually so much a problem of time, as of quality: of the vigour of the democratic forces and of those that accept change, for the most varied of reasons.

The 'residues' of the '*ancien régime*' are not as easily removed as the rubble of the Berlin Wall that many took away with them as souvenirs: museum reminders of cruelty. Authoritarianism has its roots in human behaviour; it finds its support in, and maintains itself through, the presence of living social forces, behaviour, repeated values and norms, a burden of prejudice, and the strength of 'common sense' that values violence in its physical and symbolic expressions.[10]

In Latin America, democratic transitions are, in some cases, restorations, and, in others, instaurations,[11] according to the degree to which society has been formed or the depth to which it has been penetrated by an authoritarian culture. The social sciences avoid defining authoritarianism, and thus such a definition is not easily arrived at. An authoritarian government is one of which no explanations can be demanded. A generic definition has been proposed, according to which a political regime is authoritarian when it admits no opposition and does not envisage a process for replacing itself with another. The authoritarian regime accords itself a condition of permanence *sine die* and at any price.[12]

What one associates immediately with experiences of political violence is impunity, since it is this that most clearly denies the legality and the majesty

of the judiciary in its task of defining responsibilities, judging and punishing. Processes of transition to democracy necessarily involve ways of bringing violence under the control of political power. When, on the other hand, power and violence are confused, the latter tends to become chaotic and uncontrollable. Its dynamics no longer reside in power, which was authority, but in force as an end in itself.

Many countries are experiencing real transitions with fear, an aspect that has not been duly considered in the abundant literature on the subject. Fear, when it ceases to be personal and subjective and envelops large areas of society, has unpredictable social and political effects on the behaviour of the group. The loss of fear occurs as a process of unsure self-identification, through a gradual recovery of confidence in public life. Each passing day provides new evidence that, in the process of construction of political democracy, the inheritance of authoritarian residues in the political system is something difficult to overcome.

To sum up, the experience of the past in Latin America is that it is possible to live with horror and despair. The trivialization of all this does not help democracy, although, as experience has shown, it is possible to vote with fear in the eyes and in the mind, but not to choose democratically, nor to participate politically. Only through respect for human rights, with tolerance towards each other, respect for the law, and the restored credibility of institutions, can a democratic society be constructed. Fear, however, ensconced in peoples' minds and hearts, will remain there for a long time.

The construction of electoral democracy faces the central dilemma of transitions from authoritarian societies, in which the relations between power and violence have not been resolved and still maintain a fundamental tension. It is necessary to distinguish between them analytically. In the classical theoretic tradition, still dominant, there is a tendency to identify them as two sides of the same coin. Power and violence are intimately related, but not identical. Power is rational and violence is legitimate. Weber speaks of legitimate violence as a monopoly of the state and, therefore, as an attribute that defines it. But in real life, doubts arise as to what kind of violence is illegitimate and what kind of violence is applied by a legitimate state. It might be easier to identify the quality of violence applied by an authoritarian state, a military dictatorship.

Democracy and Power without Violence

Political democracy begins, according to some authors, when the rules of the game of participation and electoral competition are accepted by all those taking part. It ceases to be a transition or a hybrid quality, when political participation is exercised by citizens having equal possibilities in the face of the institutions, or equal collective options. Consequently, the efficacy of democracy lies in limiting the use of force to exceptional situations. Demo-

cracy, in view of past experiences, implies the reduction of all the different forms of political violence.

The problem of our times is the inertia preventing the complete abandonment of the use of coercion and force, in regimes that are moving back towards legitimacy via electoral processes. It is at this stage that the weakness of the social regulations and their role in the tendency to resort to force as a normal source of power becomes patent. In most Latin American countries, there is no established political system, no community of citizens, and the political parties are only just beginning to organize themselves. It is at this point that appeals for the strengthening of civil society become important. The reference to civil society only means anything if one is thinking of social organizations as an expression of private interests that are returning to the public space, to organic participation in reference to the state; to the formation of a public opinion, that is, that can become political and thus influence the state.

Violations of human rights remain in Latin America, whether in endemic form or as residues of dictatorship. It is the question of democracies with violence and fear. A strictly formal distinction is usually made nowadays between the legal and the legitimate, something that is difficult to establish in contemporary history. There is an uncertainty at the frontiers of what is legal and what is legitimate, which defines the limits of state power, where violence seems to play a part in society's mode of functioning. These conditions are frequently found in the region and affect the democratic transition, offering the definition of a new type of democracy – hybrid democracy – which is an intermediate form on the road to the consolidation of democracy, and one that does not definitively rule out state violence. The violence applied in Latin America by authoritarian regimes, in their struggle against subversion, was permanent and total. It was, therefore, above all, an aggression against human rights and not only against politicians. This violence constituted, at certain moments, a kind of total violence. It is understandable, therefore, that in some societies, where such extremes were reached, the fundamental condition for political democracy is to guard zealously the unlimited respect for human rights.

The exercise of power in a democratic regime requires a distinction between a consolidated democratic state and one under construction, since adherence to existing legislation, the tendency to resort to violence and the confidence generated within society, are variable quantities. Modern society is organized in such a way as to limit the use of force and to achieve the aim of order and integration via forms of consensus, with the force of a political culture resting on a legitimating rationality. A democratic political culture feeds convictions and rests on the implicit recognition by citizens of the legitimacy of the existing order. In the context of this political culture, the citizen's behaviour reflects his or her appropriation of state legislation, giving credibility to public institutions, and rejecting behaviour aimed at

producing rupture. Above all – and against the Latin American tradition – this involves practising dialogue, negotiating. Agreement and obedience in a consolidated democracy rest on this kind of mechanism that at times comes close to a 'conformist attitude', but in the absence of fear.

The democratic order certainly depends on a belief in internalized legitimacy, which is not a personal, particular or individual virtue, but, rather, an attribute of citizenship, of the political system of the collectivity, and of democratic political culture. The use of force by the state, as a primary resource, breaks the mechanisms which encourage/promote the internalization of such beliefs, and credibility and confidence are adversely affected, tending to be replaced by opposition, suspicion and fear.

State violence and terrorism, which is its conspicuous form, constitute an objective limitation to political citizenship. Violence denies the law because it ignores or dilutes it, weakens the condition of the citizen, which we define as equality before the law, the institutions and collective options. Once state violence is applied, it destroys the legitimacy of its own bases. This is where power and violence become confused. Why? Because power administers (legitimate) violence and, on executing it, acquires responsibility for its results.

As a consequence of our previous history, the limits of legitimacy are being established in Latin American practice by the capacity of the judiciary to punish the guilty, and to put an end to impunity in the application of violence, because the latter becomes equivalent to crime. The inability to attribute responsibility with regard to the appalling results of the application of force is still a cause of damage in Argentina, Chile, El Salvador, Guatemala and Peru.

One of the problems of democracy as a process in construction is how to resolve adequately the legal, psycho-social and political aspects of the results of the atrocious, murderous past in Latin America. Scores of thousands of people were murdered, made to 'disappear' or tortured.[13] In some recent cases, there is a need to assign guilt, to fix responsibilities; and in other cases the need is to punish, to make an example of those responsible. In all cases, however, there is the majority will, never to let such things happen again: to turn the page, close the book on the past.

However, all this implies tensions for the consolidation of democracy. It is the tension between pardon and forgetting that affects citizens as an obsessive contradiction, since the numerous and pathological crimes perpetrated by those in power are still present in their effects. These crimes went far beyond what could be called 'repressive excesses'. No amnesty law or *ley de punto final*, setting a time limit on legal processes, could ever succeed in getting rid of the problem since, more even than the hatred, the fear remains. It is a long-term effect. At the same time, however, there is a real urgency to begin a new era, sweeping aside everything that feeds vendettas or grudges. Again, fear is fed by hatred and, together, these are elements that make the pacification of society difficult.

Violence applied (and in some cases still applied) by the state has generally been mediated by the armed forces, executors of the policies in which force (legitimate or not) appears as an instrument used to order society. It is for this reason that one of the four areas that many authors identify as points of conflict between the military and civil government (or the wishes of a significant section of society) is the establishment of the protection of human rights and the punishment that will, sooner or later, have to be applied for past violations.[14] These are decisive aspects for the consolidation of democracy. Is it necessary, then, to pursue a 'settlement of accounts' with those who murdered, tortured or caused the 'disappearance' of members of the civil population in years gone by? For many commentators, there is a clear contradiction between the collective, cultural parameters of forgiveness or forgetting, which is either an acceptance of the fact that crimes were committed and that no one will be tried for them, or that once committed there is no possibility of posterior trial. In either case, there is an appeal to an important political end, which is the consolidation of democracy. Judgment is renounced in order to avoid creating further wounds, new tensions that might endanger the fragile democratic institutions.

On the other hand, democracy needs what, in Anglo-Saxon culture, is called the rule of law, and the necessary guarantees that the law will take its due course. To secure the rule of law, and then not apply it, introduces serious weaknesses into the order and security of society. The civil authorities, in this case as in others, must be sufficiently enabled to judge those who have committed crimes. By 'enablement' I refer not to legal capacity, but rather to the political capacity to apply the law in any particular situation, no matter who is on trial.

Finally, it has not been possible to enumerate in detail the varying experiences of different countries in their attempts to punish those guilty. The most dramatic experience is that of Argentina, where President Alfonsín's democratic government tried to do so between 1984 and 1989, giving rise to at least three military rebellions. Admittedly, there was no unequivocal intention of a military coup, but these were clear expressions of military insubordination to civilian government.[15] Everything pointed to the acute problem of where does final responsibility lie for criminal acts committed in a structure of hierarchical obedience. The Ley de Obediencia Debida allowed legal processes to start against a score or so of officers, including the nine generals of the three military juntas, in December 1986; the same law laid down a deadline of sixty days for the presentation of claims, known as the Ley de Punto Final. Nearly 170 indictments were presented. In April 1987, however, the military resistance to civil power 'showed its teeth' and forced the government to make substantial changes in President Alfonsín's human rights policy. In October 1989, President Menem introduced an amnesty for practically all those implicated, including several guerrilla leaders. On that occasion, as at the time of the military revolts of 1987–88, there were massive acts of protest

against the impunity accorded to the military, which revealed the problem once again to be a question that society itself must resolve as a precondition for the achievement of new democratic dimensions. The political incapacity to punish guilty people, constitutes a serious limit on civil power, the democratic, constitutional power. There was, nevertheless, a Comissión de la Verdad, headed by the writer Ernesto Sábato, which published a wonderful document, *Nunca más*, that certainly represents a political and moral victory.

The struggle for human rights, in societies in the process of democratization, has been undergone in many societies. Another example is Uruguay, where the subject of prosecuting the violators of human rights was also raised. A Gallup poll carried out in the city of Montevideo (85 per cent of respondents were in favour of bringing offenders to trial) convinced the parties and the army of the necessity to introduce an immediate general amnesty law in order to overcome or avoid the crisis. The Congress found itself struggling with a law that would make certain offences indictable and exonerate others, which satisfied no one. The bill was submitted to referendum in April 1989, and those in favour of an amnesty won by 57 to 43 per cent in the country as a whole (but with 55 per cent of respondents in Montevideo in favour of judging the military). Throughout this process, there were clear manifestations of rebellion by the military and a rejection of the social and political basis of the amnesty, i.e. the previous recognition of guilt.

In Chile, in 1991, the democratic government of Patricio Aylwin appointed a commission entitled the Comissión de la Verdad y Reconciliación. It was also known as the Rettig Commission, after the lawyer who presided over it, and was made up of eight prestigious public figures of different political persuasions. It presented a report signalling clear violations of human rights, without giving names. Dates, other details and evidence were included in the report so that individuals are left free to act as they see fit. The army has maintained a permanent opposition. Nevertheless, with the eventual arrest of General Menéndez, in September 1995, a more than symbolic punishment was finally achieved. The incidents accompanying his trial and sentencing are another example of the quality of military legal immunity in Latin America.

Finally, in El Salvador, after the signing of the peace accords in the Palace of Chapultepec, Mexico, in January 1991, a Comissión de la Verdad was set up – provided for in the accords – including both Salvadorean and foreign members. The commission's published report was drawn up after receiving and investigating 18,000 denunciations, of which some 20 per cent could be proved. The document forms an indictment, giving details of dates and names, of the country's armed forces; 10 per cent of the violations of human rights were committed by guerrilla forces, also mentioned in the report.

Notes and References

1. Reinares, 'Conflicto social', p. 105.

2. Although the literature on these matters is extensive, I shall mention here some of the most comprehensive, such as Castañeda, *Utopía desarmada* and Wickham-Crowley, *Guerrillas and Revolution.*

3. It is arguable whether we can refer to 'governability' in the context of authoritarian regimes, given their lack of legitimacy. What should one then call the type of order achieved by military dictatorships? See Linz, *Quiebra*, pp. 45ff., and Alcántara, *Gobernabilidad*, pp. 136ff.

4. There have been numerous attempts at definition that turn around the notion of force applied on a human environment in a voluntary and conscious way by agents of the state or its representatives. Giddens refers extensively to the use of different modes of force in the art of government; see Giddens, *Nation-State and Violence.*

5. Garretón, 'Fear in military regimes', p. 14.

6. The situation of Colombia is debatable. This has for many years been the most violent country in Latin America. Violence arises from within a civil society that is armed on an unusual scale and where force has a very private dimension. The state adds its own contribution to an increasing degree, to the point where there is ever more room for doubt whether this is really a democratic society, despite the existence of regular elections, or whether it is, rather, a strange case of functional cohabitation between democracy and violence. See Wilde, *Conversaciones*, pp. 40ff.; Pécaut, *Orden y violencia.* See also Chapter 7 in this volume.

7. I refer to the rites and acts of revenge, promises of vengeance, imagined vendettas and the like, that may occur in cultures of violence, and which it is not possible to analyse here.

8. O'Donnell, 'El dilema'.

9. The mechanisms for producing fear are manifold and well-known: clear threats, surveillance, systematic house searches, checks on vehicles and persons in public places, always accompanied by force, destruction (outrages that are apparently a deliberate part of the operation), arrests without warrants (that immediately lead to torture), assassinations in the public street and, even better, in broad daylight, and finally the abduction that results in 'disappearance'.

10. President General Lucas García of Guatemala, when praising the aggressiveness of 'strong' government, described democracy contemptuously as 'feminine'. The *macho* vision in politics leads precisely to dictatorship and fear.

11. Linz, *Quiebra.*

12. The type of authoritarianism that entails impunity and corruption is inevitably associated with violence, these being characteristic not only of the formal institutions of coercion but also of the civilian institutions of the state. See Kalmanoviecki, 'Police', pp. 47ff.

13. See Zagorski, *Democracy vs. National Security*, p. 99, for figures on the numbers of victims of state repression, as well as for the size of the security forces involved, in Argentina, Brazil, Chile, Peru and Uruguay. Figures listed on number of victims of murder or 'disappearance' vary from 240 in Uruguay and 250 in Brazil to 2,000/8,000 in Chile, 3,000/8,000 in Peru and 9,000/30,000 in Argentina.It should be noted, however, that these figures, given by Zagorski, reflect adequately neither the quality nor the extent of the violence dealt out in these countries, since those responsible for the sources (Amnesty International and the UN Human Rights Commission) have been careful only to register the cases that can be considered duly proved violations of human rights.

14. The other areas are: counter-insurgency and internal security; military reform; and reform of the state. Cf. Zagorski, *Democracy vs. National Security*, p. 97.

15. Ibid., pp. 101–9.

Bibliography

Adams, Richard N., *Crucifixion by Power. Essays on the Guatemalan National Social Structure, 1944–1966.* Austin: University of Texas Press, 1970.

Agosti, Orlando Ramón, *Discursos del Comandante en Jefe de la Fuerza Aerea Argentina Brigadier General Orlando Ramón Agosti.* Author's edition, 1978.

Aguilera, Gabriel, *El fusil y el olivo. La cuestión militar en Centroamérica.* San José: FLACSO/DEI, 1989.

— *Las propuestas para la paz.* Guatemala: FLACSO (Debate 20), 1993.

Aguilera, Gabriel and Karen Ponciano, *El espejo sin reflejo. La negociación de paz en 1993.* Guatemala: FLACSO (Debate 23), 1994.

Aguilera, Gabriel et al., *Dialectica del terror en Guatemala.* San José: EDUCA, 1981.

— *Reconversión militar. Elementos para su comprensión.* Guatemala: FLACSO (Debate 19), 1993.

— *Los problemas de la democracia.* Guatemala: FLACSO, 1993.

— *Reconversión militar en América Latina.* Guatemala: FLACSO, 1994.

Aguirre Beltrán, Gonzalo, *Regiones de refugio.* Mexico: Secretaria de Educación Pública, Instituto Nacional Indigenista, 1967.

Alcántara, Manuel, *Gobernabilidad, Crisis y cambio.* Madrid: Centro de Estudios Constitucionales, 1994.

Alcántara, Manuel and Ismael Crespo (eds), *Los límites de la consolidación democrática en América Latina.* Salamanca: Ediciones Universidad de Salamanca, 1995.

Allamand, Andres, *La centroderecha del futuro.* Santiago: Editorial Los Andes, 1993.

Álvarez, Fernando, 'Peasant movements in Chiapas', *Bulletin of Latin American Research* 7(2), 1988, pp. 277–98.

Alves, Maria Helena Moreira, *Estado e oposição no Brasil, 1964–1984.* Petrópolis, RJ: Vozes, 1985.

Amnesty International, *Mexico. Human Rights in Rural Areas. Exchange of Documents with the Mexican Government on Human Rights Violations in Oaxaca and Chiapas.* London: Amnesty International, 1986.

Andrade, Regis de Castro, 'Brazil: the military in politics', *Bulletin of the Society for Latin American Studies* 26, 1977, pp. 63–82.

Anfuso, Joseph and David Sczepanski, *Efrain Rios Montt, Servant or Dictator? The Real Story of Guatemala's Controversial Born-again President.* Ventura: Vision House, 1983.

Angell, Alan, 'Chile since 1958', in Leslie Bethell (ed.), *Chile since Independence.* Cambridge: Cambridge University Press, 1993, pp. 129–202.

— 'Incorporating the left in democratic politics', in Jorge I. Domínguez and Abraham F.

Lowenthal (eds), *Constructing Democratic Governance – Themes and Issues*. Baltimore: Johns Hopkins University Press, 1996, pp. 3–25.

Ansión, Juan, 'Violencia y cultura en el Perú', in Felipe MacGregor, José Luis Rosillón and Marcial Rubio (eds), *Siete ensayos sobre la violencia en el Perú*. Lima: APEP/Friedrich Ebert, 1985, pp. 59–78.

Archdiocese de São Paulo, *Torture in Brazil*. New York: Vintage Books, 1986.

Arendt, Hannah, *The Origins of Totalitarianism*. Cleveland, OH: Meridian Books, 1968 [1951].

Arrate, Jorge, *La fuerza democrática de la idea socialista*. Barcelona: Ediciones Documentas, 1985.

Arriagada, Genaro, *Pinochet: The Politics of Power*. London: Unwin Hyman, 1988.

Ashby, Joe C., *Organized Labour and the Mexican Revolution Under Lázaro Cárdenas*. Chapel Hill: University of North Carolina Press, 1963.

Atehortua Cruz, Adolfo Leon, *El poder y la sangre, las Historias de Trujillo, Valle*. Cali: Gobernacion del Valle del Cauca, 1996.

Aubry, Andrés, 'La "lenta acumulación de fuerzas" del movimiento zapatista', Paper IN-AREMAC, San Cristóbal de las Casas, 1994.

(Autonomedia), *¡Zapatistas! Documents of the New Mexican Revolution (December 31, 1993–June 12, 1994)*. New York: Autonomedia 1994.

Avila Palafox, Ricardo, *Revolución en el estado de México?* Mexico: INAH, 1988.

Aziz, Alberto, 'San Luis Potosí: la repetición de un agravio', *Eslabones. Revista Semestral de Estudios Regionales* 3, 1992, pp. 36–52.

Balibar, Etiènne, 'Violence: idéalité et cruauté', in F. Héretier (ed.), *De la violence*. Paris: Editions Odile Jacob, 1996, pp. 55–88.

Baloyra, Enrique A., 'Democratic transitions in comparative perspective', in Enrique A. Baloyra (ed.), *Comparing New Democracies; Transition and Consolidation in Mediterranean Europe and the Southern Cone*. Boulder, CO, and London: Westview Press, 1987, pp. 9–52.

Baloyra, Enrique A. and James A. Morris (eds), *Conflict and Change in Cuba*. Albuquerque: University of New Mexico Press, 1993.

Bantjes, Adrian A., *Politics, Class and Culture in Postrevolutionary Mexico: Cardenismo and Sonora, 1929–40*. Austin: University of Texas Press, 1991.

Barber, William F. and Neale Ronning, *Internal Security and Military Power. Counterinsurgency and Civic Action in Latin America*. Ohio: Ohio State University Press for the Mershon Center for Education in National Security, 1966.

Barros Horcasitas, José Luis et al. (eds), *Transición a la democracia y reforma del estado en México*. Mexico: FLACSO/Miguel Angel Porrúa/Universidad de Guadalajara, 1991.

Barry, Tom, *Guatemala: The Politics of Counterinsurgency*. Albuquerque: InterHemispheric Education Resource Center, 1986.

Bartra, Roger, *La jaula de la melancolía. Identidad y metamorfosis del Mexicano*. México: Grijalbo, 1987.

— *Oficio Mexicano*. México: Grijalbo, 1993.

Basombrío Iglesias, Carlos, 'La estrategia del chino: supestos, instrumentos, logros y límites', *IDEELE* 5(59–60), 1993, pp. 20–7.

Baud, Michiel,'Latin American histories', *European Review of Latin American and Caribbean Studies* 57, 1994, pp. 89–95.

Baud, Michiel, Kees Koonings, Gert Oostindie, Arij Ouweneel and Patricio Silva, *Etnicidad como estrategia en América Latina y el Caribe*. Quito: Abya-Yala, 1996.

Bauman, Zygmunt, 'Modernity and ambivalence', in Mike Featherstone (ed.), *Global Culture: Nationalism, Globalization, and Modernity*. London: Sage, 1990, pp. 143–69.

Bayer, Osvaldo, 'Pequeño recordatório para un país sin memória', in Saúl Sosnowski (ed.), *Represión y reconstrucción de una cultura: el caso Argentino*. Buenos Aires: EUDEBA, 1988, pp. 203–27.

Bejarano, J. A., 'Democracia, conflicto y eficiencia económica', in J. A. Bejarano (ed.), *Construir la paz*. Bogota: Presidencia de la Republica, 1990, pp. 143–77.

Bengelsdorf, Carollee, *The Problem of Democracy: Between Vision and Reality*. New York: Oxford University Press, 1994.

Benjamin, Thomas, *A Rich Land, A Poor People. Politics and Society in Modern Chiapas*. Albuquerque: University of New Mexico Press, 1989.

Berg, Ronald, 'Peasant Response to Shining Path in Andahuyalas', in David Scott Palmer (ed.), *Shining Path of Peru*. New York: St Martin's Press, 1992.

Bétancourt, Darío and Martha L. García, *Contrabandistas, marimberos y mafiosos. Historia social de la Mafia Colombiana (1965–1992)*. Bogotá: T/M Editores, 1994.

— 'Colombie: les mafias de la drogue.' *Problèmes d'Amérique Latine* 18, 1995, pp. 73–82.

Bizberg, Ilán, 'La crisis del corporativismo mexicano', *Foro Internacional* 120, 1990, pp. 695–735.

— 'El régimen político mexicano ante la modernización', *Revista Occidental* 7(2), 1990, pp. 115–43.

— 'Modernization and corporatism in government-labour relations', in Neil Harvey (ed.), *Mexico, Dilemmas of Transition*. London: Institute of Latin American Studies/British Academic Press, 1993, pp. 299–317.

Blaffer, Sarah C., *The Black-man of Zinacantán. A Central American Legend*. Austin: University of Texas Press, 1972.

Bonasso, Miguel, *Recuerdo de la muerte*. Mexico: Ediciones Era, 1984.

Bonfil Batalla, Guillermo, *Utopía y revolución. El pensamiento político contemporáneo de los indios en América Latina*. Mexico: Nueva Imagen, 1981.

— *México profundo. Una civilización negada*. México: CyA y Grijalbo, 1990.

— *Pensar nuestra cultura. Ensayos*, Mexico: Alianza, 1991.

Borzutzky, Silvia and Jorge Pérez-López, 'The impact of the collapse of communism and the Cuban crisis on the South American left', in Carmelo Mesa-Lago (ed.), *Cuba after the Cold War*. Pittsburgh: University of Pittsburgh Press, 1993, pp. 291–322.

Bosworth, Barry P., Rudiger Dornbusch and Raúl Laban (eds), *The Chilean Economy: Policy Lessons and Challenges*. Washington: Brookings Institution, 1994.

Bot, Yvon le, *La guerre en terre Maya. Communauté, violence et modernité au Guatemala*. Paris: Editions Karthala, 1992 .

Botero, F., *Urabá: Colonización, violencia y crisis del estado*. Medellín: Ed. Universidad de Antioquia, 1991.

Brading, D.A., *Prophecy and Myth in Mexican History*. Cambridge: Cambridge University Press, 1984.

— (ed.), *Caudillo and Peasant in the Mexican Revolution*. Cambridge: Cambridge University Press, 1980.

Brewster, Keith, 'Caciquismo in rural Mexico during the 1920s: the case of Gabriel Barrios', *Journal of Latin American Studies* 28(1), 1996, pp. 105–28.

Bricker, Victoria R., *The Indian Christ, the Indian King. The Historical Substrate of Maya Myth and Ritual*. Austin: University of Texas Press, 1981.

Brinton, Daniel G., *Nagualism. A Study in Native American Folklore and History*. Philadelphia: MacCalla, 1894.

Brock, Lisa and Otis Cunningham, 'Race and the Cuban revolution: a critique of Carlos Moore's *Castro, the Blacks, and Africa*', *Cuban Studies* 21, 1991, pp. 171–85.

Bruneau, Thomas, 'Brazil's political transition', in John Higley and Richard Guenther (eds), *Elites and Democratic Consolidation in Latin America and Southern Europe*. Cambridge: Cambridge University Press, 1992, pp. 257–81.

Brunner, José Joaquín, 'La concepción autoritaria del mundo', *Revista Mexicana de Sociología* 42(3), 1980, pp. 991–1031.

— 'La cultura política del autoritarismo', *Revista Mexicana de Sociología* 44(2), 1982, pp. 559–75.

Burga, Manuel and Alberto Flores, *República aristocrática: Oligarquía, aprismo y comunismo en el Perú, 1895–1932*. Lima: Rikchay, 1979 .

Buve, Raymond, 'Peasant movements, caudillos and land reform during the Revolution (1910–1917) in Tlaxcala, Mexico', *Boletin de Estudios Latinoamericanos y del Caribe* 18, 1975, pp. 7–28.

— '¡Ir a la bola! De participatie van kleine boeren in de Mexicaanse Revolutie', in Arij Ouweneel (ed.), *Campesinos. Kleine boeren in Latijns Amerika, vanaf 1520*. Amsterdam: Thela, 1993, pp. 233–54.

Calvert, Peter, *Guatemala. A Nation in Turmoil*. Boulder, CO: Westview Press, 1985.

Camacho, M., *Cambio sin ruptura*. Mexico: Alianza, 1994.

Camín, Aguilar, *Morir en el golfo*. Mexico: Océano, 1987.

Camín, Aquilar, H., 'La obligaciòn del mundo', *NEXOS* 172, April 1992, pp. 47–53.

Camp, Roderic A., *Memórias de un político Mexicano*. Mexico: Fondo de Cultura Económica, 1989.

Campello de Souza, Maria do Carmo, 'The Brazilian "New Republic": under the "sword of Damocles"', in Alfred Stepan (ed.), *Democratizing Brazil: Problems of Transition and Consolidation*. New York and Oxford: Oxford University Press, 1989, pp. 351–94.

— 'The contemporary faces of the Brazilian rights: an interpretation of style and substance', in Douglas A. Chalmers, Maria do Carmo Campello de Souza and Atilio A. Boron (eds), *The Right and Democracy in Latin America*. New York and London: Praeger, 1992, pp. 99–127.

Campero, Guillermo, *Los Gremios Empresariales en el período 1970–1981: Comportamiento Socio-político y orientaciones ideológicas*. Santiago: ILET, 1984.

— 'Entrepreneurs under the military regime', in Paul W. Drake and Iván Jaksic (eds), *The Struggle for Democracy in Chile, 1982–1990*. Lincoln and London: University of Nebraska Press, 1991, pp. 128–58.

Camú Urzúa, Guido and Dauno Tótoro Taulis, *EZLN: El ejército que salió de la selva. La Historia del EZLN contado por ellos mismos*. Mexico: Planeta, 1994.

Cancian, Frank, *The Decline of Community in Zinacantán. Economy, Public Life, and Social Stratification, 1960–1987*. Stanford: Stanford University Press, 1992.

Cansino, César, *Construir la democracia. Límites y perspectivas de la transición en México*. Mexico: Miguel Angel Porrúa, 1995.

Cardoso, Fernando Henrique, 'O papel dos empresários no processo de transição: o caso brasileiro', *Dados* 26(1), 1983, pp. 9–27.

Carmack, Robert M., 'El impacto de la Revolución y la reforma en las culturas indígenas

de los Altos: una reseña crítica de obras recientes', *Mesoamérica* 10(18), 1989, pp. 401–25.

— (ed.), *Harvest of Violence. Guatemala's Indians in the Counterinsurgency War*. Norman: University of Oklahoma Press, 1988.

Carmagnani, Marcello, *Federalismos latinoamericanos: México, Brasil, Argentina*. Mexico: FCE/El Colegio de México, 1993.

Castañeda, Jorge G., *La utopía desarmada*. Mexico: Diana, 1994.

Catanzaro, R., 'La mafia et les recherches sur la mafia en Italie', *Déviance et Société* 19(2), 1995, pp. 201–13.

Cava, Ralph della, 'The "people's church, the Vatican, and *Abertura*"', in Alfred Stepan (ed.), *Democratizing Brazil*. Oxford: Oxford University Press, 1989, pp. 143–69.

Cavarozzi, Marcelo and Manuel Antonio Garretón (eds), *Muerte y resurrección: Los partidos políticos en el autoritarismo y las transiciones del Cono Sur*. Santiago: FLACSO, 1989.

César Lopez, Julio, 'El EPR reta al gobierno', *Proceso* 1034, 1996, pp. 6–10.

Child, John, 'Geopolitical thinking in Latin America', *Latin American Research Review* 14(2), 1979, pp. 89–111.

Cisneros, Isidro H., 'Los modelos de la transición política: México en la disyuntiva de la innovación o la conservación', in Alberto Aziz Nassif (ed.), *México: una agenda para fin de siglo*. Mexico: La Jornada Ediciones/CIICH, 1996, pp. 67–91.

CJE (Comando en Jefe del Ejército), *El ejército de hoy*. Buenos Aires: Círculo Militar, Biblioteca del Oficial, 1978.

Clapham, Christopher, 'Clientelism and the state', in Cristopher Clapham (ed.), *Private Patronage and Public Power*. London: Francis Pinter, 1982, pp. 148–64.

Cobb, Richard, *The Police and the People: French Popular Protest 1789–1820*. Oxford: Clarendon Press, 1972.

Collier, David (ed.), *The New Authoritarianism in Latin America*. Princeton, NJ: Princeton University Press, 1979.

Collier, George A., *Fields of the Tzotzil. The Ecological Bases of Tradition in Highland Chiapas*. Austin: University of Texas Press, 1975.

— 'Peasant politics and the Mexican state: indigenous compliance in highland Chiapas', *Mexican Studies/Estudios Mexicanos* 3(1), 1987, pp. 71–98.

— 'Estratificación indígena y cambio cultural en Zinacantán, 1950–1987', *Mesoamérica* 10(18), 1989, pp. 428–40.

— 'Background of the rebellion in Chiapas', Paper for the LASA 16th International Conference, Atlanta, 1991.

— 'Roots of the rebellion in Chiapas', *Cultural Survival Quarterly* 18(1), 1994, pp. 14–18.

— *Basta! Land and the Zapatista Rebellion in Chiapas*. Oakland, CA: Institute for Food and Development Policy, 1994.

Collier, Ruth Berins and David Collier, *Shaping the Political Arena*. Princeton, NJ: Princeton University Press, 1991.

Comisión de Estudios sobre la Violencia, *Colombia, violencia y democracia*. Bogotá: Universidad Nacional de Colombia, 1987.

Constable, Pamela and Arturo Valenzuela, *A Nation of Enemies: Chile under Pinochet*. New York and London: W. W. Norton, 1991.

Cook, Scott, 'Inflation and rural livelihood in a Mexican province: an exploratory analysis', *Mexican Studies/Estudios Mexicanos* 4(1), 1988, pp. 55–77.

Cornelius, Wayne A., 'Overview: the dynamics of political change in Mexico', in Wayne A. Cornelius et al. (eds), *Mexico's Alternative Political Futures*. San Diego: Center for US–Mexican Studies, 1989, pp. 1–51.

Cornelius, Wayne A. et al. (eds), *Mexico's Alternative Political Futures*. San Diego: Center for US–Mexican Studies, 1989.

Corrêa Leite Cardoso, Ruth, 'Os movimentos populares no contexto da consolidação da democracia', in Fábio Wanderley Reis and Guillermo O'Donnell (eds), *A Democracia no Brasil: Dilemas e perspectivas*. São Paulo: Vertice (Grande Brasil, Veredas 8), 1988, pp. 368–82.

Corro, Salvador, 'Operativos militares en casi todo el país', *Proceso* 1036, 1996, pp. 7–13.

Cortázar, René, *Política laboral en el Chile democrático: Avances y desafíos en los noventa*. Santiago: Ediciones Dolen, 1993.

Costa, Sílvio, *Tendências e centrais sindicais. O movimento sindical Brasileiro de 1978 a 1994*. Goiânia (GO): Editora Anita Garibaldi and Editora da Universidade Católica de Goiás, 1995.

Couto e Silva, Golbery do, *Geopolítica do Brasil*. Rio de Janeiro: Editorial José Olympio, 1967.

Craske, Nikki, *Corporatism Revisited: Salinas and the Reform of the Popular Sector*. London: University of London, 1994.

— 'Dismantling or retrenchment? Salinas and corporatism', in Rob Aitken et al. (eds), *Dismantling the Mexican State?* London: Macmillan, 1996, pp. 78–91.

Crassweller, Robert D., *Perón and the Enigmas of Argentina*. New York: W. W. Norton, 1987.

D'Araujo, Maria Celina and Celso Castro (eds), *Ernesto Geisel*. Rio de Janeiro: Editora Fundação Getúlio Vargas, 1997.

D'Araujo, Maria Celina, Gláucio Ary Dillon Soares and Celso Castro (eds), *Visões do golpe: A memória militar sobre 1964*. Rio de Janeiro: Relume Dumará, 1994.

— (eds), *Os anos de chumbo: A memória militar sobre a repressão*. Rio de Janeiro: Relume Dumará, 1994.

— (eds), *A volta aos quartéis: A memória militar sobre a abertura*. Rio de Janeiro: Relume Dumará, 1995.

DaMatta, Roberto, *Carnavais, malandros e heróis. Para uma sociologia do dilema Brasileiro*. Rio de Janeiro: Zahar, 1979.

— *A Casa e a Rua. Espaço, cidadania, mulher e morte no Brasil*. Rio de Janeiro: Editora Guanabara, 1987.

DaMatta, Roberto et al., *Brasileiro: Cidadão?* São Paulo: Cultura Editores Associados, 1992.

Danien, E. C. and R. J. Sharer (eds), *New Theories of the Ancient Maya*. Philadelphia: University of Pennsylvania, 1992.

Degregori, Carlos Iván, *Ayacucho 1969–1979. El Surgimiento de Sendero Luminoso*. Lima: IEP, 1990.

— *Qué difícil es ser Dios. Ideología y violencia política en Sendero Luminoso*. Lima: IEP/El Zorro de Abajo Ediciones, 1990.

— *La última tentación del presidente Gonzalo y otros escritos sobre el auge y colapso de Sendero Luminoso*. Lima: IEP, 1996.

Degregori, Carlos Iván and Carlos Rivera, *Peru 1980–1990. Fuerzas armadas, subversión y democracia: Redefiniciones del papel militar en un contexto de violencia subversiva y colapso del régimen democrático*. Lima: IEP, 1993.

Delli Sante, Angela. *Nightmare or Reality? Guatemala in the 1980s*. Amsterdam: Thela, 1996.

Demélas, M. D., *L'Invention politique, Bolivie, Equateur, Pérou au XIXè siecle*. Paris: ERC, 1992.

Demmers, Jolle, *Friends and Bitter Enemies. Politics and Neoliberal Reform in Yukatán, Mexico*. Amsterdam: Thela, 1998.

Derrida, Jacques, *Positions*. Chicago: University of Chicago Press, 1981.

— *Disseminations*. London: Athlone Press, 1981.

Deverre, Christian, *Transformations et crises agraries au Mexique, le cas de Chiapas*, Paris: Le Sycomore, 1978.

Diamond, Larry, Juan Linz and Seymour Martin Lipset (eds), *Democracy in Developing Countries: Latin America* (vol. 4). Boulder, CO, and London: Lynne Rienner and Adamantine Press, 1989.

Díaz Bessone, Ramón Genaro, *Guerra revolucionaria en la Argentina, 1959-1978*. Buenos Aires: Círculo Militar, Biblioteca del Oficial, 1988.

Dimenstein, Gilberto and Josias De Souza, *A História real. Trama de uma sucessão*. São Paulo: Editora Ática, 1994.

Diniz, Eli, 'O empresariado e a nova conjuntura', in Hélgio Trindade (ed.), *Brazil em perspectiva: Dilemas da abertura política*. Porto Alegre: Sulina, 1982, pp. 105-20.

— 'Empresariado e transição política no Brasil: problemas e perspectivas', in David Fleischer (ed.), *Da distensão à abertura: As eleições de 1982*. Brasília: Editora Universidade de Brasília, 1988, pp. 159-84.

Diniz, Eli, Renato Boschi and Renato Lessa, *Modernizaçao e consolidação democrática no Brasil: Dilemas da Nova República*. São Paulo: Vertice (Grande Brasil, Veredas 11), 1989.

Dix, 'Populism: authoritarian and democratic', *Latin American Research Review* 20(2), 1985, pp. 29-52.

Domínguez, Jorge I., *Cuba: Order and Revolution*. Cambridge, MA: Harvard University Press, 1978.

— 'Secrets of Castro's staying power', *Foreign Affairs* 72(2), 1993, pp. 97-107.

Domínguez, Jorge I. and Abraham F. Lowenthal (eds), *Constructing Democratic Governance: Mexico, Central America, and the Caribbean in the 1990s*. Baltimore and London: Johns Hopkins University Press, 1996.

— (eds), *Constructing Democratic Governance: South America in the 1990s*. Baltimore and London: Johns Hopkins University Press, 1996.

— (eds), *Constructing Democratic Governance: Themes and Issues*. Baltimore and London: Johns Hopkins University Press, 1996.

Dooner, Patricio, *Periodismo y política: La prensa de derecha e izquierda, 1970-1973*. Santiago: Editorial Andante, 1989.

Dopico Black, Georgina, 'The limits of expression: intellectual freedom in postrevolutionary Cuba', *Cuban Studies* 19, 1989, pp. 107-42.

Douglas, Mary, *Purity and Danger: An Analysis of Concepts of Pollution and Taboo*. London: Penguin, 1970.

Drake, Paul W. and Ivan Jaksić (eds), *The Struggle for Democracy in Chile, 1982-1990*. Lincoln and London: University of Nebraska Press, 1990.

Dreifuss, Rene, *1964: A conquista do estado. Ação política, poder e golpe de classe*. Petrópolis (RJ): Vozes, 1981.

Dresser, Denise, 'Bringing the poor back in: national solidarity as a strategy of regime legitimation', in Wayne A. Cornelius, Ann L. Craig and Jonathan Fox (eds), *Transforming State–Society Relations in Mexico*. San Diego: Center for US–Mexican Studies, 1994, pp. 212-33.

Dulles, J. W. F., *Yesterday in Mexico: A Chronicle of the Revolution.* Austin: University of Texas Press, 1961.

Earle, Duncan, 'Indigenous identity at the margin. Zapatismo and nationalism', *Cultural Survival Quarterly* 18(1), 1994, pp. 26–30.

Echandia, C., 'Colombie: dimensions économiques de la violence et de la criminalité', *Problèmes de l'Amérique Latine* 16, 1995, pp. 78–89.

Eckstein, Susan Eva, *Back from the Future: Cuba under Castro.* Princeton, NJ: Princeton University Press, 1994.

Edmonson, Munro, 'The Mayan faith', in Gary Gossen (ed.), *South and Meso-American Native Spirituality from the Cult of the Feathered Serpent to the Theology of Liberation.* New York: Crossroad, 1993, pp. 65–85.

Edwards, Sebastián and Alejandra Cox-Edwards, *Monetarism and Liberalization: The Chilean Experiment.* Cambridge, MA: Ballinger, 1987.

FAMUS, *Operación Independencia.* Buenos Aires: FAMUS, 1988.

Fauriol, Georges A. and Eva Loser, *Guatemala's Political Puzzle.* New Brunswick, NJ: Transaction Books, 1988.

Feder, Ernest, *The Rape of the Peasantry. Latin America's Landholding System.* New York: Anchor, 1971.

Fernández, Damián J., 'Youth in Cuba: resistance and accommodation', in Enrique A. Baloyra and James Morris (eds), *Conflict and Change in Cuba.* Albuquerque: University of New Mexico Press, 1993, pp. 189–211.

Figueiredo, Eurico de Lima (ed.), *Os militares e a revolução de 30.* Rio de Janeiro: Paz e Terra, 1979.

Fisher, Lilian Estelle, *The Last Inca Revolt, 1780–1783.* Norman: University of Oklahoma Press, 1966.

Fleischer, David (ed.), *Da distensão à abertura: As eleições de 1982.* Brasília: Editora Universidade de Brasília, 1988.

Flores Galindo, Alberto. *Buscando un Inca. Identidad y utopía en los Andes.* Lima: Editorial Horizonte, 1988.

Flores Olea, Víctor, 'El país ante la rebelión chiapaneca', *La Jornada Semanal* 246, 1994, pp. 23–30.

Flynn, Peter, 'Class, clientelism, and coercion: some mechanisms of internal dependency and control', Paper for the CEDLA workshop on Dependency in Latin America, Amsterdam, 1973.

Fogel, Jean-François and Bertrand Rosenthal, *Fin de siècle à La Havane. Les secrets du pouvoir Cubain.* Paris: Editions du Seuil, 1993.

Foster, George M., *Tzintzuntzán. Mexican Peasants in a Changing World.* Boston: Little Brown, 1967.

Foweraker, Joe, *Struggle for Land.* Cambridge: Cambridge University Press (Cambridge Latin American Studies 39), 1981.

Foweraker, Joe and Ann Craig, *Popular Movements and Political Change in Mexico.* Boulder, CO: Lynne Rienner, 1990.

Fox, Jonathan, 'The difficult transition from clientelism to citizenship: lessons from Mexico.' *World Politics* 46(2), 1994, pp. 151–84.

Foxley, Alejandro, *Para una democracia estable: Economía y política.* Santiago: CE PLAN, 1985.

— *Chile y su futuro: Un país posible.* Santiago: CEPLAN, 1987.

— *Economía política de la transición: El camino del dialogo*. Santiago: Ediciones Dolmen, 1993.

Frazer, James G., *The Golden Bough: A Study in Magic and Religion*. (vol.1; abridged) New York: Macmillan, 1960 [1890].

Freidel, D., L. Schele and J. Parker, *Maya Cosmos. Three Thousand Years on the Shaman's Path*. New York: William Morrow, 1993.

Freud, Sigmund, 'The uncanny', in *Standard Edition*, vol. 17. London: Hogarth Press, 1981 [1919], pp. 219–52.

Friedrich, Paul, 'The legitimacy of a cacique', in M. J. Swartz (ed.), *Local Level Politics. Social and Cultural Perspectives*. Chicago: Aldine, 1968.

— *The Princes of Naranja: An Essay in Anthrohistorical Method*. Austin: University of Texas Press, 1986.

Fuente, Alejandro de la, 'Race and inequality in Cuba, 1899–1981', *Journal of Contemporary History* 30, 1995, pp. 131–68.

Gabbert, Wolfgang, 'Ethnicity, identity, and social conflict', Paper for the CEDLA/CERLAC Joint Workshop, Amsterdam, 1991 .

Gálvez, Modesto, 'El derecho en el campesinado andino del Perú', in Diego García Sayan (ed.), *Derechos humanos y servicios legales en el campo*. Lima: Comisión Andina de Juristas/Comisión Internacional de Juristas, 1987.

Gambetta, D., *The Sicilian Mafia. The Business of Private Protection*. Cambridge, MA: Harvard University Press, 1993.

García, C.I., *Urabá, región, actores y conflicto 1960–1990*. Bogota: CEREC, 1996.

García, Alejandro, *Hijos de la violencia*. Madrid: Los Libros de Catarata, 1996.

García de León, Antonio, *Resistencia y utopía. Memorial de agravios y crónicas de revueltas y profecías acaecidas en la Provincia de Chiapas durante los últimos quinientos años de su historia*, (2 vols), Mexico: Era, 1985.

Garma Navarro, Carlos, 'Liderazgo protestante en una lucha campesina en México', *América Indígena* 44(1), 1984, pp. 127–41.

Garretón, Manuel Antonio, 'The political evolution of the Chilean military regime and problems in the transition to democracy', in Guillermo O'Donnell, Philippe C. Schmitter and Lawrence Whitehead (eds), *Transitions from Authoritarian Rule: Latin America*. Baltimore: Johns Hopkins University Press, 1986, pp. 95–122.

— 'Fear in military regimes: an overview', in Juan F. Corradi, Patricia Weiss Fagen and Manuel Antonio Garretón (eds), *Fear at the Edge. State Terror and Resistance in Latin America*. Berkeley: University of California Press, 1992, pp. 13–25.

Garretón, Manuel Antonio and Tomás Moulian, *La Unidad Popular y el conflicto político en Chile*. Santiago: CESOC-LOM, 1993.

Garza Toledo, Enrique de la, 'The restructuring of state–labour relations in Mexico', in Maria Lorena Cook et al. (eds), *The Politics of Economic Restructuring. State–Society Relations and Regime Change in Mexico*. San Diego: Center for US–Mexican Studies, 1994, pp. 195–217.

Gasparini, Juan, *Montoneros: Final de cuentas*. Buenos Aires: Puntosur, 1988.

Giddens, Anthony, *The Nation-State and Violence*. Cambridge: Polity Press, 1985.

Gilbert, M. Joseph, 'Caciquismo and the revolution: Carrillo Puerto in Yucatán', in D. A. Brading (ed.), *Caudillo and Peasant in the Mexican Revolution*. Cambridge: Cambridge University Press, 1980, pp. 193–221.

Gillespie, Richard, *Soldiers of Perón: Argentina's Montoneros*. Oxford: Clarendon Press, 1982.

Girard, René, *The Scapegoat*. Baltimore: Johns Hopkins University Press, 1989.

Giussani, Pablo, *Montoneros: La soberbia armada*. Buenos Aires: Editorial Sudamericana/ Planeta, 1984.

Gledhill, John, *Casi Nada: A Study of Agrarian Reform in the Homeland of Cardenismo*. Albany, NY: Institute for Mesoamerican Studies, University at Albany, 1991.

Gleijeses, Piero, 'Guatemala: crisis and response', in *Report on Guatemala. Findings of the Study Group on United States–Guatemalan Relations*. Boulder, CO: Westview Press, 1985, pp. 51– 74.

— *Shattered Hope. The Guatemalan Revolution and the United States, 1944–1954*. Princeton, NJ: Princeton University Press, 1991.

Góes, Walder de, 'Militares e política: uma estratégia para a democracia', in Fábio Wanderley Reis and Guillermo O'Donnell,(eds), *A democracia no Brasil: Dilemas e perspectivas*. São Paulo: Vertice (Grande Brasil, Veredas 8), 1988, pp. 229–55.

Golte, Jürgen, *Repartos y rebeliones. Tupac Amaru y las contradicciones de la economía colonial*. Lima: IEP, 1980.

Golte, Jürgen and Norma Adams, *Los caballos de Troya de los invasores. Estrategias campesinas en la conquista de la Gran Lima*. Lima: IEP, 1990.

Gómez, Leopoldo and John Bailey, 'Transición política y dilemmas del PRI', *Foro Internacional* 31(1), 1990.

Gómez Tagle, Silvia, 'Electoral reform and the party system, 1977–1990', in Neil Harvey (ed.), *Mexico, Dilemmas of Transition*. London: Institute of Latin American Studies/British Academic Press, 1993, pp. 64–90.

— 'Electoral violence and negotiations, 1988–1991', in Neil Harvey and Mónica Serrano (eds), *Party Politics in 'An Uncommon Democracy'. Political Parties and Elections in Mexico*. London: Institute of Latin American Studies, 1994, pp. 77–92.

Gonzáles, Efraín, *La economía regional de Lima*. Lima: CIE/IEP, 1992.

González, Soledad and Alejandro Patiño, *Memoria campesina. La historia de Xalatlaco Contada por su gente*. Mexico: INAH, 1994.

González y González, Luis, *San José de Gracia. Mexican Village in Transition*. Austin: University of Texas Press, 1983 [1972].

Gorriti Ellenbogen, Gustavo, *Sendero Luminoso. Historia de la guerra milenaria en el Perú. Tomo I*. Lima: Editorial Apoyo, 1990.

Gosner, Kevin, 'Conceptualización de comunidad y jerarquía: enfoques recientes sobre la organización política maya colonial en el altiplano', *Mesoamérica* 12, 1991, pp. 151–62.

— *Soldiers of the Virgin. The Moral Economy of a Colonial Maya Rebellion*. Tucson: University of Arizona Press, 1992.

— 'Historical perspectives on Maya resistance: the Tzeltal revolt of 1712', in Kevin Gosner and Arij Ouweneel (eds), *Indigenous Revolts in Chiapas and the Andean Highlands*. Amsterdam: CEDLA, 1996, pp. 27–42.

Gosner, Kevin and Arij Ouweneel (eds), *Indigenous Revolts in Chiapas and the Andean Highlands*. Amsterdam: CEDLA, 1996.

Gossen, Gary H., 'Una diáspora maya moderna: desplazamiento y persistencia cultural de San Juan Chamula, Chiapas', *Mesoamérica* 4, 1983, pp. 253–76.

— 'The other in Chamula Tzotzil cosmology and history: reflections of a Kansan in Chiapas', *Cultural Anthropology* 8(4), 1993, pp. 443–75.

— 'Comments on the Zapatista Movement', *Cultural Survival Quarterly* 18(1), 1994, pp. 19– 21.

— 'Who is the Comandante of Subcomandante Marcos?', in Kevin Gosner and Arij Ouweneel (eds), *Indigenous Revolts in Chiapas and the Andean Highlands*. Amsterdam: CEDLA, 1996, pp. 107–20.

— 'Maya Zapatistas move to the ancient future', *American Anthropologist* 98(3), 1996, pp. 528–38.

— (ed.), *South and Meso-American Native Spirituality from the Cult of the Feathered Serpent to the Theology of Liberation*. New York: Crossroad, 1993.

Gramajo Morales, Héctor Alejandro, *Tesis de la estabilidad nacional*. Guatemala: Ministerio de la Defensa/Editorial del Ejercito, 1989.

— *Liderazgo militar y el futuro del ejercito de Guatemala*. Guatemala: Ministerio de la Defensa/ Editorial del Ejercito, 1990.

Granados Chapa, Miguel Angel, *Nava sí, Zapata no! La hora de San Luis Potosí: Crónica de una lucha que Triunfó*. Mexico: Grijalbo, 1992.

Green, Lina, 'Living in a state of fear', in Caroline Nordstrom and Antonius C. G. M. Robben (eds), *Fieldwork under Fire. Contemporary Studies of Violence and Survival*. Berkeley: University of California Press, 1995, pp. 105–27 .

Greenberg, James B., *Blood Ties. Life and Violence in Rural Mexico*. Tucson: University of Arizona Press, 1989.

Gruening, Ernest, *Mexico and its Heritage*. New York: Greenwood, 1968 [1928].

Guerra, Francisco Xavier, *Le Mexique. De L'Ancien Régime a la Révolution* (vol. 2). Paris: L'Harmattan, 1985.

— *México: Del antiguo régimen a la revolución* (vol. 1). Mexico: Fondo de Cultura Económica, 1988.

Guerrero, Javier, *Los años de olvído. Boyacá y los origenes de la violencia*. Bogotá: Tercer Mundo Editores, 1991.

Guillén López, Toniatuh, 'The social basis of the PRI', in Wayne A. Cornelius et al. (eds), *Mexico's Alternative Political Futures*. San Diego: Center for US–Mexican Studies, 1989, pp. 243–64.

— 'Baja California, una década de cambio político', in Toniatuh Guillén López (ed.), *Frontera Norte. Una década de política electoral*. Mexico and Tijuana: El Colegio de México/El Colegio de la Frontera Norte, 1992, pp. 139–85.

— 'Political culture from the northern border of Mexico. Elements for a debate', in Wil Pansters (ed.), *Citizens of the Pyramid. Essays on Mexican Political Culture*. Amsterdam: Thela (Latin America Studies 7), 1997, pp. 337–62.

Guillermoprieto, Alma, 'Letter from Mexico: Zapata's heirs', *New Yorker*, 16 May 1994, pp. 52–63.

— 'The shadow war', *New York Review of Books* 42(4), 1995, pp. 34–43.

Guzmán, Abimael, *'Por la nueva bandera', en Guerra popular en el Perú. El pensamiento Gonzalo*. Brussels: Luis Arce Borja Editor, 1989, pp. 139–60.

Gúzman Campos, Germán, Orlando Fals Borda and Eduardo Umaña Luna, *La Violencia en Colombia* (2 vols). Bogotá: Carlos Valencia Editores, 1980.

Haber, Paul, 'Cárdenas, Salinas and the urban popular movement', in Neil Harvey (ed.), *Mexico, Dilemmas of Transition*. London: The Institute of Latin American Studies/British Academic Press, 1993, pp. 218–48.

Haggard, Stephan and Robert R. Kaufman, *The Political Economy of Democratic Transitions*. Princeton, NJ: Princeton University Press, 1995.

Hagopian, Frances, 'Traditional power structures and democratic governance in Latin America', in Jorge I. Domínguez and Abraham F. Lowenthal (eds), *Constructing Democratic Governance – Themes and Issues*. Baltimore and London: Johns Hopkins University Press, 1996, pp. 64–86.

Harvey, Neil, 'Personal networks and strategic choices in the formation of an independent peasant organization: the OCEZ of Chiapas, Mexico', *Bulletin of Latin American Research* 7(2), 1988, pp. 299–312.

— 'The difficult transition: neoliberalism and neocorporatism', in Neil Harvey (ed.), *Mexico, Dilemmas of Transition*. London: Institute of Latin American Studies/British Academic Press, 1993, pp. 4–26.

— *Rebellion in Chiapas. Rural Reforms, Campesino Radicalism, and the Limits to Salinismo*. San Diego: Center for US–Mexican Studies, 1994.

Harvey, Neil and Mónica Serrano (eds), *Party Politics in 'An Uncommon Democracy'. Political Parties and Elections in Mexico*. London: Institute of Latin American Studies, 1994.

Hayden, Brian and Rob Gargett, 'Big man, big heart? A Mesoamerican view of the emergence of complex society', *Ancient Mesoamerica* 1, 1990, pp. 3–20.

Hayes, Robert A., *The Armed Nation: The Brazilian Corporate Mystique*. Tempe: Center for Latin American Studies, Arizona State University, 1989.

Hernández, Luis, 'The new Mayan war,' *NACLA Report on the Americas* 27(5), 1994, pp. 6–10.

Hernández Rodríguez, Rogelio, 'La difícil transición política en México', *Mexican Studies/Estudios Mexicanos* 8(2), 1992, pp. 237–57.

— 'What to do with the PRI? Salinas and the ruling party', in Wil Pansters (ed.), *Citizens of the Pyramid. Essays on Mexican Political Culture*. Amsterdam: Thela (Latin America Studies 7), 1997, pp. 209–24.

Herthoghe, Alain and Alain Labrousse, *Le Sentier Lumineux du Pérou. Un nouvel intégrisme dans le Tiers Monde*. Paris: Éditions la Découverte, 1989 .

Higley, John and Richard Guenther (eds), *Elites and Democratic Consolidation in Latin America and Southern Europe*. Cambridge: Cambridge University Press, 1992.

Hilton, Stanley E., 'The Armed Forces and industrialists in modern Brazil: the drive for military autonomy' *Hispanic American Historical Review* 62(4), 1982, pp. 629–73.

Hirmas, María Eugenia, 'La franja entre la alegría y el miedo', in Diego Portales and Guillermo Sunkel (eds), *La política en pantalla*. Santiago: ILET/CESOC, 1989, pp. 107–55.

Huber, Ludwig, *Después de Dios y la Virgen está la ronda. Las rondas campesinas de Piura*. Lima: IEP/IFEA, 1995.

Huizer, Gerrit, 'Emiliano Zapata and the peasant guerrillas in the Mexican Revolution', in Rodolfo Stavenhagen (ed.), *Agrarian Problems and Peasant Movements in Latin America*. New York: Anchor, 1970, pp. 375–406.

Huneeus, Carlos, 'Los partidos políticos y la transición a la democracia en Chile hoy', *Estudios Públicos* 15, 1984, pp. 57–88.

Hunter, Wendy, *Eroding Military Influence. Politicians against Soldiers*. Chapel Hill and London: University of North Carolina Press, 1997.

Hurtado, Javier, 'Características y dificultades de la transición démocratica de México con relación a la naturaleza de su régimen político', in José Luis Barros Horcasitas et al. (eds), *Transición a la Democracia y Reforma del Estado en México*. Mexico: FLACSO/Miguel Angel Porrúa/Universidad de Guadalajara, 1991, pp. 121–41.

Irwin, Constance, *Fair Gods and Stone Faces*. New York: Praeger, 1963.

Isbell, Billie Jean, 'Shining Path and peasant responses in rural Ayacucho', in David Scott Palmer (ed.), *Shining Path of Peru*. New York: St Martin's Press, 1992.

Jacobs, Ian, 'Rancheros of Guerrero: the Figueroa brothers and the Revolution', in D. A. Brading (ed.), *Caudillo and Peasant in the Mexican Revolution*. Cambridge: Cambridge University Press, 1980, pp. 169–86.

James, Daniel, *Resistance and Integration: Peronism and the Argentine Working Class, 1946–1976*. Cambridge: Cambridge University Press, 1988.

Jelin, Elizabeth, 'Cómo construir ciudadanía? Una vision desde abajo', *European Review of Latin American and Caribbean Studies* 55, 1993, pp. 21–37.

Jiménez Castillo, Manuel, *Huáncito. Organización y Práctica Política*. Mexico: Instituto Nacional Indigenista, 1985.

Jonas, Suzanne, *The Battle for Guatemala. Rebels, Death Squads and US Power*. Boulder, CO: Westview Press, 1991.

Kalmanoviecki, L., 'Police, people and preemption in Argentina', in Martha K. Huggins (ed.), *Vigilantism and the State in Modern Latin America*. New York: Praeger, 1991.

Kaufman, Robert R., 'Liberalization and democratization in Latin America: perspectives from the 1970s', in Guillermo O'Donnell, Philippe C. Schmitter and Lawrence Whitehead (eds), *Transitions from Authoritarian Rule: Comparative Perspectives*. Baltimore: Johns Hopkins University Press, 1986, pp. 85–107.

Keane, John, *Reflections on Violence*. London and New York: Verso, 1996.

Kirk, Robert, *Grabado en piedra. Las mujeres de Sendero Luminoso*. Lima: IEP, 1993.

Klaiber S. J. and L. Jeffrey, *Religion and Revolution in Peru, 1824–1976*. London: University of Notre Dame Press, 1977.

Knight, Alan, *The Mexican Revolution* (2 vols). Cambridge: Cambridge University Press, 1986.

— 'Historical continuities in social movements', in Joe Foweraker and Ann Craig (eds), *Popular Movements and Political Change in Mexico*. Boulder, CO: Lynne Rienner, 1990, pp. 78–102.

— 'Mexico's elite settlement: conjuncture and consequences', in John Higley and Richard Guenther (eds), *Elites and Democratic Consolidation in Latin America and Southern Europe*. Cambridge: Cambridge University Press, 1992, pp. 113–45.

— 'El obrigo de Arturo Alessandri', in María Luisa Tarrés (ed.), *Transformaciones Sociales y Acciones Colectivas*. Mexico: El Colegio de México/Centro de Estudios Sociológicos, 1994, pp. 37–58.

— 'Habitus and homicide: political culture in revolutionary Mexico', in Wil Pansters (ed.), *Citizens of the Pyramid: Essays on Mexican Political Culture*. Amsterdam: Thela (Latin America Series 7), 1997, pp. 107–29.

Knight, Franklin W., 'Ethnicity and social structure in contemporary Cuba', in Gert Oostindie (ed.), *Ethnicity in the Caribbean. Essays in Honor of Harry Hoetink*. London: Macmillan, 1996, pp. 106–20.

Köhler, Ulrich, 'Estructura y funcionamiento de la administración comunal en San Pablo Chalchihuitán', *América Indígena* 42(1), 1982, pp. 117–45.

— 'Ciclos de poder en una comunidad indígena de México: política local y sus vínculos con la vida nacional', *América Indígena* 46(3), 1986, pp. 435–51.

Koonings, Kees, Dirk Kruijt and Frits Wils, 'The very long march of history', in Henk Thomas (ed.), *Globalization and Third World Trade Unions*. London: Zed, 1995, pp. 99–129.

Krauze, Enrique, *Por una democracia sin adjetivos.* Mexico: Joaquín Mortiz Planeta, 1986.

Krieger, Emilio, 'Derecho electoral en julio de 1988', in Pablo González Casanova (ed.), *Segundo informe de la democracia: México el 6 de Julio de 1988.* Mexico: Siglo XXI, 1990, pp. 159–78.

Kristeva, Julia, *Etrangers à Nous-Mêmes.* Paris: Fayard, 1988.

Kruijt, Dirk, 'Perú: relaciones entre civiles y militares, 1950–1990', in Dirk Kruijt and Edelberto Torres-Rivas (eds), *América Latina: Militares y sociedad* (vol. 2). San José: FLACSO, 1991, pp. 29–142.

— *Revolution by Decree. Peru, 1968–1975.* Amsterdam: Thela (Latin America Series 1), 1994.

— 'El futuro de las fuerzas armadas en Centroamérica', in F. Barahona Riera and M. Carballo Quintana (eds), *Reconversión militar en Centroamérica.* San José: Friedrich Ebert Stiftung/Universidad para la Paz, 1995, pp. 55–70.

— 'Ethnic civil war in Peru: the military and Shining Path', in Kevin Gosner and Arij Ouweneel (eds), *Indigenous Revolts in Chiapas and the Andean Highlands.* Amsterdam: CEDLA, 1996, pp. 241–56.

— 'Politicians in uniform: dilemmas about the Latin American military', *European Review of Latin American and Caribbean Studies* 61, 1996, pp. 7–19.

Kruijt, Dirk et al., *Changing Labour Relations in Latin America.* Amsterdam: Thela, 1996.

— *La evolución del estado de seguridad nacional. El caso de Guatemala.* Guatemala: CITGUA (Cuadernos 19), 1991.

Lamounier, Bolivar, '*Authoritarian Brazil* revisited: the impact of elections on the *Abertura*', in Alfred Stepan (ed.), *Democratizing Brazil. Problems of Transition and Consolidation.* Oxford: Oxford University Press, 1989, pp. 43–79.

— 'Brazil: toward parliamentarism?', in Juan J. Linz and Arturo Valenzuela (eds), *The Failure of Presidential Democracy: The Case of Latin America* (vol. 2). Baltimore and London: Johns Hopkins University Press, 1994, pp. 179–219.

— 'Brazil: inequality against democracy', in Larry Diamond, Juan J. Linz and Seymour Martin Lipset (eds), *Politics in Developing Countries. Comparing Experiences with Democracy.* Boulder, CO: Lynne Rienner, 1995, pp. 119–69.

— 'Brazil: the hyperactive paralysis syndrome', in Jorge I. Domínguez and Abraham F. Lowenthal (eds), *Constructing Democratic Governance – South America.* Baltimore: Johns Hopkins University Press, 1996.

Landsberger, Henry and Tim McDaniel, 'Hypermobilization in Chile, 1970–1973', *World Politics* 28(4), 1976, pp. 502–41.

Langer, Susanne K., *Philosophy in a New Key: A Study in the Symbolism of Reason, Rite, and Art.* New York: Penguin, 1948.

Lara, Patricia, *Siembra vientos y recogerás tempestades. La historia del M-19, sus protagonistas y sus destinos.* Bogotá: Planeta, 1991.

Leal Buitrago, F., *El oficio de la guerra: La seguridad nacional en Colombia.* Bogotá: Tercer Mundo, 1994.

Lechner, Norbert, *Los patios interiores de la democracia: Subjetividad y política.* Santiago: FLACSO, 1988.

— 'Some people die of fear', in Juan E. Corradi, Patricia Weiss Fagen and Manuel Antonio Garretón (eds), *Fear at the Edge. State Terror and Resistance in Latin America.* Berkeley: University of California Press, 1992, pp. 3–21.

Leeds, Elizabeth, 'Cocaine and parallel politics in the Brazilian urban periphery: constraints on local-level democratization', *Latin American Research Review* 31(3), 1996, pp. 47–84.

Letts, Ricardo, *La izquierda Peruana*. Lima: Mosca Azul, 1981 .

Linden, Ronald H., 'Analogies and the loss of community: Cuba and Eastern Europe in the 1990s', in Carmelo Mesa-Lago (ed.), *Cuba after the Cold War*. Pittsburgh: University of Pittsburgh Press, 1993, pp. 17–58.

Linz, Juan, *La quiebra de las democracias*. Madrid: Alianza, 1987.

Loaeza, Soledad, 'México, 1968: los origenes de la transición', in Ilàn Semo et al. (eds), *La transición interrumpida. México, 1968–1988*. Mexico: Universidad Iberoamericana/Nueva Imagen, 1993, pp. 15–47.

Loaeza, Soledad et al., 'La erupción de Chiapas', *Cuaderno de Nexos* 68, 1994, pp. 3–17.

Lockhart, James, *Spanish Peru 1532–1560. A Colonial Society*. Madison: University of Wisconsin Press, 1968.

Lopez, George and Michael Stohl, 'Liberalization and redemocratization in Latin America: the search for models and meanings', in George Lopez and Michael Stohl (eds), *Liberalization and Redemocratization in Latin America*. New York: Greenwood, 1987, pp. 1–13.

López Martínez, Héctor, *Rebeliones de Mestizos y Otros Temas Quinientistas*. Lima: Talleres Gráficos P.L. Villanueva, 1972.

López Velasco, Vicente Paulino, *Y surgió la unión ... Génesis y desarrollo del Consejo Nacional de Pueblos Indígenas*, Mexico: Secretaría de la Reforma Agraria, 1989.

Loret de Mola, Carlos, *Los caciques*. Mexico: Grijalbo, 1979.

Lovell, W. George, 'Surviving conquest: the Maya of Guatemala in historical perspective', *Latin American Research Review* 23(2), 1988, pp. 25–57.

Lovemann, Brian, 'Protected democracies and military guardianship: political transitions in Latin America, 1978–1993', *Journal of Interamerican Studies and World Affairs* 36(2), 1994, pp. 105–90.

Lowenthal, Abraham F., *Partners in Conflict: The United States and Latin America in the 1990s*. Baltimore: Johns Hopkins University Press, 1990.

McGarrity, Gayle L., 'Race, culture, and social change in contemporary Cuba', in Sandor Halebsky and John M. Kirk (eds), *Cuba in Transition: Crisis and Transformation*. Boulder, CO: Westview Press, 1992, pp. 193–205.

MacLeod, M. J. and Robert Wasserstrom (eds), *Spaniards and Indians in Southeastern Mesoamerica. Essays on the History of Ethnic Relations*. Lincoln: University of Nebraska Press, 1983.

Mainwaring, Scott, Guillermo O'Donnell and J. Samuel Valenzuela (eds), *Issues in Democratic Consolidation: The New South American Democracies in Comparative Perspectives*. Notre Dame: University of Notre Dame Press, 1992.

Mallon, Florencia, *Peasant and Nation*. Berkeley: University of California Press, 1995.

Mandela, Nelson and Fidel Castro, *How Far We Slaves Have Come! South Africa and Cuba in Today's World*. New York: Pathfinder, 1991.

Manrique, Nelson, 'La década de la violencia', *Márgenes* 5/6, 1989, pp. 137–82.

— 'La caída de la cuarta espada y los senderos que se bifurcan', *Márgenes* 13/14, 1995, pp. 11–42.

Manz, Beatriz, *Refugees of a Hidden War. The Aftermath of Counterinsurgency in Guatemala*. Albany: State University of New York Press, 1988.

Marín, Juan Carlos, *Los hechos armados: Un ejercício posible*. Buenos Aires: CICSO, 1984.

Márquez, Enrique, 'Gonzalo N. Santos o la naturaleza del "tanteómetro político"', in Carlos Martínez Assad (ed.), *Estadistas, caciques y caudillos*. Mexico: UNAM, Instituto de Investigaciones Sociales, 1988, pp. 143–68 .

— *Por qué perdió Camacho. Revelaciones del asesor de Manuel Camacho Solís*. Mexico: Océano, 1995.

Márquez, Gabriel, '¿Cual arte alienante?', *El Diario*, 24 May 1989, p. 16.

Martin, G., *Desarrollo económico, sindicalismo y proceso de paz en Urabá*. Bogotá: Universidad de los Andes, 1986.

Martínez, Javier, 'Miedo al Estado, miedo a la sociedad', *Proposiciones* 12, 1986, pp. 34–42.

Martínez Assad, Carlos, 'Nava: de la rebelión de los coheretos al juicio político', in Carlos Martínez Assad (ed.), *Municipios en conflicto*. Mexico: UNAM, Instituto de Investigaciones Sociales, 1985, pp. 96–113.

Martinez Peláez, Severo, *La patria del criollo*. San José: EDUCA, 1973 .

Martins, Luciano, 'The "liberalization" of authoritarian rule in Brazil', in Guillermo O'Donnell, Philippe C. Schmitter and Laurence Whitehead (eds), *Transitions from Authoritarian Rule: Latin America*. Baltimore: Johns Hopkins University Press, 1986, pp. 72–94.

Masi, Juan José, 'Lucha contra la subversión', *Revista de la Escuela Superior de Guerra* 45 (373), 1967, pp. 36–90.

Masterson, Daniel M., *Militarism and Politics in Latin America. Peru from Sánchez Cerro to Sendero Luminoso*. New York: Greenwood, 1991.

Matos Mar, José, *Desborde popular y crisis del estado. El nuevo rostro del Perú en la década de 1980*. Lima: Instituto de Estudios Peruanos (Perú Problema 21), 1984.

Mattini, Luis, *Hombres y mujeres del PRT-ERP*. Buenos Aires: Editorial Contrapunto, 1990.

Mauss, Marcel, *The Gift: Forms and Functions of Exchange in Archaic Societies*. New York: W. W. Norton, 1967 [1925].

Melgar Bao, Ricardo, 'Las utopías indígenas en América, lectura de un año nefasto', *Memoria* 62, 1994, pp. 24–31.

Mesa-Lago, Carmelo, *Cuba after the Cold War*. Pittsburgh: University of Pittsburgh Press, 1993.

Mesa-Lago, Carmelo and Horst Fabian, 'Analogies between East European socialist regimes and Cuba: scenarios for the future', in Carmelo Mesa-Lago (ed.), *Cuba after the Cold War*. Pittsburgh: University of Pittsburgh Press, 1993, pp. 353–80.

Meyer, Lorenzo, *La segunda muerte de la Revolución Mexicana*. Mexico: Cal y Arena, 1992.

Middlebrook, Kevin J., *Political Liberalization in an Authoritarian Regime: the Case of Mexico*. San Diego: University of California Press, 1985 .

Millett, Richard, 'The Central American militaries: predators or patriots?', in Robert Leiken (ed.), *Central America: Anatomy of a Conflict*. New York: Pergamon Press, 1984.

Mir, Luís, *A revolução impossível. A esquerda e a luta armada no Brasil*. São Paulo: Editora Best Seller, 1994.

Moisés, José Álvaro, *Os brasileiros e a democracia. Bases sócio-políticas da legitimidade democrática*. São Paulo: Editora Ática, 1995.

Moksnes, Heidi, 'Reflections on representing "Indians"', *Anthropological Newsletter* 35 (3), 1994, pp. 26–7.

Molinar Horcasitas, Juan, *El tiempo de la legitimidad. Elecciones, autoritarismo y democracia en México*. Mexico: Cal y Arena, 1991.

Monsivais, C. 'Duración de la eternidad', *NEXOS* 172, April 1992, pp. 37–45.

Montejo, Victor, *Testimony: Death of a Guatemalan Village*. Willimantic: Curbstone Press, 1987.

Montoya, Rodrigo et al. *La sangre de los cerros. Urqukunapa Tawarnin*. Lima: CEPES/Mosca Azul, 1987.

Moore, Barrington, *Social Origins of Dictatorship and Democracy. Lord and Peasant in the Making of the Modern World*. London: Penguin, 1967.

Moore, Carlos, *Castro, the Blacks and Africa*. Los Angeles: Center for Afro-American Studies, University of California, 1988.

Moulian, Tomás and Pilar Vergara, 'Estado, ideología y políticas económicas en Chile: 1973–1978'. *Estudios Cieplan* 3, 1980, pp. 65–120.

Munck, Ronaldo, *Argentina: From Anarchism to Peronism. Workers, Unions and Politics, 1855–1985*. London: Zed, 1987.

— 'After the transition: democratic disenchantment in Latin America', *European Review of Latin American and Caribbean Studies* 55, 1993, pp. 7–19.

Munizaga, Giselle, *El discurso público de Pinochet: Un análisis semiológico*. Santiago: CESOC/CENECA, 1988.

NACLA, 'Injustice for all. Crime and impunity in Latin America', *NACLA Report on the Americas* 30(2), 1996, pp. 16–43.

Nations, James D., 'The ecology of the Zapatista revolt', *Cultural Survival Quarterly* 18(1), 1994, pp. 31–3.

Navarrete, Carlos, *San Pascualito Rey y el culto a la muerte en Chiapas*. Mexico: UNAM, 1982.

Navarro, Zander (ed.), *Política, protesto e cidadania no campo*. Porto Alegre: Editora da Universidade/UFRGS, 1996.

Nordstrom, Caroline and Antonius C. G. M. Robben (eds), *Fieldwork under Fire. Contemporary Studies of Violence and Survival*. Berkeley: University of California Press, 1995.

Nun, José, 'The middle class military coup', in Claudio Véliz (ed.), *The Politics of Conformity in Latin America*. Oxford: Oxford University Press, 1967, pp. 66–118.

Obando Arbulú, Enrique, 'Diez años de guerra antisubversiva: una pequeña historia', *Qué Hacer* 72, 1991, pp. 28–39.

— 'Subversion and antisubversion in Peru, 1980–1992: a view from Lima', *Low Intensity Conflict and Law Enforcement* 2(2), 1993, pp. 318–30.

O'Brien, Philip and Jackie Roddick, *Chile: The Pinochet Decade. The Rise and Fall of the Chicago Boys*. London: Latin American Bureau, 1983.

O'Donnell, Guillermo, *Modernization and Bureaucratic-Authoritarianism: Studies in South American Politics*. Berkeley: Center for International Studies, University of California, 1973.

— 'Reflections on the patterns of change in the bureaucratic-authoritarian state', *Latin American Research Review* 13(1), 1978, pp. 3–38.

— 'El dilema de las transiciones', in *Nuestra América*. São Paulo: Memorial de América Latina, 1992.

O'Donnell, Guillermo and Philippe C. Schmitter, *Transitions from Authoritarian Rule: Tentative Conclusions about Uncertain Democracies*. Baltimore: Johns Hopkins University Press, 1986.

O'Donnell, Guillermo, Philippe C. Schmitter and Laurence Whitehead (eds), *Transitions from Authoritarian Rule: Latin America*. Baltimore: Johns Hopkins University Press, 1986.

— (eds), *Transitions from Authoritarian Rule: Comparative Perspectives*. Baltimore: Johns Hopkins University Press, 1986.

Oliven, Ruben, *Violência e cultura no Brasil*. Petrópolis, RJ: Vozes, 1986.

Oostindie, Gert and Patricio Silva, 'Europa en de Cubaanse crisis', *Internationale Spectator* 51, 1997, pp. 26–31.

O'Phelan Godoy, Scarlett, *Rebellions and Revolts in Eighteenth Century Peru and Upper Peru*. Cologne and Vienna: Böhlau Verlag, 1985.

Oppenheim, Lois Hecht, *Politics in Chile: Democracy, Authoritarianism, and the Search for Development*. Boulder, CO: Westview Press, 1993.

Oppenheimer, Andres, *Castro's Final Hour: The Secret Story Behind the Coming Downfall of Communist Cuba*. New York: Simon and Schuster, 1992.

Ordóñez Cifuentes, José Emilio R., *Reclamos jurídicos de los Pueblos Indios*. Mexico: UNAM, 1993.

Orsolini, Mario H., *Montoneros: Sus proyectos y sus planes*. Buenos Aires: Círculo Militar, Biblioteca del Oficial, 1990.

Ouweneel, Arij, *Onderbroken groei in Anáhuac. De ecologische achtergrond van ontwikkeling en armoede op het platteland van Centraal-Mexico (1730–1810)*. Amsterdam: CEDLA, 1989.

— *Alweer die Indianen. De jaguar en het konijn in Chiapas Mexico*. Amsterdam: Thela, 1994.

— 'Het verleden leefde voort in Antonio Pérez. Indiaanse "standennijd" in centraal Mexico, 1757–1761', *Tijdschrift voor Geschiedenis* 1995, pp. 24–49.

— 'Away from prying eyes: the Zapatista revolt of 1994', in Kevin Gosner and Arij Ouweneel (eds), *Indigenous Revolts in Chiapas and the Andean Highlands*. Amsterdam: CEDLA, 1996, pp. 79–106.

— *Shadows over Anáhuac. An Ecological Interpretation of Crisis and Development in Central Mexico, 1730–1800*. Albuquerque: University of New Mexico Press, 1996.

— (ed.), *Campesinos. Kleine Boeren in Latijns Amerika, vanaf 1520*. Amsterdam: Thela, 1993.

Page, Joseph A., *Perón: A Biography*. New York: Random House, 1983.

Painter, James, *Guatemala: False Hope, False Freedom. The Rich, the Poor and the Christian Democrats*. London: Catholic Institute for International Relations/Latin America Bureau, 1987.

Paixão, Antonio Luiz, 'Crime, controle social e consolidação da democracia: as metáforas da cidadania', in Fábio Wanderley Reis and Guillermo O'Donnell (eds), *A democracia no Brasil: dilemas e perspectivas*. São Paulo: Vértice, pp. 168–99.

Palacio, Germán (ed.), *La irrupción del Paraestado. Ensayos sobre la crisis Colombiana*. Bogotá: ILSA/CEREC, 1992.

Palmer, David Scott, 'The Shining Path in Peru: insurgency and the drug problem', in Edwin G. Corr and Stephen Sloan (eds), *Low Intensity Conflicts. Old Threats in a New World*. Boulder, CO: Westview Press, 1992, pp. 151–70.

— 'Peru, the drug business and Shining Path: Between Scylla and Charybdis?', *Journal of Interamerican Studies and World Affairs* 32(3), 1992, pp. 65–88.

— (ed.), *The Shining Path of Peru*. New York: St Martin's Press, 1992.

Panizza, Francisco and Alexandra Barahona de Brito, 'The politics of human rights in Brazil under democratic rule', Paper for the LASA 20th International Conference, Guadalajara, 1997.

Pansters, Wil, *Politics and Power in Puebla. The Political History of a Mexican State 1937–87*. Amsterdam: CEDLA, 1990.

— 'Citizens with dignity. Opposition and government in San Luis Potosí, 1938–1993', in Rob Aitken et al. (eds), *Dismantling the Mexican State?* London: Macmillan, 1995, pp. 244–66.

— 'El hambre por la democracia. Recuento de un pequeño drama a grandes rasgos', in Hubert Hermans et al. (eds), *Las crisis socioeconomicas y sus soluciones*. Groningen: Centro de Estudios Mexicanos, 1996, pp. 63–80.

— 'Theorizing political culture in modern Mexico', in Wil Pansters (ed.), *Citizens of the Pyramid. Essays on Mexican Political Culture*. Amsterdam: Thela (Latin America Series 7), 1997, pp. 1–37.

— (ed.), *Citizens of the Pyramid. Essays on Mexican Political Culture*. Amsterdam: Thela (Latin America Series 7), 1997.

Pansters, Wil and Arij Ouweneel (eds), *Region, State and Capitalism in Mexico. Nineteenth and Twentieth Centuries*. Amsterdam: CEDLA, 1989.

Paré, Luisa, *El proletariado agrícola en México: Campesinos sin tierra o proletarios agrícolas?* Mexico: Siglo XXI, 1977.

Payne, Arnold, *The Peruvian Coup d'Etat of 1962: The Overthrow of Manuel Prado*. Washington: Institute for the Comparative Study of Political Systems, 1968.

Pécaut, Daniel, *L'ordre et la violence: Evolution socio-politique de la Colombie entre 1930 et 1953*. Paris: Editions de l'Ecole des Hautes Etudes en Sciences Sociales, 1987.

— *Orden y Violencia: Colombia 1930–1964*. Bogotá: Siglo XXI, 1987.

— 'Présent, passé, future de la violence', in J. M. Blanquer and C. Gros (eds), *La Colombie à l'aube du troisième millénaire*. Paris: Editions de l'Institut des Hautes Etudes de l'Amérique Latine, 1996, pp. 48–63.

PEN (Poder Ejecutivo Nacional), *Decreto 2770–2772*. 6 October 1975.

Peña, Guillermo de la, 'Poder local, poder regional: perspectivas socio-antropológicas', in Jorge Padúa and Alain Vanneph (eds), *Poder local, poder regional*. Mexico: El Colegio de México/CEMCA, 1986, pp. 27–56.

Perelli, Carina, 'The military's perception of threat in the southern cone of South America', in Louis W. Goodman, Johanna S. R. Mendelson and Juan Rial (eds), *The Military and Democracy. The Future of Civil–Military Relations in Latin America*. Lexington, MA and Toronto: Lexington Books, 1990, pp. 93–105.

Perera, Victor, *Unfinished Conquest. The Guatemalan Tragedy*. Berkeley: University of California Press, 1993.

Pérez Arce, Francisco, 'The enduring struggle for legality and democracy', in Joe Foweraker and Ann Craig (eds), *Popular Movements and Political Change in Mexico*. Boulder, CO: Lynne Rienner, 1990, pp. 105–20.

Pérez Correa, F. (ed.), 'Reflexiones sobre la pertinencia de la aplicación del concepto de transición democràtica para el caso mexicano', in J. L. Barros Horcasitas et al. (eds), *Transición a la democracia y reforma del estado en México*. Mexico: FLACSO/ Miguel Angel Porrúa/ Universidad de Guadalajara, 1991, pp. 279–85.

Pérez-López, Jorge F. (ed.), *Cuba at a Crossroads: Politics and Economics After the Fourth Party Congress*. Gainesville: University Press of Florida, 1994.

Pérez-Stable, Marifeli, *The Cuban Revolution: Origins, Course and Legacy*. New York: Oxford University Press, 1993.

Petras, James E. and Fernando Ignacio Leiva, *Democracy and Poverty in Chile: The Limits to Electoral Politics*. Boulder, CO: Westview Press, 1994.

Petras, James E. and Morris H. Morley, 'Cuban socialism: rectification and the new model of accumulation', in Sandor Halebsky and John M. Kirk (eds), *Cuba in Transition: Crisis and Transformation*. Boulder, CO: Westview Press, 1992, pp. 15–36.

Piñeyro, José Luis, 'Las Fuerzas Armadas en la transición politica de Mexico', *Revista Mexicana de Sociologia* 59(1), 1997, pp. 163–89.

Pinheiro, Sérgio, 'Democracies without citizenship', in NACLA, 'Injustice for all. Crime and impunity in Latin America', *NACLA Report on the Americas* 30(2), 1996, pp. 17–23.

Pion-Berlin, David, *The Ideology of State Terror: Economic Doctrine and Political Repression in Argentina and Peru*. Boulder, CO: Lynne Rienner, 1989.

Plant, Roger, *Guatemala: Unnatural Disaster*. London: Latin America Bureau, 1978.

Poitevin, René, 'Guatemala: La crisis de la democracia'. Dudas y esperanzas en los golpes de estado de 1993. Guatemala: FLACSO (Debate 21), 1994.

Politzer, Patricia, Fear in Chile: Lives under Pinochet. New York: Pantheon, 1989.

Portales, Diego and Guillermo Sunkel (eds), La política en pantalla. Santiago: ILET/CESOC, 1985.

Portocarrero, Gonzalo and Patricia Oliart, El Perú desde la escuela. Lima: IAA, 1989.

Przeworski, Adam, Democracy and the Market. Cambridge: Cambridge University Press, 1991.

Puig, Carlos and Rodrigo Vera, 'La petición de Zedillo de suprimir los programas de nota roja en television, desestimada', Proceso 1035, 1996, pp. 24–6.

Quartim de Moraes, João, Dictatorship and Armed Struggle in Brazil. New York and London: Monthly Review Press, 1971.

— 'A função das Forças Armadas num Brasil democrático', in João Quartim de Moraes, Wilma Peres Costa and Eliézer Rizzo de Oliveira, A tutela militar. São Paulo: Vertice (Grande Brasil, Veredas 3), 1987, pp. 82–104.

— A esquerda militar no Brasil (vol. 1: da conspiração republicana à guerilla dos tenentes). São Paulo: Siciliano, 1991.

Quirk, Robert E., Fidel Castro. New York: W. W. Norton, 1993.

Raby, David L., Educación y revolución social en México. Mexico: Sepsetentas, 1974.

Radu, Michael, 'Cuba's transition: institutional lessons from Eastern Europe', Journal of Interamerican and World Affairs 37, 1995, pp. 83–111.

Rangel Suarez, Alfredo, 'Colombia: la guerra irregular en el fin de siglo', Análisis Político 28, 1996, pp. 74–84.

Reinares, Fernando, 'Conflicto social, violencia colectiva y cambio político: un apunte teórico', in Manuel Alcántara and Ismael Crespo (eds), Los límites de la consolidación democrática en América Latina. Salamanca: Ediciones Universidad de Salamanca, 1995, pp. 103–10.

Remmer, Karen L., Military Rule in Latin America. Boulder, CO: Westview Press, 1991.

Report on Guatemala, Findings of the Study Group on United States–Guatemalan Relations. Boulder, CO: Westview Press, 1985.

Reveiz, Edgar, Democratizar para sobrevivir. Bogotá: Poligrupo Comunicacion, 1989.

Reyes Matta, Fernando, Carlos Ruiz and Guillermo Sunkel (eds), Investigación sobre la prensa en Chile (1974–1984). Santiago: CERC-ILET, 1986.

Rial, Juan, 'The armed forces and the question of democracy in Latin America', in Louis W. Goodman, Johanna S. R. Mendelson and Juan Rial (eds), The Military and Democracy. The Future of Civil–Military Relations in Latin America. Lexington, MA, and Toronto: Lexington Books, 1990, pp. 3–21.

— 'Makers and guardians of fear', in Juan F. Corradi, Patricia Weiss Fagen and Manuel Antonio Garretón (eds), Fear at the Edge. State Terror and Resistance in Latin America. Berkeley: University of California Press, 1992, pp. 90–103.

Ricoeur, P., Temps et récités (vol. 1). Paris: Seuil, 1983.

— Soi-même comme Autre. Paris: Seuil, 1990.

Rizzo de Oliveira, Eliézer, 'O aparelho militar: papel tutelar na Nova República', in João Quartim de Moraes, Wilma Peres Costa and Eliézer Rizzo de Oliveira, A tutela militar. São Paulo: Vertice (Grande Brasil, Veredas 3), 1987, pp. 54–81.

— 'Constituinte, Forças Armadas e autonomia militar', in Eliézer Rizzo de Oliveira et al., As Forças Armadas no Brasil. Rio de Janeiro: Espaço e Tempo, 1987, pp. 145–85.

Robben, Antonius C. G. M., 'Deadly alliance: leaders and followings in transactionalism and mass psychology', in Jojada Verrips (ed.), *Transactions: Essays in Honor of Jeremy F. Boissevain*. Amsterdam: Het Spinhuis, 1994, pp. 229–50.

Rodríguez, Victoria, 'The politics of decentralization in Mexico: from *Municipio Libre* to *Solidaridad*, *Bulletin of Latin American Research* 12(2), 1993, pp. 133–45.

Rodríguez Araujo, Octavio, *La reforma política y los partidos políticos en México*. Mexico: Siglo XXI, 1982.

Rodríguez Rabal, César, *La violencia de las horas. Un estudio psicoanalítico sobre la violencia en el Perú*. Caracas: Nueva Sociedad, 1995.

Roldán, Mary, 'Citizenship, class and violence in historical perspective: the Colombian case', Paper for the LASA 20th International Conference, Guadalajara, 1997.

Romanucci-Ross, Lola, *Conflict, Violence and Morality in a Mexican Village*. Sacramento: National Press Books, 1973.

Romero Jacobo, César, *Los Altos de Chiapas. La voz de las armas*. Mexico: Planeta, 1994.

Roniger, Luis, *Hierarchy and Trust in Modern Mexico and Brazil*. New York: Praeger, 1990.

Rosada-Granados, Héctor Roberto, *Indios y ladinos. Un estudio antropológico-sociológico*. Guatemala: Editorial Universitaria, 1987 .

Ross, John, *Rebellion from the Roots: Indian Uprising in Chiapas*. New York: Common Courage Press, 1994.

Ross, John et al. (eds), *Shadows of Tender Fury. The Letters and Communiqués of Subcomandante Marcos and the Zapatista Army of National Liberation*. New York: Common Courage Press, 1995.

Rouquié, Alain, *The Military and the State in Latin America*. Berkeley: University of California Press, 1989.

Rovira, Guiomar, *¡Zapata Vive! La rebelión indígena de Chiapas contada por sus protagonistas*. Barcelona: Virus, 1994.

Rubin, Jeffrey W., 'Popular mobilization and the myth of state corporatism', in Joe Foweraker and Ann Craig (eds). *Popular Movements and Political Change in Mexico*. Boulder, CO: Lynne Rienner, 1990, pp. 247–67.

Rubio, M., *Homicidios, justicia, mafia y capital social. Otro ensayo sobre la violencia Colombiana*. Bogota: CEDE/Universidad de los Andes, 1996.

— *Capital Social, educación y delincuencia juvenil en Colombia*. Bogotá: CE DE/Universidad de los Andes, 1996.

Rus, Jan, 'Whose caste war? Indians, ladinos, and the "Caste War" of 1869', in Murdo MacLeod and Robert Wasserstrom (eds), *Spaniards and Indians in Southeastern Mesoamerica. Essays on the History of Ethnic Relations*. Lincoln: University of Nebraska Press, 1983, pp. 127–68.

— 'Local adaptation to global change: the reordering of native society in highland Chiapas, Mexico, 1974–1994', *European Review of Latin American and Caribbean Studies* 58, 1995, pp. 71–89.

Rus, Jan, and Robert Wasserstrom, 'Civil–religious hierarchies in Central Chiapas: a critical perspective', *American Ethnologist* 7(3), 1980, pp. 466–78.

Sábato, Ernesto, *On Heroes and Tombs*. London: Jonathan Cape, 1990 [1961].

Salazar, Alonso J., *Mujeres de fuego*. Medellín: Corporación Fuego, 1993.

Salazar, Alonso J., *No nacimos pa' semilla. La cultura de las bandas juveniles de Medellín*. Bogotá: CINEP, 1993.

Salazar, Alonso J. and Ana María Jaramillo, *Medellín: Las subculturas del narcotráfico.* Bogotá: CINEP, 1992.

Salazar, Gabriel, *Violencia política popular en las 'Grandes Alamedas'.* Santiago: SUR, 1990.

Salimovich, Sofia, Elizabeth Lira and Eugenia Weinstein, 'Victims of fear: the social psychology of repression', in Juan F. Corradi, Patricia Weiss Fagen and Manuel Antonio Garretón (eds), *Fear at the Edge. State Terror and Resistance in Latin America.* Berkeley: University of California Press, 1992, pp. 147–73.

Sanderson, Steven E., *Agrarian Populism and the Mexican State.* Berkeley: University of California Press, 1981.

Santos, Gonzalo N., *Memorias.* Mexico: Grijalbo, 1986.

Santos, Wanderley Guilherme dos, Violeta Maria Monteiro and Ana Maria Lustosa Caillaux, *Que Brasil é Este?* São Paulo: Vertice, 1990.

Santucho, Julio, *Los últimos Guevaristas: Surgimiento y eclipse del Ejercito Revolucionario del Pueblo.* Buenos Aires: Puntosur, 1988.

Saragoza, Alex M., *The Monterrey Elite and the Mexican State, 1880–1940.* Austin: University of Texas Press, 1988.

Scarry, Elaine, *The Body in Pain: The Making and Unmaking of the World.* Oxford and New York: Oxford University Press, 1985.

Scheper-Hughes, Nancy, *Death without Weeping. The Violence of Everyday Life in Brazil.* Berkeley: University of California Press, 1992.

Schiller, Herman, et al., *Hubo dos terrorismos?* Buenos Aires: Ediciones Reencuentro, 1986.

Schirmer, Jennifer, 'Guatemala: los militares y la tesis de estabilidad nacional', in Dirk Kruijt and Edelberto Torres-Rivas (eds), *América Latina: Militares y sociedad* (vol. 1). San José: FLACSO, 1991, pp. 183–219.

— 'The Guatemalan military project: an interview with Gen. Hector Gramajo', *Harvard International Review* 13(3), 1991, pp. 41–76.

— 'The looting of democratic discourse by the Guatemalan military and its implications for human rights', Paper for the SSRC-CEDES Conference and Proceedings 'Derechos Humanos, Justicia y Sociedad' (Human Rights, Justice and Society), Buenos Aires, 1992.

Schlesinger, Stephen and Stephen Kinzer, *Bitter Fruit. The Untold Story of the American Coup in Guatemala.* London: Sinclair Browne, 1982.

Schmitt, Carl, *Der Begriff des Politischen.* Berlin: Duncker & Humblot, 1979 [1932].

Schmitz, Mathias, *Die Freund–Feind Theorie Carl Schmitts.* Cologne: Westdeutscher Verlag, 1965.

Schneider, Ronald M., *Communism in Guatemala, 1944–1954.* New York: Praeger, 1959.

— *Brazil: Politics and Culture in a New Industrial Powerhouse.* Boulder, CO: Westview Press, 1996.

Schryer, Frans J., *The Rancheros of Pisaflores.* Toronto: University of Toronto Press, 1980.

— *Ethnicity and Class Conflict in Rural Mexico.* Princeton, NJ: Princeton University Press, 1990.

Schulz, Donald E. (ed.), *Cuba and the Future.* Westport, CT: Greenwoood Press, 1993.

Scott, James, *Weapons of the Weak. Everyday Forms of Peasant Resistance.* New Haven: Yale University Press, 1985.

Scully, Timothy R., *Rethinking the Center: Party Politics in Nineteenth and Twentieth Century Chile.* Stanford: Stanford University Press, 1992.

Semo, Ilán (ed.), *La tranisición interrumpida. México, 1968–1988.* Mexico: Universidad Iberoamericana/Nueva Imagen, 1993.

Seoane, María, *Todo o nada*. Buenos Aires: Planeta, 1991.

Sesereses, Cesar, 'The Guatemalan legacy: radical challengers and military politics', in *Report on Guatemala. Findings of the Study Group on United States–Guatemalan Relations*. Boulder, CO: Westview Press, 1985, pp. 17–49.

— 'Guatemalan insurgency and counterinsurgency: the highlands war, 1978–1982', in Georges A. Fauriol (ed.), *Latin American Insurgencies*. Washington: National Defense University Press, 1985, pp. 97–113.

Sexton, James D. (ed.), *Campesino: the Diary of a Guatemalan Indian*. Tucson: University of Arizona Press, 1985.

Sheridan, Thomas E., *Where the Dove Calls*. Tucson: University of Arizona Press, 1988.

Shumway, Nicholas, *The Invention of Argentina*. Berkeley: University of California Press, 1991.

Silva, Patricio, 'The state, politics and the peasant unions in Chile', *Journal of Latin American Studies* 20(2), 1988, pp. 433–52.

— 'Technocrats and politics in Chile: from the Chicago Boys to the CIEPLAN Monks', *Journal of Latin American Studies* 23(2), 1991, pp. 385–410.

— 'Social democracy, neoliberalism, and ideological change in the Chilean socialist movement, 1973–1992', *Nordic Journal of Latin American Studies* 23(1–2), 1993, pp. 92–115.

— 'Modernization, consumerism and politics in Chile', in David Hojman (ed.), *Neo-Liberalism with a Human Face? The Politics and Economics of the Chilean Model*. Liverpool: University of Liverpool Monograph Series No. 20, 1995, pp. 118–32.

— 'Empresarios, neoliberalismo y transición democrática en Chile', *Revista Mexicana de Sociología* 57(3), 1995, pp. 238–65.

Simon, Jean-Marie, *Guatemala. Eternal Spring, Eternal Tyranny*. New York: W. W. Norton, 1987.

Simpson, John and Jana Bennett, *The Disappeared and the Mothers of the Plaza*. New York: St Martin's Press, 1985.

Siverts, Henning, 'The "cacique" of K'ankujk. A study of leadership and social change in highland Chiapas, Mexico', *Estudios de Cultura Maya* 5, 1965, pp. 340–60.

Smith, Carol A., 'The militarization of civil society in Guatemala: economic reorganization as a continuation of war', *Latin American Perspectives* 17(4), 1990, pp. 8–41.

— (ed.), *Guatemalan Indians and the State, 1540 to 1988*. Austin: University of Texas Press, 1990.

Smith, Lois M. and Alfred Padula, 'The Cuban family in the 1980s', in Sandor Halebsky and John M. Kirk (eds), *Transformation and Struggle: Cuba Faces the 1990s*. New York: Praeger, 1992, pp. 175–88.

Smith, Wayne S., 'Cuba's long reform', *Foreign Affairs* 75, 1996, pp. 99–112.

Smith, William C., Carlos H. Acuña and Eduardo A. Gamarra (eds), *Latin American Political Economy in the Age of Neoliberal Reform. Theoretical and Comparative Perspectives for the 1990s*. Miami: North–South Center, 1994.

Sola, Lourdes, 'Heterodox shock in Brazil: *técnicos*, politicians, and democracy', *Journal of Latin American Studies* 23(1), 1991, pp. 163–95.

— *Estado da transição: Política e economia na Nova República*. São Paulo: Vertice (Grande Brasil, Veredas 9), 1988.

Solares, Ignacio, *El Gran Elector*. Mexico: Joaquín Mortiz, 1993.

Solares, Jorge, 'Guatemala: etnicidad y democracia en tierra arrasada', in Gabriel Aguilera et al., *Los problemas de la democracia*. Guatemala: FLACSO, 1992, pp. 47–72.

Sorj, Bernardo, 'Reforma agrária e democracia', in Fábio Wanderley Reis and Guillermo O'Donnell (eds), *A democracia no Brasil: Dilemas e perspectivas*. São Paulo: Vertice (Grande Brasil, Veredas 8), 1988, pp. 136–49.

Soto, Henando de, *The Other Path. The Invisible Revolution in the Third World*. New York: Harper and Row, 1989.

Spalding, Karen, 'Class structures in the southern Peruvian highlands, 1750–1920', in Benjamin S. Orlove and Glynn Custred (eds), *Land and Power in Latin America*. New York: Holms and Meier, 1980, pp. 79–97.

Spooner, Mary Helen, *Soldiers in a Narrow Land: The Pinochet Regime in Chile*. Berkeley and Los Angeles: University of California Press, 1994.

Stallings, Barbara and Robert R. Kaufman (eds), *Debt and Democracy in Latin America*. Boulder, CO: Westview Press, 1989.

Starn, Orin, *Rondas Campesinas de Paimas-Piura*. Lima: Tarea, 1987 .

— 'Noches de ronda', *Quehacer* 69, 1991, pp. 76–92.

— 'Con los llanques todo barro': *Reflexiones sobre Rondas Campesinas, protesta rural, y nuevos movimientos sociales*. Lima: IEP, 1991 .

— *Hablan los Ronderos. La búsqueda por la paz en los Andes*. Lima: IEP, 1993 .

Steinhauf, Andreas, 'Diferenciación étnica y redes de larga distancia entre migrantes andinos: el caso de Sanka y Colcha', *Boletin del Institut Français de Etudes Andines* 20(2), pp. 93–114.

Stepan, Alfred, *The Military in Politics. Changing Patterns in Brazil*. Princeton, NJ: Princeton University Press, 1971.

— 'The new professionalism of internal warfare and military role expansion', in Abraham F. Lowenthal (ed.), *Armies and Politics in Latin America*. New York and London: Holmes and Meier, 1976, pp. 244–60.

— *The State and Society. Peru in Comparative Perspective*. Princeton: Princeton University Press, 1978.

— 'State power and the strength of civil society in the southern cone of Latin America', in Peter Evans, Dietrich Rueschemeyer and Theda Skocpol (eds), *Bringing the State Back In*. New York: Cambridge University Press, 1985, pp. 317–43.

— *Rethinking Military Politics: Brazil and the Southern Cone*. Princeton, NJ: Princeton University Press, 1988.

Stern, Steve J., 'Nuevas aproximaciones al estudio de la consciencia y las rebeliones campesinas: las implicaciones de la experiencia andina', in Steve J. Stern (ed.), *Resistencia, rebelión y consciencia campesina en los Andes, siglos XVIII al XX*. Lima: IEP, pp. 25–41.

— (ed.), *Resistance, Rebellion and Consciousness in the Andean Peasant World, 18th to 20th Centuries*. Madison: University of Wisconsin Press, 1987.

Stoll, David, *Between Two Armies in the Ixil Towns of Guatemala*. New York: Columbia University Press, 1993.

Strong, Simon, *Shining Path, the World's Deadliest Revolutionary Force*. London: HarperCollins, 1992.

Szulc, Ted, *Fidel: A Critical Portrait*. New York: Avon, 1987.

Tamayo Flores-Alatorre, Sergio, 'Origen y novedad en el EZLN', *La Jornada Semanal* 245, 1994, pp. 39–43.

Tapia, Carlos, *Autodefensa armada del campesinado*. Lima: CEDEP, 1995.

— *Del 'equilibrio estratégico' a la derrota de Sendero Luminoso*. Lima: IEP, 1996.

Tapia, Jorge, *El terrorismo de estado: La doctrina de la seguridad nacional en el Cono Sur*. Mexico: Editorial Nueva Imagen, 1980.

Tarazona-Sevillano, Gabriela and John B. Reuter, *Sendero Luminoso and the Threat of Narco-Terrorism.* New York: Praeger, 1990 .

Tavares de Almeida, Maria Hermínia, 'Novas tendências do movimento sindical', in Hélgio Trindade (ed.), *Brazil em perspectiva: Dilemas da abertura política.* Porto Alegre: Sulina, 1982, pp. 81–103.

— 'Difícil caminho: sindicatos e política na construção da democracia', in Fábio Wanderley Reis and Guillermo O'Donnell (eds), *A democracia no Brasil: Dilemas e perspectivas.* São Paulo: Vertice (Grande Brasil, Veredas 8), 1988, pp. 327–67.

Tedlock, Dennis, *Breath on the Mirror. Mythic Voices of the Living Maya.* San Francisco: Harper, 1993.

Tella, Torcuato di, 'Populism and reform in Latin America', in Claudio Véliz (ed.), *Obstacles to Change in Latin America.* Oxford: Oxford University Press, 1972.

Tello, Maria del Pilar, *Sobre el volcán: Diálogo frente a la subversión.* Lima: CELA, 1989.

— *Perú: El precio de la paz.* Lima: Ediciones PETROPERU, 1991.

Thoumi, Francisco, *Economia, política y narcotráfico.* Bogotá: Tercer Mundo, 1994.

Tilly, Charles, *Coercion, Capital, and European States, AD 990–1992.* Cambridge, MA, and Oxford: Blackwell, 1992.

Tironi, Eugenio, *El liberalismo real: La sociedad Chilena y el régimen militar.* Santiago: Ediciones Sur, 1986.

— *Autoritarismo, modernización y marginalidad: El caso de Chile 1973–1989.* Santiago: Ediciones Sur, 1990.

Tompkins, Peter, *Mysteries of the Mexican Pyramids.* New York: Harper and Row, 1976.

Toriello, Guillermo, *La batalla de Guatemala.* Santiago: Editorial Universitaria, 1955.

Torres Arias, Edgar, *Mercaderes de la muerte.* Bogotá: Intermedio Editores, 1995.

Torres-Rivas, Edelberto, *Centroamérica: La democracia posible.* San José: EDUCA, 1987 .

— *Repression and Resistance.* Boulder, CO: Westview Press, 1989.

— 'Democracy and the metaphor of good government', in Joseph S. Tulchin et al. (eds), *The Consolidation of Democracy in Latin America.* Boulder, CO: Lynne Rienner, 1995, pp. 45–57.

Touraine, Alain, *America Latina: Política y Sociedad.* Madrid: Espasa-Calpe, 1989.

Tulchin, Joseph S. and Augusto Varas (eds), *From Dictatorship to Democracy: Rebuilding Political Consensus in Chile.* Boulder, CO: Lynne Rienner, 1991.

Turner, Bryan, *Citizenship and Capitalism.* London: Allen and Unwin, 1986.

Tutino, John, *From Insurrection to Revolution in Mexico. Social Bases of Agrarian Violence, 1750–1940.* Princeton, NJ: Princeton University Press, 1986.

Uribe, María Victoria, *Matar, rematar y contramatar. Las masacres de la violencia en el Tolima.* Bogotá: CINEP, 1992.

Uribe, María Victoria and T. Velazquez, *Enterrar y callar.* Bogotá: Comite Permanente por la Defensa de los Derechos Humanos, 1996.

Valenzuela, Arturo, *The Breakdown of Democratic Regimes: Chile.* Baltimore and London: Johns Hopkins University Press, 1978.

Valenzuela, Arturo (ed.), *Military Rule in Chile: Dictatorship and Oppositions.* Baltimore and London: Johns Hopkins University Press, 1986.

Valenzuela, J. Samuel, 'Democratic consolidation in post-transitional settings: notion, process, and facilitating conditions', in Scott Mainwaring, Guillermo O'Donnell and J.

Samuel Valenzuela (eds), *Issues in Democratic Consolidation: The New South American Democracies in Comparative Perspectives.* Notre Dame: University of Notre Dame Press, 1992, pp. 57–104.

Varese, Stefano, 'Think locally, act globally', *NACLA Report on the Americas* 25(3), 1991, pp. 13–17.

Vargas Foronda, Jacobo, *Guatemala: Sus recursos naturales, el militarismo y el imperialismo.* Mexico: Claves Latinoamericanas, 1985 .

Vargas Llosa, Mario, *El pez en el agua. Memorias.* Barcelona: Seix Barral, 1993 .

Vázquez León, Luis, *Ser indio otra vez. La purepechización de los Tarascos Serranos.* Mexico: CyA y Grijalbo, 1992.

Velasco e Cruz, Sebastião C. and Carlos Estevam Martins, 'De Castello a Figueiredo: uma incursão na pré-história da "abertura"', in Bernardo Sorj and Maria Hermínia Tavares de Almeida (eds), *Sociedade e política no Brasil pós-1964.* São Paulo: Brasiliense, 1984, pp. 13–61.

Ventura, Zuenir, *Cidade partida.* São Paulo: Companhia das Letras, 1994.

Vergara, Abilio, 'Subregión de Huanta. Apuntes para su comprensión', in *Gonzáles Vigil. Libro jubilar 1933–1983.* Huanta: UNSCH, 1983, pp. 125–77.

Vergara, Abilio et al., 'Calluchaca. Algunos elementos sobre la ideología comunal', in *Comunidades campesinas de Ayacucho.* Ayacucho: IER/José María Arguedas/CCTA Editores, 1985.

Vergara, Pilar, *Auge y caída del neoliberalismo en Chile.* Santiago: FLACSO, 1985.

Villagran Kramer, Francisco, *Bibliografía política de Guatemala. Los pactos políticos de 1944 a 1970.* Guatemala/San José: FLACSO, 1993.

Vogt, Evon Z., 'Possible sacred aspects of the Chiapas rebellion', *Cultural Survival Quarterly* 18(1), 1994, p. 34.

Vos, Jan de, *Viajes al desierto de la soledad. Cuando la Selva Lacandona aún era selva.* Mexico: Fondo de Cultura Economica, 1988.

— *No queremos ser cristianos. Historia de la resistencia de los Lacandones, 1530–1695, através de testimonios españoles e indígenas.* Mexico: Fondo de Cultura Economica, 1990.

— *Vivir en frontera. La experiencia de los indios de Chiapas.* Mexico: INAH, 1994.

— 'El encuentro de los Mayas de Chiapas con la teología de la liberación: ¿"vino nuevo en cueros nuevos?" (Marcos, 2:22)', Paper for the CEDLA Workshop on Rebellion in Chiapas and the Andean Highlands, Amsterdam, 1996.

Vylder, Stefan de, *Allende's Chile: The Political Economy of the Rise and Fall of the Unidad Popular.* Cambridge: Cambridge University Press, 1976.

Walker, Ignacio, 'Un nuevo socialismo democrático para Chile', *Estudios Cieplan* 24, 1988, pp. 5–36.

Warman, Arturo and Arturo Argueta (eds), *Movimientos idígenas contemporáneos en México.* Mexico: UNAM, 1993.

Wasserman, Mark, *Persistent Oligarchs. Elites and Politics in Chihuahua, Mexico, 1910–1940.* Durham: Duke University Press, 1993.

Wasserstrom, Robert, *Class and Society in Central Chiapas.* Los Angeles: University of California Press, 1983.

Weffort, Francisco, *O Populismo na política brasileira.* Rio de Janeiro: Paz e Terra, 1978.

Weiss Fagen, Patricia, 'Repression and state security', in Juan F. Corradi, Patricia Weiss Fagen and Manuel Antonio Garretón (eds), *Fear at the Edge. State Terror and Resistance in Latin America.* Berkeley: University of California Press, 1992, pp. 39–71.

Whitehead, Laurence, 'The peculiarities of transition a la mexicana', in N. Harvey and M. Serrano (eds), *Party Politics in an Uncommon Democracy. Political Parties and Elections in Mexico*. London: ILAS, 1994, pp. 109–30.

Wiarda, Howard, *Corporatism and National Development in Latin America*. Boulder, CO: Westview Press, 1981.

— (ed.), *Politics and Social Change in Latin America. Still a Distinct Tradition?* Boulder, CO: Westview Press, 1992.

Wickham-Crowley, Timothy P., 'Terror and guerrilla warfare in Latin America, 1956– 1970', *Comparative Studies in Society and History* 32(2), 1990, pp. 201–37.

— *Guerrillas and Revolution in Latin America. A Comparative Study of Insurgents and Regimes since 1956*. Princeton, NJ: Princeton University Press, 1992.

Wieviorka, Michel, *Société et terrorisme*. Paris: Fayard, 1988.

Wilde, Alexander, *Conversaciones de caballeros: La quiebra de la democracia en Colombia*. Bogotá: Ediciones Tercer Mundo, 1982.

Wimmer, Andreas, 'Mexikos Vergessener Suden. Rebellion gegen die Institutionalisierte Revolution', *Neue Zürcher Zeitung* Fernausgabe 20, 26 January 1994, p. 6.

Womack, John, *Zapata and the Mexican Revolution*. New York: Pelican, 1969.

Yurrita, Alfonso, 'The transition from military to civilian rule in Guatemala', in Louis W. Goodman, Johanna S. R. Mendelson and Juan Rial (eds), *The Military and Democracy. The Future of Civil–Military Relations in Latin America*. Lexington, MA, and Toronto: Lexington Books, 1991, pp. 75–89.

Zagorski, Paul W., *Democracy vs. National Security. Civil–Military Relations in Latin America*. Boulder, CO, and London: Lynne Rienner, 1992.

Zermeño, Sergio, 'Crisis, neoliberalism, and disorder', in J. Foweraker and A. Craig (eds), *Popular Movements and Political Change in Mexico*. Boulder, CO: Lynne Rienner, 1990, pp. 160–80.

— 'Intellectuals and the state in the "lost decade"', in Neil Harvey (ed.), *Mexico, Dilemmas of Transition*. London: Institute of Latin American Studies/British Academic Press, 1993, pp. 279–98.

— 'De Tlatelolco a San Cristóbal: el laberinto de la sociedad', *La Jornada Semanal* 247, 1994, pp. 29–35.

— 'Society and politics in contemporary Mexico', in Wil Pansters (ed.), *Citizens of the Pyramid. Essays on Mexican Political Culture*. Amsterdam: Thela (Latin America Series 7), 1997, pp. 183–208.

Zogbaum, Heidi, *B. Traven: A Vision of Mexico*. Wilmington: Scholarly Resources Books, 1992.

Index